6

7

13

5

8

12

29

4-25

26-27

28

29

29

35

37-38

42

42

36

39-41

50

51

51

54

56

56

52

56

56

51

53

55

57

66

67

67

68

68

69

69

70

70

71-72

82

82

83

84

85

85

91

92

93

93

94

95

96

Numbers given next to the images refer to the plates where that family/genus
can be found. Figures are only approximately to scale.

A Field Guide to the Birds

of the

Indian Subcontinent

A FIELD GUIDE TO THE BIRDS

OF THE

INDIAN SUBCONTINENT

Krys Kazmierczak

Illustrated by Ber van Perlo

YALE UNIVERSITY PRESS
NEW HAVEN AND LONDON

Published in the United Kingdom by Pica Press (an imprint of Helm Information Ltd) and in
the United States by Yale University Press.

ISBN 0-300-07921-4

Library of Congress Catalog Card Number: 99-62421
Printed in Hong Kong.

A catalogue record for this book is available in the British Library.

The paper in this book meets the guidelines for permanence and durability of the
Committee on Production Guidelines for Book Longevity of the Council on Library
Resources.

10 9 8 7 6 5 4 3 2 1

Cover illustrations by John Cox
Front: Scarlet Minivets and Red-wattled Lapwings
Spine: Fire-tailed Myzornis
Back: Wallcreeper and Grandala

CONTENTS

ACKNOWLEDGEMENTS

We have been very fortunate in having the support and active help of many people during the preparation of this guide. First of all we would like to thank Nigel Redman and Christopher Helm of Pica Press for conceiving this work, entrusting us with its creation and providing encouragement throughout.

We are indebted to all past and present ornithologists and birders active in South Asia, without whose extensive work and literature this guide would never have been possible. The monumental publications of Salim Ali, E. C. S. Baker, A. O. Hume and S. Dillon Ripley in particular cannot go unacknowledged. We are also indebted to many more recent authors for the work they have done in furthering our understanding of the taxonomy, status, field identification and behaviour of birds. In this regard the work of Per Alström, Peter Clement, Richard Grimmett, Carol and Tim Inskipp, Urban Olsson, Pamela Rasmussen, T. J. Roberts and Philip Round deserves especial mention.

Much research was carried out at the British Museum of Natural History at Tring where the staff were always extremely helpful and supportive. Our special thanks go to Mark Adams, Robert Prys-Jones, Don Smith, Frank Steinheimer, Cyril Walker, Michael Walters and Effie Warr. The illustrator also wishes to thank René Dekker from Naturalis, the Natural History Museum at Leiden, the Netherlands. A great debt of gratitude is owed to the many collectors who have in the past contributed to the priceless collections of bird specimens in these undervalued international museums.

We much appreciate the work of all those who have devoted of their spare time to check and suggest improvements to the illustrations and various sections of the draft text: Neil Arnold, David Bishop, Nigel Cleere, Chris Feare, David Gibbs, David James, Ragupathy Kannan, Tim Loseby, Nigel Redman, Barry Taylor, Gehan de Silva Wijeyeratne and Tim Worfolk. The contributions of Des Allen, Brian Gee, Paul Holt, Jon Hornbuckle and Per Undeland were particularly substantial and invaluable.

Our heartfelt thanks go to the many people who have assisted us by providing reference photographs, sound recordings, details of their observations and other information: Shahid Ali, Des Allen, Per Alström, John Anderton, Neil Arnold, Ramana Athreya, Vidya Athreya, Ashley Banwell, Hem Sagar Baral, Maan Barua, Phil Bawden, Nigel Bean, David Bishop, Jim Bland, Neil Bostock, Michael Bowman, Seb Buckton, Geoff Carey, Anwaruddin Choudhury, Alan Cole, Jon Curson, Edward C. Dickinson, Raf Drijvers, Nick Dymond, Göran Ekström, David Fisher, John Flynn, Tony Forster, Brian Gee, Smaran Ghosal, Gayatri Gogoi, Bikram Grewal, Richard Grimmett, John Groombridge-Harvey, Simon Harrap, Henk Hendriks, Thilo Hoffmann, John Holmes, Paul Holt, Jon Hornbuckle, Carol and Tim Inskipp, David James, Björn Johansson, Julia Jones, Ragupathy Kannan, S Karthikeyan, David Knights, Michael Knoll, Günter Lamsfuss, Terry Lee, Alan Lewis, Nigel Lindsey, Tim Loseby, Eric Lott, Lionel Maumary, Iwein Mauro, Krister Mild, Dhananjai Mohan, Peter Morris, Kushal Mookherjee, Tony Palliser, Otto Pfister, Aasheesh Pittie, Vibhu Prakash, Anand Prasad, J. N. Prasad, Asad Rahmani, Richard Ranft, Pam Rasmussen, Nigel Redman, Andrew Robertson, Craig Robson, Malcolm Roxby, Harkirat S. Sangha, the late Narayan C. Sarmah, Tom Schultz, Pratap Singh, Raj Singh, P. S. Sivaprasad, Subbu Subramanya, Vivek Tiwari, Per Undeland, Edward Vercruysse, Steve Whitehouse and Gehan de Silva Wijeyeratne. Tim Loseby's selfless help in the photographic department was greatly appreciated. Many others have contributed both directly and indirectly. We are most grateful to them all even though it is not possible to single everyone out by name.

The following were particularly helpful in providing much new distributional data: Otto Pfister (Ladakh), Aasheesh Pittie (Andhra Pradesh), Harkirat Singh Sangha (Rajasthan), Pratap Singh (Arunachal Pradesh), Paul Thompson (Bangladesh) and Per Undeland (Punjab).

Marc Dando and Julie Dando deserve many thanks for the care and creativity they showered on the book during its layout and design phase. Our gratitude extends to Nigel Redman and Nigel Collar for selflessly executing the thankless task of editing.

We would especially like to thank our families as well as both our birding and non-birding friends for their support, patience and encouragement during the long incubation of this work.

INTRODUCTION

This book arose from the long-felt need for a field guide which would help observers to identify all the bird species occurring in the Indian subcontinent, but would be user-friendly and easily portable at the same time. We hope we have achieved this aim by illustrating all the species on 96 colour plates and, in most cases, condensing the species texts onto the page facing the relevant plate. For most birds the illustrations are sufficient to allow their positive identification and a complete description was considered unnecessary. Only groups such as warblers and larks, which are hard to identify in the field, have received a somewhat fuller treatment.

Any work of this kind draws heavily on previous publications, and this one is no exception. While we have tried to incorporate as much relevant material as possible, inevitably there will be a few errors and omissions. Our knowledge of the field identification, habits, habitats, vocalisations and current distribution of many species is still far from complete. Any information which can help with improving, correcting and updating this guide for future editions would be gratefully received by the author (c/o Pica Press, The Banks, Mountfield, near Robertsbridge, East Sussex TN32 5JY, UK).

THE REGION

The region covered by this guide comprises Bangladesh, Bhutan, India, the Maldives, Nepal, Pakistan and Sri Lanka – see map on inside back cover. Borders shown in this, and the species distribution maps, are neither correct nor authenticated and do not constitute an opinion on the part of the authors, publishers or distributors as to the position of any national or international boundaries.

THE SPECIES

We have tried to cover all 1300 or so species reliably recorded from the subcontinent up to mid-1999. Where space has allowed we have also included some species which can be met with in neighbouring countries and might occur in our region. Recent research has shown that records of some species previously reported from South Asia are erroneous or doubtful. We have nevertheless considered it helpful to illustrate most of them as they could occur. In cases where birds have not conclusively been recorded in the subcontinent, this is clearly indicated by the inclusion of the relevant text within bold square brackets [ ].

Records of Eared Pitta *Pitta phayrei* and Pallas's Reed Bunting *Emberiza pallasi* as well as probable, but as yet unpublished, records of Rough-legged Buzzard *Buteo lagopus*, Swinhoe's Minivet *Pericrocotus cantonensis*, Chinese Leaf Warbler *Phylloscopus sichuanensis* and Japanese Grosbeak *Eophona personata*, and the separation of Golden-spectacled Warbler *Seicercus burkii* into three separate species, came to our notice too late for inclusion on the plates, but we have included short descriptions in the text. Over 1330 species are illustrated in total.

TAXONOMY, SYSTEMATIC ORDER AND NOMENCLATURE

The taxonomy and scientific nomenclature followed herein are broadly that of *An Annotated Checklist of the Birds of the Oriental Region* by Inskipp, Lindsey & Duckworth (1996). In a few cases we have accepted more recent published revisions:

Correcting the spelling of *Columba torringtoni* to *Columba torringtonii* (Wijesinghe 1998).

Correcting the spelling of *Centropus chlororhynchus* to *Centropus chlororhynchos* (Warren 1966 and Wijesinghe 1998).

Specimens from Great Nicobar formerly thought to belong to *Otus scops* and subsequently *Otus magicus* are now assigned to a new species – Nicobar Scops Owl *Otus alius* (Rasmussen 1998).

Reinstating the Forest Owlet to its original monotypic genus as *Heteroglaux blewitti* (Rasmussen & Collar 1999).

Splitting Rufous-winged Bushlark *Mirafra assamica* into Bengal Bushlark *Mirafra assamica* and Jerdon's Bushlark *Mirafra affinis* (Alström 1998).

Correcting the scientific name of White-faced Starling from *Sturnus senex* to *Sturnus albofrontatus* (Mees 1997).

Splitting Great Myna *Acridotheres grandis* from the now extralimital White-vented (Orange-billed Jungle) Myna *Acridotheres cinereus* (*javanicus*) (Feare & Craig 1998).

Splitting Hill Myna *Gracula religiosa* into Common Hill Myna *Gracula religiosa* and Southern Hill Myna *Gracula indica* (Feare & Craig 1998).

Correcting the scientific name of Russet Bush Warbler from *Bradypterus seebohmi* to *Bradypterus mandelli* (Dickinson *et al.* 1998).

Splitting Lesser Whitethroat *Sylvia curruca* into Lesser Whitethroat *Sylvia curruca* Hume's Lesser Whitethroat *Sylvia (curruca) althaea* and Desert Lesser Whitethroat *Sylvia (curruca) minula* (Martens & Steil 1997).

Splitting Golden-spectacled Warbler *Seicercus burkii* into Golden-spectacled Warbler *Seicercus burkii*, Whistler's Warbler *Seicercus whistleri* and Grey-crowned Warbler *Seicercus tephrocephalus* (Alström and Olsson 1999).

There are a number of instances where further study may show that taxa, until now regarded as subspecies, would be better treated as distinct species. We have indicated where this is the case in the relevant texts.

At the request of the publishers we have largely followed the older and more familiar Peters-based systematic order as used in the works of Ali & Ripley (specifically Ripley's 1982 *Synopsis*), in preference to that of Inskipp *et al.*, subject to a few modifications necessitated by the logistics of the plate layout.

There is a profusion of English bird names in current use. The same species can sometimes have as many as five or six different English names, e.g. *Anthus hodgsoni* is variously known as Olive-backed Pipit, Olive Tree Pipit, Indian Tree Pipit, Oriental Tree Pipit, Hodgson's Tree Pipit and Hodgson's Pipit. Conversely, the same name may be applied to totally different species, as in works by Ali & Ripley where both *Cettia diphone* and *Bradypterus tacsanowskius* are referred to as Chinese Bush Warbler. This obviously leads to much confusion, and a concerted attempt by the International Ornithological Congress (IOC) is now being made to achieve a common standard set of internationally acceptable English names. In this book we largely follow the nomenclature of Inskipp *et al.*, which is a major step forward in resolving this issue, though the final set of names approved by the IOC may well differ to some extent. Alternative names are given in parentheses in the indexes.

CONSERVATION

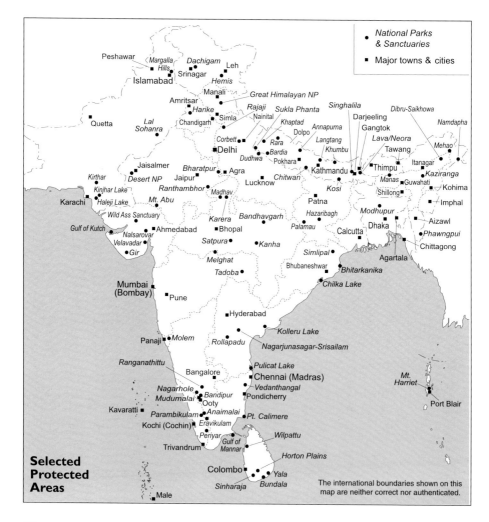

10

The peoples of South Asia have always shown great respect for the creatures they shared their living space with, and there is a long tradition of wildlife conservation in the region. The great religious writings of the Hindus, Buddhists and Jains in particular teach non-violence and respect for even the lowliest of life-forms. The Emperor Ashoka, in the 3rd century BC, famously laid down some of the earliest conservation laws known to mankind, forbidding the killing of certain animals and the burning of forests. These socio-religious values still persist to a great extent today, but pressures of a growing population with ever-increasing demands on land and other natural resources are taking their toll. The problems for the wildlife and natural habitats of the subcontinent were foreseen fairly early on, and there is now an extensive network of national parks and sanctuaries throughout the region. The number of protected areas in India alone is fast approaching 600. Bhutan is exemplary in having put 22% of its land area under protection, covering representative areas of all its major ecosystems. The result is that there have been relatively few extinctions of bird species in the last 100 years or so, but pressures of deforestation, 'reclamation' of wetlands, habitat destruction through increased farming, road-building, hydroelectric projects and other industrial developments are continually eating away at what is left of the natural world, and the outlook for some species is bleak. The larger birds especially, such as bustards, cranes, hornbills and raptors, which are hunted in some areas, are showing worrying declines in population levels. Everything possible must be done to support the region's governments and NGOs in their efforts to educate people in nature-awareness and to preserve the environment. Birdwatchers are often in the forefront of such difficult work, and everyone using this book is encouraged to join at least one of the various organisations concerned with birds and conservation in the subcontinent and take an active part in their work. Contact addresses can be found in the section on Useful Organisations on p. 316.

How To Use This Book

THE ILLUSTRATIONS

The illustrations are the most important part of any field guide. Wherever possible the illustrator has drawn on photographic reference material of live birds to supplement field experience, study of museum skins and literature during the preparation of the artwork.

Generally speaking the birds illustrated on any given plate are drawn to the same scale, with the exception of flying birds which are normally shown smaller. Where a species is clearly sexually dimorphic (or dichromatic) both sexes are illustrated. If only one bird is illustrated this implies that the sexes are alike, though close scrutiny in the field may reveal minor differences, females often being slightly duller in plumage than males. The word race is used in this book to mean subspecies. Where more than one race of a species occurs in the region, we have tried to show those which are most distinctive in order to illustrate the range of plumage variation within a species, but please note that not all races are illustrated. Juvenile, immature and/or first-winter plumages are also shown if considered helpful and space allowed.

Species regarded as globally threatened, or near-threatened (Collar *et al.* 1994), are indicated on the plates by a red ⌄.

THE SPECIES TEXTS

The need for brevity has necessitated the use of symbols in the species texts, as well as a degree of simplification and a rather telegraphic style in places. The information for each species is presented in the following order:

Name
The English name is given first in bold type, e.g. **Red-vented Bulbul**, followed by the currently accepted scientific name in italics, e.g. *Pycnonotus cafer.*

Ali & Ripley number
To make cross-reference easier for those who are familiar with the works of Ali and Ripley, we have included their reference numbers in parentheses, as given in Ripley's 1982 *Synopsis.* This makes it easier to see where species have since been split or lumped. The absence of such a reference number indicates that the species is extralimital or a more recent addition to the avifauna of the region (clarified by the status code at the end of the paragraph).

Size
This is given as the approximate average length of a bird as measured from bill tip to tail tip. All measurements are to the nearest centimetre (cm), except in the case of very small birds where measurements may be given to the nearest half-centimetre.

Identification notes

These are usually limited to those features which distinguish the bird from similar species, e.g. the flamebacks form a fairly distinctive group within the woodpeckers but can be difficult to identify to species level. We therefore only describe such field marks that serve to differentiate flamebacks from each other, but not from other woodpeckers. Field marks that are not discernible in the illustrations are also mentioned, e.g. a wing-patch that is normally only visible in flight. The combination of field marks described usually suffices for the correct identification of a species, but in many cases a knowledge of habits, habitat, voice and distribution can be helpful. Identification notes are not given if a bird is considered distinctive enough not to be confusable with any other species.

It is generally assumed that the observer can assign the species to the correct family. The birdwatcher unfamiliar with particular families or groups of birds is recommended to read the family descriptions in the following section. Please note that family descriptions only take into account those species which occur within the Indian subcontinent and some characteristics mentioned may not apply to extralimital members of the family.

Where comparisons are made with other species on the same plate they are referred to by their number. If the referenced species is on another plate, then the species number is preceded by the plate number, e.g. 58.11 refers to species number 11 on plate 58.

Abbreviations

ad   adult
br   breeding
nbr   non-breeding
imm   immature (a bird that has not yet attained adult plumage; usually includes juvenile)
juv   juvenile (a bird in its first full plumage after fledging)
nom   nominate (see glossary)
vs   versus; as opposed to
♂   male (adult unless otherwise stated)
♀   female (adult unless otherwise stated)
○   pale morph
●   dark morph
◐   intermediate morph

⌘ Altitudinal range, habitat (and behaviour)

Where it is known, we have given the broadest altitudinal range (in metres) in which each species may be found, but the optimum altitudinal zone may vary from one part of the subcontinent to another. For example, many species inhabit a lower altitudinal zone in the Himalaya but range to higher levels in the more temperate hills of South India and Sri Lanka. Exceptional or local values appear in parentheses.

A short simplified description of each species's preferred habitat is given. For species which have only occurred as vagrants to the region we have included notes based on the favoured habitat within their usual range at the time of year they might be expected to occur. Please note, however, that vagrants and birds on migration are particularly likely to turn up in atypical habitats. By and large, birds do tend to keep to definite habitat types and this can often be a clue to their identity. For example, a small black and white bird perched on a rock in a desert is likely to be a wheatear; a similar one on a tree in a Himalayan forest could be a Little Pied Flycatcher, a Bar-winged Flycatcher-shrike or a Pied Falconet; standing on a rock in a Himalayan torrent it is more likely to be a forktail; in an urban park or garden setting it will probably be a Magpie Robin. Where space allows, extra notes on behaviour may be included in the section on habitat.

Symbols:

<   below, e.g. <1600(2440) indicates that the species is chiefly found below 1600m but it does sometimes occur at altitudes up to 2440m
>   above, e.g. >850(plains) indicates that the species normally occurs above 850m but may sometimes be found down as far as plains level
S   summer
W   winter

∇ **Voice**

The most characteristic calls and songs have been included wherever they were considered useful for identification purposes. Nearly all bird species use vocalisations in order to communicate in certain basic situations. These vocalisations are usually fairly specific to a given species so that with practice it is possible to identify most birds simply by their calls. It is, however, notoriously difficult to transcribe bird calls using the English alphabet and different observers often 'hear' the same call in different ways. The calls and songs transcribed here are gathered from many sources including the author's own notes and recordings and will give some indication of a bird's usual repertoire, which can often be quite varied. Normally the call most likely to be heard by the observer is given first, and the (usually longer) song follows. The latter is sometimes omitted as most passage migrants and non-breeding visitors sing rarely, if at all, during their stay in the subcontinent. While the transcriptions we give may not create the exact sound in the reader's mind, we hope they may be recognisable when the bird is heard.

Identification by voice alone has to be made with care, though to the experienced observer this is often the best means to identify certain groups such as cuckoos, owls and nightjars, as well as some warblers and pipits. It should be borne in mind that many related species have similar-sounding calls and some species are very skilled in imitating others. In addition there can be a degree of geographical variation in a species's vocalisations; and any given individual may perform variations on a theme.

With vocalisations gathered from so many disparate sources, it has not been possible to maintain consistency in the transcriptions, but we have endeavoured to use the following system:

too	transcriptions (as opposed to descriptions) are given in italics
too	underscoring indicates that a vocal element is stressed
TOO	upper-case letters indicate that an element is distinctly louder than the rest of the strophe
(too)	optional elements, or ones that are inaudible except at close range, are given in parentheses, e.g. *too-too-(too)-(too)* indicates that a bird usually calls with two *too* notes but sometimes with three or four.
...	at the end of a transcription indicates that the call continues with similar notes or phrases
´	indicates a rise in tone, e.g. *too ´too* indicates that the second note is at a higher pitch than the first
`	indicates a fall in tone, e.g. *too`too* indicates that the second note is at a lower pitch than the first

Pauses are indicated in several ways to give a rough indication of their length, e.g.

tootootoo	continuous without any apparent break
too-too-too	very short breaks between notes
too too too	short pauses between notes
too, too, too	slightly longer breaks
too...too...too	longer pauses between notes

Some of the traditional interpretations of bird calls, such as the *brain fever* of the Common Hawk Cuckoo, are not always phonetically accurate, but have been included because of their usefulness as mnemonics.

Unfortunately, space precludes us from acknowledging the source of each individual transcription. As well as drawing from the literature and audio sources listed in the appendix under *References and Further Reading*, we have studied unpublished recordings from Des Allen, Hem Sagar Baral, David Bishop, Raf Drijvers, Brian Gee, Paul Holt, Alan Lewis, Nigel Lindsey, Craig Robson, Pratap Singh, Edward Vercruysse and Steve Whitehouse.

Status

At the end of the paragraph for each species we have indicated its status within the subcontinent as follows:

E	endemic to the Indian subcontinent (resident unless otherwise indicated)
N	near-endemic (resident unless otherwise indicated)
R	resident
B	breeder
S	summer visitor
A	altitudinal migrant
M	migrates within the subcontinent (e.g. breeds in the Himalaya and winters in southern India and/or Sri Lanka)
P	passage migrant

W	winter visitor
V	vagrant, accidental or rare visitor
I	introduced
X	extralimital (not recorded in the Indian subcontinent)
●	subject to some (local) seasonal movement or nomadism
*	localised or patchily distributed (e.g. **B*** = breeds locally)
†	probably extinct
?	status uncertain

1	abundant or very common
2	common
3	fairly common
4	uncommon
5	scarce or rare

When the symbol **●** or * is used, it refers to the preceding letter, not the one after. Note that some species may be assigned more than one status code, e.g. **R●W3** would indicate a fairly common resident species which may undertake some seasonal wanderings and is augmented by migrants from the north in winter; **RA2** would describe a common species as partly resident and partly an altitudinal migrant; **V(W?5)** would be a vagrant (or possibly a scarce winter visitor).

If an observer locates a very rare or vagrant species, he or she should make careful notes, drawings and thorough descriptions on the spot, backed up by photographic evidence if possible. These should then be written up together with the circumstances of the observation and sent for verification and/or publication to the editor of *Forktail*, the journal of the Oriental Bird Club, or the *Journal of the Bombay Natural History Society*. In the case of Sri Lankan observations, submissions should be made to the Ceylon Bird Club. See section on Useful Organisations. The author (address c/o the publishers) would also welcome copies of such reports.

DISTRIBUTION MAPS

The distribution maps presented in this guide were compiled from information available up to mid-1999. Primary sources include Ali & Ripley (1971-1999), Ash & Shafeeg (1994), Grimmett, Inskipp & Inskipp (1998), Harvey (1990), Inskipp & Inskipp (1991), Lamsfuss (1998), Ripley (1982) and Roberts (1991-2). These have been supplemented with the author's own observations together with numerous additional references. The result we believe to be the most accurate and up-to-date maps of subcontinental bird distributions currently available. Future authors will, no doubt, be able to refine these further as more information emerges. Please note: where a species is not explicitly shown as scarce, this does not imply that it may not be scarce in some or all parts of that range.

For ease of reference the distribution maps have been incorporated into the main body of the book. Where there is space available they are included on the same page as the relevant text. Otherwise, they can be found on the page immediately adjoining the plate/text unit to which they refer. In a few cases, the distribution information is given in the species text, rather than in map form. Extralimital species have not been mapped. Please refer to the key to the distribution maps on the inside back cover.

In most cases it has not been possible to separate out the summer and winter ranges of altitudinal migrants where these overlap. Birds may be expected at higher altitudes in summer and at lower altitudes in winter within the (resident) range shown.

The maps reflect actual records of species as far as these have been judged to be reliable.

Many species are under-recorded due to difficulties in identification, lack of observer coverage in some areas, or because records have not been published, and are doubtless more widespread than the maps suggest.

Extreme care should be taken with the identification of rare birds or those which appear 'off range'. On closer examination such records often prove to be cases of mistaken identity. Resident species with a restricted distribution are extremely unlikely to be found at any great distance from their usual range, e.g. if a bird seen in southwestern India is initially identified as a Blue Whistling Thrush, reference to the maps will show that this is most implausible and that the most likely explanation is that the bird was in fact a Malabar Whistling Thrush. It should be borne in mind that birds may occasionally appear 'out of season', e.g. it is not uncommon for a few individuals of a widespread wintering species, such as Green Sandpiper, to oversummer. It has not been possible to indicate this on the maps.

TOPOGRAPHY

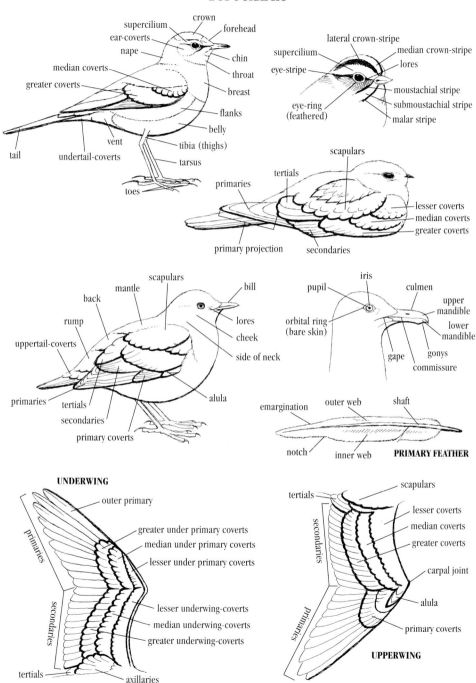

15

REFERENCES

Ali, S. & Ripley, S. D. (1971-1999) *Handbook of the Birds of India and Pakistan*. 10 vols. 1st & 2nd edns. OUP, Delhi & Oxford.

Alström, P. (1997) Field identification of Asian *Gyps* vultures. *Oriental Bird Club Bull*. 25: 32-49.

Alström, P. (1998) Taxonomy of the *Mirafra assamica* complex. *Forktail* 13: 97-107.

Alström, P. & Olsson, U. (1999) The Golden-spectacled Warbler: a complex of sibling species, including a previously undescribed species. *Ibis* 141(4): 545-568.

Ash, J. S. & Shafeeg, A. (1994) Birds of the Maldive Islands, Indian Ocean. *Forktail* 10: 3-32.

Collar, N. J., Crosby, M. J. & Stattersfield, A. J. (1994) *Birds to Watch 2 – The World List of Threatened Birds*. BirdLife International, Cambridge.

Dickinson, E. C., Rasmussen, P. C., Round, P. D. and Rozendaal, F. G. (1998) Reinstatement of *Bradypterus seebohmi* to the Indian Avifauna, and revalidation of an earlier name. P. 399 in Adams, N. J. and Slotow, R. H. (eds.) *Ostrich* 69: Proceedings of the 22nd Int. Ornithol. Congr. Duban.

Feare, C. & Craig, A. (1998) *Starlings and Mynas*. Christopher Helm, London.

Grimmett, R., Inskipp, C. & Inskipp, T. (1998) *Birds of the Indian Subcontinent*. Christopher Helm, London.

Harvey, W. G. (1990) *Birds in Bangladesh*. University Press, Dhaka.

Inskipp, C. & Inskipp, T. (1991) A Guide to the Birds of Nepal. 2nd edn. Christopher Helm, London.

Inskipp, T., Lindsey, N. & Duckworth, W. (1996) *An Annotated Checklist of the Birds of the Oriental Region*. Oriental Bird Club, Sandy, UK.

Lamsfuss, G. (1998) *Die Vögel Sri Lankas : ein Vogel- und Naturführer* [The Birds of Sri Lanka: a bird and nature guide]. Max Kasparek Press, Heidelberg.

Martens, J. & Steil, B. (1997) [Territorial songs and species differentiation in the Lesser Whitethroat superspecies *Sylvia (curruca)*.] (In German with an English summary.) *Journal für Ornithologie* 138: 1-23.

Mees, G. F. (1997) On the identity of *Heterornis senex* Bonaparte. *Bull. Brit. Orn. Club* 117: 67-68.

Rasmussen, P. C. (1998) A new Scops-owl from Great Nicobar Island. *Bull. Brit. Orn. Club* 118: 141-153.

Rasmussen, P. C. and Collar, N. J. (1999) Major specimen fraud of the Forest Owlet *Heteroglaux* (*Athene* auct.) *blewitti*. *Ibis* 141: 11-21.

Ripley, S. D. (1982) *A Synopsis of the Birds of India and Pakistan*. 2nd edn. Oxford University Press/Bombay Nat. Hist. Soc., Bombay.

Roberts, T. J. (1991-2) *The Birds of Pakistan*. 2 vols. OUP, Karachi.

Warren, R. L. M. (1966) *Type-specimens of Birds in the British Museum* (*Natural History*). Vol. 1: Non-passerines. British Museum (Natural History), London.

Wijesinghe, D. P. (1998) Review of Inskipp *et al.*, 1996, *An Annotated Checklist of the Birds of the Oriental Region*. *Ceylon Bird Club Notes*, June 1998: 65-68.

FAMILY INTRODUCTIONS

Plate 1: Shearwaters and Petrels

This group of seabirds is highly pelagic, normally keeping well out to sea except when breeding. Observations are limited to sea voyages, watches from strategic headlands along the coast and occasional storm-blown birds or beached corpses. Given the difficulty of observing and identifying these species it is perhaps not surprising that our knowledge of their distribution and movements in subcontinental waters is extremely limited. **Shearwaters** and **petrels** belong to the group of birds known as tubenoses due to their salt-filtering nostrils being located in a tube on top of the hook-tipped bill. **Shearwaters** can be distinguished from the petrels of the region by their relatively long, slender bills and straight, rigidly-held wings. Most of them spend long periods gliding just above the sea. The **petrels** have short stubby bills and tend to hold their wings bowed and flexed at the wrist. The manner in which a bird flies can be a useful, though not conclusive, identification feature.

Plate 2: Frigatebirds and Boobies

Frigatebirds are large pelagic species with long rakish wings and deeply forked tails. They are extremely aerial, feeding on fish or scraps snatched from other seabirds or the surface of the water. Adult males are distinguished by their bright red gular pouches (rarely visible at a distance) which are inflated during courtship display. Adult females have blackish heads without the red throat-patch. Young birds have rusty, buffy or whitish heads. For specific identification it is important to note the exact pattern of white on the underparts, and the presence or absence of white 'spurs' on the axillaries. Only the first immature stage (juvenile), adult male and female plumages are illustrated, and it should be borne in mind that these birds take several years to reach maturity and many confusing immature plumages occur. It may not always be possible to identify a particular individual. **Boobies** are related to the cormorants, darters and pelicans but have adapted to live in a strictly marine environment. The 'cigar-shaped' body is characteristic. Note also the long, narrow, pointed wings, wedge-shaped tail and webbed feet. They plunge-dive (often from a great height) to catch their prey with the serrated conical bill. Flight is normally direct with powerful flaps of the wings interspersed with gliding. As with all pelagic species, sightings of boobies and frigatebirds are infrequent: mostly from islands, mainland coasts and ships, though storm-blown individuals may occur inland.

Plate 3: Storm-petrels, Tropicbirds and Loons

Storm-petrels are relatively small ocean-going birds with long pointed wings and square or forked tails. Plumage is predominantly dark- or greyish-brown with more-or-less diagnostic white/pale features. They usually feed by picking items from the surface of the sea, often while 'walking' or skipping on the water. **Tropicbirds** are medium-sized, largely white, pelagic species. Adults have distinctive long tail-streamers which together with bill colour and black plumage markings are the main identification features. Predominantly aerial, they have a high graceful flight and feed by plunge-diving, sometimes resting on the water with cocked tail. **Loons** (or **divers**) are large, swimming, fish-eating birds which breed on lakes well to the north of our region. Breeding plumage is distinctive but vagrants to the subcontinent are more likely to be non-breeding/immature birds, which are identified with some difficulty by shape of bill, pattern of grey on neck and spotting on upperparts.

Plate 4: Pelicans, Darter, Cormorants and Grebes

Pelicans are very large, mainly white, aquatic birds with webbed feet. Wings are long and broad, tail short and rounded. The huge bill is equipped with a large elastic pouch used for scooping up fish, often in a co-operative group effort. They nest on trees in colonies. **Cormorants** are dark, medium-large waterbirds with webbed feet and a strong straight bill with a hooked tip. The longish stiff tail often appears ragged. They swim and dive for fish from the surface of the water. Flight is direct with long neck outstretched. They often perch with outstretched wings and usually nest in colonies on trees. **Darters** are like cormorants but have a long thin pointed bill used for spearing fish. The longer, slimmer, snake-like neck has given rise to the alternative name of Snakebird, particularly manifest when the bird swims with body submerged. **Grebes** are small to medium-sized waterbirds with fairly thin pointed bills, upright necks and a characteristic tailless shape. Strictly aquatic, they feed by diving for fish and other small water animals. They patter along the surface of the water to assist take-off, and build their nests on floating vegetation.

Plate 5: Egrets and Herons

Egrets and **herons** are medium to large, long-legged waterbirds with long necks and sharp dagger-like bills. They are diurnal and prey mainly on fish, frogs, crustaceans and insects which they stalk in shallow water, marshes, mud or wet fields. Flight is slow on broad rounded wings, usually with neck drawn in. Many species breed in colonies on trees in wetlands.

Plate 6: Little Heron, Pond Herons, Bitterns and Night Herons

The **herons** and **bitterns** on this plate are medium-sized to large birds, generally squatter than the birds on plate 5 with shorter, stouter necks and shorter legs. Generally similar in habits except that the bitterns are rather secretive and shy, preferring to keep to dense marshy vegetation, and the night herons are largely nocturnal.

Plate 7: Storks, Spoonbill, Flamingos and Ibises

Storks are large, long-legged birds with long necks and very long, heavy bills. All except the adjutants fly with their necks outstretched, a feature which helps distinguish them from herons, and often soar on thermals. They prey on a variety of small fish, mammals, birds, reptiles, snails etc., primarily in wetlands but also in grass and arable land. Adjutants also feed on carrion. **Flamingos** are very large, extremely long-necked and long-legged wading birds with characteristic pink tones in the plumage. The uniquely shaped bill is specially adapted for filtering tiny food particles (algae, diatoms and small invertebrates) from the water while holding the head upside-down. They build huge colonies of nest mounds made of mud. **Spoonbills** are similar in habits and general proportions to the storks but for the spatulate bill which is swept from side to side in mud and shallow water to feel for small animal prey. **Ibises** are closely related to spoonbills, but the long, downcurved bill is used to probe for food in the mud or peck at prey items on the ground.

Plates 8, 9 & 10: Geese, Swans and Ducks

Geese are large-bodied waterfowl with fairly long necks, broad bills and webbed feet. Winter visitors throughout most of the subcontinent (though some Bar-headed Geese breed in Ladakh), they usually congregate in flocks which may occasionally contain an individual of one of the rarer species. Their presence is often advertised by loud honking calls. They graze on grass and crops as well as aquatic vegetation, and are good swimmers. Flocks fly high, usually in V-formation. **Swans** are easily distinguished from geese by their very long necks. The adults are largely white; juveniles have grey plumage. They normally feed in shallow water, submerging the head and up-ending in deeper water. Jizz, bill shape and colour are the key identification features. **Ducks** are similar to geese but generally somewhat smaller and often more tied to water. Most are sexually dichromatic, the brighter males of many species attaining a duller female-type (eclipse) plumage during the post-breeding moult but retaining some features which identify them as males. Flight is fast and direct; many species are readily identifiable by the colour of the patch on the secondaries (speculum). The majority are winter visitors.

Plate 11: Honey-buzzard, Bazas and Kites

Honey-buzzards are medium-large birds of prey which feed on honey, bees, wasps and their larvae. The relatively small head has a distinctive cuckoo-shaped profile. In flight they show fairly long, broad wings rounded at the tip and a long, quite narrow tail, both marked with characteristic barring below. They soar on flat wings. **Bazas** are small to medium-sized raptors characterised by very broad rounded wings, fairly long squarish tail, jaunty crest and forest-dwelling habits. They feed mainly on large insects, frogs and lizards and are somewhat crepuscular. The name **kite** is usually applied to a fairly heterogeneous group of small to medium-sized hawks with forked tails. The Brahminy Kite is an exception but resembles the true kites (genus *Milvus*) in its scavenging habits. The adult has a highly distinctive chestnut and white plumage.

Plate 12: Accipiters

Accipiters are small to medium-sized hawks with broad rounded wings and relatively long tails. Most are forest-dwelling, principally hunting for birds by cruising just above or through the canopy and then dashing after their prey with a fast agile flight weaving between the trees, or by pouncing on birds and small mammals from a concealed perch. The white undertail-coverts are conspicuously fluffed up during the undulating courtship display-flight. Females are generally browner and noticeably larger than males. The various species, especially the immatures, are confusingly similar and specific identification may not always be possible in the field. It is important to note the exact shade of colour of the upperparts and the pattern of barring and streaking on the underparts and tail, as well as the presence or absence of a mesial streak (may be poorly marked in some immatures). In flight the broad rounded wings differentiate them from similar-sized falcons. Generally rather solitary. Familiarity with Shikra, the commonest species, will help when identifying other birds in the family.

Plate 13: Buzzards

The true ***Buteo*** **buzzards** are medium-sized raptors with characteristic rounded wings, stout bodies, relatively small heads, short thick necks and fairly broad tails, rounded when fanned. They are smaller and less powerful than the eagles but larger than most of the accipiters. The body and underwing-coverts are unbarred and usually contrast with the flight feathers when seen from below in flight. Each species has a confusing variety of colour morphs varying from almost entirely dark brown to very pale individuals. They are normally birds of more open, dry habitats where they perch on convenient lookout posts and hunt by pouncing on small mammals and lizards. The **Butastur** buzzards (also known as **buzzard-eagles**) are smaller and slimmer-winged than the *Buteo* species and have longer, narrower tails. The White-eyed Buzzard is the commonest raptor in some parts of the Deccan, while the Grey-faced Buzzard is unlikely to occur anywhere but on the Andaman and Nicobar Islands. Compare also the Oriental Honey-buzzard on Plate 11.

Plate 14: Hawk Eagles

The **hawk eagles** of the genus *Spizaetus* are fairly large raptors with broad rounded wings which bulge markedly on the inner trailing edge before narrowing again where they meet the body. The tail is relatively long and broad, and the legs are feathered down to the base of the toes. The **eagles** of the genus *Hieraaetus* were formerly also known as hawk eagles but differ from *Spizaetus* in being smaller and having longer, slimmer wings.

Plates 15 & 16: *Aquila* Eagles

The *Aquila* eagles are large, mainly dark eagles with long broad wings and fairly broad, medium-length tails. Plumages are confusing with many individual variations and successions during the several years taken to attain maturity. Some of the more typical plumages are illustrated and the more helpful field marks described. Separation requires care and practice and it will not always be possible to assign an individual seen in the field to a particular species.

Plate 17: Osprey, Sea and Fish Eagles

All the birds on plate 17 are large raptors which specialise in preying on fish and are hence almost always found near water. They may also opportunistically take other prey and scavenge on carrion and refuse. The **Osprey** is smaller than the other fishing eagles and rather more rakish with fairly long angular wings and tail. It is the only representative of its genus and is found throughout most of the world. The *Haliaeetus* sea eagles are very large with massive bills. In flight the wings are characteristically long, broad and parallel-sided (plank-like). The tails of the adults are strongly patterned, rather short but broad and rounded or wedge-shaped. The *Ichthyophaga* fish eagles are similar to the *Haliaeetus* but slightly smaller with bulging secondaries producing a rather different flight outline.

Plates 18 & 19: Vultures

Vultures are large, broad-winged birds of prey which feed almost exclusively on dead animals. Their feeding habits often result in large gatherings at a carcass. Such groups often consist of several different species, allowing comparisons to be made. Most vultures have unfeathered heads or at least partly so. They search for carrion while cruising at great height, at the same time keeping an eye on their brethren and following any other vulture that appears to be descending towards a meal. Vultures are largely silent except for an assortment of cackles, hisses, squeals, croaks and screams when squabbling over a corpse. There appears to have been a very worrying population crash in the region in recent years. It can be difficult to identify *Gyps* vultures to species. It takes several years for a bird to become adult and intermediate plumages can be confusing, although younger immatures more closely resemble juveniles and older subadult birds are more similar to adults. It helps to become familiar with the adults and commoner species first. In the plains the White-rumped Vulture is by far the commonest, while in the Himalaya above 1,000m the Himalayan Griffon is the species most frequently encountered, though even this species may descend to the foothills and plains in winter. It is best to age a bird first: the feathers of a juvenile are uniformly long and pointed whereas those of an adult are for the most part rounded. This difference is most easily seen on the lesser and median coverts of a perched bird; however, in flight the trailing edge of a juvenile's wing appears serrated, but not so in the adult. In adults (except *tenuirostris* Long-billed Vulture) the bill is largely pale, whereas juveniles usually have a blackish bill, sometimes pale on the culmen. A compact fluffy white ruff (rather than long and straggly) identifies a bird as an adult (except Himalayan Griffon).

Plate 20: Harriers

Harriers are slim, medium-sized raptors with relatively long slender wings and tail. They are birds of wide open spaces and hunt by quartering fairly near the ground in order to surprise their prey. During this they use a flap-and-glide technique with the wings held in a characteristic V during the glide. To identify the males it is important to note the exact distribution of black in the plumage. Juveniles are generally more rufous than females and both are difficult to identify to species in the field without good views and some experience. An encounter with such a bird will often result in the bird simply being noted as a 'ringtail' harrier, so-called because of the bars, or rings, on the tail. At rest the best identification features are the head pattern and the ratio of wing-length to tail length. The former can be difficult to see on a flying bird, when the underwing pattern may be more helpful. There is much individual and age-related variation and only the more helpful features are indicated here.

Plate 21: Snake and Serpent Eagles

As the name suggests these medium-sized to large raptors are specialised in preying on snakes and other reptiles. The **Short-toed Snake Eagle** inhabits dry open areas. The **serpent eagles** are largely forest raptors, though they may often be found near jheels and rivers. The crest of the serpent eagles gives the birds a rather full-headed appearance but is not otherwise apparent unless raised.

Plates 22 & 23: Falcons and Falconets

Falcons are small to medium-sized compact raptors with relatively long, pointed wings which enable them to achieve high speeds in flight. Most of them are inhabitants of fairly open biotopes and specialise in preying on smaller birds, mammals, reptiles and insects which they hunt from the air. In soaring flight the wings may sometimes appear slightly rounded, like those of the accipiters, but generally the difference in structure is readily apparent. The females are usually noticeably larger then the males. The plumage of the larger falcons can be rather variable making specific identification difficult, especially between Saker and Laggar. **Falconets** are diminutive falcons with the same distinctive shape and hooked bill as their relatives but are not much larger in size than sparrows. They inhabit forest clearings, forest edge and more open wooded habitats, preying mainly on insects and small birds.

Plates 24–28: Galliformes

The so-called **galliformes** (or gamebirds) are generally plump with rounded wings, relatively small head, short thick bill and strong unfeathered legs. They are adapted to a lifestyle of scratching around on the ground for food – seeds, fruit, berries, shoots, leaves, tubers etc., as well as worms, snails and insects. Many roost in trees at night. Most nest on the ground. Generally rather shy and difficult to observe, when disturbed they may freeze or fly a short distance, sometimes up into a tree, but most prefer to run. Many are globally threatened because of habitat destruction and hunting for food and feathers. **Scrubfowl**, or **megapodes** as they are also known, share many of the characteristics of other galliformes but have exceptionally strong legs and feet and unusual nesting habits. They bury their eggs in a large mound of sand and vegetation near the seashore, the temperature produced by the decaying vegetation being sufficient to incubate the eggs. The young hatch fully fledged and immediately begin fending for themselves. **Partridges** and **francolins** are medium-sized with shorter tails. **Quails** are similar in build and habits but smaller. Some are migratory unlike most galliformes. The unrelated **buttonquails** are similar in appearance to the true quails but lack a hind toe. In flight they can be distinguished from true quails by the contrast between the pale upperwing-coverts and darker flight feathers. They are unusual in that the females are larger and brighter than the males and, being polyandrous, they leave the raising of the young entirely to the males. Most **pheasants** and **tragopans** are strongly sexually dimorphic. The colourful males usually have a very striking courtship display. **Peafowl** are large colourful birds with iridescent plumage, long crest and distinctive ocelli ('eyes') adorning the cock's long train of feathers. **Peacock pheasants** are similar in having ocelli, but the plumage overall is grey-brown; ocelli are also found on the upperparts, and the crest is short and bushy. **Junglefowl** will be recognisably familiar to almost everyone due to their resemblance to farmyard cocks and hens. Usually shy, they often come out onto paths and clearings in the early morning and towards dusk, frequently in small groups of a cock and 3–5 hens.

Plate 29: Cranes, Bustards and Floricans

Cranes are very large wading birds with long necks and legs, distinguished from storks by the bill being no longer than the length of the head, and by the inner secondary plumes which project beyond the tail in a 'bustle'. They fly with neck outstretched in contrast to the herons. Their loud trumpeting calls are unlike those of any other birds of the region. **Bustards** and **floricans** are tall, long-necked terrestrial birds with long, powerful legs, muscular bodies and short straight bills. Male bustards are larger than females; the reverse is the case with the floricans. They are inhabitants of open plains, grasslands and standing crops but omnivorous in their feeding habits. Most are polygamous and by nature gregarious in the non-breeding season, although the severe declines in their populations due to loss of habitat and persecution means that they are now rarely seen in any great numbers.

Plate 30: Rails, Crakes, Gallinules and Finfoot

Rails and **crakes** are small to medium-sized plump wading birds with long legs and toes, fairly short rounded wings and a short tail which is often held cocked and frequently flicked upwards. The body is usually held horizontally and appears plump from the side but is relatively narrow to facilitate movement through reeds and dense vegetation. Most are shy inhabitants of marshes and dense waterside scrub and thus rarely observed. The best opportunities are usually in the twilight of dawn and dusk when they often emerge into more open areas. Except on migration, flight appears weak with drooping legs, the birds usually dropping back into cover after a short distance. **Gallinules** are similar in structure but less shy, with Common Coot in particular spending much time swimming on open water. The unrelated **Finfoots** share many of the characteristics of the gallinules but the neck is comparatively long and thick, the bill is thick and tapering, the toes have wide lobes, and the tail is relatively long and stiff. They swim, dive and run well but rarely fly.

Plate 31: Waders I (Jacanas, Thick-knees, Oystercatcher, Crab-plover, Avocet, Ibisbill, Stilt, Pratincoles, Coursers)

The term **wader** is used to describe a large, somewhat heterogeneous group of species that are united by certain anatomical characters. For the most part they are long-legged birds frequenting shallow wetlands and their margins, with some having evolved to occupy drier habitats. Most feed terrestrially, subsisting largely on animal matter such as worms, molluscs, insects and crustaceans. A large proportion of species only come to the subcontinent in winter when their rather drab grey and brown non-breeding plumage makes identification difficult. **Jacanas** are distinguished by their very long toes which enable them to walk on floating vegetation, earning them the alternative name of lily-trotter. The sex roles are reversed, the female being polyandrous and the male looking after the eggs and young. **Thick-knees** have long strong legs, stout body, large head with big yellow eyes, short neck and thick bill. They are relatively crepuscular and nocturnal. **Oystercatchers** are pied waders generally frequenting seashores where they use their long, strong orange-red bills to open the shells of their mollusc prey. The **Crab-plover** is a mainly white wader with black on the wings and back, and long pale legs. The distinctively shaped, thick black bill is adapted for preying on crabs and other crustaceans, which it hunts chiefly on coastal mudflats and reefs. **Avocets** are graceful pied waders with very long legs and diagnostic long, slender, strongly upcurved bills. The **Ibisbill** is easily distinguished by its long decurved red bill used for probing for small aquatic animals among stones in the shallows of mountain rivers. **Stilts**, as the name implies, are extremely long-legged. This together with the black upperparts, white underparts, long neck, relatively small head and long straight thin black bill give a distinctive appearance. **Pratincoles** are short-legged with a short, broad, decurved bill, forked tail and long, pointed swept-back wings. Unlike other waders they catch most of their insect prey on the wing. **Coursers** are long-legged, fast-running, plover-like birds with moderately long rounded wings and decurved bills. They inhabit arid habitats.

Plate 32: Waders II (Lapwings, Dotterels and Plovers)

Lapwings are medium-sized waders with long legs, fairly large head, short straight bill and rounded wings. Stance is fairly upright with birds usually running or walking a few steps before stopping to pick a prey item from the ground and then changing direction. **Dotterels** and **Plovers** are of similar build but mostly smaller with a shorter neck, relatively shorter pointed wings and less upright stance.

Plate 33: Waders III (Godwits, Dowitchers, Curlews, Ruff, Golden and Grey Plovers, Turnstone and Phalaropes)

Godwits, **dowitchers**, **curlews** and **whimbrels** are large, relatively tall, long-legged waders with long slender bills used to feed by probing in the mud for small invertebrates. The bills of godwits are slightly upcurved; those of dowitchers straight; those of curlews and whimbrels downcurved. **Golden** and **Grey Plovers** are similar in build and habits to the lapwings (plate 32) but have shorter necks, more pointed wings, spangled upperparts and, in breeding plumage, a largely black face and underparts. **Turnstones** are squat, thrush-sized waders with short legs and a short, strong, slightly up-tilted bill used for turning over stones in search of prey items. **Phalaropes** are much more aquatic than other waders, and are usually found swimming, often far out to sea. The thin, straight medium-length bill, dark smudge behind the eye in non-breeding plumage and spinning action when feeding are characteristic. In breeding plumage females are larger and brighter than males which take care of rearing the young.

Plate 34: Waders IV (Shanks, Tattler, Sandpipers, Snipes, Painted-snipe and Woodcock)

Shanks, **tattlers** and *Tringa* **sandpipers** are small to medium-sized waders with fairly long legs and longish bill used to probe in the mud for invertebrate prey on mudflats and the margins of waterbodies. **Snipes** are medium-sized, stout-bodied waders with very long, fairly straight bill and highly cryptic plumage. Generally found in grassy marshland and soft margins of vegetated waterbodies probing vertically in the mud for prey. Specific identification is difficult but key features to note are overall colour, length of bill, exact pattern and width of supercilium and head-stripes, pattern and colour of scapulars, extent of barring on underparts, presence/absence of white trailing edge to the secondaries in flight and flight pattern. Tail pattern (page 311) is often diagnostic but usually difficult to see in the field. **Painted-snipes** are superficially similar in build to the snipes but the brighter plumage is distinctive. Males are duller than females. **Woodcocks** though similar in appearance to snipe are distinguished by the cross-barring on the head and their woodland habitat. Usually crepuscular and nocturnal, they are difficult to see unless flushed.

Plate 35: Waders V (Calidrids – Sandpipers, Sanderling, Dunlin, Knots and Stints)

Calidrids are small to medium-sized, plump migratory waders with medium to longish bill, medium-long legs and fairly slim pointed wings. All are winter visitors or vagrants to the subcontinent and thus usually seen in the less distinctive non-breeding plumage. Identification usually rests on a combination of features including size, jizz, bill length and shape, supercilia, upperpart patterning, leg length and colour, extent of underpart wash or spotting, and in flight the pattern of white on the rump, tail and wings.

Plate 36: Jaegers and Skuas

These medium-large, stout seabirds are related to the gulls but distinguished by their largely brown and white plumage, strongly hooked bills, long sharp claws and more piratical habits. They chase other seabirds forcing them to drop prey or regurgitate food, but also feed directly on fish, birds, eggs, chicks, small mammals, carrion, insects and berries. Largely pelagic, they breed in higher latitudes. Plumages are confusingly variable, with some species occurring in dark, pale and an assortment of intermediate morphs as well as undergoing both seasonal and age-related changes. The illustrations only show a selection of typical examples, and positive identification may not always be possible, even if birds are seen well, which is seldom the case. Skuas and jaegers are usually silent away from their breeding grounds, so that voice is not of any significant diagnostic value. Jizz is often the best way of identifying species in this group, but the experience needed to familiarise oneself with this aspect is unlikely to be acquired in the subcontinent due to the scarcity of opportunities for observation. Females are generally similar to males but slightly larger. The characteristic central tail projections of the jaegers develop with age and are lacking in juveniles. They are often broken off, absent or reduced due to tail moult, particularly in the non-breeding birds more likely to occur in the subcontinent. Jaegers do not show the striking white blaze at the base of the primaries characteristic of skuas. Non-breeding birds show barring to varying degrees on some or all of rump, vent, flanks and breast-band. Immatures are characterised by the barred underwing-coverts.

Plates 37 & 38: Gulls

Gulls are robust, medium-sized seabirds with webbed feet, strong bills, long wings and fairly short, rounded or square-cut tails. Adult plumages are mostly a mixture of grey and white, often with black markings, while browner, more mottled feather tracts are characteristic of immature birds. Identification rests primarily on head and wing pattern, sometimes together with bill and leg coloration. The larger species take up to four years to reach adulthood and non-adult plumages can be very confusing. In the Indian region gulls are largely coastal species though some may be found on inland waterbodies. Versatile feeders, they subsist largely on animal matter such as fish, molluscs, carrion, birds, eggs, etc. The taxonomy of the so-called **Herring Gull group** (38.2–38.6) is in a state of flux and the arrangement followed here is provisional. The forms wintering in the Indian subcontinent are poorly known and there has been much confusion regarding their taxonomic affinities, birds variously being treated as subspecies of Herring Gull *Larus argentatus* and/or Lesser Black-backed Gull *Larus fuscus*, neither of which (as presently defined) is now considered to occur in the region. The group is characterised by large size; white head, underparts and tail; powerful yellow bill with red gonydeal spot; grey upperparts; contrastingly dark primaries tipped with white and usually showing 1 or 2 white 'mirrors' on the outer feathers. Size alone distinguishes them from all the other gulls in the region except Pallas's (37.7), which has a black hood in breeding plumage and a tricoloured bill. Field identification is extremely difficult and the subtle differences between the different forms are often only appreciable when direct comparison is possible. Assessment of features such as upperpart colour may depend on light conditions and viewing angle. Most characteristics are in any case variable, with a degree of overlap between species, and our understanding of them is still evolving. Important attributes to note are the exact shade of grey of the upperparts; bill size and shape; head shape; leg colour and length; degree of moult; exact pattern of the primaries; extent of streaking on the head and neck. A thorough study of the birds wintering in the subcontinent needs to be undertaken. All the species on this plate are winter visitors/vagrants to the sea coasts, but can turn up on larger waterbodies inland, especially on migration. Descriptive notes primarily refer to adult winter plumage. A treatment of the complex and often poorly known immature plumages is beyond the scope of this guide.

Plates 39–41: Terns, Noddies and Skimmers

Terns are similar to gulls but generally smaller and slimmer, with a slender pointed bill, slim pointed wings, forked tail and short legs. They generally feed by flying and plunge-diving for fish or dipping to pick prey items from the surface of the water or ground. Juveniles are distinguished from adults by scalloping on the upperparts. **Noddies** are often lumped with terns but are overall sooty-brown with longer bill and long wedge-shaped tail showing a shallow fork when spread. They are more pelagic than most other terns. **Skimmers** are related to terns but distinguished by the long, strong, scissor-like bill with elongated lower mandible. The feeding method is unique: skimming the surface of the water with bill open and lower mandible partly immersed to snap up any fish that may be encountered.

Plates 42 & 43: Sandgrouse and Pigeons

Sandgrouse are medium-sized terrestrial birds, similar in some respects to pigeons with short neck, small head, long pointed wings, longish wedge-shaped tail, short legs with feathered tarsi and toes. Plumage blends in well with their desert and semi-desert biotopes. An interesting adaptation is the ability of the males to carry water soaked into the belly feathers over long distances back to the nest. Flight is fast and direct, often in sizeable flocks. Gait is mincing and pigeon-like. All species are granivorous and ground-nesters. **Pigeons** and **doves** are plump medium-sized birds with small head, short bill and legs, broad longish tail. Largely granivorous and frugivorous, some are almost exclusively arboreal while others feed mainly on the ground. Flight is fast and direct. Most are quite gregarious. They nest in trees or on ledges of cliffs and buildings. Some species are quite nomadic outside the breeding season, following the availability of seasonal fruit and grain. The terms pigeon and dove are often interchangeable, though they are generally used to refer to the larger and smaller species respectively.

Plate 44: Parakeets and Hanging Parrots

Parakeets are medium-sized birds with largely green plumage, large head, short neck, strong, rounded hooked bill and long tail with elongated central tail feathers. Gregarious and chiefly arboreal, they feed mainly on fruit and grain and will often gather in huge flocks where food is abundant. They often use their bills to give extra purchase when clambering about in trees. Flight is swift and direct, and the flight call is more-or-less a harsh scream, which can with practice be used for identifying the species. We have not illustrated young birds, which are difficult to identify specifically as they generally lack the distinctive markings of the adults. Such birds are, in any case, usually found in the company of adults of the same species. The related **hanging parrots** are much smaller with short tails lacking streamers. They habitually sleep upside-down, whence the name.

Plate 45: Cuckoos and Malkohas

Cuckoos are medium-sized zygodactylous birds with long graduated tails and characteristic, slightly decurved bills. They are brood-parasitic, laying their eggs in the nests of other birds, which then raise the young as their own. In most species sexes are alike, although some females also have a hepatic (rufous-brown) morph. Some cuckoos are very similar in plumage and are best distinguished by their distinctive loud calls which are monotonously repeated in the breeding season, often from an exposed perch; they are inconspicuous at other times of the year. They are largely solitary and arboreal, but may descend to the ground to feed. **Malkohas** are related to cuckoos but are larger, plumper-bodied with a stouter bill and very long graduated tail; they raise their own young and are usually found singly or in pairs frequenting the mid-storey.

Plate 46: Koel, Coucals, Frogmouths and Nightjars

The **Koel** is a kind of cuckoo (see previous plate). **Coucals** are related to cuckoos and malkohas but are much larger with stout bodies and broad tails. They frequent bushes, scrub and grassland as well as low to mid-storey forest. They are not brood-parasitic. Omnivorous. **Nightjars** are medium-sized, cryptically-mottled species with broad gapes adapted for hawking insects. Eyes are large, tail is long, and wings are long and pointed. Their nocturnal habits and similar plumages make them normally very difficult to observe adequately and identify except by voice. They spend the day roosting on the ground or perched along a horizontal branch, when they may be fairly closely approached, allowing identification by the following features: size; pattern of white in tail and wing (absent in females of most species); amount of streaking on crown; pattern of scapulars. **Frogmouths** are similar to nightjars but with larger head, much broader heavier bill, more rounded wings and habit of roosting in an upright position.

Plates 47 & 48: Owls

Owls are birds of prey with a large rounded head, short neck, rounded wings and short tail. Most, but not all, species are partly, if not wholly, nocturnal. Adaptations to a life of hunting by night include the facial disk which helps focus sound to the asymmetrically placed ears so that the bird can pinpoint the location of its prey aurally, soft plumage to enable soundless flight, and large eyes with good night-vision. Important features to note for identification: presence or absence of 'horns' (ear-tufts); overall coloration; shape of facial disc; pattern and strength of barring and streaking on underparts; eye colour; tail barring. Note that the 'horns', which some owl species have, may be raised or lowered. They are usually fairly obvious where present. Calls are often the most useful diagnostic feature. Fish owls can be distinguished from other owls by their unfeathered tarsi, and from eagle owls additionally by the dark tail with narrow buffy bars.

Plate 49: Swifts, Swiftlets, Needletails and Treeswift

Swifts are superficially similar to swallows (plate 58) but have longer scythe-like wings and a generally stiffer flight consisting of rapid wing-beats interspersed with long glides. Overall plumage is dark brown or black, occasionally with a blue or green gloss, relieved in many species with distinctive patches of white. Their very short legs reflect the fact that they spend most of their time in the air hawking for insects and are only seen perched at roosting or nesting sites, which are usually in caves, old buildings, rock faces or hollow trees. They often fly very high and are frequently seen at the edge of an approaching weather front feeding on the clouds of insects which it stirs up. **Swiftlets** are smaller with square-ended or notched tails. They breed colonially using hardened saliva in the construction of the nests, which are highly prized by some Asiatic peoples for their supposed medicinal properties and for making birds' nest soup. The collection of these nests is endangering the species' survival. **Needletails** are among the fastest flying birds in the world. They are bulkier then other swifts with broader wings and short square-ended tails tipped with needle-like projections (only visible at close range). **Treeswifts** are unlike other swifts in being less aerial, more colourful, sporting a crest, and building their nests in the forks of branches. Since species on this plate are mostly seen on the wing, identification notes primarily refer to birds in flight.

Plate 50: Rollers, Trogons and Kingfishers

Rollers are heavily-built, medium-sized birds with colourful, predominantly blue and purple plumage. The head is large; bill strong and broad; neck and legs short; tail broad; wings long and broad. They hunt from a lookout perch by hawking for insects or dropping onto small animals on the ground; they usually occur singly or in loose pairs. The striking wing-pattern is shown to great advantage in their rolling acrobatic display-flight. **Trogons** are shy, brightly coloured, medium-sized inhabitants of broadleaved evergreen forests. Appearance is chunky with characteristic long, broad square-cut tail; short rounded wings; short, thick, broad bill; short legs; upright posture. Generally found singly or in pairs, sometimes with mixed flocks, usually frequenting the mid-storey from where they sally forth after insects. **Kingfishers** are small to medium-sized birds with long strong bill; large flat head; short neck; compact body; short rounded wings; and short weak legs. Many are tied to aquatic habitats, subsisting largely on fish caught by diving from an exposed position, but some prey chiefly on insects and small animals well away from water.

Plate 51: Bee-eaters, Barbets and Hoopoe

Bee-eaters are mostly slim and medium-sized; plumage is essentially green with splashes of blue, yellow and chestnut; longish, slim, pointed decurved bill; long triangular pointed wings; long tail, often with elongated central tail feathers; short weak legs. Gregarious. They hawk for insects or catch them in graceful sallies from an exposed perch, and nest in burrows. **Barbets** are brightly coloured chunky birds, predominantly green with diagnostic patches of red, orange, blue, yellow and/or brown on the head. Strong stout bill; short rounded wings; short to medium-length tail. Strictly arboreal, frequenting the canopy. Chiefly frugivorous, often attracted in large numbers to fruiting trees. They generally excavate their own nesting holes. The single South Asian species of **hoopoe** is a highly distinctive fawn colour with black wings and tail barred white; long erectile crest tipped with black; long downcurved bill. Usually solitary or in small loose groups feeding on the ground. Nests in tree hollows.

Plate 52: Hornbills

Hornbills are large birds with broad wings, long tails and very large bills. In most species the bill is surmounted by a distinctive casque which grows in size as the bird reaches maturity over a period of several years. Most inhabit forests, though some frequent open wooded areas, including parks and gardens. They subsist largely on fruit, being particularly partial to figs; their movements are thus to some extent dictated by the fruiting of trees. They will, however, also feed on small animals and birds. The flight is slow and direct; the larger birds are audible from some distance due to the loud whooshing noise made by their wings. Outside the breeding season some species congregate in flocks. In flight most hornbills can be readily identified by the tail pattern. On perched birds it can be important to note the shape and pattern of the casque as well as the coloration of the bare parts. Hornbills are also unusual in that the entrance to the nesting cavity is sealed up with the female inside. She is fed by her mate through a narrow slit and does not emerge for several weeks or months until the young are partly grown or even fully fledged. Their size and habit of breeding in tree hollows mean that the hornbills' survival depends on the continued existence of large mature trees in primary forest which provide the necessary nesting sites. Progressive deforestation and hunting by man have resulted in population decreases in almost all species of hornbill.

Plates 53–55: Woodpeckers, Piculets, Wryneck and Honeyguide

Woodpeckers specialise in hunting for insects and larvae in the bark and wood of trees. To this end they have evolved a strong, conical, chisel-like bill for excavating and a very long sticky tongue for extracting their prey from deep crevices and bore-holes in the wood. The tail is specially adapted with stiff central feathers used as a support when climbing trees. Most are zygodactylous. They work their way up a treetrunk or branch in short erratic bursts, their bill-tapping often giving away their presence. Many species also feed terrestrially on ants. The flight is typically strong and undulating. Generally non-migratory. Usually solitary, in pairs or small family groups, though many regularly associate with mixed hunting parties. Most have more-or-less loud calls as well as territorial drumming displays produced in the breeding season by a rapid hammering of their bills on a resonant piece of wood. Nesting cavities are excavated in trees and sometimes in ants' or termites' nests. **Piculets** are tiny, plump, short-tailed woodpeckers. Chiefly forage for ants, their pupae and eggs on small branches, twigs and bamboo in the manner of a nuthatch. They often tap loudly with their bills. Usually occur singly or in pairs but often with mixed hunting parties. They excavate nesting holes in rotten branches and bamboo. **Wrynecks** are cryptically coloured birds in a subfamily of the woodpeckers. When perched on a tree they may look like part of an old broken branch. They mostly forage on the ground for ants and other invertebrates. Usually solitary or in pairs. **Honeyguides** are small, zygodactylous arboreal birds which specialise in feeding on insects, larvae and the wax from wild bees' honeycombs. They often bear a superficial resemblance to bulbuls but the sole South Asian species could also be mistaken for a finch. More or less restricted to forests in the vicinity of rock bees' nests which are usually found hanging from steep cliffs of Himalayan river gorges. Rather solitary, birds may defend a colony of bees' nests against others of their own species. African species are said to lead humans to honeycombs, whence the name.

Plate 56: Broadbills, Ioras, Leafbirds, Fairy Bluebird, Orioles, Waxwing and Pittas

Broadbills are brightly coloured, medium-sized birds with largish heads and broad flattened bills. Usually in family parties, often in mixed flocks, moving from tree to tree in the mid and upper storeys. They feed mainly on grasshoppers, insects, bugs and spiders and can be quite tame and approachable. **Ioras** are slim, sparrow-sized, greenish-yellow birds with a slender straight bill. They generally keep to the foliage of trees and bushes and feed on insects, grubs and caterpillars. Normally singly or in pairs, often in mixed flocks. Breeding male more brightly coloured than female but attains drabber plumage in the winter months. **Leafbirds** are medium-sized green and yellow birds with slender downcurved bills. They merge in well with their preferred habitat of dense canopy foliage. Often attracted to flowering trees, they feed on nectar and fruit as well as invertebrates. Leafbirds can be quite vocal; some are skilled mimics. **Fairy bluebirds** are large, stout-bodied, thrush-like birds related to the leafbirds but coloured blue and black. Small loose parties of non-breeding birds rove around forests in search of fruit and nectar. Generally arboreal but also descend to fruit-bearing bushes. **Orioles** are sturdy colourful thrush-sized birds. Males are usually black and yellow or similarly conspicuous colours; females and young often duller. Normally solitary or in pairs feeding on berries, fruit and insects in the tree canopy. Flight fast and slightly undulating. Song mellow with a flute-like quality; calls often harsh with a cat-like nasal tone. **Waxwings** are gregarious inhabitants of temperate and boreal regions of the Northern Hemisphere. Somewhat starling-shaped with a distinctive crest and short broad bill. The name derives from waxy red droplets often found on the tips of the secondaries. Chiefly subsist on fruit and berries. Rather nomadic; in some winters they appear in regions well to the south of their usual range, a few having strayed as far as South Asia. **Pittas** are colourful, long-legged birds the size of a thrush but plumper and shorter-tailed. They generally hop around on the forest floor, over fallen logs and in dense undergrowth, usually singly or in loose pairs. They feed on insects, beetles, grubs, snails, worms etc. Very shy, and best located by characteristic whistling calls. More likely to be seen in the open just after dawn or at dusk and may take to trees to sing or roost.

Plate 57: Larks

Larks are generally small to medium-sized ground-feeding birds of open arid regions. For the newcomer to birdwatching they can be confusingly similar to the pipits, some of which inhabit the same habitats. With practice the larks can be distinguished from the latter by their shorter-tailed, dumpier appearance, heavier bills, shorter legs and habit of crouching down when approached before taking flight if the intruder comes too near. Some species are particularly fine songsters often with characteristic song-flights, making up vocally for what they lack in visual appeal. The subdued streaked brown and grey patterns blend in well with their surroundings, the underpart coloration in some species being slightly variable and tending to match the locally predominant soil colour. Specific identification can be difficult with the exception of the rather distinctive Horned Lark, Greater Hoopoe Lark and sparrow lark males. Sexes are similar in all but the sparrow larks. Flight is normally strong and undulating. **Bushlarks** can be distinguished from most other larks by the more-or-less obvious rufous wing-patch and the jerky, stiff wing-beats. The tips of their tertials reach the tips of the primaries. They do not usually call when flushed. *Ammomanes* larks are separated from most other larks by their comparatively unstreaked upperparts. **Skylarks** have short indistinct crests that are not obvious unless raised. **Short-toed larks** are all rather small with more-or-less streaked upperparts and relatively short stubby bills. (The toe length is rarely a helpful feature in the field.) The rather large, stout-billed *Melanocorypha* larks usually have a distinct black patch at the sides of the neck, a feature that is otherwise only shown by the much smaller Hume's and Greater Short-toed Larks. **Crested larks** are easily identified by the long pointed crest which is usually upstanding and obvious.

Plate 58: Swallows and Martins

Swallows and **martins** are small slim birds which spend much of their time on the wing hawking for insects. Wings are long and pointed; bill small but with a comparatively wide gape; legs short and weak; tail more-or-less forked in most species.

Often confused with the unrelated swifts (plate 49), but have shorter, relatively broader wings, a more fluttering flight and they frequently perch on wires and other lookouts which true swifts almost never do. Gregarious, often roosting or assembling in large gatherings. Collectively referred to as hirundines, the name swallow is usually applied to the longer-tailed species. The **crag martins** show a band of white tail-spots which helps distinguish them from the **sand martins**.

Plate 59: Woodswallows and Drongos

Woodswallows are small chunky birds with broad triangular wings, short square tails and short broad-based bill with a wide gape. They feed by catching insects on the wing in a characteristic gliding flight. They perch openly on tops of bare trees, telegraph wires etc., often in close contact with neighbouring birds. **Drongos** are medium-sized birds with strong, slightly downcurved bills and medium to very long tails that are forked or otherwise characteristic, but beware of birds with broken or moulting tail feathers. In most species the plumage is largely black with varying degrees of gloss. Rather upright when perched, they are very agile in flight when chasing winged insects. Some species which are otherwise solitary may congregate around swarms of insects. All but the Black Drongo are primarily forest birds. With practice some species can be identified by voice, but many have a wide range of vocalisations and are adept at confusing the observer by their superb mimicry of other birds.

Plate 60: Hypocolius, Flycatcher-shrike, Woodshrikes and Shrikes

The **Hypocolius** is the only member of its family and is reminiscent of both bulbuls and shrikes with an elongated body, long tail, slight bushy crest and the male's dark mask. **Flycatcher-shrikes** are small pied birds with arboreal flycatching habits and an upright stance when perched. They are related to cuckoo-shrikes and minivets (plate 64) rather than flycatchers and shrikes. **Woodshrikes** are medium-sized, fairly thickset, grey/brown birds with a strong, hook-tipped bill, rounded wings, medium-length tail and a dark mask through the eye. Largely insectivorous and arboreal. **Shrikes** are small to medium-sized passerines with strong, hook-tipped bill, largish head, short, fairly thick neck, medium-length pointed wings, long, slightly graduated tail, strong legs with sharp claws and upright stance. They hunt from an exposed perch, swooping down on their insect and small animal prey, sometimes impaling prey on thorns. They utter a variety of harsh and squeaky notes.

Plate 61: Starlings and Mynas

Starlings are medium-sized birds with a straight pointed bill, relatively short triangular wings and a shortish, squarish tail. The flight is fast and direct. On the ground they walk or run rather than hop. They are often highly gregarious especially in winter when huge flocks may form. Some species are largely arboreal feeding on the nectar of flowers, fruit and insects while others also forage on the ground. Most are rather noisy with a variety of loud chattering, squeaking and whistling calls. Some are good mimics. The **mynas**, while related to the starlings, are bulkier with a strong, slightly decurved bill. The wings are more rounded and adorned by a pale wing-patch (at the base of the primaries), more obvious in flight. Some species have distinctively coloured bare skin around the eye. They enjoy a fairly catholic diet and are equally at home on the ground as on trees, bushes and buildings. They are rather noisy with a range of loud chattering, ringing and squeaking notes. The Common Myna is one of the most familiar birds in the Indian subcontinent as it is commonly found around human habitation. The **hill mynas** (or **grackles**) are equal in size or somewhat larger than the other myna species. They are glossy black birds with distinctive yellow wattles on the head and a white wing-patch. Largely arboreal, they feed on fruit, flowers, nectar and insects. They are quite sociable and noisy. In the wild they can be recognised by their loud whistling notes but their skills as mimics in captivity make them popular cagebirds.

Plate 62: Corvids (Jays, Magpies, Treepies, Nutcracker and Groundpecker)

Corvids are medium-sized to large powerful passerines with strong bills and legs. Most are omnivorous, noisy and gregarious. Flight is usually direct and heavy. Most have untidy nests of twigs placed in trees. **Jays** are bright medium-sized corvids with rounded wings, bushy crest and medium-long tail. They inhabit temperate Himalayan forests and utter a variety of harsh notes but also with some mimicry. **Magpies** and **treepies** are colourful members of the crow tribe with very long tails and similar omnivorous, noisy and sociable habits. The **nutcrackers** have a similar build to the jays but the tail is comparatively short, the plumage brown with white spotting and the bill is longer, more conical, adapted to feeding on nuts and pine seeds. **Groundpeckers** (**ground-jays**) are thrush-sized terrestrial birds rather unlike other corvids, with strong decurved bill, long legs and an upright stance somewhat reminiscent of a wheatear.

Plate 63: Black Corvids (Crows, Rook, Ravens, Jackdaws and Choughs)

The **crows** (including Rook) and **ravens** are perhaps the most typical of the corvids with their largely black plumage, strong build and heavy bill. They are noisy and gregarious, and often wary but not shy. The House Crow is among the most familiar of Indian birds. **Jackdaws** are relatively small compact crows with comparatively small head and bill, and rounded wings.

Choughs are intermediate in size between jackdaws and crows with the typical black plumage, comparatively long, slim, red or yellow downcurved bill and rounded, long-fingered wings. Flight is graceful and acrobatic, often utilising the updraughts in the mountains they frequent. Gregarious and often tame.

Plate 64: Cuckooshrikes, Triller and Minivets
Small to medium-sized birds of forests and open woodland, with relatively long pointed wings and somewhat graduated tails. They generally keep to the canopy and mid-storey, feeding chiefly on insects and the like. **Cuckooshrikes** are robust, medium-sized birds with predominantly grey plumage and strong blackish bills. For specific identification note the shade of grey and exact pattern of barring on the underparts. **Minivets** and **trillers** are pied or brightly coloured with fairly long tails and strong, slim black bills. Plumage is predominantly black, red/orange, grey and white in males, the red/orange colour largely replaced by yellow in females. They often move around in flocks which may consist of more than one species of minivet; sometimes also in mixed hunting parties. Truly red males can be identified to species by the exact pattern of red on the wings. Females can be more confusing, it being important to note the exact pattern of yellow on the wing, forehead, chin and throat.

Plate 65: Bulbuls
Bulbuls are medium-sized birds with short rounded wings, medium-long tails and short-medium bills. Several species have distinctive crests. They chiefly inhabit trees, shrubs and bushes feeding on fruit, berries and insects. Many species are rather vocal and gregarious; some are among the more familiar birds of parks and gardens. Sexes alike.

Plate 66: Babblers I (Jungle and Wren Babblers) and Winter Wren
Babblers form a diverse group of small to medium-sized passerines with soft plumage, short rounded wings and strong legs. They are largely insectivorous inhabitants of forest and scrub. Many species are gregarious and noisy with a variety of musical notes as well as chattering, rattling and babbling calls. Most are sedentary, some moving to higher or lower altitudes according to season. Sexes usually alike. **Jungle** and **wren babblers** are generally small, dumpy brown birds that spend most of their time foraging on or near the ground in the undergrowth of dense forests, bamboo and thick scrub. Many have conspicuously short tails. Their habits and habitat tend to make them inconspicuous, though not always shy. Most species are solitary or in pairs. The **Winter Wren** is superficially similar to the smaller wren babblers. Its stubby tail is characteristically cocked. Occurs in high altitude rocky and bushy habitats in the Himalaya.

Plate 67: Babblers II (Scimitar, Tree and Tit Babblers)
The **scimitar babblers**, as the name suggests, are principally distinguished by their long downcurved bills. They are usually found in pairs or small parties, sometimes in mixed hunting groups with other species, feeding on the forest floor, in the undergrowth and low trees. They are quite vocal with male and female often calling to each other in short resonant antiphonal duets. The female reply is usually so immediate that the two parts sound as though given by one bird. The remaining babblers on this plate are mainly small, more-or-less gregarious inhabitants of forest undergrowth.

Plate 68: Babblers III (*Turdoides*, Leiothrix, Mesia, Cutia and Shrike Babblers)
The *Turdoides* babblers are a group of largish dumpy babblers with long, broad, floppy-looking tails. Plumage is rather monochrome with few, if any, markedly contrasting patches of colour. They generally live in family groups of up to a dozen or more, roosting close together and frequently indulging in mutual preening. They mainly keep to the ground, low undergrowth, scrub, grass and bushes, though individual 'lookouts' often ascend higher in trees. The **Leiothrix** and **Mesia** are small, colourful, gregarious inhabitants of humid forest undergrowth. The **Cutia** is the only member of its genus and a rather heavyset multicoloured bird with habits like those of a slow-moving nuthatch. **Shrike babblers** are small, stocky arboreal birds distinguished from other babblers by the somewhat hook-tipped bill. Usually found in bird waves.

Plate 69: Babblers IV (Fulvettas, Minlas and Sibias)
Fulvettas (**tit babblers**) are small, chiefly gregarious babblers with short rounded wings, rounded head, short bill, short thick neck, and medium-length tail. Usually found in flocks, both single species and mixed, frequenting forest undergrowth and mid-storey. **Minlas** are colourful slim babblers with short straight bill and medium-long square-ended tail. Gregarious. **Sibias** are medium-sized with strong decurved bill and very long graduated tail. Arboreal and gregarious.

Plate 70: Babblers V (Parrotbills, Yuhinas, Myzornis and *Timalia*)
Parrotbills are distinguished by the short deep, parrot-like bill with curved cutting edges to the mandibles used for cutting grass and bamboo stems. Gregarious but shy inhabitants of bamboo and grassland. **Yuhinas** are somewhat like fulvettas (plate 69) but generally slimmer, crested, not so bull-necked, with somewhat finer more pointed bill, longer, more pointed

wings and more arboreal habits. The **Myzornis** is a small babbler in a genus of its own. It has distinctive bright green plumage with red and black tail and wing markings.

Plates 71 & 72: Babblers VI (Babaxes, Barwings and Laughingthrushes)

Babaxes are large, distinctly streaked, montane babblers with longish, slightly decurved bills, more closely related to the *Turdoides* babblers than the laughingthrushes. Usually in pairs or small parties hopping around on the ground, in bushes and trees. **Barwings** as the name suggests show distinctive black barring on the wings (and tail). Outside the breeding season they are generally found in groups of up to a dozen or more birds, sometimes together with sibias and laughingthrushes, working their way through bushes and lower trees. **Laughingthrushes** are large, stocky, long-tailed babblers which usually feed on the ground and in the undergrowth. Most species are gregarious, keeping together in large family groups of six to a dozen, sometimes even 50 or more, particularly outside the breeding season. They tend to move in follow-my-leader fashion, and are usually rather wary, trying to keep plenty of vegetation between themselves and the observer. When disturbed they may strike up a cacophony of cackling, squealing, babbling, chattering or laughing notes – hence the name.

Plates 73 & 74: Mangrove Whistler and Flycatchers

Whistlers are reminiscent of chats and flycatchers but more strongly-built with a thick rounded head, short thick neck and short heavy bill. They pick insects from branches and foliage but also fly-catch. **Flycatchers** form a large varied group of insectivorous passerines which feed mostly by making short sallies from a perch to catch flying insects but some also glean prey items from foliage. Bill is generally short, slightly broad and flat and surrounded by rictal bristles; legs thin. Usually perch rather upright. Occur singly, in loose pairs or small family groups. Calls are harsh or ticking; songs usually thin and warbling.

Plate 75: Monarch Flycatchers, Fantails, Flycatcher-warblers, Goldcrest, Tesias and Tit Warblers

Fantails are small birds with short rounded wings and long broad tail habitually held cocked and fanned. Usually found in the lower and mid-storey, they often switch from side to side in order to disturb their insect prey. **Warblers** form a large diverse group of mainly small compact passerines with short slender bill, thin short to medium legs and medium wings. They feed chiefly on insects. Mostly non-gregarious. **Goldcrests** are tiny, brightly coloured arboreal warblers. **Tesias** have very short tails and long legs. Unlike most other warblers they spend most of the time on the ground and in low undergrowth. Warblers of the genera *Seicercus*, *Abroscopus* and *Tickellia* are fairly robust-looking with yellow on the underparts and distinctive head markings. Alström and Olsson (1999 – too late for inclusion on the plate) suggest that the species previously known as Golden-spectacled Warbler *Seicercus burkii* should in fact be treated as several separate species of which three occur in our region: Golden-spectacled Warbler *Seicercus burkii*, Whistler's Warbler *S. whistleri* and Grey-crowned Warbler *S. tephrocephalus*. They are very similar, but the following summary of the main distinguishing features should be of help with identification:

    S. burkii has black lateral crown stripes, usually distinct in front of the eye and almost reaching the bill; median crown stripe green with sparse, thin, pale greyish streaks; green border immediately below lateral crown stripes; upperparts average brighter, more yellowish-green than *whistleri*; underparts average deeper, more saturated yellow than on *whistleri*; greater covert wing-bar usually faint or absent but can be distinct; little or no white on third outermost tail feather; no white on outer web of outer tail feather or only very thin pale stripe along shaft at base. Call is a soft 'whiplash' *huit*. Song is distinguished from *whistleri* by the presence of tremolos and trills. It breeds along the main Himalayan range, generally at lower altitudes than *whistleri* though with some overlap (in Uttar Pradesh recorded singing/breeding between c. 2085 and 2600m, in Kalimpong district of NE India between c. 1700 and 2050m).

    S. whistleri has greyish-black lateral crown stripes, becoming indistinct in front of the eye; median crown stripe as *burkii* or slightly paler greenish with less grey; green border immediately below lateral crown stripes; upperparts dull greyish-green; underparts yellow with some greenish/brownish on sides of breast and flanks; greater covert wing-bar usually distinct but can be faint or absent; distinct long white wedge on inner web of third outermost tail feather; basal part of outer web of outermost tail feather has broad white stripe along shaft or is all white. Call is a *tiu* or *tiu(-)du* or *chip*, softer and lower-pitched than *burkii*. Song lacks the tremolos and trills of the other two species. It breeds along the main Himalayan range, generally at higher altitudes than *burkii* (in Uttar Pradesh recorded singing/breeding between c. 2775 and 3050m, in Kalimpong district of NE India between c. 2000 and 2300m) and in the hills south of the Brahmaputra near the Burmese border.

    S. tephrocephalus is similar to *burkii* but forehead/median crown stripe usually grey with little or no green; border immediately below dark lateral crown stripes grey. Call is poorly-known but has been described as a short, comparatively faint *chup* and a double *chu(-)du* or *tu(-)ru* in China. Song is insufficiently known for reliable separation from *burkii*. Breeds in the hills south of the Brahmaputra near the Burmese border (and in western Myanmar/Burma).

Wintering distributions are not fully studied, but as a group they appear to winter within their breeding ranges with some movement to lower altitudes, as well as southerly migration as far as Bangladesh, central India, the Eastern Ghats of northeastern Andhra Pradesh and SE Asia.

Plate 76: Bush and Grasshopper Warblers

Bush and **grasshopper warblers** are small insectivorous birds which generally keep inside dense bushes, long grass and undergrowth, where they are difficult to observe. Plumage patterns are not highly differentiated, being largely a mixture of greys and browns. Observation of any individual bird requires a degree of patience and is often a piecing together of incomplete views; however, be aware that more than one species may often be present in the same bush! Species diagnosis generally requires being sure of several characteristics and specific identification of a given bird may not always be possible in the field. With practice an observer can become familiar with the call notes and during the breeding season some species are most easily identified by their rather distinctive songs. Many species are under-recorded and poorly understood due to the difficulties involved in observation and identification. **Cettia warblers** are medium-sized, unstreaked bush warblers with rounded wings and square-ended, often notched tails. There is normally a little white showing on the edge of the bend in the closed wing. They generally prefer more wooded or scrubby areas than the *Bradypterus* warblers and hop through the brushwood rather than run. **Bradypterus bush warblers** are also unstreaked with obviously rounded tails, the pattern on the undertail-coverts being important for identification. They generally prefer grassier habitats and often scuttle along the ground, rather like a small rodent. **Grasshopper warblers** of the genus *Locustella* have streaked upperparts and rather broad, rounded tails with elongated undertail-coverts. They inhabit wet and scrubby vegetation and are very skulking, often creeping around in thick grass, bushes and reeds.

Plate 77: Prinias, Scrub Warbler, Grassbirds and Cisticolas

The birds on this plate are largely insectivorous inhabitants of various types of grassland, though some also make use of adjoining scrub and mixed habitats. **Prinias** are small to medium-sized warblers with short rounded wings and long thin graduated tails often held cocked and/or rather loosely waved around. Tail is usually shorter in breeding season; rectrices show white tips (subterminally blackish), which may be lost by abrasion. Several species are confusingly similar. Age-, season- and latitude-related plumage variation add to the complexity. They often forage in loose parties with birds in different stages of plumage. Range, habitat and voice are frequently useful additional clues. **Grassbirds** are medium to large warblers with fairly broad graduated tails. Very skulking except for Striated Grassbird. **Cisticolas** are small warblers with short graduated tails, short rounded wings and streaked upperparts.

Plate 78: Reed and 'Tree' Warblers

The two groups of warblers illustrated here present some of the most difficult identification challenges to birdwatchers. With practice and patience it is, however, possible to sort out these tricky 'little brown jobs' but even experienced observers may not be able to identify every bird seen. The **reed warblers** of the genus *Acrocephalus* are typically fairly slim with relatively long bill, flat crown and head, and rounded tails. The plumage is brown above and pale below. The song is usually repetitive and churring but can include mimicry. As the English name implies 'acros' are usually found in marshy habitats but this does not apply to all species. They are mostly fairly skulking, keeping low down in dense vegetation, and the best chances of observation are often in the early morning when they may climb to the top of a reed or bush to preen and sun themselves. The *Hippolais* **warblers** are very similar to the unstreaked reed warblers but generally greyer and without rufous tones in the more uniform plumage. The tails are square-ended, or only slightly rounded at the corners, with white on the outer feathers, and the undertail-coverts relatively short, though may be long on Olivaceous Warblers. Recent mitochondrial DNA research indicates that the latter and Booted Warbler may in fact be more closely related to the *Acrocephalus* group.

Plate 79: Tailorbirds and *Sylvia* Warblers

Tailorbirds are small warblers with fairly long thin graduated tails, greenish upperparts, rufous crowns and long, thin, slightly downcurved bills. They are named after their habit of stitching leaves together to build a nest. Dark-necked and Mountain Tailorbirds are strictly forest species inhabiting dense undergrowth in the north-eastern part of the subcontinent, while the Common Tailorbird is a familiar widespread species found in parks, gardens and scrubby margins of woodland throughout most of the region. The *Sylvia* **warblers** are fairly small, sturdy and mostly round-headed with relatively short stubby bills compared to other warblers. The tail is usually square-ended, often with whitish outer tail feathers. They generally inhabit scrub, semi-desert, light woodland, thorn forest, parks and gardens in drier habitats.

Plate 80: Leaf Warblers

The **leaf warblers** of the genus *Phylloscopus* are small active birds which mainly feed on insects and spiders among the foliage of trees and bushes. Their plumage is generally dominated by brown and olive tones with contrasting dark, yellow, buff or white markings. All species show a more-or-less distinct supercilium and dark line through the eye. The tail is normally fairly square-cut with a slight notch and rounded corners. With many of the species being rather similar in pattern and coloration, specific identification within this group is among the most challenging of tasks for the birdwatcher. It is important to note as many of the following features as possible: the exact colour of under- and upperparts; number and colour of wing-bars; presence or absence of crown-stripe, pale rump, white in the outer tail feathers and pale fringes to the tertials; exact length, shape, colour and distinctness of the supercilium; length of primary projection; bill shape and colour; leg colour. All characteristics show some variability within any given species, so that birds should generally not be identified solely on the basis of one or two field marks. Although the number of wing-bars is an important feature it should be borne in mind that some individuals of species which normally show wing-bars may lose them due to abrasion of the feather tips, and conversely some birds which normally have no wing-bar may occasionally show a faint one if observed closely. In addition to considerable individual variation, moult and feather wear seasonally affect plumage coloration, with most species appearing brighter in fresh plumage. In general, an intermediate winter plumage has been illustrated. The best identification feature is often the call. Range, behaviour and habitat may be useful additional pointers.

Plates 81 & 82: Robins and Redstarts, Rock Chat, Shama, Forktails and Dippers

Robins form a large varied group consisting of the genera *Luscinia, Tarsiger, Irania, Cercotrichas, Myiomela, Cinclidium, Copsychus* and *Saxicoloides* in the thrush family. They are small to medium-sized insectivorous birds with short, fairly slim bill, medium wings, and medium to longish tails. Stance is normally quite upright. Mostly shy in bushes, undergrowth and on the ground. **Redstarts** are generally distinguished from robins and other chats by the rufous flashes in the medium-long tail, which is often shivered or spread. They frequently sit on low perches in the open. **Forktails** are members of the thrush family with pied plumage and long deeply forked tails. Mostly found along forested Himalayan mountain streams, hopping from rock to rock or walking along the banks, feeding on insects and other aquatic invertebrates. Usually fly low over the water. Shrill calls carry above the noise of the water. **Dippers** are rotund brown birds with short wings and tail. Tied to fast-flowing montane rivers where they swim and walk under water searching for invertebrate prey beneath the stones. Fast direct flight low over the water.

Plate 83: Wheatears, Stonechats and Bushchats

Wheatears are slim pied and buffy/brown birds with distinctive tail patterns shown when the tail is spread (see page 311). Largely terrestrial inhabitants of open arid regions (virtually restricted to the north-western part of the subcontinent). Usually perch on rocks, low walls and bushes watching out for insects, beetles, lizards and other small prey. **Bush-** and **stonechats** are generally somewhat smaller, dumpier and shorter-tailed than wheatears. Ordinarily inhabit less arid, better vegetated open areas than the latter group. Spend most of the time conspicuously perched fairly upright on low bushes or other lookouts flying down occasionally to pick up insect prey from the ground. Often flick their wings and fan their tails. When flushed, birds of both groups usually only fly a short distance before settling on another exposed perch.

Plate 84: Rock, Whistling and *Zoothera* Thrushes, Grandala, Cochoas

In build **rock thrushes** are fairly typical thrushes (see next paragraph). Sexually dichromatic. The ♂♂ are coloured blue with various proportions of chestnut, red or white. Perch with a rather upright stance. **Whistling thrushes** are medium to large dark blue thrushes with pale blue markings. Generally frequent hill/montane watercourses and neighbouring moist vegetated areas. Calls are shrill and carry above the sound of running water. The **Grandala** is a slim long-winged bird somewhat between a starling and a thrush in build. Inhabits high-altitude open country, usually in large flocks. Feeds on the ground. Upright stance when perched. **Cochoas** are fairly large, robust, colourful, thrush-like birds with fairly broad bills. Shy, unobtrusive, arboreal and frugivorous. **Zootheras** are distinguished from other thrushes by broad pale bands on the underwing. Usually found singly or in pairs feeding on the ground in forested habitats. Often fly up into a tree when disturbed.

Plate 85: Shortwings and *Turdus* Thrushes

Thrushes are fairly robust, medium-sized passerines with a relatively slim bill, fairly long wings and legs. Largely insectivorous, some supplement their diet with fruit. Some are chiefly arboreal while others are more terrestrial and move by hopping, rather than walking. Most thrushes found in the subcontinent are relatively solitary though some may gather in flocks, particularly in winter. Many are good songsters as judged by the human ear. Juveniles are usually spotted in contradistinction to those of warblers and babblers. **Shortwings** are small thrushes with short rounded wings and short square tail. Chiefly insectivorous, feeding on the ground and in moist dense undergrowth. Solitary, shy and skulking. Members of the genus *Turdus* are typical thrushes.

Plate 86: Tits

Small active acrobatic birds with short conical bill, short to medium rounded wings, medium to long tail, short strong legs. Subsist chiefly on insects, but also take seeds and fruit. Mostly arboreal, though may feed on the ground. Usually in small flocks, often mixed with other species. *Parus* and *Sylviparus* are chiefly tree cavity-nesters. The others mostly build hanging balls of moss, lichens, hair, feathers etc.

Plate 87: Creepers and Nuthatches

Treecreepers are small plump passerines with long, slender downcurved bill, short pointed tail and short slim legs. Upperparts are largely brown above, spotted and barred with buff and white; underparts chiefly whitish. They creep up treetrunks and branches, usually in spiral fashion using the stiff tail as a support, probing in crevices for their insect prey. Often solitary but may join bird waves outside the breeding season. Voices are thin and high-pitched. The **Spotted Creeper** is similar but has spotted underparts and the tail is not stiff. **Nuthatches** are small and stocky with short tails and strong, straight pointed bill. Plumage largely blue/grey above, white/rusty/chestnut/buff below. Arboreal (except Eastern Rock Nuthatch which lives on rocky cliffs). They feed on insects, spiders, nuts and seeds and forage mainly on treetrunks and branches climbing up, sideways, down or upside-down with equal facility. Solitary or in pairs, sometimes in mixed flocks. The related **Wallcreeper** is unmistakably unique with its long slender bill and broad, rounded, butterfly wings marked with deep red, which are often flicked open to disturb its insect prey as it creeps over the cliff faces of its montane habitat.

Plate 88: Pipits

Pipits are small, rather nondescript, ground-feeding birds. They are quite similar to larks in coloration but relatively slimmer with longer legs, tail and wings, finer bill and frequently a more upright stance. In most species the outer tail feathers are white. Some wag tail up-and-down while walking, somewhat in the manner of a wagtail, a habit which helps to distinguish them from larks. Flight is also different, typically rather undulating, less fluttery. Specific identification can be difficult and demands patience, good views and attention to detail. They often give diagnostic call in flight.

Plate 89: Wagtails

Small, slim ground-feeding birds with slender pointed bill, pointed wings, fairly long legs and long tail habitually wagged up-and-down (side-to-side in Forest Wagtail). Unlike the related pipits, plumage is unstreaked and generally brighter, more contrasting. They feed primarily on insects. Often call in flight. Some species gather in large loose flocks in favourable habitat and roost communally outside the breeding season.

Plate 90: Spiderhunters, White-eyes and Sunbirds

Spiderhunters are small, robust, arboreal forest birds with very long decurved bill. Very active with fast dashing flight. Usually found singly or in pairs. Food similar to sunbirds. **White-eyes** are small active birds reminiscent of warblers with rounded wings, fairly short legs, medium-length, slightly decurved bill and distinct white eye-ring. Arboreal, usually keeping in flocks feeding on insects, nectar and berries. **Sunbirds** are the Old World equivalent of hummingbirds: small with long slender decurved bill, short rounded wings, square-cut tail, often hovering in front of flowers. They feed on nectar, insects, spiders and small berries. Male is usually brightly plumaged, female usually drab. Most *Aethopyga* males have elongated central tail feathers. Some *Nectarinia* males have an eclipse plumage. *Nectarinia* females are largely yellow below, *Aethopyga* generally olive.

Plate 91: Flowerpeckers, Avadavats and Munias

Flowerpeckers are small, plump and short-tailed with short bills. They feed on berries, nectar and insects. Very partial to *Loranthus*. Rather restless, flitting about from tree canopy to tree canopy; sometimes descend to bushes. Quite vocal with characteristic short sharp notes often given in flight. In some species sexes alike; in others female much duller than male and difficult to identify. **Munias** are small, strongly patterned, finch-like birds which live in tight flocks. Strong conical bills are an obvious adaptation to their granivorous diet. Usually found in grassland, scrub and cultivation, often feeding on the ground. Young birds mostly drab and difficult to identify, but flocks usually contain some distinctive adults. In our region this group includes the avadavats, Indian Silverbill and locally introduced Java Sparrow.

Plate 92: Sparrows, Petronias, Weavers, and Finches (Chaffinch and Brambling)

Sparrows and **petronias** are small birds with largely brown and grey plumage, short conical pointed bills and lightly notched tails. They generally subsist on seeds and grain for which they forage on the ground or in ripening fields of cereal and grass. Most species tend to associate in flocks, particularly in the non-breeding season, and will often roost and nest together in colonies. The House Sparrow is a common commensal of man throughout much of the subcontinent and worth studying in order to compare similar species. **Weavers** are superficially sparrow-like birds with heavier bills and colourful black-and-yellow patterning in breeding males. They have a similar diet of seeds and grains but are less likely to be found in urban settings. They build distinctive hanging woven nests in colonies, usually near or over water. They forage in large gatherings during the winter months.

31

Plate 93: Accentors, Mountain Finches and Snowfinches

Accentors are small birds, superficially like sparrows, but distinguished by their much thinner bills. They feed on insects, seeds and berries on the ground and in low bushes. Most species inhabit montane regions above the tree-line, descending to lower altitudes in winter, where they can often be found in the vicinity of upland villages, frequenting hedges and bushes around fields and orchards. **Mountain finches** are, as the name suggests, more or less restricted to high Himalayan regions. They are small dark nondescript birds with short conical bills typical of finches. They congregate in large flocks feeding on the ground in rather open areas, avoiding steeper slopes. **Snowfinches** also inhabit barren alpine regions. Similar in size and build to the mountain finches but rather more strongly patterned with distinctive white patches in the plumage. Almost entirely terrestrial in feeding habits. They gather in large flocks outside the breeding season.

Plates 94 & 95: Finches

The **Finches** form a large varied group of small or medium-sized passerines with short, heavy, conical bill and medium narrow notched tail. They chiefly subsist on seeds but will also take fruit and insects. Some are relatively arboreal, others are more terrestrial in their feeding habits. Most are fairly colourful though females are usually duller than males. Often congregate in large flocks. Flight fast and undulating.

Plate 96: Buntings

Buntings are small birds similar to finches, but the conical bill is usually finer, tail often longer, frequently with white outer tail feathers. Plumage of males often duller in the non-breeding season. They forage predominantly on the ground, generally preferring grass seeds. Gregarious, often forming large flocks outside the breeding season. Many species have similar *tzick* calls. Most are migratory, only visiting the subcontinent in winter.

PLATE 1

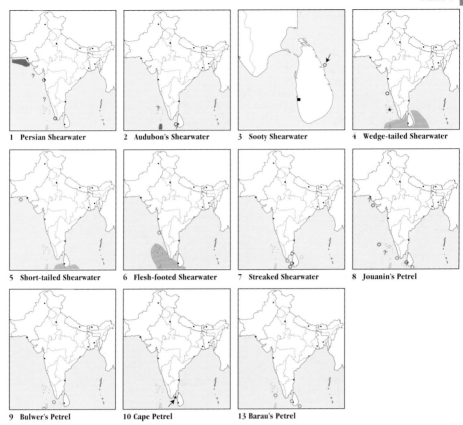

1 Persian Shearwater 2 Audubon's Shearwater 3 Sooty Shearwater 4 Wedge-tailed Shearwater

5 Short-tailed Shearwater 6 Flesh-footed Shearwater 7 Streaked Shearwater 8 Jouanin's Petrel

9 Bulwer's Petrel 10 Cape Petrel 13 Barau's Petrel

PLATE 1: SHEARWATERS AND PETRELS

1 Persian Shearwater *Puffinus persicus* (12) 31cm. Very similar to 2 with which it was previously considered to be conspecific. Differs by having a longer bill, a darker underwing, and streaking on the flanks and axillaries. Flight: as 2. **R*?4**

2 Audubon's Shearwater *Puffinus lherminieri* (11) 31cm. Slightly shorter-billed than 1; flanks and axillaries unstreaked. Flight: a rapid flutter followed by a short banking glide. **RB2**

3 Sooty Shearwater *Puffinus griseus* 43cm. An overall sooty-brown bird but the conspicuous white wing-lining separates it from other dark shearwaters. The dark feet and more rapid direct flight help to distinguish it from 6 and the dark morph of 4. Longer-billed than 5 with paler underwing-coverts. Flight: strong and direct with rapid mechanical wingbeats. **V**

4 Wedge-tailed Shearwater *Puffinus pacificus* (9) 43cm. (●) Dark morph is separated from 3 and 5 by entirely dusky underwing; from 6 by dark bill. (○) The pale morph is less common than the dark. Distinguished from 1, 2 and 7 by longer tail which normally appears slender and pointed. Despite the bird's name the tail only looks wedge-shaped when the bird banks. Flight: slow and lazily drifting; in windy weather a more erratic hither and thither. **S3**

5 Short-tailed Shearwater *Puffinus tenuirostris* (10) 42cm. Similar to 3 but has greyer underwing-coverts, shorter bill, whitish chin, and steeper forehead. Flight: burst of short rapid wingbeats followed by a stiff-winged glide. **S5**

6 Flesh-footed Shearwater *Puffinus carneipes* (8) 43cm. Conspicuous pink bill separates this from other dark shearwaters. From 3 and 5 also by dark underwing; from 4 by shorter rounded tail. Flight: a stiff-winged glide interspersed with slow lazy flaps. **PS3-4**

7 Streaked Shearwater *Calonectris leucomelas* (7) 48cm. Distinguished from other shearwaters by large size and whitish face. The streaking on head is only visible at close range. Flight: languid glides on loose down-curved wings. **V?R?5**

8 Jouanin's Petrel *Bulweria fallax* (13a) 31cm. Similar to 9 but note the oddly shaped tail with short outer feathers, larger size, bigger head, broader wings, and pale area around bill (when seen closely). Flight: strong and fast in wide weaving sweeps, gliding or swooping into the troughs between the waves from 15-20m above the sea. **V?**

9 Bulwer's Petrel *Bulweria bulwerii* (13b) 27cm. From 8 by the tail shape which is long and pointed when held closed, wedge-shaped when open. Note that 8 in worn plumage may also show a pale bar across the upperwing-coverts, though not usually as extensive. Flight: twisting low over the waves with wings held forward; over calm water deliberate and straight – a few wingflaps alternating with a short glide. **V**

10 Cape Petrel *Daption capense* (6) 39cm. The pied plumage is fairly unmistakable. Likes to follow ships feeding on the waste. Flight: several rapid wingflaps followed by a glide. **V**

11 [Trinidade Petrel *Pterodroma arminjoniana* 37cm. A polymorphic species whose underbody varies from white to slaty-brown. Intermediate birds show variable amounts of white on the underbody, often leaving a dark breast-band. The wings are dark below with white patches at the base of the primaries. The upperparts are ashy-brown. The dark morph is similar to 3 but is overall bulkier with a shorter bill and a somewhat different underwing pattern. Flight: generally like a typical gadfly petrel but in calmer weather conditions rather like 3. **V** (The first record for the subcontinent was of a storm-blown bird found in South India in 1996, unpublished at the time of writing.)]

12 [White-headed Petrel *Pterodroma lessonii* 43cm. The white head is diagnostic. Flight: fast and swooping with wings held bowed and angled forward, moving over the ocean in high sweeping arcs. **V?** (A single possible sighting off Colombo.)]

13 Barau's Petrel *Pterodroma baraui* 38cm. The combination of white forehead and dark cap is distinctive, as are under- and upperwing patterns. Flight: fast and swooping. **V**

14 [Mascarene Petrel *Pterodroma aterrima* (13). 36cm. Could be mistaken for 8 or 9 but is much larger, more heavily built and has a squarer tail. Flight: high and swooping. **X** (The single 1940 specimen, now missing, was probably of a Jouanin's Petrel, a species not recognised at the time.)]

15 [Soft-plumaged Petrel *Pterodroma mollis* 35cm. From other shearwaters and petrels of the region by the extensive, dark grey patches at the sides of the breast which on some birds join to form a complete breast-band. Flight: a fast zigzag of glides interspersed with bursts of quick wingflaps. **X** (Possible vagrant but records to date unacceptable.)]

PLATE 2: FRIGATEBIRDS AND BOOBIES

1 **Christmas Island Frigatebird** *Fregata andrewsi* (30) 95cm. ♂ black below but for narrow, semi-circular white patch on lower belly; no 'spurs'. ♀ black hood, narrow white hind-collar, white breast and belly extending as 'spurs' onto underwing, small black 'hook' on flank below leading edge of wing. **Imm** from other imms by broader blackish breast-band (some have distinctly longer, broader 'spur' on the underwing than imm 2); from imm 3 by less triangular belly-patch with 'spurs' attached to, not incorporated in, belly-patch. **V**

2 **Great Frigatebird** *Fregata minor* (31) 93cm. ♂ entirely black below. ♀ white breast, no 'spurs', small greyish-white throat, without hind-collar, thus not hooded. **Imm** white belly with narrow breast-band; white 'spur' sometimes present on underwing. From imm 1 and 3 by rounded white patch on underbody, and usually by absence of spurs. **Occasional non-breeding visitor 3-4**

3 **Lesser Frigatebird** *Fregata ariel* (32) 76cm. ♂ black except white 'spurs' extend from flanks onto underwing. ♀ black hood with narrow white hind-collar, white breast and flanks extending as spurs on underwing, black of vent extends up centre of belly in a V- or U-shape. **Imm** has triangular white belly-patch with apex at vent, straightish base-line across the breast (rounded in imm 2), and spurs on underwing forming the corners; older immatures develop black V up centre of belly; from imm 1 and imm 2 by triangular white belly-patch; older immatures by blackish V on belly. **B* and occasional non-breeding visitor 2**

4 **Masked Booby** *Sula dactylatra* (23) 80cm. **Ad** from 6 by black face-mask and tail, and yellow bill. Leg colour variable from yellow/orange to dark grey. **Imm** from ad 5 by white hind-collar and different underwing pattern. **Non-breeding visitor 5**

5 **Brown Booby** *Sula leucogaster* (25) 76cm. **Ad** dark brown upperparts, head and upper breast contrasting with white of remaining underbody; lacks white hind-collar of imm 4. **Occasional non-breeding visitor 3-4**

6 **Red-footed Booby** *Sula sula* (24) 41cm. **Ad** red feet and pink at base of bill diagnostic. (○) white morph separated from 4 by dark carpal patch; (●) dark morph. Intermediate morphs occur with all or some of the head, neck, tail, tail-coverts, rump and/or underparts whitish. **Juv** (not shown) is entirely ashy-brown with dark bill, purplish facial skin and greyish legs. **V**

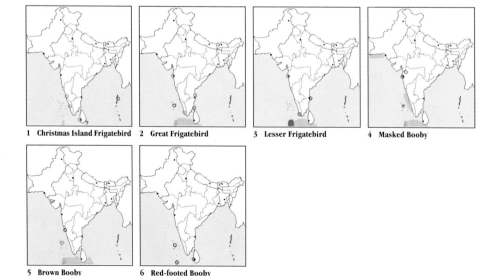

1 Christmas Island Frigatebird   2 Great Frigatebird   3 Lesser Frigatebird   4 Masked Booby

5 Brown Booby   6 Red-footed Booby

36

PLATE 3: STORM-PETRELS, TROPICBIRDS AND LOONS

1 **[Matsudaira's Storm-petrel** *Oceanodroma matsudairae* 24cm. All dark with pale bar on upperwing-coverts. Distinct white patch at base of outer primaries diagnostic. Larger and broader-winged than 2. Flight usually flapping interspersed with short glides, slower and lazier than 2. ⌘ Open sea. Follows ships. **X(V?)** – not definitely recorded from the region though there have been a couple of possible sight records just to the south of the subcontinent.]

2 **Swinhoe's Storm-petrel** *Oceanodroma monorhis* (16) 20cm. All dark with pale bar on upperwing-coverts. Lacks the obvious white forewing patch of 1 (white shaft-streaks only visible at close range); smaller; narrower wings. Flight fast and weaving with short glides on bowed wings; may patter or rest on surface of water. ⌘ Open sea. Does not usually follow ships. **V**

3 **White-faced Storm-petrel** *Pelagodroma marina* 20cm. From other storm petrels by brownish-grey upperparts with grey rump. Face pattern diagnostic at close range. Erratic weaving flight with jerky wingflaps and short glides; more direct when feeding. ⌘ Open sea. Does not usually follow ships. **P5**

4 **Black-bellied Storm-petrel** *Fregetta tropica* (15) 20cm. From 6 by rounded tail and white on underwing and flanks. From 5 by dark band down centre of abdomen and darker upperparts. Erratic weaving flight. ⌘ Open sea. May accompany whales, dolphins or ships. **V**

5 **White-bellied Storm-petrel** *Fregetta grallaria* 20cm. From 6 by rounded tail and white on underparts. Lacks dark ventral band of 4; paler upperparts; wing-bar less well marked. Similar flight to 4. ⌘ Open sea. Does not usually follow ships. **V**

6 **Wilson's Storm-petrel** *Oceanites oceanicus* (14) 17cm. Combination of broad white band across base of tail extending onto outer undertail-coverts and pale crescent on upperwing. From 4 & 5 also by forked tail and dark underparts. Flight direct; patters on water. ⌘ Open sea. Follows ships. **S2**

7 **Red-billed Tropicbird** *Phaethon aethereus* (17) 48cm (tail ribbons 50cm). **Ad** blackish barring on upperparts; black line through eye extends back to nape; red bill and white tail-streamers. **Imm** black eye-stripe almost joining across hind-crown and denser barring on upperparts separates from imm 8 & 9. ⌘ Ocean; sea-coast. May follow ships. **(Scarce non-breeding visitor)5**

8 **White-tailed Tropicbird** *Phaethon lepturus* (19) 39cm (tail ribbons 38cm). **Ad** diagonal black line on upperwing diagnostic; black eye-stripe does not extend onto nape. Note also white tail-streamers and yellow or orange bill. **Imm** lacks black hind-collar of 7; yellow bill and distinct black patch on outer primaries separate from 9. ⌘ Ocean; sea-coast. Sometimes follows ships. **R*4**

9 **Red-tailed Tropicbird** *Phaethon rubricauda* (18) 46cm (tail ribbons 33cm). **Ad** red tail-streamers diagnostic. Entirely white upperparts except for black shafts of outer primaries and black inner secondaries edged white; often shows rosy tinge to body and/or wings. Note also red bill. **Imm** from 7 & 8 by blackish bill (yellow at base) and relatively little black on outer primaries. ⌘ Ocean; sea-coast. Sometimes follows ships. **V**

10 **Red-throated Loon** *Gavia stellata* (2) 61cm. **Winter ads** told from next species by thinner, slightly upcurved bill, white speckling on upperparts (only visible at close range) and more extensive white on sides of neck. ⌘ In winter mainly coastal waters but also lakes and large rivers. **Winter vagrant**

11 **Black-throated Loon** *Gavia arctica* (1) 65cm. **Winter ads** show dark hind-neck extending round to mid-way on the sides of the neck; bill often seems slightly decurved; rear flanks usually show an obvious white patch. ⌘ In winter mainly coastal waters but also lakes and large rivers. **Winter vagrant**

PLATE 3

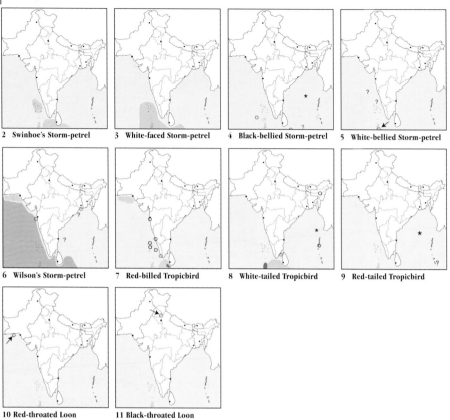

2 Swinhoe's Storm-petrel
3 White-faced Storm-petrel
4 Black-bellied Storm-petrel
5 White-bellied Storm-petrel

6 Wilson's Storm-petrel
7 Red-billed Tropicbird
8 White-tailed Tropicbird
9 Red-tailed Tropicbird

10 Red-throated Loon
11 Black-throated Loon

PLATE 4

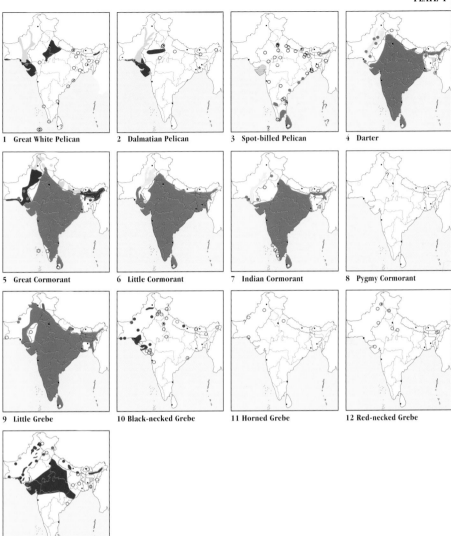

1 Great White Pelican

2 Dalmatian Pelican

3 Spot-billed Pelican

4 Darter

5 Great Cormorant

6 Little Cormorant

7 Indian Cormorant

8 Pygmy Cormorant

9 Little Grebe

10 Black-necked Grebe

11 Horned Grebe

12 Red-necked Grebe

13 Great Crested Grebe

PLATE 4: PELICANS, DARTER, CORMORANTS AND GREBES

1 **Great White Pelican** *Pelecanus onocrotalus* (20) 183cm. From 2 & 3 by black flight feathers on underwing (dark brown with an additional line across underwing coverts on imm). **Br** by large area of pink bare skin around eyes, drooping nuchal crest, (orange-)yellow gular pouch, pinkish (vs grey) legs, white of plumage tinged with pink/orange. ✤ Large waterbodies. **R*W3**

2 **Dalmatian Pelican** *Pelecanus crispus* (22) 183cm. Note white underwing with blackish trailing edge. **Br** by deep orange gular pouch; from 1 by curly nuchal crest, greyish cast to plumage, dark grey legs, small area of pinkish bare skin around eye. ✤ Large waterbodies. **WP4**

3 **Spot-billed Pelican** *Pelecanus philippensis* (21) 152cm. Note dusky flight feathers on underwing. Line of spots along upper mandible diagnostic (only visible at close range). **Br** by deep purple/pinkish gular pouch; and from 1 by greyish tone to plumage, blackish legs, short untidy nuchal tuft, and small area of pinkish/yellowish bare skin around eye. ✤ Large waterbodies. **R•3**

4 **Darter** *Anhinga melanogaster* (29) 90cm. Long thin kinked neck and dagger-like bill distinctive. Frequently swims partly submerged leaving the head and neck above water, resulting in a snake-like appearance; hence the alternative name of Snakebird. ✤ Lakes and jheels. **R•3**

5 **Great Cormorant** *Phalacrocorax carbo* (26) 80cm. From other cormorants by much larger size and yellow gular skin extending to eyes. **Br** by white patch on thighs, white facial skin, (variable amount of) white feathering on sides of head and brownish-bronze sheen to upperparts. ✤ Lakes, rivers, jheels, creeks etc. **R•2**

6 **Little Cormorant** *Phalacrocorax niger* (28) 51cm. From other cormorants (except 8 which see) by small size, short stubby bill and lack of yellow on gular pouch. Often shows a fairly domed head with a steep forehead. **Br** from 7 also by greenish/bluish sheen to upperparts, short crest on forecrown. **Nbr** from 7 by greyish-pink gular skin. ✤ Lakes, rivers, jheels, creeks etc. **R•2**

7 **Indian Cormorant** *Phalacrocorax fuscicollis* (27) 63cm. Distinctly smaller than 5. Hard to separate from 6 on size unless seen together but note the long slender bill (and shallow forehead). **Br** distinguished by white tuft behind ear-coverts, purplish-black gular skin, greenish-bronze sheen to upperparts, and emerald-green eyes. **Nbr** by yellow gular skin not usually extending to eye. ✤ Lakes, rivers, jheels, creeks etc. **R•3**

8 **Pygmy Cormorant** *Phalacrocorax pygmeus* (28a) 51cm. A very rare vagrant to the subcontinent. **Br** from other cormorants by warm brown head and scattering of white plumes throughout the glossy black plumage. **Nbr** probably not safely distinguishable from 6 in similar plumage but note the warmer brown head and neck, extensive white belly and fairly distinct brown breast-band. ✤ As for other cormorants. **V**

9 **Little Grebe** *Tachybaptus ruficollis* (5) 27cm. **Nbr** by small size, short neck, stubby bill and high blunt rear. In flight lacks white on wings. ✤ Mainly inland on standing waterbodies. ▽ High whinnying trill; *whit, whit.* **R•MW1**

10 **Black-necked Grebe** *Podiceps nigricollis* (4) 31cm. **Nbr** by thin, slightly upturned bill and high domed forehead; from 11 also by dusky ear-coverts (not clear-cut) and foreneck. In flight white on secondaries and inner primaries, very little or none on forewing. ✤ Lakes and jheels. ▽ Usually silent in winter; high squeaky *beekit; whit, whit....* **W3-4**

11 **Horned Grebe** *Podiceps auritus* 34cm. **Nbr** from 10 by thicker straight bill, dusky cap sharply demarcated from white cheeks, white foreneck, and pale spot on lores. In flight from all but 12 by white patches on secondaries and forewing, the latter not extending down along inner wing as in 13. ✤ Lakes and jheels. ▽ Usually silent in winter; similar calls to 12 but higher-pitched. **V**

12 **Red-necked Grebe** *Podiceps grisegena* (4a) 45cm. Note yellow at base of dark bill; dark eye. **Nbr** from 13 by shorter and thicker neck, dark cap extending below eye. From 11 by grey cap extending below eye to fade into white and by grey foreneck. From 10 by large size, long straight bill and shallow forehead. In flight wing pattern like 11 but more extensive white on forewing. ✤ Lakes and jheels. ▽ Usually silent in winter; *uweb, uweb...; ooa-eb.* **V**

13 **Great Crested Grebe** *Podiceps cristatus* (3) 49cm. **Nbr** by large size, long neck, long flesh-coloured bill, white of face extending above eye except for dark lores. In flight by white patches on secondaries and forewing, the latter extending along inner wing to secondaries. ✤ Mainly on larger waterbodies. ▽ Usually silent in winter; harsh deep *errgh, errgh; krrrrreb,* etc. **B*W3**

PLATE 5: EGRETS AND HERONS

1 Great Egret *Casmerodius albus* (45-6) 90cm. Large size separates this from most other white egrets except 2 when not seen together. Distinguished from latter by long thin neck with a sharp, almost rectangular kink in it when not fully extended, and long slim dagger-like bill (appears longer than head); gape extends back behind eye; **Nbr** yellow bill usually without dusky tip; **Br** plumes only on back, black bill, turquoise facial skin, legs tinged with red. In flight the slower, more deliberate wingbeats are apparent. ⌘ Mainly lowland jheels, margins of lakes, rivers, creeks etc. **R•2**

2 Intermediate Egret *Mesophoyx intermedia* (47-8) 80cm. **Nbr** from 3 by larger size, yellow bill and dark feet; from 1 by proportionally shorter, thicker neck without latter's sharp kink, bill relatively shorter and thicker (appears shorter than head), gape not extending behind eye. **Br** distinguished from both 1 & 3 by plumes on breast and back but not on head, orange-yellow facial skin. ⌘ Mainly low-altitude jheels, wet paddies, margins of lakes, rivers, creeks etc. **R•2**

3 Little Egret *Egretta garzetta* (49) 63cm. Separated from most similar white egrets by black legs with contrasting yellow feet; **Nbr** by all-black bill; **Br** by plumes on nape, back and breast; facial skin changes from yellow to purplish-pink to greenish- or greyish-blue. For differences from white morph 4 & 5 see below. ⌘ <1530. Jheels, wet fields, margins of lakes, rivers, rarely coastal. **R•2**

4 Western Reef Egret *Egretta gularis* (50) 63cm. Sometimes treated as a race of 3. **Br** separated from the similar 5 by the crest of two fine plumes (vs bushy nuchal crest). Occurs in two morphs. **Nbr dark morph** is easily distinguishable from all except the dark morph of 5; from latter by the distinct white patch on throat and upper foreneck (rather than a narrow white streak down centre of chin and throat); ranges do not normally overlap. Sometimes shows white patches on forewing, more obvious in flight. **White morph** is very similar to 3 but bill appears thicker, slightly decurved and usually has at least some yellow on it though it may be all dark; legs are usually greener and yellow of the feet normally extends further up the tarsus and is less sharply demarcated; its salt water habitat is often a good pointer as 3 almost always prefers freshwater situations. ⌘ Saline coastal wetlands. **R•3**

5 Pacific Reef Egret *Egretta sacra* (51) 58cm. Very similar in plumage and habits to 4, (which see); note also the stouter bill and shorter, heavier legs. Range and coastal habitat indicative. ⌘ Rocky seashore, mangroves, mudflats etc. **R2-3**

6 Cattle Egret *Bubulcus ibis* (44) 51cm. **Br** has distinctive orangy wash on head and neck. **Nbr** separated from other white egrets by small size; relatively short, thick neck; short bill and round-headed appearance. Has a habit of following cattle not usually observed in other egrets. ⌘ <1500. Open grazing areas, wet fields. **RA1**

7 [Great-billed Heron *Ardea sumatrana* 110cm. Could be confused with 10 or 11 but has uniform, brownish-tinged, slaty-grey plumage without any contrasting dark markings; develops a nuchal crest and whitish plumes on the lower neck and scapulars in the breeding season. In flight note the uniform brownish-grey upperwing (two-toned in 10 & 11). The similar 8 has a white belly and underwing-coverts and is unlikely to be found in the same habitat. ⌘ Island coasts and mangroves. **X(V?)** – A scarce resident of coasts around neighbouring South-East Asia and thus a potential vagrant. There are old unconfirmed sightings of this species from the Nicobar Islands.]

8 White-bellied Heron *Ardea insignis* (33) 127cm. The brownish-tinged, slaty-grey upperparts and lack of contrasting dark marks on head and neck separate this from all other herons except 7 which does not have white belly. In flight from 10 & 11 by uniform brownish-grey upperwing; from 7 by the white belly and underwing-coverts. ⌘ Marshes and forest rivers in the east Himalayan foothills and adjacent plains. **R5**

9 Goliath Heron *Ardea goliath* (34) 147cm. Superficially similar to 11 but much larger, bill black with paler lower mandible, absence of black markings on rich, vinous-chestnut head. **Juv** has duller rufous head and neck, some rufous on grey upperparts, white underparts streaked with brown. ⌘ Lowland lakes, mangroves, creeks, estuaries. **V**

10 Grey Heron *Ardea cinerea* (35-6) 96cm. Pattern of grey, black and white distinctive. ⌘ All kinds of larger, open inland and coastal waters. **RW2**

11 Purple Heron *Ardea purpurea* (37-7a) 86cm. Similar to 10 but more slender with darker, chestnut-buffy to purplish-brown tones, particularly to neck and underparts; in flight by the chestnut-buffy or purplish-brown wing-coverts and sharp angle in the folded neck. Usually shy, keeping to more densely vegetated areas than 10. ⌘ Plains-level marshes, jheels and vegetated lake margins. **R•2**

PLATE 5

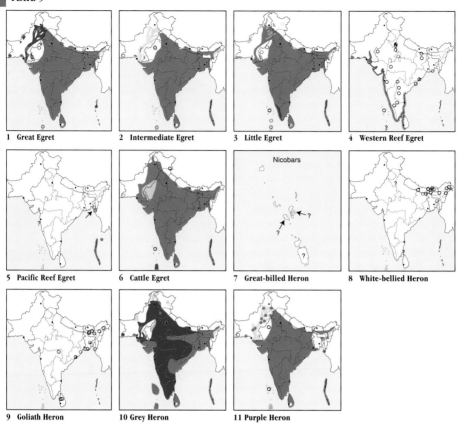

1 Great Egret

2 Intermediate Egret

3 Little Egret

4 Western Reef Egret

5 Pacific Reef Egret

6 Cattle Egret

7 Great-billed Heron

Nicobars

8 White-bellied Heron

9 Goliath Heron

10 Grey Heron

11 Purple Heron

PLATE 6

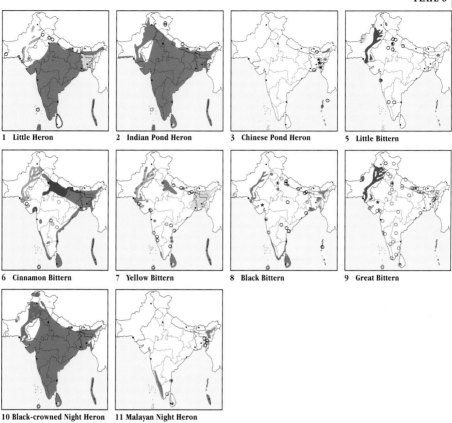

1 Little Heron

2 Indian Pond Heron

3 Chinese Pond Heron

5 Little Bittern

6 Cinnamon Bittern

7 Yellow Bittern

8 Black Bittern

9 Great Bittern

10 Black-crowned Night Heron

11 Malayan Night Heron

47

PLATE 6: LITTLE HERON, POND HERONS, BITTERNS AND NIGHT HERONS

1 **Little Heron** *Butorides striatus* (38-41) 44cm. Small size, entirely slaty upperparts (slight greenish tinge not always obvious) and greenish-black crown and nuchal crest distinguish this from other similar herons and bitterns. ⌘ Mainly plains (1500). Edges of streams, lakes, ponds, creeks, mangroves etc. Solitary. ▽ *k'yow* when flushed. **R3**

2 **Indian Pond Heron** *Ardeola grayii* (42-2a) 46cm. **Br** from br3 by deep maroon back with pale brownish-yellow head, neck and breast. **Nbr** an inconspicuous dull earthy-brown bird that suddenly becomes startlingly obvious when it spreads its white wings in flight; indistinguishable from nbr3. ⌘ <2150. All kinds of shallow wetlands, both large and small. Breeds and roosts colonially; feeds alone. ▽ Harsh croak when flushed. **R•1**

3 **Chinese Pond Heron** *Ardeola bacchus* (43) 52cm. **Br** from br2 by dark slaty back with dark chestnut head, neck and breast. **Nbr** not safely distinguishable from nbr2. ⌘ and ▽ as 2. **R*5**

4 [**Squacco Heron** *Ardeola ralloides* 46cm. Could occur as a vagrant to the northwestern part of the region in winter when it is doubtfully distinguishable from 2, though generally rather paler. Birds attaining summer plumage can be separated by the dark streaking on crown and hindneck, the pale vinous back and bluish bill tipped with black. ⌘ and ▽ similar to 2. **X**]

5 **Little Bittern** *Ixobrychus minutus* (55) 36cm. ♂ distinguished from most other bitterns by large pale wing-panels (on coverts) contrasting with black flight feathers and back; but see 7 & 10. ⌘ <1800. Reedbeds and dense waterside vegetation. Crepuscular and shy. ▽ *wuk*; deep *krok* repeated every two seconds; *keck eck eck eck eck eck.* **R*•4**

6 **Cinnamon Bittern** *Ixobrychus cinnamomeus* (56) 38cm. Identified by the entire upperparts being rich chestnut both at rest and in flight. **Imm** is browner but with chestnut flight feathers and tail, and buffy spots on wing-coverts. Crepuscular and shy. ⌘ <1800. Reedbeds, marshes, long wet grass, wet paddies, mangroves. ▽ Rather silent; *kok-kok*; *ek-ek-ek.* **R•3**

7 **Yellow Bittern** *Ixobrychus sinensis* (57) 38cm. ♂ from ♂5 by brown back and rump. ♀ can be warm buff but never as richly coloured as 6 and always has contrasting dark tail and flight feathers. **Imm** is like ♀ but more boldly streaked. Brown markings of ♀/imm warmer, more rufous then those of ♀/imm 5. ⌘ <1200. Reedbeds and other dense marsh vegetation, wet paddies, mangroves. Crepuscular and shy. ▽ Usually silent; rasping *krik-kriko krek*; *harrr*; *kak-kak-kak.* **R•3**

8 **Black Bittern** *Dupetor flavicollis* (58) 58cm. Overall almost black (♀ dark brown) with contrasting buffy-yellow band down sides of neck. In flight note entirely blackish or dark brown upperparts. Rather secretive. ⌘ <1200. Marshes, edges of paddyfields, overgrown streams and canals. ▽ Usually silent; harsh *queh.* **R•M4**

9 **Great Bittern** *Botaurus stellaris* (59) 71cm. Large size and stout long neck together with the dark brown mottling, streaking and cross-barring on golden-buff plumage make this a distinctive bird. In flight note the dark barring on flight feathers. Imm 5 is much smaller, lacks vermiculations on wings and sides of neck, and the dark brown flight feathers contrast with pale wing-coverts; imm 10 is smaller and has white spots on brown wings; imm 11 is smaller and darker greyish-brown above with narrow dark barring. Low owl-like flight. ⌘ Dense reedbeds. Very shy. ▽ Usually silent in its winter quarters; *aurr* in flight; far-carrying, deep booming song like someone blowing across the top of an empty bottle. **W5**

10 **Black-crowned Night Heron** *Nycticorax nycticorax* (52) 58cm. From ♂5 by stout black (vs orange) bill, contrasting white forehead, grey (vs black) flight feathers, absence of buff tones to underparts and wings, greenish gloss to back and cap; in flight note grey wings. **Imm** when perched distinguished from imm 2 & 3 by heavy pale spotting on upperparts; in flight by brown wings (spotted with white). ⌘ <1900. Jheels, marshes, paddyfields, ponds, mangroves. Usually roosts communally in the daytime and flies out at dusk to feed at night. ▽ *weck* or *kwock*, often in flight. **RM3**

11 **Malayan Night Heron** *Gorsachius melanolophus* (53-4) 51cm. **Ad** at rest looks similar to 6 but note black cap and crest, bulky build, and shorter, thicker bill; fine blackish vermiculations on the upperparts are visible at close range; in flight the contrasting blackish flight feathers (tipped with white on the primaries) make separation easy. **Imm** from similar birds by the vermiculated wings and white spotting on crest and nape. ⌘ <1800. Vicinity of streams and swampy areas in dense forest. Nocturnal; very shy. ▽ Short croak; repeated deep *oo.* **RM5**

PLATE 7: STORKS, SPOONBILL, FLAMINGOS AND IBISES

1 **Woolly-necked Stork** *Ciconia episcopus* (62) 83cm. Distinguished from other storks by the fluffy white neck contrasting with black body and wings. ✿ <920(1800). Marshy areas and wet grassland; also within forest. **R3**

2 **Black Stork** *Ciconia nigra* (65) 98cm. Black head and neck separates this from all other storks except 11 which has a longer black bill and white mantle. ✿ Along rivers and marshy areas. **WP3**

3 **White Stork** *Ciconia ciconia* (63) 105cm. From 4 by red bill and blackish patch around eye. In flight from all storks except 4 by white head, neck, body, tail and underwing-coverts contrasting with black flight feathers. See also 9. ✿ Marshy areas; wet and dry fields. **W4**

4 **Oriental Stork** *Ciconia boyciana* (64) 110cm. Separated from 3 by heavier greyish-black bill, red skin around eye and extensive whitish edging to primaries. ✿ Marshy areas, rivers, cultivation. **W*5**

5 **Lesser Adjutant** *Leptoptilos javanicus* (68) 110cm. From 6 by uniformly black upperwing, lack of gular pouch and pure white undertail-coverts. ✿ Marshy areas, wet fields, mangroves. **R●4**

6 **Greater Adjutant** *Leptoptilos dubius* (67) 130cm. From 5 by gular pouch (sometimes concealed among the breast feathers), white neck ruff, pale grey panel on blackish upperwing and grey undertail-coverts; in flight best distinguishing feature is upperwing pattern. ✿ Marshes, jheels. Also scavenges in towns in NE India. **R●5**

7 **Greater Flamingo** *Phoenicopterus ruber* (73) 110cm. When difference in size not apparent, most easily separated from 8 by the bill colour which is pale pink with a contrasting black tip in ad (greyish in juv); in flight by entire underwing-coverts red and proportionately longer neck. ✿ Jheels, shallow brackish lakes, lagoons, saltpans. **R●MW2**

8 **Lesser Flamingo** *Phoenicopterus minor* (74) 90cm. Very similar to 7. A deep pink bird will usually be of this species though ads of both this and 7 often look entirely white in the field. The best distinguishing feature is the very dark red bill, subterminally paler (at a distance looks black); in flight shows contrasting reddish patch on pale pinkish underwing-coverts and proportionately shorter neck. ✿ Mainly brackish lakes; lagoons; saltpans. **R●M3**

9 **Asian Openbill** *Anastomus oscitans* (61) 76cm. Superficially similar to 3 & 4 but bill shape and colour diagnostic; white of plumage tinged grey; in flight by the black tail (white in 3 & 4). **Juv** much greyer and initially without the bill opening. ✿ Marshes, jheels, flooded fields. **R●2**

10 **Painted Stork** *Mycteria leucocephala* (60) 93cm. **Ad** fairly unmistakable. **Juv** brownish-grey; could be confused with one of the other juv storks but note the long bill with slightly decurved tip. ✿ Marshes, jheels, flooded fields, large rivers. **R●2**

11 **Black-necked Stork** *Ephippiorhynchus asiaticus* (66) 135cm. The large size, black head, neck and long, slightly upcurved bill are distinctive. In flight the broad black stripe through the white underwing separates this from all other storks. ✿ Large marshes, jheels and rivers. **R*4**

12 **Eurasian Spoonbill** *Platalea leucorodia* (72) 82cm. The long spatulate bill is unique among the larger waterbirds. In flight note the entirely white plumage (washed yellow on throat and breast of **br ad**; primaries tipped black in **juv**). ✿ Marshes, jheels, rivers, mudflats. **R●3**

13 **Black-headed Ibis** *Threskiornis melanocephalus* (69) 60cm. Distinguished in flight by the black head and neck contrasting against the white underparts; note also the red/pink streak along the underwing-coverts. **Imm** has greyish-white neck making it look superficially like 12, but note the black head and bill shape. ✿ Marshes, jheels, rivers, wet fields, mudflats. **R●2**

14 **Glossy Ibis** *Plegadis falcinellus* (71) 60cm. Could be confused with imm 15 but lacks the latter's white shoulder-patch; in flight legs project well beyond tail. ✿ Marshes, jheels. **R●W3**

15 **Black Ibis** *Pseudibis papillosa* (70) 73cm. From 14 by blacker plumage, red nape and white shoulder-patch (can be obscured at rest); in flight legs do not project beyond tail. ✿ Drying margins of lakes and jheels; fields and grassland. **R●3**

PLATE 7

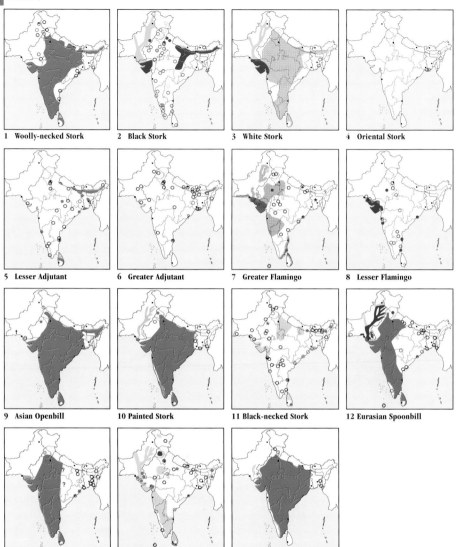

1 Woolly-necked Stork 2 Black Stork 3 White Stork 4 Oriental Stork

5 Lesser Adjutant 6 Greater Adjutant 7 Greater Flamingo 8 Lesser Flamingo

9 Asian Openbill 10 Painted Stork 11 Black-necked Stork 12 Eurasian Spoonbill

13 Black-headed Ibis 14 Glossy Ibis 15 Black Ibis

PLATE 8

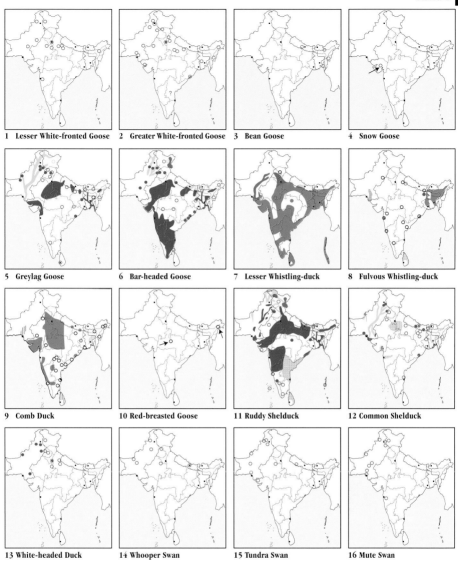

1 Lesser White-fronted Goose 2 Greater White-fronted Goose 3 Bean Goose 4 Snow Goose

5 Greylag Goose 6 Bar-headed Goose 7 Lesser Whistling-duck 8 Fulvous Whistling-duck

9 Comb Duck 10 Red-breasted Goose 11 Ruddy Shelduck 12 Common Shelduck

13 White-headed Duck 14 Whooper Swan 15 Tundra Swan 16 Mute Swan

PLATE 8: GEESE, SWANS AND DUCKS I

1 **Lesser White-fronted Goose** *Anser erythropus* (80) 53cm. Similar to 2 but smaller; more obviously dark head; yellow eye-ring; steeper, angular forehead; small bill; slightly larger area of white extending further back on forehead; shorter neck; overall plumage slightly darker. ⌘ Marshes, jheels, lakes, grasslands, estuaries. ▽ Like 2 but often higher-pitched. **V(W5)**

2 **Greater White-fronted Goose** *Anser albifrons* (79) 68cm. From 3 & 5 by obvious white face and irregular dark bars on the belly. Larger than 1, more rounded head, longer bill, no yellow eye-ring, less extensive white on forecrown, slightly paler overall. ⌘ Marshes, jheels, lakes, grasslands, estuaries. ▽ Varied nasal calls; *yih-yee* in flight. **V(W5)**

3 **Bean Goose** *Anser fabalis* (76-7) 76cm. Note the orange-yellow band through the dark bill, lacks white forehead and dark belly bars of 1 & 2, has relatively dark head and orange legs compared with 5. ⌘ Grass- and arable land near water. ▽ Nasal *kayew*; *kayayayayew*; *naehaehaeh*. **V**

4 **Snow Goose** *Anser caerulescens* (83) 75cm. Forms (○) snow or white phase (●) blue phase. ⌘ In usual winter range mainly on agricultural land but roosts on water. ▽ Cackling nasal *keck* in flight. **V**

5 **Greylag Goose** *Anser anser* (81) 81cm. Note pink bill and legs, relatively pale head and neck, large heavy build. In flight the contrasting pale grey forewings and rump are distinctive. ⌘ Marshes, jheels, lakes, estuaries, grasslands, cultivation. ▽ Nasal *ahng...(ahng)...(ahng)...*, more rasping than other geese. **W2**

6 **Bar-headed Goose** *Anser indicus* (82) 75cm. Diagnostic barring on head. Highly gregarious. ⌘ S High-altitude marshy areas by lakes in Ladakh. W Large lakes, rivers, jheels and farmland. ▽ Nasal honking and cackling, lower-pitched than 5. **MW2**

7 **Lesser Whistling-duck** *Dendrocygna javanica* (88) 42cm. Similar to 8 but smaller, chestnut uppertail-coverts, dark brown centre of crown, white streaking on flanks indistinct, contrasting chestnut shoulder diagnostic if exposed. ⌘ Well-vegetated lakes and jheels in the plains. ▽ Repeated wheezy whistling *whi-whee* or *seasick* in flight; wings also make a whistling noise. **R●2**

8 **Fulvous Whistling-duck** *Dendrocygna bicolor* (89) 51cm. Like 7 but larger, buffy-white uppertail-coverts, warm brown crown merging onto sides of head, dark streak down back of neck, prominent white streaking on flanks (indistinct on 7) often hidden beneath wing. ⌘ As 7. ▽ *pew-ee* similar to 7 but louder and higher-pitched. Wings also make a whistling sound. **R●4**

9 **Comb Duck** *Sarkidiornis melanotos* (115) 76cm. **Nbr**♂ lacks knob but bill is usually swollen compared with ♀. ⌘ Well-vegetated lowland marshes; jheels and rivers; usually near woodland. Generally nests in tree-hollows. ▽ Usually silent; low croak; wheezy whistles; hisses. **R●4**

10 **Red-breasted Goose** *Branta ruficollis* (75) 61cm. Unmistakable. May associate with other geese. ⌘ Usually winters on grass- and arable land near water. ▽ Squeaky *kik-yoik* in flight. **V**

11 **Ruddy Shelduck** *Tadorna ferruginea* (90) 66cm. Unmistakable. ⌘ S Around high-altitude lakes in Ladakh. W Large lakes and broad rivers in the plains. ▽ *or-r-r-r*; nasal trumpeting *whaeh*; *go-go-go-go-go*; *chuk-a-wa*. **MW2**

12 **Common Shelduck** *Tadorna tadorna* (91) 61cm. Unmistakable. ⌘ Open lakes and broad rivers. ▽ *wwweh*; *whi-whi-whi-...*; *geg-geg-geg-....* **W5**

13 **White-headed Duck** *Oxyura leucocephala* (123) 46cm. ♂ unmistakable; ♀ note small size and face pattern. ⌘ Mainly large, shallow lakes and lagoons with underwater weeds. ▽ *uwee*; *uweeoo*; short rapid *pee-piu*; long rattling *r-r-r-rrrrr....* **W4-5**

14 **Whooper Swan** *Cygnus cygnus* (86) 152cm. From 16 by yellow lores and base to bill (without knob); neck usually held straight and wings never arched when swimming; from 15 by larger size; more extensive wedge-shaped yellow on bill usually coming to a sharp point nearer the black tip; longer neck appears more slender; at close range an orange stripe is often visible along the side of the bill (not much more than a small triangle at base of bill on 14). ⌘ Lakes, large rivers, sheltered coastal waters. ▽ Various loud trumpetings. **V**

15 **Tundra Swan** *Cygnus columbianus* (84-5) 122cm. Forms **(a)** eastern '*jankowskii*' **(b)** western '*bewickii*'. From 16 by yellow lores and base to bill (without knob); neck usually held straight and wings never arched when swimming; from 14 by smaller size; less extensive yellow on bill not reaching beyond nostrils, the yellow being square-ended or rounded distally; relatively shorter, thicker neck. ⌘ Lowland lakes, marshes, jheels, lagoons, arable land. ▽ Similar to 14 but usually less raucous. **V**

16 **Mute Swan** *Cygnus olor* (87) 152cm. From 14 & 15 by largely orange-red bill with black lores, base and knob; long wedge-shaped tail; when swimming the neck is usually held in an S-shape and the wings are often arched. ⌘ Lakes, marshes, wet fields, farmland, sheltered bays. ▽ Usually silent. Wings noisy in flight. **V**

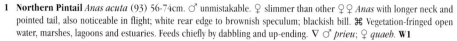

PLATE 9: DUCKS II

1 **Northern Pintail** *Anas acuta* (93) 56-74cm. ♂ unmistakable. ♀ slimmer than other ♀♀ *Anas* with longer neck and pointed tail, also noticeable in flight; white rear edge to brownish speculum; blackish bill. ♋ Vegetation-fringed open water, marshes, lagoons and estuaries. Feeds chiefly by dabbling and up-ending. ▽ ♂ *prieu*; ♀ *quaeb*. **W1**

2 **Common Teal** *Anas crecca* (94) 38cm. ♂ distinctive. At a distance when head pattern is not clear, note the white flank stripe and yellow 'triangle' at the side of the tail. Drab ♀ best identified by small size and green speculum; from ♀10 by pale stripe at side of tail and lack of dark cheek-bar. See also 3. ♋ Mainly freshwater lakes, jheels and marshes. Dabbles and up-ends. ▽ ♂ *preep*; *krick*; ♀ *quaeb*. **W1**

3 **Baikal Teal** *Anas formosa* (95) 40cm. ♀ from ♀2 by distinct white spot at base of bill and break in the supercilium above the eye; from ♀10 by this and absence of dark cheek-bar. ♋ In winter can occur on most types of waterbody. Dabbles; may feed on crops and stubble. ▽ ♂ low *wot-wot-wot*; *proop*; ♀ *quaeb*. **W5**

4 **Sunda Teal** *Anas gibberifrons* (96). 43cm. In our region represented by the race *albogularis*, restricted to the Andaman Islands, sometimes treated as a full endemic species. Amount of white around eye rather variable. ♋ Marshes, pools, creeks, wet grass and arable land. Dabbles. ▽ Soft whistle; low quack. **R*3-4**

5 **Spot-billed Duck** *Anas poecilorhyncha* (97-9) 61cm. Races **(a)** *zonorhyncha* uncommon winter visitor to eastern Assam **(b)** nom [**(c)** *haringtoni* of eastern Assam with very small/no red spots and green speculum is not shown]. Note large size, two-tone bill, dark cap and eye-line. Red spots at base of bill diagnostic when present; in flight green speculum (blue in *zonorhyncha*) bordered white; large white tertial patch (much reduced in *zonorhyncha*). ♋ <1200(1800) Vegetated lakes, marshes, jheels, slow-moving rivers. Usually in pairs, small groups. Dabbles, up-ends. ▽ Like 6. **R•MW2**

6 **Mallard** *Anas platyrhynchos* (100) 61cm. ♂ easily recognised. ♀ could be confused with a number of other ♀♀, especially 7, but note the yellowish-orange bill with dark centre and purple-blue speculum edged white (entirely white in 7). ♋ Vegetated lakes, jheels and marshes. Dabbles, up-ends and grazes. ▽ ♂ rasping *quaehp*; ♀ accelerating *quaeh quaeh-quaeh-quae-que-que...*decreasing in volume towards the end. **B*W3**

7 **Gadwall** *Anas strepera* (101) 51cm. ♂ overall greyish; black stern and white speculum diagnostic. ♀ from similar ♀♀ by white speculum; note also different bill pattern compared to ♀6. ♋ Vegetated lakes, jheels, marshes, (reservoirs). Dabbles; sometimes grazes and up-ends. ▽ Like 6 but softer. **W1**

8 **Falcated Duck** *Anas falcata* (102) 51cm. ♂ distinctive. ♀ difficult to separate from other drab brown ♀♀ but note the blackish bill and legs, buffish belly, unmarked head; in flight grey-brown forewing separated from black and green speculum by buffy-white bar. ♋ Lakes, jheels, rivers, reservoirs. Dabbles and up-ends. ▽ Rather silent in winter; ♂ short piercing whistle; ♀ hoarse quack. **W4-5**

9 **Eurasian Wigeon** *Anas penelope* (103) 49cm. ♂ distinctive. ♀ from ♀8 by white belly, rusty tinge to flanks, pale grey bill, black speculum (sometimes glossed green), lack of buffy-white wing-bar. ♋ Vegetated lakes, jheels, marshes (creeks, mangroves). Grazes more than other ducks but also dabbles. ▽ ♂ whistling *wheeooh*; ♀ *errr, errr, errr....* **W1**

10 **Garganey** *Anas querquedula* (104) 41cm. Long, well-demarcated, white supercilium extending back to hind-neck of ♂ unique among Indian ducks. ♀ similar to ♀2 but note more distinct eye-stripe, pale patch at base of longer bill, no pale stripe at side of tail. See also ♀3. ♋ All kinds of wetland. Dabbles and up-ends. ▽ ♂ dry rattle; ♀ *waeb*. **W1**

11 **Northern Shoveler** *Anas clypeata* (105) 51cm. The very large spatulate bill is distinctive even in flight, when the bluish-grey forewing and whitish underwing-coverts (contrasting with brown body) are additional pointers on the ♀. ♋ Inland waterbodies. Uses bill to sift organisms from the water, dabbles and up-ends. ▽ ♂ *veck-veck-veck*; ♀ *kwaeb*. **W1**

12 **White-winged Duck** *Cairina scutulata* (116) 81cm. ♂ illustrated; ♀ has more heavily speckled head, making it appear darker. Could be confused with a Comb Duck (8.9) but note the dark breast and belly; white forewing and underwing-coverts; pale bill. Rare variant has all-white head and breast. ♋ Slow-moving rivers and pools in lowland evergreen and swamp forest, canebrakes and tall elephant grass. Largely nocturnal, roosting in well-foliated trees. Singly or in pairs. Dabbles; dives occasionally. ▽ Rather silent; wailing *cronk*, sometimes followed by nasal whistle. **R5**

13 **Marbled Duck** *Marmaronetta angustirostris* (92) 48cm. Spotted plumage and dark eye-patch diagnostic. In flight distinguished from most similar-sized ducks by absence of any strong pattern; ♀ Garganey (10) is the most similar but has a white-edged speculum. ♋ Well-vegetated waterbodies, both freshwater and brackish. Dabbles, up-ends and sometimes dives. ▽ Relatively silent; *whee-wheeu*; squeaky notes. **B*W5**

14 **Pink-headed Duck** *Rhodonessa caryophyllacea* (106) 60cm. Not reliably sighted since 1935. Was probably always rare. Mostly confused with ♂ Red-crested Pochard (10.4) but note bright pink (vs orange-chestnut) head, entirely dark flanks (vs large white patch), head shape, pink (vs red) bill and different habitat. ♋ Secluded pools in lowland grass jungle, forests and swamps. Mainly a dabbler, observed to dive. ▽ Said to have had a wheezy whistle and low quack. †**(R•)**

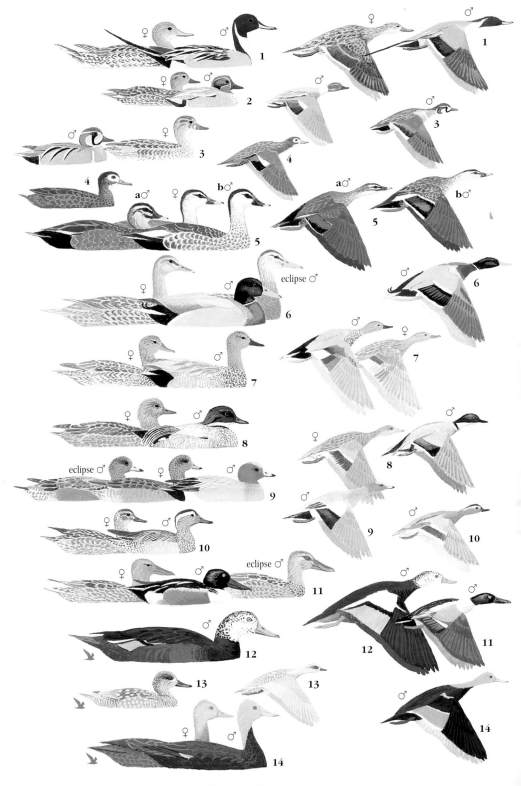

PLATE 9

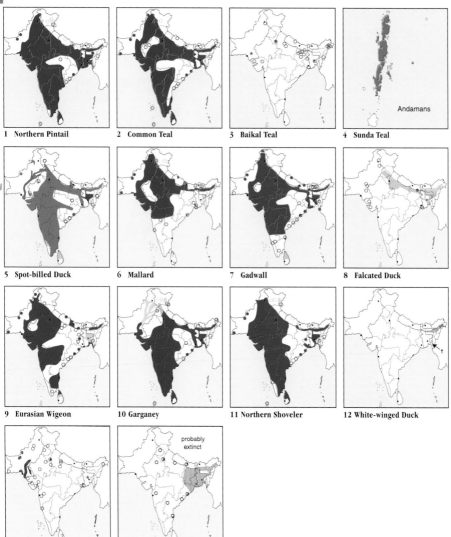

1   Northern Pintail

2   Common Teal

3   Baikal Teal

4   Sunda Teal

Andamans

5   Spot-billed Duck

6   Mallard

7   Gadwall

8   Falcated Duck

9   Eurasian Wigeon

10 Garganey

11 Northern Shoveler

12 White-winged Duck

13 Marbled Duck

14 Pink-headed Duck

probably extinct

PLATE 10

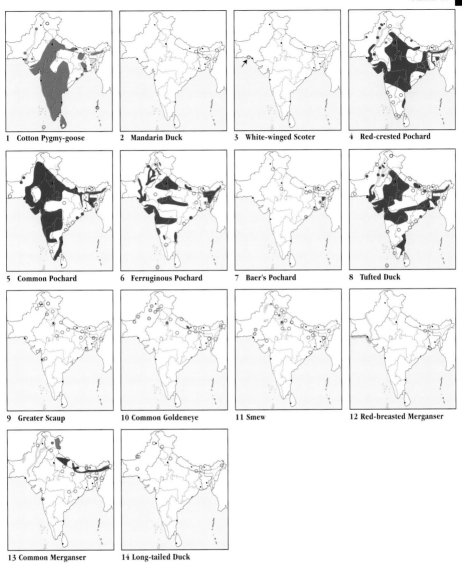

1 Cotton Pygmy-goose

2 Mandarin Duck

3 White-winged Scoter

4 Red-crested Pochard

5 Common Pochard

6 Ferruginous Pochard

7 Baer's Pochard

8 Tufted Duck

9 Greater Scaup

10 Common Goldeneye

11 Smew

12 Red-breasted Merganser

13 Common Merganser

14 Long-tailed Duck

PLATE 10: DUCKS III

1 **Cotton Pygmy-goose** *Nettapus coromandelianus* (114) 33cm. Unlikely to be confused with any other species in the region. ⌘ Mainly freshwater, shallow, well-vegetated waterbodies. Dabbles and sometimes dives. ∇ Short rapid cackling *geh geggy-geh* resembling *fix baygonets* or *quack, quack-quackyduck*, chiefly in flight. **R*●2**

2 **Mandarin Duck** *Aix galericulata* (113) 48cm. Distinctive. ⌘ Forest streams and pools. Dabbles. ∇ Usually silent; ♂ high whistled *hwick*; *tweek*; ♀ low clucking. **V**

3 [**White-winged Scoter** *Melanitta fusca* 55cm. Note that the intensity of the pale patches on face of ♀ can be very variable, almost totally absent in some birds. ⌘ In winter usually frequents coastal waters but may turn up on inland lakes. ∇ *wuhuhuh*; *quh...quh...quh....* **V?** (Photographed in Pakistan but as yet unpublished.)]

4 **Red-crested Pochard** *Rhodonessa rufina* (107) 54cm. ♂ could be mistaken for ♂ Pink-headed Duck (9.14) but has orange-chestnut (vs pink) head, different head shape and large white flank-patch (vs dark brown flanks). ⌘ Larger, mainly inland waterbodies with submerged and fringing vegetation. Dabbles, up-ends, dives and grazes. ∇ soft rasping *uwheh*; *gick*; *perr-perr-perr....* **W3**

5 **Common Pochard** *Aythya ferina* (108) 48cm. ♂ from ♂4 by dark chestnut head, silver-grey back, grey band on black bill; in flight by greyish-white (vs black) belly and less contrast between upperwing-coverts and flight feathers. ♀ could be confused with other ♀♀ but note the two-toned bill; dark brown head, neck and breast contrasting somewhat with the greyer body and back; indistinct pale post-ocular stripe; in flight grey upperwing-coverts and pale grey flight feathers. Other pochards have white wing-bars. ⌘ Open areas on lakes, jheels and lagoons. Dives; occasionally up-ends. ∇ Usually silent; ♂ soft wheezy whistle; ♀ low *krrr...krrr...krrr....* **W2**

6 **Ferruginous Pochard** *Aythya nyroca* (109) 41cm. Note dark chestnut head, breast and flanks contrasting with white undertail; white iris of ♂. ⌘ All kinds of wetlands. Diving duck which also dabbles and up-ends. ∇ Usually silent in winter; *wheeoo*; *keck*; *gaaa*; *kerrr.* **B*W3**

7 **Baer's Pochard** *Aythya baeri* (110) 46cm. ♂ green-glossed black head separates from other *Aythya* except 9 which has grey back, blackish breast and undertail; from ♂ Mallard (9.6) by grey bill, pale iris, chestnut and white flanks, white wing-bar. Brighter brown patches flanking the grey bill separate ♀ from similar ducks. From 6 also by white on fore-flanks. ⌘ Lakes, jheels, marshes, slow rivers, (coastal waters). Diving duck. ∇ Usually silent harsh *graak.* **W4-5**

8 **Tufted Duck** *Aythya fuligula* (111) 43cm. Tuft diagnostic but not always obvious. ♀ from ♀6 & 7 by dark undertail and yellow eye; see also ♀5 & 9. ⌘ Generally prefers more open, deeper waters. Usually feeds by diving but may also dabble and up-end. ∇ Usually silent; *whu-wuwuwu...*; dry *gerrr*; soft whistle. **W1**

9 **Greater Scaup** *Aythya marila* (112) 46cm. From 8 by lack of tuft; ♂ by vermiculated grey back; ♀ usually has broad white patch (vs little or none) at base of bill. ⌘ Lakes, jheels, coastal waters. Diving duck. ∇ *quarrer*; *qurr*; *whee-wheeoo.* **V(W)**

10 **Common Goldeneye** *Bucephala clangula* (118) 46cm. ♂ unmistakable. ♀ could be confused with some other ♀♀ but note the short stubby bill, head shape, white neck-ring and large white wing-patches. ⌘ Lakes, rivers, creeks, lagoons. Diving duck. ∇ Usually silent; *(ke)-queh*; *karr...karr...karr....* **W4-5**

11 **Smew** *Mergellus albellus* (119) 46cm. White throat and sides of neck separates ♀ from others with chestnut head and neck. ⌘ Lakes, jheels, rivers. Diving duck. ∇ Normally silent; low croaks, whistles and growls. **W5**

12 **Red-breasted Merganser** *Mergus serrator* (122) 58cm. Scraggy crest and mottled reddish-brown breast separate ♂ from 13. ♀like ♀13 but reddish-brown of head and neck fades into whitish throat and breast and greyish-brown upperparts; in flight by dark line across white speculum. ⌘ Lakes and inshore coastal waters. Diving duck. ∇ Usually silent; *krrr-krrr-krrr....* **V(W)1**

13 **Common Merganser** *Mergus merganser* (120-1) 66cm. White underparts often tinged with pink. ♀ like ♀12 but reddish-brown of head and neck clearly demarcated from remaining plumage. ⌘ Rivers and lakes. Dives; may hunt fish co-operatively. ∇ Usually silent; *kreh-kreh*; deep *karr.* **R*B*W3**

14 **Long-tailed Duck** *Clangula hyemalis* (117) 42cm. A distinctive diving duck. ⌘ Normally maritime but subcontinental records are from inland waterbodies. ∇ *(uh)-eh-euwuah*; low quack. **V**

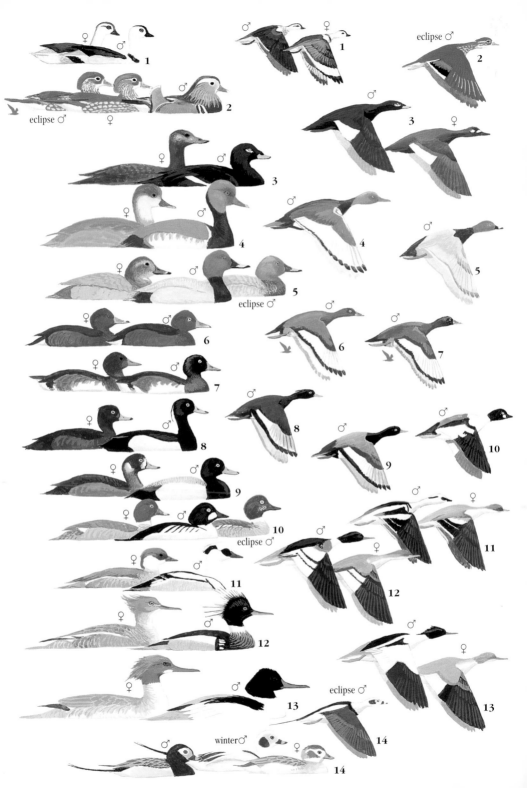

PLATE 11: HONEY BUZZARD, BAZAS AND KITES

1 **Oriental Honey-buzzard** *Pernis ptilorhynchus* (129-30) 65cm. Extremely variable in plumage coloration ranging from very dark to rather pale or sometimes rufous with differing degrees of barring on the underparts. Males are usually greyer than females. In overhead flight the tail pattern on most adult birds – a single broad dark band towards the tip and two narrower ones near the base of the tail – is diagnostic. The basal two bands tend, however, to merge into one on adult ♂♂ and younger birds may show up to five narrower, often indistinct bands. With practice it is possible to identify the species from true buzzards (Plate 13) by its relatively long-necked, pigeon-headed appearance, also a useful feature on a perched bird. The slight crest on the nape is seldom raised and thus not a very helpful field mark. Races (**a**) *ruficollis* (**b**) *orientalis*. ❄ <1800. Well-wooded areas, forest clearings and groves of trees. Feeds on honey and larvae of wild bees and wasps, but also on insects, small mammals, lizards and birds. ▽ High pitched screaming *whe-yeeuw*; *whee-ew*; *piha*; rather silent outside the breeding season. **R●W2**

2 **Black Baza** *Aviceda leuphotes* (127-8a) 33cm. Unmistakable. ❄ <1200. Clearings in evergreen forest, preferring the vicinity of streams in the foothills. Often found in small groups with up to a maximum of 20 individuals having been recorded in a single gathering. ▽ Soft, quavering plaintive squeal. **RM4**

3 **Jerdon's Baza** *Aviceda jerdoni* (125-6) 48cm. Could be confused with Crested Goshawk (12.8) but on a perched bird note the long, jaunty black crest tipped with white, grey cere and longer wings reaching down ²/₃ to ³/₄ of the way along the tail. In flight note the unusually broad and rounded wings with extremely ample hands. Mountain Hawk Eagle (14.1) is much larger, its crest is not usually held vertically and wing-tip only extends ¹/₃ to ²/₃ down the tail. **Ad** usually has diagnostic broad rufous bars on the wing linings; the uppertail shows 3 evenly spaced dark bars with the terminal bar much broader than the other two (usually 4 narrower even bars on Crested Goshawk 12.8). **Imm** is similar to ad but is streaked with brown on the breast and shows 4-5 dark bars on the tail. ❄ 150-1800. Evergreen hill forest. ▽ *kip-kip-kip*; *kikiya, kikiya,...*; loud, plaintive mewing *pee-ow*; usually silent outside the breeding season. **R5**

4 **Black-shouldered Kite** *Elanus caeruleus* (124) 33cm. A fairly distinctive small raptor with pointed wings. Could be mistaken for a harrier (Plate 20), but note the black shoulder. Commonly hovers when searching for prey, a habit not usually shared by the harriers which are much larger, slimmer and longer-winged. ❄ <1200(2100). Generally in drier open country of the lowlands. ▽ Soft melodious *pleewit pleewit*; rapid *ge-ge-ge-ge...*; usually silent in winter. **R2**

5 **Brahminy Kite** *Haliastur indus* (135) 48cm. **Ad** has unique bright chestnut and white plumage. **Imm** can be difficult to separate from other large raptors with pale bars across the upperwing; note the unbarred, rounded tail, large pale patch on the primaries and the pale head and breast merging into the darker colour of the belly and vent when seen from below. ❄ Low country (<1800). More common round the sea-coasts but also frequents larger inland waterbodies. ▽ Quavering nasal *myeah*; *meeah*; short high-pitched scream. **R●3**

6 **Red Kite** *Milvus milvus* (131) 61cm. Note very deeply forked tail, prominent white primary-patch below, rufous-brown body and wing lining; slimmer and more angular 7. ❄ Within its usual range an inhabitant of open country and farmland interspersed with woodland or groves of trees. ▽ *wheeeaw-wheew-wheew-wheeaw*. **Winter vagrant**

7 **Black Kite** *Milvus migrans* (132-4) 61cm (*lineatus* 66cm). The only common large dark raptor with a forked tail, though the latter may appear slightly rounded when spread and tail feathers are being moulted. Beware of other raptors occasionally giving a fork-tailed appearance because of lost or moulting tail feathers. Races (**a**) nom (**b**) *govinda* (**c**) *lineatus*. The latter is sometimes considered a separate species. In flight told from the other races by its larger size and conspicuous white primary-patch on the underwing; at rest the slightly paler underparts without any hint of rufous are indicative. ❄ <2200 (*lineatus* up to 4500, exceptionally 5300). Common scavenger around many human settlements and surrounding areas. ▽ Long drawn-out squealing *kweeeeeeee-(wi-wi-wi-wi-wi)*. **RM1**

PLATE 11

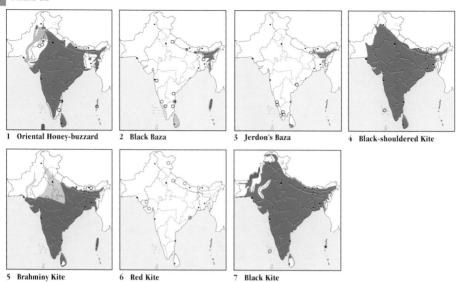

1 Oriental Honey-buzzard 2 Black Baza 3 Jerdon's Baza 4 Black-shouldered Kite

5 Brahminy Kite 6 Red Kite 7 Black Kite

PLATE 12

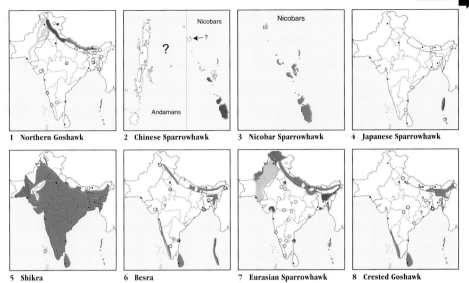

1 Northern Goshawk

2 Chinese Sparrowhawk

3 Nicobar Sparrowhawk

4 Japanese Sparrowhawk

5 Shikra

6 Besra

7 Eurasian Sparrowhawk

8 Crested Goshawk

PLATE 12: ACCIPITERS

1 **Northern Goshawk** *Accipiter gentilis* (136) ♂50cm ♀61cm. Separable from most other accipiters on size alone, being nearly twice as big as the sparrowhawks (though a large ♀7 may approach the size of a small ♂). Note the distinct white supercilium and absence of mesial streak, separating from 8. ♀ is like ♂ but browner. ⌘ (150)2400-4900. Himalayan forests, preferring oak; occasionally above treeline. ▽ Short squeal *kweeah*; chattering *yiek-yiek-yiek*.... **B*W3**

2 **Chinese Sparrowhawk** *Accipiter soloensis* (143) 30cm. **Ad** most easily identified in flight by unmarked white underwing (sometimes washed with pinkish-orange) with contrasting broad blackish primary tips. When perched note the upperparts somewhat darker than 5 and the white underparts washed pinkish-orange with no barring, though some ♀♀ may show barring. **Imm** very similar to other imm accipiters but usually has a whiter underwing and a darker slaty-coloured crown and nape. ⌘ Open forest and scrub. ▽ *pyew pyew pi-pi-pi; kewe kewe kewe kewe*. **W*5**

3 **Nicobar Sparrowhawk** *Accipiter butleri* (141-2) 30cm. Like 5 but smaller and more richly coloured. ♂ shows a single dark subterminal band on the undertail. ♀ and **imm** are rich rufous-brown with 3-5 dark bands on the uppertail. A juv collected from Great Nicobar was browner and darker. ⌘ Forest. **E*3**

4 **Japanese Sparrowhawk** *Accipiter gularis* (152) 29cm. The smallest accipiter. From 6 by wing extending half-way along tail, narrower dark bands on tail. ♂ lacks mesial streak; peachy wash on underparts shows some white mottling on breast and thin white barring on belly and flanks. ♀ has thin hair-fine mesial streak. ⌘ Open country, forest and mangroves. ▽ *peew peew peewpipi*. **W*(R?)4**

5 **Shikra** *Accipiter badius* (137-40) 35cm. It is worth familiarising oneself with this, the commonest accipiter of the region, in order to use it as a benchmark for comparison with the other species on this plate. ♂ has the palest (bluish) grey upperparts of all the accipiters. The chin and throat are white with a grey mesial streak. The breast, belly and flanks are variably covered with narrow pale rusty bars, most prominent on the breast. In some birds, especially at a distance, this may appear as a uniform pale rufous wash. In flight the underwing is whitish with dark tips (not as dark or extensive as on 2). The barring on the flight feathers is faint grey, often not visible from a distance, and the wing linings usually show some pale rufous barring. The tail shows little or no barring on a perched bird. ♀ is similar but upperparts are browner. **Imm** is dark brown above, usually with some rufous and white streaking on the nape. It has a white supercilium (streaked with brown) and a bold dark mesial streak on the otherwise white throat. The rest of the underparts are heavily streaked with brown and rufous-brown drop-shaped spots tending more towards barring at the sides of the breast and flanks. The tail has 5-7 dark bars. ⌘ <1800(2250). Mainly plains and lower hills. Open wooded and arable country, vicinity of villages. ▽ loud harsh *titu-titu*; *ki-weew*; long-drawn screaming *iheeya, iheeya*; high piping *kyeew*; noisy sharp *ti-tui* during breeding season. **RM2**

6 **Besra** *Accipiter virgatus* (149-51) 32cm. **Ad** has the darkest upperparts of all the accipiters. The distinctly bold mesial streak, together with orange-streaked breast (orange, spotted with white in ♀) and barred belly, separate this species from all accipiters except 8 which is much larger, has a short crest and underpart markings dark brown. Generally smaller and much darker with more heavily barred tail (3-4 broad dark bars) and underwing than 5. From 4 also by wings only extending ¹/₃ of the way along tail. **Imm** from imm 5 by darker upperparts and broader dark bars on the tail. ⌘ <2800(3450). Dense hill forest but also more open wooded habitats in winter when Himalayan birds may descend to the adjoining plains. ▽ *tchew-tchew-tchew*.... **RA4**

7 **Eurasian Sparrowhawk** *Accipiter nisus* (147-8) 34cm. Similar to 5 but darker and more heavily marked. Absence of mesial streak separates this from 5 & 6. In flight from 5 by the distinctly barred underwing and tail. Underparts of ♀ and **imm** are barred with dark grey or brown distinguishing from all but 1, which is much larger and generally only found in the higher Himalaya, and 4 which is smaller and lacks whitish supercilium. ⌘ S 1400-3500(5200). W <2400. Well-wooded country, open forest, groves and orchards. Races **(a)** *melaschistos* **(b)** *nisosimilis*. ▽ *keew-keew-kikikikiki*. **AW3**

8 **Crested Goshawk** *Accipiter trivirgatus* (144-6) 43cm. At rest the short nuchal crest (not always visible) distinguishes from other accipiters. The dark brown mesial streak, breast streaking, barring on belly and flanks separate from all except 6 which is much smaller and has orange-brown markings on underparts. The shorter crest, yellow cere, shorter wings (only extending down basal third of the tail) and 4 narrow dark bars of even width on the uppertail distinguish it from Jerdon's Baza (11.3). ⌘ <2100. Most types of forest, preferring broadleaved in foothills and broken country. ▽ shrill prolonged yelp; shrill screaming *he, he, hehehehe*. **R4**

PLATE 13: BUZZARDS

1 **Long-legged Buzzard** *Buteo rufinus* (153) 61cm. Typical adults are identified by their pale cinnamon-coloured tails, but beware of some Common and Upland Buzzards which have pale rufous tails. In the most usual colour phase Long-legged has a pale creamy unstreaked head and breast (paler than the other *Buteo* species) contrasting with chestnut belly. Structurally the species is larger and longer-winged than Common Buzzard but not as heavy and massive as Upland Buzzard. Dark phase and immature birds may show heavy dark barring on the tail. ✇ **S** 1500-3700. Hill forest with clearings. **W** Down to the plains where it generally prefers open semi-desert and cultivation, but may also frequent deciduous forest. ∇ Usually silent in winter; call similar to that of Common Buzzard but less plaintive. **(A)W2**

1 Long-legged Buzzard

2 **Upland Buzzard** *Buteo hemilasius* (154) 71cm. To the observer familiar with the other buzzards the sheer size of this species is diagnostic. Most individuals show large white patches at the base of the primaries on the upperwing, a feature which distinguishes them from other buzzards which show very little if any such pale patch. On typical birds the whitish head usually shows some brown streaking at least on the nape and malar region, not usually found on pale-headed Long-legged Buzzards. At close range it can be seen that the feathering extends at least three-quarters down the length of the tarsus compared with half-way on Common and Long-legged Buzzards. The tail is never cinnamon-coloured as in the latter. ✇ Open country in the Himalaya. Frequently hovers. ∇ Usually silent in winter. **W4-5**

2 Upland Buzzard

3 **Common Buzzard** *Buteo buteo* (155-6) 54cm. The smallest and most compact of the *Buteo* species. A pale 'V' on the breast when present is indicative. For differences see 1 & 2. Occurs in at least three races each exhibiting a range of colour variation **(a)** *vulpinus*, **(b)** *refectus* and **(c)** *japonicus*. ✇ <4000. Open country with scattered perches, forest edge, open forest. Despite its name this species is not particularly common in the subcontinent. ∇ Mewing *meeee-ew*. **W3**

4 **[Grey-faced Buzzard** *Butastur indicus* 44cm. Separated from the similar 5 by grey cheeks, absence of pale shoulder; in flight by barring on underwing and tail. ✇ Forest, open country with scattered trees, second growth, plantations. ∇ *ti-viiih....* **V?** (Sight reports from Narcondam Island and South Andaman require documentation.)]

3 Common Buzzard

5 **White-eyed Buzzard** *Butastur teesa* (157) 43cm. The combination of dark mesial streak on white throat, white nape-patch and pale shoulder separates this species from other buzzards. Only adults have the distinctive white eye. ✇ <1200. Open country (including cultivation) with scattered bushes and trees, open broadleaved forest, forest edge. ∇ *ki-weeahr...* up to 5 or 6 times. **R3**

6 **[Rough-legged Buzzard** *Buteo lagopus* – **not illustrated.** 55cm. **Ad** separated from other *Buteo* species by white tail with broad black (sub)terminal band. Note also black belly; whitish head, breast and underwing-coverts variably streaked blackish; black carpal patches; black primary tips and trailing edge to the underwing. ♂ sometimes shows further dark bands on uppertail; head and upper breast can be quite heavily streaked, appearing dark. **Juv** shows diffuse or faint dark tail band and trailing edge to the wing. ✇ Open areas. Frequently hovers. ∇ Usually silent; like 3 but longer and higher-pitched. **V?** (Single published sight record from Bhutan needs confirmation.)]

5 White-eyed Buzzard

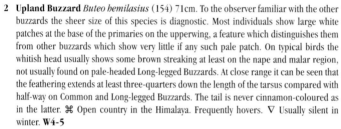
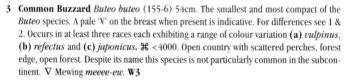
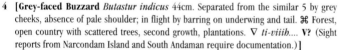

PLATE 14: HAWK EAGLES

1 **Mountain Hawk Eagle** *Spizaetus nipalensis* (158-9) 72cm. The typical pattern of streaked upper breast with the remainder of the underparts barred brown and white distinguishes from 2. Can be mistaken for Jerdon's Baza (11.3) but the crest is not usually held quite so upright; the streaking and barring is not so rufous below; **ad** shows 4 broad, evenly spaced dark bars on the uppertail with the terminal bar only slightly broader than the others; wing-tip only extends ¹/₃ to ²/₃ down the tail. **Imm** doubtfully distinguishable from imm 2 except in the northern part of its range where the latter only shows a rudimentary crest. ✴ (150)600-2400(3050) (generally at higher altitudes than 2 but range overlaps). Hill forest. ▽ Usually silent; shrill metallic whistle *peee-(peee)-peeeeoo*; sharp *kee-kikik*. **R(A)3**

1 **Mountain Hawk Eagle**

2 **Changeable Hawk Eagle** *Spizaetus cirrhatus* (160-2) 71cm. The much reduced crest of the northern race (**a**) *limnaeetus* distinguishes it from the southern race (**b**) *cirrhatus*. Pale birds separated from 1 by the underpart barring being absent or restricted to the lower flanks and thighs. Dark phase similar to Black Eagle (16.3) but when seen from below the flight feathers are much paler than the wing-coverts and the tail is paler at the base becoming dark on the terminal half; Black Eagle shows thin pale bands on the blackish undertail at close range. ✴ Plains and foothills (1900). Generally prefers well-wooded areas but may sometimes be seen in more open habitats with scattered trees. ▽ High whistling *(ki)-(ki)-(ki)-ki-ki-ki-ki-kee-keew*; normally silent outside the breeding season. **R2**

2 **Changeable Hawk Eagle**

3 **Rufous-bellied (Hawk) Eagle** *Hieraaetus kienerii* (165) 57cm. **Ad** quite distinctive, the white throat and upper breast contrasting with the rufous belly, vent and wing lining and the black hood. At a distance looks all dark with contrasting bright white upper breast and throat. **Juv** in flight looks almost completely white below with dark smudges on the lower flanks and base of the shoulder. If seen head-on the front edge of the inner wing looks white. Could be confused with a very pale buzzard but the perched bird shows a short crest, a distinct white supercilium and a dark mask through the eye. ✴ (Plains) foothills-1500. Humid evergreen and deciduous forest. ▽ Plaintive scream. Usually silent. **R4**

3 **Rufous-bellied (Hawk) Eagle**

4 **Bonelli's (Hawk) Eagle** *Hieraaetus fasciatus* (163) 70cm. **Ad** in flight has a unique combination of white underbody (variably streaked black on the breast), three-toned underwings and dark terminal band to the pale tail. The whitish patch on the upper back is also a good field mark. **Imm** underbody and wing lining vary from light buff to rufous in colour; the flight feathers and tail have indistinct fine barring; there is a large pale 'comma' patch at the base of the dark-tipped primaries. ✴ <2400. Well-wooded areas. ▽ Chattering *kie, kie, kikiki; cheu-cheu-....* **RW4**

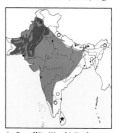

4 **Bonelli's (Hawk) Eagle**

5 **Booted (Hawk) Eagle** *Hieraaetus pennatus* (164) 52cm. Usually has a round white spot on each side of the neck at the base of the forewing showing up as a diagnostic pair of 'spotlights' when seen from the front. On pale-phase birds seen from below the creamy-white body and wing-lining contrasting with the blackish flight feathers are a combination not shown by any other large raptor. (Some juv *Aquila* eagles show a similar pattern but with buffier body and wing lining.) On dark-phase birds seen from below, the rounded tail with square corners and a dark wedge between the pale outer feathers, together with the broad dark band across the base of the wing-lining, are features which separate this species from Black Kite (11.7) and imm Brahminy Kite (11.5); distinguished from above by the whitish 'V' of the uppertail-coverts. ✴ <2400. Well-wooded areas, cultivation, semi-desert. ▽ Rapid *kwik-kwik-kwik....* **RW3**

5 **Booted (Hawk) Eagle**

70

1 **Golden Eagle** *Aquila chrysaetos* (166) 95cm. **Ad** from most other large eagles by overall dark plumage with golden hind-crown, nape and hind-neck, but see 2. **Imm** birds are fairly easily identified in flight by the characteristic white patch extending from the base of the primaries across the base of the inner secondaries, combined with the white basal half of tail, becoming less distinct as birds get older. In soaring flight holds its wings in a shallow 'V' unlike other *Aquila* species. Note also long wings with bulging secondaries broader than the primaries. ✹ >1800 in desolate rocky mountainous country. ▽ Usually silent. A thin shrill yelping *kiew*; a barking cry. **R4**

2 **(Eastern) Imperial Eagle** *Aquila heliaca* (167) 85cm. **Ad** similar to ad 1 but slightly smaller, back of head and neck generally much paler and pale 'braces' on the shoulders. The latter field mark is diagnostic but can be difficult to see on a bird overhead. The buffy-white back of head distinguishes from 3 & 4, as does the longer greyish tail with blackish distal third. **Imm** can be difficult to separate from 3 & 4 but lacks the clear white band on greater coverts of the underwing of 4 and is streakier on breast than other *Aquila* species; the sandy-coloured body, underwing and upperwing-coverts contrast with the darker flight feathers. Does not have the creamy or tawny coloration associated with 3. Pale wedge on inner primaries; pale trailing edge to wings and tip of tail. Creamy patch on lower back and rump is larger than on young 3 & 4 and merges into white of uppertail-coverts. Soaring flight generally on flatter more horizontal wings than 1, with fuller wing-tips and tending to show a narrower, squarer tail. ✹ Mainly open country. ▽ Normally silent. **WR*4**

3 **Tawny Eagle** *Aquila rapax* (168) 67cm. Variable in plumage. Large creamy-white to white patch on lower back, rump and uppertail-coverts on most individuals in all plumages. **Ad** dark morph similar to 4 but with fairly uniform dark brown underparts; barring on tail and flight feathers indistinct. Pale morph has rufous-buff to creamy-white body and coverts contrasting with darker flight feathers, some with a pale wedge on inner primaries. **Imm** similar to pale morph ad with some going through transitional plumages to become dark morph ads. Lacks white underwing-bar of young 4. When soaring wings are slightly arched. Iris yellowish on subadult and adult birds. ✹ Semi-desert, cultivation, and other dry open habitats. ▽ Not very vocal. Guttural *kra*; harsh grating *kekeke*. **R3**

4 **Steppe Eagle** *Aquila nipalensis* (169) 78cm. Treated in older works as a race of 3 from which it is often difficult to separate. On perched birds at reasonably close range it can be seen that the yellow gape extends to the rear edge of the eye as opposed to the centre of the eye on 3. **Ad** is overall dark to mid-brown below with many birds showing bold dark barring on the tail and the slightly paler flight feathers along with a broad dark trailing edge to both, features which also separate this from Greater Spotted (16.1) and Lesser Spotted (16.2) Eagles. Upperparts dark brown, often with paler coverts; sometimes a small rusty-yellow patch on nape; small whitish patch on rump and dark terminal band on tail. **Imm** broad white band through the centre of the underwing is a good field mark which becomes fainter with age but is still indicated on many subadult birds; white trailing edge to wings and tail is lost with feather wear; white on lower back restricted to uppertail-coverts; white bar formed by tips of greater coverts. When soaring and gliding holds wings slightly arched. Iris brown at all ages. ✹ Open country, often near water. ▽ Generally rather silent. **W2**

1 Golden Eagle 2 (Eastern) Imperial Eagle 3 Tawny Eagle 4 Steppe Eagle

PLATE 16: *AQUILA* EAGLES II AND BLACK EAGLE

1 Greater Spotted Eagle *Aquila clanga* (170) 67cm. A large dark eagle separated from 2 by the underwing-coverts being darker than, or as dark as, the flight feathers. From 3 and Imperial Eagle (15.2) by its shorter, more rounded tail. The basic colour of the upperparts is blackish-brown. Has neater 'trousers' than 15.3 & 15.4. **Ad** shows little or no difference in colour between the flight feathers and the underwing-coverts, though the inner primaries may be slightly translucent and there is a small pale patch at the base of the outer primaries; there is no pale patch on the hindneck and little or none at the base of the primaries on the upperwing. Young birds have distinctly darker coverts than flight feathers below. **Juv** has a white trailing edge to the wings and tail; white spots on the coverts and scapulars form white bars on the wings in flight, generally more extensive than on 2. The rare *fulvescens* form has a creamy-white body, upperwing-coverts and underwing-coverts; from juv 15.2 by unstreaked underbody and no prominent pale wedge on inner primaries of underwing. Gliding and soaring birds tend to hold the wings slightly arched below the horizontal. ⌘ The vicinity of lakes, jheels, canals and marshes. ∇ Wild clanging *jeb-jeb-jeb*. **W(B*)3**

2 Lesser Spotted Eagle *Aquila pomarina* (171) 64cm. The south Asian race *hastata* is sometimes treated as a separate species. The slightly smaller size and slimmer build compared with 1 is not generally apparent unless birds are seen together. Best separated in flight by the underwing-coverts being distinctly paler than the flight feathers. The upperwing-coverts are paler than the flight feathers with pale patches at the base of the inner primaries (smaller but still distinct on ad). **Juv** is normally less heavily spotted above than juv 1. ⌘ A rare bird of low country woodland and cultivation, sometimes also in similar habitat to 1. ∇ High-pitched cackling laugh. **R4-5**

3 Black Eagle *Ictinaetus malayensis* (172) 75cm. In flight the wings are a different shape from other large dark eagles, being broadest on the inner primaries, becoming 'pinched' near the body; the tail is longer, more square-ended. **Ad** is a large, very dark, almost black eagle with a pale patch at the base of the outer primaries; contrasting bright yellow feet and cere; at close range the long tail shows thin pale barring. **Juv** is paler and browner than ad with dark brown streaking on the underbody and pale underwing-coverts. When soaring the wings are held in a 'V'; slightly arched while gliding when the tail is usually held closed giving a square-cut appearance. ⌘ <2700. Largely a bird of forested hilly areas where it hunts by cruising just above the tree-tops in its search for birds, their nestlings and eggs. ∇ Normally silent; *kee, kee, kee*. **R3**

1   Greater Spotted Eagle   2   Lesser Spotted Eagle   3   Black Eagle

fulvescens

juv

1

juv

juv *fulvescens*

1

2

juv

2

juv

juv

2

juv

juv

3

3

3

PLATE 17: OSPREY, SEA AND FISH EAGLES

1 **Osprey** *Pandion haliaetus* (203) 56cm. Distinguished by the pale head with dark brown band through the eye. In flight note the long narrow wings sharply angled at the carpal when gliding; pale underparts with dark carpal patch and band across centre of underwing. ♀ and **imm** show a dark breast-band. ⌘ <900(3970). Large rivers and waterbodies, both inland and coastal. ▽ Generally silent on wintering grounds; *pew pew pew...; kieek kieek.* **WR*B*3**

2 **White-tailed Eagle** *Haliaeetus albicilla* (172a) 77cm. **Ad** easily recognised by wholly white tail contrasting with brown wings and body. **Imm** confusable with other large dark eagles but note the characteristic broad wings. Lacks the pale patches at the base of the primaries of 3 & 4. ⌘ Normally a coastal species on its breeding grounds but in the subcontinent generally occurs in the vicinity of larger inland lakes and rivers. ▽ Yelping *kew kew klee klee...;* hoarse *kurr kurr kurre....* **W5**

3 **White-bellied Sea Eagle** *Haliaeetus leucogaster* (173) 68cm. **Ad** very distinctive with white head, underbody and tail (black at base only). ⌘ Sea-coasts, lagoons and estuaries; occasionally some way along adjoining rivers and creeks. ▽ Loud nasal goose-like honking. **R3**

4 **Pallas's Fish Eagle** *Haliaeetus leucoryphus* (174) 80cm. **Ad** from other sea and fish eagles by black tail with broad white subterminal band; lacks white vent and lower flanks of 6. **Imm** from 2 by large pale patch on inner primaries. ⌘ <1800. Vicinity of larger inland rivers, lakes, jheels, marshes and tidal creeks. ▽ Loud, far-carrying raucous shrieks very like the creaking of the unoiled wooden block tackle of a village well. **RM4**

5 **Lesser Fish Eagle** *Ichthyophaga humilis* (177) 64cm. **Ad** from 6 by tail colour, dark at tip fading to white at the base. **Imm** extremely like 6 but lacks latter's white streaking on brown head and breast; in flight by uniformly coloured tail. ⌘ Foothills and adjoining plains-1500(4250). Himalayan forest rivers and streams; occasionally jheels, tanks and more open rivers. ▽ 'Querulous shouts and cackles' in the breeding season. **RA5**

6 **Grey-headed Fish Eagle** *Ichthyophaga ichthyaetus* (175-6) 74cm. **Ad** from 5 by contrastingly two-tone tail; from 4 by grey head, white vent and lower flanks. **Imm** very similar to 5 but is streaked with white on the brown head and breast. ⌘ Plains level. Vicinity of large lakes and slow rivers in open wooded country. ▽ *krraah...krraah...krraah;* unmusical weird *awh awhrr...* **R4**

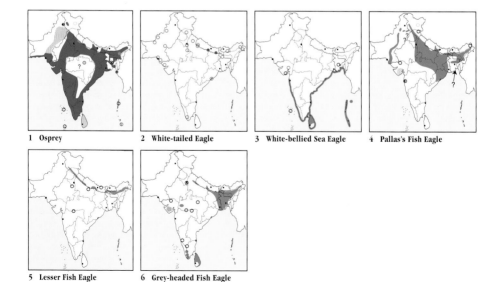

1 Osprey   2 White-tailed Eagle   3 White-bellied Sea Eagle   4 Pallas's Fish Eagle

5 Lesser Fish Eagle   6 Grey-headed Fish Eagle

PLATE 18: VULTURES I

1 Red-headed Vulture *Sarcogyps calvus* (178) 84cm. **Ad** easily distinguished at rest by the bare red skin of its head and legs. These are also quite prominent in overhead flight when the white patches at the sides of the thighs are another conspicuous diagnostic feature. Note also the white on the upper breast and the whitish line along the underwing lining. **Imm** browner, the head covered in white down. In overhead flight shows the same diagnostic pattern of white on dark as the ad with the addition of a white lower belly and undertail-coverts. ⌘ <2000(3050). Open country, deciduous wood-land, semi-desert; often near human habitation. Usually seen singly or in pairs, often outnumbered by other vulture species at a carcass, though up to 20 birds have been observed together. It is relatively timid and not very high in the pecking order. More solitary than most other vultures. **R4**

2 Cinereous Vulture *Aegypius monachus* (179) 105cm. In flight the all-dark plumage differentiates this from 1 and the *Gyps* vultures on plate 19; pale legs visible at closer range. On a perched bird the angular head shape separates from all vultures but 1. In flight from Greater Spotted Eagle (16.1) and Black Eagle (16.3) by the typical vulture jizz, relatively broad wings, small head and short, slightly wedge-shaped tail. ⌘ Open savanna, semi-desert and cultivation. Top of the vulture pecking order. Usually seen singly though may occur in groups of up to 20 locally in parts of Pakistan. **R*W4**

3 Egyptian Vulture *Neophron percnopterus* (186-7) 64cm. **Ad** is quite distinctive looking – rather handsome in flight but somewhat scruffy when seen perched. **Imm** is dingy brown; the head-ruff is diagnostic on a perched bird while in over-head flight the diamond-shaped tail separates from all but the much larger, longer-tailed and longer-necked 4. ⌘ More common in the plains and foothills, though some breed in the mountains (up to 3800). Generally scavenges on carrion and refuse in the vicinity of human habitation. Will drive off House Crows but gives way to most other vultures. **R(A)3**

4 Lammergeier *Gypaetus barbatus* (188) 122cm. Rather untypical for a vulture. Very large and long-winged. In flight note the long wedge-shaped tail, a feature not shown by any other large raptor except 3, which is half the size with a much shorter and more pointed tail. **Ad** seen at reasonably close range is unmistakable; at a distance note the golden (or creamy) head and underbody contrasting with the dark mantle, wings and tail. **Imm** in flight looks all dark and when size is not apparent could be mistaken for imm 3, but note the longer blunter tail and longer head and neck; in good light the blackish head contrasting with the dark brown underparts may be apparent. On a perched bird in profile the 'beard' is distinctive. ⌘ (300)1200-4100(7500). Himalayas. More of a montane species than 3 but altitudinal range overlaps. Usually found singly or in pairs. This species has the interesting habit of feeding on bone-marrow by carrying bones up to a great height and dropping them onto rocks to break them open. Will usually wait to take its turn until other vultures have finished feeding. ∇ Normally silent; *whueeeoo*; sharp guttural *koolik, koolik*. **R3**

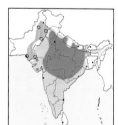 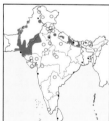  

1 Red-headed Vulture   2 Cinereous Vulture   3 Egyptian Vulture   4 Lammergeier

PLATE 19: VULTURES II

1 **Eurasian Griffon** *Gyps fulvus* (180, 183) 100cm. When seen together is appreciably larger than 3 & 4 but smaller than 2. Usually has a distinctive rufous or cinnamon tone to the plumage (especially underparts). Head and neck are usually covered in short whitish feathers (vs mainly unfeathered black in adult 3 & 4). The adult's compact white ruff is another feature which distinguishes from 2. In flight note the mid/dark-brown underbody, pale head and ruff, dark remiges and tail, paler brown wing lining with variably broad whitish patagial and central bars. ⌘ <3050. Barren mountains, open savanna, semi-desert. Nests singly or in small groups on cliffs. **RAM4**

2 **Himalayan Griffon** *Gyps himalayensis* (181) 120cm. The largest of the *Gyps*. Seen together with 1, 3 or 4 the much larger size is apparent. **Ad** is the palest *Gyps*, readily identified by being overall very pale sandy/creamy coloured (white on underwing-coverts) with contrastingly dark flight feathers and tail. In contrast the **juv** is very dark brown overall with a whitish feathered head and neck; pale streaks especially obvious on upperwing-coverts and underbody; almost no contrast between the flight feathers and underwing-coverts; the pale bar on underwing-coverts is often indistinct. ⌘ (plains) 900-4000(6100). Mountains of the Himalaya, sometimes straying to the adjacent plains. Pairs or small groups nest on cliffs. **A3**

3 **Long-billed Vulture** *Gyps indicus* (182, 184) 92cm. Races (**a**) nom **ad** perched is distinguished by the pale brown lesser and median coverts, dark brown remiges, pale brown almost unstreaked underparts, blackish unfeathered head, and pale horny-yellow or greenish-yellow bill with greenish leaden cere. Normally nests in colonies on cliffs. (**b**) *tenuirostris* **ad** perched is darker than nom and has blackish bill and cere with a pale culmen. **Ads** of both races and **juv** *tenuirostris* in flight from below by pale brown body and wing-coverts contrasting with dark flight feathers, rectrices, head and neck; an intermediate dark bar with pale fringes runs through the greater coverts. The two races may be split in future. ⌘ Plains (up to 1530). All habitats. Normally nests in trees. **R(A)3**

4 **White-rumped Vulture** *Gyps bengalensis* (185) 85cm. **Ad** is the most easily identifiable of the *Gyps*. The overall black colour with greyish-black secondaries and contrasting fluffy white ruff identify a perched bird. When the wings are spread the clearly white back and rump are visible. In flight the white underwing-coverts contrasting with black flight feathers and body are diagnostic. **Juv** is rather dark brown with pale streaking on upperwing-coverts and underbody and lacks the white back and rump of adult; in flight confusingly similar to several other immature *Gyps* but note the dark brown tail and flight feathers are not much darker than the body and wing-coverts, both above and below, with the latter showing whitish patagial and central bars. ⌘ <1000(3100). All habitats. Normally nests in trees. **R2**

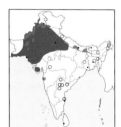

1　Eurasian Griffon　　　2　Himalayan Griffon　　　3　Long-billed Vulture　　　4　White-rumped Vulture

PLATE 20: HARRIERS

1 **Hen Harrier** *Circus cyaneus* (189) 50cm. In flight ♂ from ♂2 by broader black wing-tip; from ♂3 by lack of black bands at base of secondaries, but note the dark trailing edge to underwing. ♀ patch on ear-coverts not contrastingly darker than brown on rest of head; white supercilium joins or almost joins with white below eye; distinct whitish collar behind ear-coverts; on underwing the dark secondary bars continue as distinct lines on the primaries; wing lining unbarred. **Juv** is like ♀ but rufous-brown underbody and wing lining; from juv 2 & 3 by dark brown streaking on underparts. ⌘ <3000 (much higher on passage). Open country. The commonest harrier at higher elevations. **W3-4**

1 Hen Harrier

2 **Pallid Harrier** *Circus macrourus* (190) 48cm. Perched birds from 3 by the wing-tip falling well short of the tail tip; longer legs; more erect stance, usually more upright than shown. Longer, more pointed wings than 1. ♂ paler than ♂1 & 3, particularly on breast; in flight by thinner black wedge on wing-tip; from ♂3 also by lack of black lines across upper- and underwing. ♀ dark line through eye separates white supercilium from white patch below eye; fairly distinct white line around dark ear-coverts; on underwing secondaries look darker than on ♀1 due to broader barring, becoming broken on primaries; wing lining unbarred. **Juv** shows little or no supercilium; broad dark eye-stripe joins distinct dark ear-covert patch which extends to bill and is clearly bordered by buffy collar; the sides of the neck (behind the collar) are blackish contrasting with the rest of underbody; on underwing a boomerang-shaped pale patch at base of primary coverts diagnostic when present. ⌘ <3000(3350). Open country. **W(S)3**

2 Pallid Harrier

3 **Montagu's Harrier** *Circus pygargus* (191) 48cm. Perched birds from 2 by the wing-tip reaching the tail-tip; shorter legs; more horizontal stance. Longer, more pointed wings than 1. On ♂ dark bar across secondaries diagnostic if visible. In flight ♂ from ♂1 & 2 by black lines on the secondaries (both above and below). ♀ has very white face, contrasting dark patch on ear-coverts and the collar behind fairly indistinct; strongly barred underwing-coverts and axillaries; pattern of barring on secondaries below different from that of 1 & 2 (see illus.). On **juv** the clear dark patch on the ear-coverts does not usually connect with bill; eye-stripe and collar behind ear-coverts are indistinct or absent; distinct white supercilium above and behind eye; lacks blackish neck-sides of juv 2. A rare melanistic form (♂ illustrated) sometimes occurs but has not thus far been recorded from the Indian subcontinent. ⌘ Mainly lowlands (2650 on passage). Open country. **W3**

3 Montagu's Harrier

4 **Pied Harrier** *Circus melanoleucos* (192) 48cm. ♂ has distinctive pied plumage though could be confused with older ♂5a which see. ♀ has relatively plain brown head without the pale collar behind ear-coverts; whiter underwing with flight feathers less heavily barred than other ♀♀. **Juv** more uniformly dark brown above than 1, 2 & 3 juvs and rich cinnamon-brown below. ⌘ Mainly lowlands (3810). Grasslands, marshes and cultivation. **W(B•)4**

4 Pied Harrier

5 **Eurasian Marsh Harrier** *Circus aeruginosus* (193-4) 56cm. Larger, bulkier and slower-flapping flight than other harrier species. The swampy habitat is often a clue to the identity of the Marsh Harrier as 1, 2 & 3 usually prefer drier areas. ♂ readily separated from other harriers by the creamy, or whitish, crown and throat contrasting with the overall dark brown colour; ♀ has creamy leading edge to wing. **Juv** may have brown crown. Races **(a)** *spilonotus* sometimes treated as a separate species from nom but intermediates occur. Illustrated are perched subadult ♂ and flying adult ♂. Older ♂ (rare in our region) has blackish head like ♂4 but is larger, bulkier and lacks the white forewing. **(b)** nom ♂ in flight has fairly distinctive grey upperwings with black tips, brown greater coverts and creamy leading edge. ⌘ Mainly lowlands <920(3050). Marshes, jheels, wet paddy-fields, grassland. **W2**

5 Eurasian Marsh Harrier

PLATE 21: SNAKE AND SERPENT EAGLES

1 **Short-toed Snake Eagle** *Circaetus gallicus* (195) 66cm. Note the dark head and upper breast contrasting with the white underside of the body which is dotted with scattered broken bars. Quite distinctive in flight when it also shows the fine banding and barring on the underwing; 3 (or 4) dark, evenly spaced bands on the undertail, the terminal band somewhat broader. When perched note the rather large, owl-like head; the wing-tips reaching the tip of the tail; greyish cere. The tarsi are unfeathered and vary in colour from greyish-brown to yellowish-white. ⌘ <1000(2300). Semi-desert, open dry stony scrub and cultivation. ▽ Kite-like wailing whistle *pieeou, pieeou*; *wheeo kow-kow-kow....* **R3**

2 **Crested Serpent Eagle** *Spilornis cheela* (196-200) 74cm (*davisoni* 56cm). **Ad** the distinctive pattern of banding on the flight feathers and tail is diagnostic in flight. On a perched bird note the rufous-brown underparts spotted with silvery-grey; black crown and nape finely streaked with white; cere and unfeathered legs yellow. **Imm** is quite variable with up to six dark bands on the undertail and in flight can be confused with an imm hawk eagle (plate 14). Races **(a)** nom **(b)** *davisoni* (endemic to the Andaman Islands; birds from the Nicobars appear closest to *malayensis* – not shown). ⌘ <2000(3350). Forest, woodland, mangroves. ▽ Quite a vocal species often giving away its presence by the characteristic calls: (*kli*)-(*kli*)-*klee-klee-kleeuu*. **R(M)2**

3a **Small Serpent Eagle** *Spilornis minimus* (201) 48cm. Like a diminutive version of 2, of which it is sometimes regarded as an endemic race. The evidence is conflicting and the taxonomic status of the various forms of Serpent Eagle found in the Nicobars requires further study. ⌘ Both primary and disturbed forest. ▽ Has been reported as very like 2 but this needs confirmation. **E3** (The central Nicobar islands of Camorta, Katchal, Nancowry and Teressa; ?Great Nicobar.)

3b **Small (Great Nicobar) Serpent Eagle** *Spilornis minimus klossi* (202) 46cm. Sometimes treated as a separate species in its own right. See 3a for comments re taxonomy. The absence of markings on the buffy-brown underparts separate **ad** from all other serpent eagles of the region. ⌘ Dense primary forest. ▽ No description available, though has been reported as being very different from 3a. **E3** (Great Nicobar group of islands.)

4 **Andaman (Dark) Serpent Eagle** *Spilornis elgini* (202a) 50cm. Much darker chocolate-brown underparts separate this species from 2b, the local *davisoni* race of Crested Serpent Eagle; in flight note also narrow (vs broad) pale bands through the tail and flight feathers. Compare also 14.2, the local race of which is relatively small and dark. ⌘ Primary (and secondary) evergreen forest. Where they inhabit the same islands *elgini* generally prefers primary evergreen forest while *davisoni* is usually found in littoral, secondary and mangrove forest. There is, however, some degree of ecological overlap. ▽ Clear whistles unlike 2. **E2** (Andaman Islands; record from Nicobars may be a case of mislabelling.)

   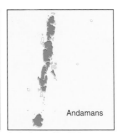

1 Short-toed Snake Eagle   2 Crested Serpent Eagle   3 Small Serpent Eagle   4 Andaman (Dark) Serpent Eagle

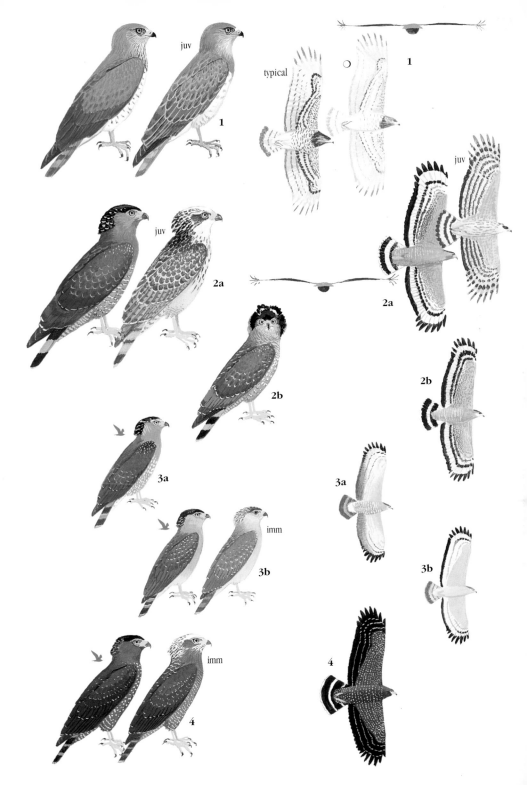

juv

1

typical

1

juv

2a

2a

2b

2b

3a

3a

3b

3b

imm

4

imm

4

PLATE 22: LARGER FALCONS

1 **Saker Falcon** *Falco cherrug* (206-7) 52cm. Larger and more heavy-bodied than all the other falcons of the region. **Ad** is much browner than adult Peregrine 3 but very similar to ad Laggar Falcon 2. Distinguished from the latter by the paler brown upperparts, the feathers usually boldly edged with orange-buff giving a more barred appearance; less distinct moustachial stripe; uppertail usually barred at least on all but central tail feathers; underparts paler, less heavily spotted and without the dark brown thighs of Laggar. Races **(a)** nom **(b)** *milvipes* (sometimes known as Shanghar Falcon). Both are rare winter visitors to the region. Usually solitary at that time of year. ✿ Desert, semi-desert, mountains. ▽ Usually silent outside the breeding season; similar to that of the Peregrine but somewhat harsher and more squealing. **W5**

2 **Laggar Falcon** *Falco jugger* (208) 45cm. **Ad** from Saker by smaller size; darker, greyer-brown upperparts; dark thighs; pale-tipped uppertail with little or no barring; lacks the upperpart spotting of 1b. Often in pairs. ✿ Plains. Relatively dry open regions including semi-desert, cultivation and areas with sparse scrub. Not normally found in the high mountains of the Himalaya. ▽ In the breeding season a shrill *whi-ee-ee*, otherwise rather silent. **NR(M*)3**

3 **Peregrine Falcon** *Falco peregrinus* (209, 211) 43cm. Races **(a)** *peregrinator*, sometimes known as Shaheen Falcon, is a widespread but localised resident. Northern form is illustrated. Southern forms lack the barring on the rich rufous underparts and are very similar to the much smaller Oriental Hobby (23.9) but note the white area separating the broad black moustachial region from the black of the nape. ✿ Hilly country, usually in the vicinity of rocky crags where it nests. **(b)** *japonensis* and **(c)** *calidus* are winter and passage visitors to the subcontinent and could be confused with Saker 1 or Laggar 2 but **ad** is slaty-grey above; underparts are barred; blackish hood extends down the face in a distinctly broad moustachial stripe; the hood is distinctly darker than the remaining upperparts. The latter two features distinguish the brown **imm** from Saker and Laggar. ✿ Chiefly open wetland and coastal areas where they hunt the wintering waterbirds. ▽ Non-breeding birds are normally silent; hoarse *kwaeh*; *kek-kek-kek*; *kiyook*; *chirr-r-r*. **RW**

3d **Peregrine (Barbary) Falcon** *Falco peregrinus babylonicus* (210). 40cm. Often regarded as a race of Barbary Falcon *Falco (peregrinus) pelegrinoides*, which is treated by some authorities as a separate species. Recent studies have shown that both are best considered as subspecies of Peregrine Falcon. **Ad** similar to Red-necked Falcon (23.5) but does not have the entire crown and nape rufous; from Merlin (23.10) by larger size; broad dark malar; barred (vs streaked) underparts; dark feather-centres to upperparts create a scalloped/barred effect appearing darker grey at a distance; several dark bars on tail merging towards tip; unstreaked crown. ♀ is distinctly larger than ♂. **Juv** rather like ♀/juv 23.5 but much larger and bulkier; bold broad (vs narrow) malar; unstreaked crown; more contrastingly barred uppertail. ✿ Barren semi-desert with scattered vegetation; open dry fields. Breeds locally in hot arid mountain regions. ▽ Similar to other races. **B*W4**

1 Saker Falcon   2 Laggar Falcon   3 Peregrine Falcon

PLATE 23: SMALLER FALCONS AND FALCONETS

1 Collared Falconet *Microhierax caerulescens* (204) 18cm. Diminutive size separates from all falcons except 2 which lacks the white collar on the hindneck and rufous in the plumage. The amount of rufous on the underparts of adult birds is quite variable with some birds almost entirely rufous below. ⌘ <920(2000). Forest edge, clearings and abandoned cultivation with tall lookout trees. ▽ Shrill whistle. **R4**

2 Pied Falconet *Microhierax melanoleucos* (205) 20cm. Diminutive size separates from all falcons except 1, which see. ⌘ <1500. Forest edge, clearings and tea plantations. ▽ Shrill scream; low chattering. **R4-5**

3 Common Kestrel *Falco tinnunculus* (222-4) 36cm. See 4 for differences. Frequently hovers looking for terrestrial prey. Solitary or in pairs. ⌘ <3300(5500). Open grassland, cultivation and semi-desert. ▽ Shrill *ki-ki-ki-ki-....* **RW2**

4 Lesser Kestrel *Falco naumanni* (221) 34cm. ♂ from ♂3 by lack of spotting on the rufous upperparts and bluish-grey wing-panel. In flight from below looks paler with spotting almost absent. On some birds the central tail feathers are somewhat elongated, a feature not normally shown by 3. ♀ can only safely be told from ♀3 at very close range by the pale colour of the claws (black in 3); the absence of a dark line behind the eye is another pointer. ⌘ Open grassland and cultivation. Gregarious. ▽ Hoarse *kye-kye*; *kye-kiki*. **P(W)4**

5 Red-necked Falcon *Falco chicquera* (219) 34cm. Separated from all other falcons by the entire crown and nape being reddish, but compare 10 and 22.3d. ⌘ Open lowlands with cultivation and groves of trees; thorn forest; often near human habitation. ▽ Rapid twittering; chattering screeches; high-pitched squeal. **R(M)4-5**

6 Sooty Falcon *Falco concolor* (216) 38cm. ⌘ Arid coastal habitat. ▽ Fairly slow *kee-keee-keee-....* **B*5** (Rare and localised summer breeder on the coast of western Pakistan.)

7 Amur Falcon *Falco amurensis* (220) 30cm. ♂ note grey throat, breast and upper belly contrasting with rusty lower belly and vent; in flight the pure white underwing-coverts contrasting with dark flight feathers are distinctive. ♀ has rich buffy vent and orange legs which may make it appear quite similar to ♂8 at a distance; separated by dark barring on upperparts; dark bands on uppertail; dark trailing edge to underwing. ⌘ Mainly lowland and foothills forest. Often hovers. Gregarious on passage. ▽ Shrill *kew-kew-kew....* **P(B*)4-5**

8 Eurasian Hobby *Falco subbuteo* (212-3) 33cm. **Ad** note streaked underparts, rusty vent and thighs. **Imm** like miniature imm Peregrine (22.3); from ♀ & imm 3, 4 & 10 by distinct face pattern. See also 7. ⌘ **S** 1200-4000. **W** >plains. Open woodland, forest edge, cultivation, semi-desert. ▽ *tee-tee-tee-....* **RAMW3**

9 Oriental Hobby *Falco severus* (214-5) 29cm. **Ad** note unmarked rufous underparts. From Shaheen Falcon (22.3a) by smaller size; no white cheeks; slimmer build. ⌘ Foothills-2400. Well-wooded foothills, forest edge, cultivation. ▽ Loud squealing *ki-ki-ki-ki-....* **RAM4**

10 Merlin *Falco columbarius* (217-8) 29cm. ♂ like miniature Peregrine (22.3) but streaked (vs barred) below; narrow malar stripe often indistinct; bright grey upperparts with distinct dark shaft-streaks visible at close range; single broad dark subterminal tail-bar (white tips may abrade away). ♀ similar to ♀♀ of 3 & 4 but smaller; upperparts dark brown without the rufous tinge; tail evenly banded. Races **(a)** *insignis* **(b)** *pallidus.* ⌘ Lowlands. Open country. ▽ Usually silent in winter; hoarse *yee-yee-yee....* **W5**

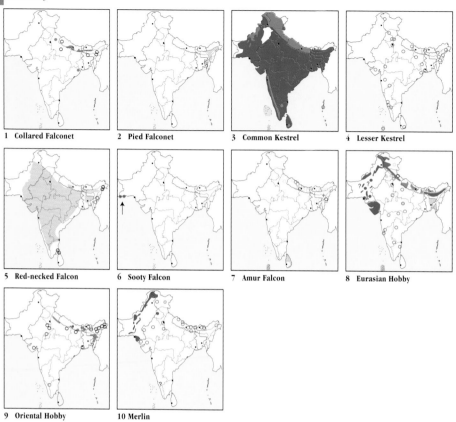

PLATE 23

1 Collared Falconet

2 Pied Falconet

3 Common Kestrel

4 Lesser Kestrel

5 Red-necked Falcon

6 Sooty Falcon

7 Amur Falcon

8 Eurasian Hobby

9 Oriental Hobby

10 Merlin

PLATE 24

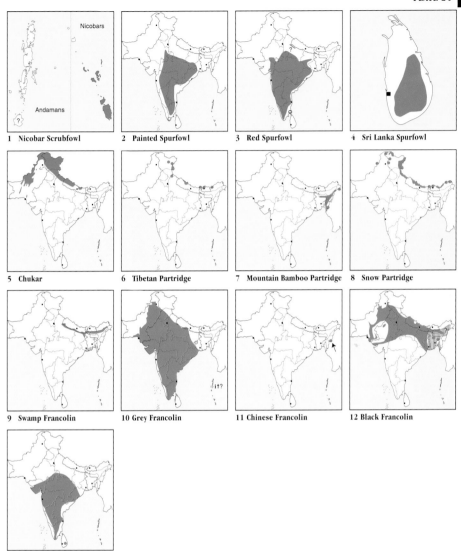

1 Nicobar Scrubfowl

2 Painted Spurfowl

3 Red Spurfowl

4 Sri Lanka Spurfowl

5 Chukar

6 Tibetan Partridge

7 Mountain Bamboo Partridge

8 Snow Partridge

9 Swamp Francolin

10 Grey Francolin

11 Chinese Francolin

12 Black Francolin

13 Painted Francolin

PLATE 24: SCRUBFOWL, SPURFOWL, PARTRIDGES AND FRANCOLINS

1 **Nicobar Scrubfowl** *Megapodius nicobariensis* (225-6) 43cm. ⌘ Coastal evergreen forest. In pairs or coveys. Partially nocturnal. ▽ *kuk-a-kuk-kuk*; ringing clanging turning to cackling *urr-rak, urr-rak, ur-r-rak, rak, rak, rak, rak.* **E*3**

2 **Painted Spurfowl** *Galloperdix lunulata* (278) 32cm. ⌘ <1100. Dense thorn, bamboo and grass scrub in drier rocky/broken country. In pairs or coveys. ▽ Cackling; *chur, chur, chur.* **E3**

3 **Red Spurfowl** *Galloperdix spadicea* (275-7) 36cm. Races **(a)** nom **(b)** *stewarti.* ⌘ <1250. Scrub and bamboo jungle, forest edge, coffee, lantana. In pairs or coveys. ▽ *kuk-kuk-kuk-kuk-karak*; rattling *k-r-r-kwek, kr-kwek, kr-kwek.* **E3**

4 **Sri Lanka Spurfowl** *Galloperdix bicalcarata* (279) 34cm. ⌘ <2000. Dense humid forest. In pairs or coveys. ▽ Loud ringing cackle – *kik-kik-kik-kirrik-kirrik*; *yuhuhuhu, yuhu, yuhu, yuhu, yuhuhéehéeyu.* **E3**

5 **Chukar** *Alectoris chukar* (234-6) 38cm. ⌘ (1200)2000-4000(5000). Hillsides with sparse scrub and adjacent cultivation. Gregarious. ▽ Rapid *chukchukchukchukchuk...*; *kak-kak-kak-(kak)-(kak)-kawak-kak-kawak-kak-kawak-kak....* **R2-3**

6 **Tibetan Partridge** *Perdix hodgsoniae* (248-9) 31cm. ⌘ **S** 3600-5600. **W** 2800-4000. Stony hillsides and plateaux with scattered bushes, dwarf juniper and rhododendron scrub. Pairs or large coveys. ▽ Rattling *scherrrreck-scherrrreck*; shrill *chee, chee, chee, chee, chee.* **R*3**

7 **Mountain Bamboo Partridge** *Bambusicola fytchii* (274) 35cm. ⌘ <2000. Scrub jungle, long grass, forest edge, often near streams; not particularly in bamboo. In coveys. Note restricted range. ▽ *Che-chirree-chirree-chirree-chirree*; discordant squawks. **R*4**

8 **Snow Partridge** *Lerwa lerwa* (227) 38cm. ⌘ (2500)3000-5000. Open hillsides covered with grass, lichens or other low vegetation. Gregarious. ▽ Similar to 10; low whistle. **R3**

9 **Swamp Francolin** *Francolinus gularis* (247) 37cm. Separated from other francolins by rusty throat and the long white streaks edged with black on the underparts. ⌘ Tall damp grassland and swamps, mainly in the floodplains of the terai. In pairs or small groups. ▽ *kye*; *kyew-kyew-kyew-ka-ka-ka*; *chukeroo chukeroo chukeroo*; *kaw-care.* **E*3**

10 **Grey Francolin** *Francolinus pondicerianus* (244-6) 33cm. Fairly nondescript greyish-brown plumage finely cross-barred above and below, upperparts with long narrow pale streaks. The commonest francolin of the plains. Races **(a)** nom **(b)** *mecranensis.* ⌘ Plains. Dry, fairly open, scrubby areas and adjacent cultivation. In pairs or family groups. ▽ ♂Repeated ringing *pukee-jew...pukee-jew...*; *pateela...pateela...*; high *tee tee tee*; *kirrr..kirrr..kirrr.* **R2**

11 **Chinese Francolin** *Francolinus pintadeanus* (243) 33cm. ♂ could be confused with ♂ 12 but note the rufous-brown supercilium, white throat, absence of chestnut collar, black upperparts spotted and barred with white and chestnut on shoulders. ♀ distinguished from similar francolins by the buffy-white cheek, rufous-buff supercilium and distinct dark post-ocular stripe; lacks the rufous nuchal patch of ♀12. Note restricted range. ⌘ Low oak scrub and grassy forest clearings. Singly or in pairs. ▽ *(kik) krik kriki, krich kaka.* **R*5**

12 **Black Francolin** *Francolinus francolinus* (237-9) 34cm. ♂ not unlike ♂11(which see) but much more widespread and common; in most cases separable by range. ♀ is the only francolin with a distinct rufous nuchal patch. ⌘ <1200(2500). Chiefly tall grassland near rivers and cultivation. Singly, in pairs or small groups. ▽ *(click)...chik-chirrik cheek-chereek.* **R2**

13 **Painted Francolin** *Francolinus pictus* (240-2) 31cm. Best distinguished by the pale chestnut sides of head with little or no dark eye-line and by the contrasting brown central crown-stripe which may be raised slightly to give a crest-like effect. Lacks the dark throat edging of 10. ♂ from 10 by black underparts and mantle heavily spotted with large round white spots. ⌘ Usually prefers drier, scrubbier habitats than 12 but not such arid ones as 10. Scattered pairs and family parties. ▽ Very like 12 *(click)...cheek-cheek-kerrag*; metallic *klak-kok-kok-ko-kok.* **E•3**

PLATE 25: PARTRIDGES, QUAILS AND BUTTONQUAILS

1 **Hill Partridge** *Arborophila torqueola* (266-9) 28cm. ♂ chestnut crown and ear-coverts; black throat separated from grey breast by white gorget. ♀ brown crown streaked black. ✼ (550)1500-4000. Hillsides and ravines in broadleaved evergreen forest. Gregarious. ▽ Loud, far-carrying, whistled *hwoaa* (c. 20/min). **R3**

2 **Rufous-throated Partridge** *Arborophila rufogularis* (270-1) 27cm. Rufous throat separated from grey breast by black gorget. Races **(a)** nom **(b)** *intermedia.* ✼ 600-2400. Evergreen hill forest undergrowth and secondary scrub. Gregarious. ▽ Long clear whistles like 1 leading into a series of *wheea-whu* ascending in pitch. **R3**

3 **White-cheeked Partridge** *Arborophila atrogularis* (272) 28cm. White cheek-patch bordered by black eye-stripe and throat. ✼ <750(1900). Undergrowth and bamboo in evergreen forest. In pairs and scattered coveys. ▽ Slightly wavering *kokoko* repeated c10 times at 2-3sec accelerating and rising in pitch. **R3**

4 **Chestnut-breasted Partridge** *Arborophila mandellii* (273) 28cm. Chestnut breast separated from rufous throat by black and white gorgets. ✼ 350-2450. Dense undergrowth in evergreen forest. ▽ repeated *hwrrooa whe-whe-ee.* **R*4**

5 **Jungle Bush Quail** *Perdicula asiatica* (255-8) 17cm. From 6 by rich chestnut throat, chestnut and buffy-white supercilium. ✼ <1500. Dry grass and scrub, grassy open forest, edges of fields. In coveys. ▽ Rallying soft *whi-whi-whi-whi...; chee-chee-chuck, chee-chee-chuck....* **E3**

6 **Rock Bush Quail** *Perdicula argoondah* (259-61) 17cm. From 5 by lack of chestnut supercilium; usually fewer or no dark spots on upperparts; throat patch of ♂ dull brick-red (vs chestnut). Races **(a)** nom **(b)** *salimalii.* ✼ Dry, stony areas with sparse scrub. In coveys. ▽ Similar to 5 **E4**

7 **Painted Bush Quail** *Perdicula erythrorhyncha* (262-3) 16cm. Red bill and large black spots on flanks diagnostic except for allopatric 9. ♂ has dark forehead, demarcated white throat and relatively dark upperparts. ✼ 600-2000. Long grass, scrub, forest edge. In coveys. ▽ *weep...weep...; tu-tu-tu-tu-tutu-tutu-tuttu; kirikee, kirikee....* **E3**

8 **Manipur Bush Quail** *Perdicula manipurensis* (264-5) 20cm. Only quail with slaty-grey upperparts. ✼ <1000. Damp elephant grass (swamps). In coveys. ▽ Clear soft *whit- 'it- 'it- 'it- 't- 't*, repeated 3 or 4 times, louder each time. **E*5**

9 **Himalayan Quail** *Ophrysia superciliosa* (280) 25cm. Not recorded since 1876. ✼ 1650-2100. Grass and brushwood on steep hillsides in the Dehra Dun – Nainital region; similar habitat to Cheer Pheasant (27.5). In coveys of 5-6. ▽ Low, short, quail-like contact note; shrill whistled alarm. **†(E?)**

10 **Blue-breasted Quail** *Coturnix chinensis* (253-4) 14cm. ♀ superficially similar to 16 but bright yellow legs; less heavily barred on breast; lacks rufous flanks and buffy barring on secondaries. ✼ Mainly plains (up to 2000). Wet grassland, secondary scrub, road verges, marshes, paddyfield edges, tea gardens. In pairs and small coveys. ▽ *tir-tir-tir.* **R•*4**

11 **Rain Quail** *Coturnix coromandelica* (252) 18cm. ♂ diagnostic black breast-patch and bold flank streaking. ♀ not safely separable from 12 & 13. ✼ Mainly plains (up to 2000). Grass, scrub, crops, stubble. Singly or in scattered pairs (or small groups). ▽ Clear *whit-whit* repeated at c. 1sec intervals. **R•M3**

12 **Common Quail** *Coturnix coturnix* (250) 20cm. See 13. ♀ not safely separable from 11 & 13. ✼ <2500. Grass, crops, stubble. In pairs. ▽ *(mau-wau)* followed by liquid *whic we-wic* or 'wet-me-lips' repeated persistently; *queep...queep; chack-chack-chack-chack* in flight. **R*W3**

13 **Japanese Quail** *Coturnix japonica* (251) 20cm. ♂ from 12 by brick-red throat and sides of head with black reduced or absent; richer upperpart coloration. ♀ not safely separable from 11 & 12. ✼ Grassland and cultivation. ▽ Mainly silent in winter; harsh *kwa kaoh.* **W4-5**

14 **Small Buttonquail** *Turnix sylvatica* (313) 13cm. From 15 & 16 by distinctly pointed tail, dark rump (a pointer in flight) and chestnut spots bordered with black on sides of neck/breast; from 15 by pale fleshy or blue-grey legs and grey bill. ✼ <2400. Grassland, grassy scrub and crops. Singly; occasionally in pairs or small groups. ▽ Muffled resonant 'drumming' like 16 but softer. **R•M4**

15 **Yellow-legged Buttonquail** *Turnix tanki* (314-5) 15cm. From 14 & 16 by yellowish bill, yellow legs (trailing in flight) and black spotting on buffy wings. ✼ <1200(2000). Grassland mixed with scrub; standing crops. Singly; occasionally in pairs or small groups. ▽ Unobtrusive 'drumming' similar to 16. **R•M4**

16 **Barred Buttonquail** *Turnix suscitator* (316-9) 15cm. Races **(a)** *leggei* **(b)** *taigoor.* From other buttonquails by barring on breast and flanks. ♀ by black throat. ✼ <2500. Grassland, scrub, cultivation and open woodland. Singly; occasionally in pairs or small groups. ▽ Increasingly loud 'drumming' *(groo groo) drr-r-r-r-r...* for 15sec+ ending abruptly; booming *hoo-oo-oon.....hoo-oo-oon....* **R•3**

17 **See-see Partridge** *Ammoperdix griseogularis* (228) 26cm. ✼ <2000. Dry, rocky hillsides with sparse scrub; edges of fields. In pairs or small groups. ▽ *chuck-chuck*; far-carrying, monotonously repeated *whou-it*; in flight *bit-bit-bit* and a whirring noise produced by the wings. **R3**

PLATE 25

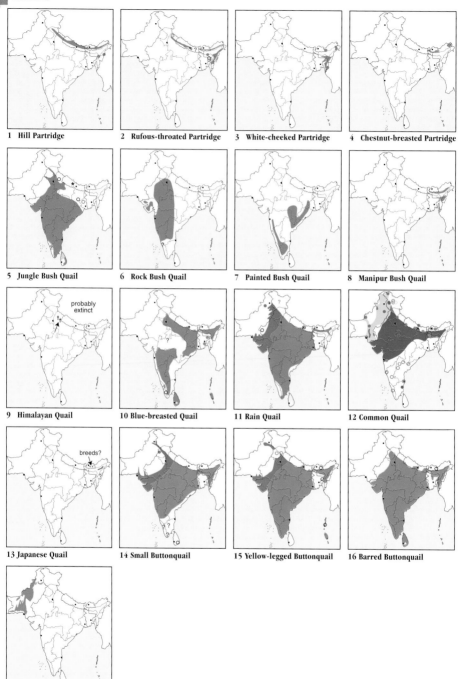

1 Hill Partridge

2 Rufous-throated Partridge

3 White-cheeked Partridge

4 Chestnut-breasted Partridge

5 Jungle Bush Quail

6 Rock Bush Quail

7 Painted Bush Quail

8 Manipur Bush Quail

9 Himalayan Quail

10 Blue-breasted Quail

11 Rain Quail

12 Common Quail

13 Japanese Quail

14 Small Buttonquail

15 Yellow-legged Buttonquail

16 Barred Buttonquail

17 See-see Partridge

PLATE 26

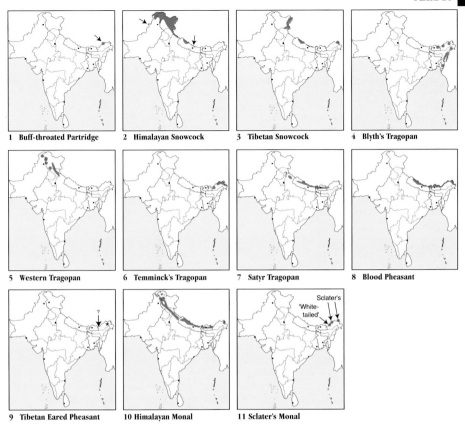

1 Buff-throated Partridge

2 Himalayan Snowcock

3 Tibetan Snowcock

4 Blyth's Tragopan

5 Western Tragopan

6 Temminck's Tragopan

7 Satyr Tragopan

8 Blood Pheasant

9 Tibetan Eared Pheasant

10 Himalayan Monal

11 Sclater's Monal

97

PLATE 26: BUFF-THROATED PARTRIDGE, SNOWCOCKS, TRAGOPANS AND PHEASANTS

1 **Buff-throated Partridge** *Tetraophasis szechenyii* (233) 46cm. ✻ 3350-4600. Well-vegetated rocky ravines in coniferous forest and rhododendron scrub. In small coveys. ▽ Loud harsh series of notes. **R*5**

2 **Himalayan Snowcock** *Tetraogallus himalayensis* (232) 68cm. From 3 by chestnut markings on head and bordering throat; grey lower breast and belly; flanks narrowly streaked with black and chestnut. In flight shows a white patch on primaries. ✻ **S** 4000-5500. **W** >c. 2400. Steep arid hillsides, alpine meadows, rocky ridges above the tree-line. Gregarious when not breeding. ▽ Rising whistled *courlee-whiyi*; accelerating *kuk kuk kuk-kuk-kuk-kuk-kukukukukuk*. **RA3**

3 **Tibetan Snowcock** *Tetraogallus tibetanus* (229-31) 51cm. From 2 by grey head and neck, white underparts broadly streaked with black on lower breast and belly. In flight shows a white patch on secondaries. ✻ **S** 4500-5800. **W** >(c. 3000) 3650. Similar habitat to 2. ▽ Accelerating *wup-wup-wup-wup-wup-wup-wuwuwuwuwuwu-wukkow-wukkow-(wuwuwu)*; whistle and curlew-like calls similar to 2. **RA4**

4 **Blyth's Tragopan** *Tragopan blythii* (287-8) ♂68cm ♀59cm. ♂ from ♂6 & 7 by yellow facial skin, greyish-buff lower breast and belly. ♀ not safely separable from other ♀ tragopans in the field but crimson tinge to shoulder (when apparent) distinguishes from allopatric 5 & sympatric 6; extremely similar to ♀7 but range may be indicative. ✻ 1600-3300. Dense undergrowth in evergreen forest, often on steep slopes. ▽ Loud, far carrying *hwaau, oowaaa, oowaau,...; gock... gock... gock.* **RA5**

5 **Western Tragopan** *Tragopan melanocephalus* (285) 71cm. ♀ rather similar to other ♀ tragopans but is the only one that looks greyish overall; underparts dotted with narrow white streaks edged with black. ✻ **S** 2400-3600. **W** >1350. Thick undergrowth in mixed coniferous forest and alpine shrubbery on steep slopes. Usually singly, in pairs or small family groups. ▽ Nasal, wailing *khuwaah; whaah.* **EA4-5**

6 **Temminck's Tragopan** *Tragopan temminckii* (289) 64cm. ♂ by bright cobalt-blue facial skin (yellow in ♂4, dark blue in ♂7); from ♂7 by grey spots (not edged with black) on crimson underparts; crimson back and rump. ♀ doubtfully separable in the field from ♀4 & 7 but lacks crimson tinge to shoulder, a feature difficult to see in the field. ✻ 2100-3500. Habitat similar to 7. Usually solitary. ▽ Similar to other tragopans. **R*5**

7 **Satyr Tragopan** *Tragopan satyra* (286) ♂68cm ♀59cm. ♂ from ♂4 & 6 by dark blue facial skin; from ♂6 by white spots edged with black on crimson underparts; olive-brown back and rump. ♀ not safely separable from other ♀ tragopans in the field but crimson tinge to shoulder (when evident) distinguishes from 5 & 6; extremely similar to ♀4 but range may be indicative. ✻ (1800)2400-4250. Dense undergrowth and ringal bamboo in evergreen forest, often in ravines and on steep slopes. Usually singly, in pairs or small family groups. ▽ Loud, far-carrying, wailing *guwaa...guwaah... guwaaah... (guwaaah)* increasing in volume. **RA4**

8 **Blood Pheasant** *Ithaginis cruentus* (281-4) 46cm. Races (a) *kuseri* (b) nom. ✻ (1500)2600-4600. Steep forest; dwarf rhododendron; juniper scrub; ringal bamboo near the snowline. Gregarious and often tame. ▽ Long high-pitched squeal; *chuck; kzeeuuk-cheeu-cheeu-chee.* **RA3**

9 [**Tibetan Eared Pheasant** *Crossoptilon harmani* (292) 72cm. Unmistakable. ✻ (2400)3000-5000. Grassy slopes adjacent to rhododendron and juniper scrub. In coveys. ▽ Loud resonant calls reminiscent of guineafowl; heron-like *wrack.* (Resident in south-east Tibet. Old record from Arunachal Pradesh disputed. Recent records unconfirmed.)]

10 **Himalayan Monal** *Lophophorus impejanus* (290) 72cm. Similar to 11 but ♂ has long distinctive crest; blue rump with white lower back; entire tail cinnamon-rufous. ♀ very similar to ♀11 but dark rump (uppertail-coverts white); strongly demarcated white chin and throat; pale streaking on underparts. ✻ 2500-5000. Steep grassy slopes; oak, deodar and rhododendron forest; cultivation. Singly or in small groups. ▽ Loud ringing whistle *wheee-(uw).* **A2**

11 **Sclater's Monal** *Lophophorus sclateri* (291) 72cm. Similar to 10 but ♂ crest consists of very short curly feathers; has bronze shoulders; white rump, uppertail-coverts and distal half of tail. ♀ from ♀10 by pale greyish rump and uppertail-coverts; greyish-white chin and upper throat only; finely vermiculated underparts. ✻ (2500?)3000-4000. Forest with thick undergrowth of rhododendron and bamboo; rhododendron scrub; usually in steep rocky terrain. ▽ Similar to 10. **R*5**

A population of monals recently discovered in W Arunachal Pradesh is similar to Sclater's but ♂ has all-white tail. Further research is needed to determine its taxonomic status.

PLATE 27: PHEASANTS

1 **Kalij Pheasant** *Lophura leucomelanos* (293-8) 64cm. Generally the commonest and most widespread Himalayan pheasant. Races and distinguishing features for ♂♂ **(a)** *lathami* – black underparts and crest; rump feathers edged with white. [**(b)** *williamsi* – silvery upperparts and tail. Resident in Myanmar (Burma). May occur in adjacent parts of Mizoram.] **(c)** *moffitti* – all-black upperparts and underparts. **(d)** *melanota* – black upperparts and crest, greyish underparts. **(e)** *hamiltonii* – white crest; greyish underparts; feathers of the rump usually broadly edged with white (vs narrowly in nom) but this feature variable. **(f)** nom – black crest, rump feathers edged with white; greyish underparts. ♀ distinguished from ♀ of other pheasant species by long drooping crest, large bare red patch around eye, tail shape similar to that of ♂ but smaller. ⌘ Commoner at lower altitudes but recorded up to 3700m. Forest undergrowth, forest edge, cultivation, often in the vicinity of streams. Will emerge onto the road at dawn and dusk. Singly, in pairs or family parties. ∇ Low contact *kurr-kurr-kurrchi-kurr; kerwik-kerwik*; squeals, clucks, chuckles and chirrups; courting male drums by rapidly beating wings against the breast-sides. **A2**

2 **Koklass Pheasant** *Pucrasia macrolopha* (303-6) ♂61cm ♀53cm. Races and distinguishing features for ♂♂ **(a)** *nipalensis* – sides and flanks mainly black; no chestnut collar. **(b)** *biddulphi* – chestnut collar but not mantle. **(c)** *castanea* – chestnut collar and mantle. **(d)** nom – sides and flanks mainly grey; no chestnut collar. ⌘ **S** c.2000-4000. **W** 1000-2300. Conifer, oak and rhododendron forest, preferring steep slopes and ravines with good undergrowth and grassy clearings. In pairs or small groups. ∇ *ka-ka-ka khwa khwa; kok-kok-(kok)...koklas; qui-quik qui-quik...; kwak-kwak-kwak; wo-kok*. **A3**

3 **Mrs Hume's Pheasant** *Syrmaticus humiae* (308) ♂90cm ♀60cm. ♀ lacks the crest of ♀1 & 5 and is also distinguished by tail shape which is similar to ♂ but smaller; red facial skin separates from ♀4. Note restricted range. ⌘ 900-2000. Steep open forest with grass and bracken. ∇ Varied. Loud *chuck*; high-pitched chirping calls; muttering *buk-buk-buk-buk-buk*; wing whirring. **R*5**

4 **Common Pheasant** *Phasianus colchicus* ♂80cm ♀60cm. ♀ similar to ♀1, 3 & 5 but lacks red facial skin; absence of crest also separates from ♀1 & 5. ⌘ Habitat in most of its usual range is varied from grassland to scrub, forest and cultivation. Usually in small groups. ∇ *kuchuk-kuchuk-kuchuk...*; ♂ has loud *kok kok korrok* followed by wing-flapping. **I*5** (Locally introduced into Bhutan and Himachal Pradesh.)

5 **Cheer Pheasant** *Catreus wallichii* (307) ♂90-118cm ♀61-76cm. ♀ can be separated from other ♀ pheasants by general shape (similar to that of male though tail somewhat shorter) and marked dark spotting on breast. ⌘ 1400-3500(4545). Prefers steep, rugged, south-facing grassy hillsides, but also occurs in scrub with scattered trees, wooded ravines and early second growth in cleared forest. In coveys. ∇ Cackling *waak*; sharp *tuk tuk*; loud, far-carrying *chir-a-pir, chir-a-pir, chir, chir, chirwa, chirwa...*; high piercing *chewewoo* whistles interspersed with short *chut* calls; squeaks and chuckles. **E4**

1 Kalij Pheasant   2 Koklass Pheasant   3 Mrs Hume's Pheasant   5 Cheer Pheasant

PLATE 28: PEAFOWL, JUNGLEFOWL AND PEACOCK PHEASANT

1 **Indian Peafowl** *Pavo cristatus* (311) ♂ 110cm without train (c. 2-2.5m in full plumage) ♀86cm. ✺ <1800(2000). In the wild state usually in deciduous forest, often near water; commonly semi-feral in the vicinity of villages and cultivation. Usually in small groups of a male and 3-5 hens in the breeding season; otherwise often in separate groups of ♂♂ and ♀♀/imms. Forages on the ground. Roosts in tall trees. ▽ Loud *mayaah*, repeated 4-5 times. **E2**

2 **Green Peafowl** *Pavo muticus* (312) Now probably extinct in the subcontinent. ♂ 110cm without train (c. 2-2.5m in full plumage) ♀ 86cm. ✺ Deciduous forest, second growth and cultivation, usually in the vicinity of streams. ▽ ♂ Loud *aow-aaw*; ♀ *aa-ow*. †(R*5?)

3 **Sri Lanka Junglefowl** *Gallus lafayetii* (302) ♂69cm ♀36cm. ♂ similar to ♂4 & 5 but plumage streaked with dark brown, reddish belly and breast, elongated comb with yellow centre. ♀ from ♀4 & 5 by prominent barring on wings. Endemic to Sri Lanka; range indicative. ✺ Forest undergrowth and scrub in all zones of Sri Lanka up to the highest hills. ▽ ♂ loud *kwek...kaw-choyik*; ♀ *kwikkuk, kwikkukkuk....* **E2**

4 **Grey Junglefowl** *Gallus sonneratii* (301) ♂ 70cm ♀46cm. ♂ similar to ♂3 & 5 but overall greyer with spangled neck-ruff. ♀ from ♀5 by white spotting on underparts; lacks the conspicuous wing-barring of ♀3. ✺ Undergrowth in forest and abandoned plantations. ▽ *kúk`ka...kurra-kuh(ah)*. **E2**

5 **Red Junglefowl** *Gallus gallus* (299-300) ♂ 66cm ♀43cm. The ancestor of all domestic varieties. There are probably few, if any, pure wild strains remaining because of hybridisation with domestic birds. For ♂ differences see 3 & 4. ♀ lacks white underpart spotting of ♀3 & 4 and the prominent barring on wings of ♀3. ✺ Mainly foothills and plains (up to 2000). Moist deciduous forest, often on the edge and in second growth. ▽ Recognisably like the familiar domestic chicken. **R2**

6 **Grey Peacock Pheasant** *Polyplectron bicalcaratum* (309-10) ♂64cm ♀48cm. ✺ <1200. Dense primary evergreen forest. Usually found singly or in pairs. ▽ 6-8 hoarse notes on ascending scale *kraa´kraa´kraa´kraa´kraa´kraa´(kraa) ´(kraa)*; tremolo *kuraaaaaa-a-a*. **R3**

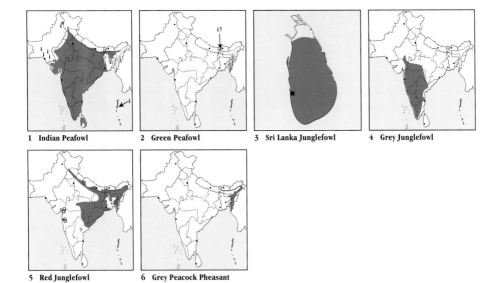

1 Indian Peafowl   2 Green Peafowl   3 Sri Lanka Junglefowl   4 Grey Junglefowl

5 Red Junglefowl   6 Grey Peacock Pheasant

PLATE 29: CRANES, BUSTARDS AND FLORICANS

1 **Common Crane** *Grus grus* (320) 114cm. From 2 by white behind eye extending down back of nape. See also 5. ✳ Crop fields, jheels, marshes, river banks. In large flocks, often together with 5. ▽ Loud trumpeting *kraarrh*. **W3**

2 **Black-necked Crane** *Grus nigricollis* (321) 139cm. At rest looks grey with black head, neck and rear end. In flight similar to 1 & 5 but overall paler with all-black neck. ✳ **S** 4300-4600. Boggy areas around lakes. In pairs. **W** >1500. Open fallow fields and swampy areas. Gregarious. ▽ Loud whooping *kr-kra-kruw*, slightly higher-pitched than 4. **MW5**

3 **Hooded Crane** *Grus monacha* (322) 97cm. Dark grey with white neck and head (black and red forecrown). ✳ Open wetlands, fields, river banks. ▽ Loud trumpeting *trrreeow*. **V**

4 **Sarus Crane** *Grus antigone* (323-4) 152cm. Largely red head and upper neck diagnostic. World's tallest flying bird. ✳ <1700. Jheels, marshes, open agricultural fields, village tanks etc. In pairs or family groups. ▽ Loud trumpeting, often in duet. **R*3**

5 **Demoiselle Crane** *Grus virgo* (326) 95cm. Most similar to 1 but black of neck continues down onto elongated breast feathers; long white feathery plumes behind eye. In flight from 1 by black of neck extending far down onto breast. ✳ Crop fields, stubble, jheels, marshes, fluvial sandbanks. In large flocks, often associating with 1. ▽ Loud trumpeting. **W3**

6 **Siberian Crane** *Grus leucogeranus* (325) 135cm. At rest looks completely white with red face. In flight white with contrasting black primaries. ✳ Open marshes and jheels. Gregarious; Indian wintering population on the verge of extinction. ▽ Soft, musical *koonk-koonk*. **W5**

7 **MacQueen's Bustard** *Chlamydotis macqueeni* (355) 65cm. Diagnostic black ruff down side of neck (less marked in ♀ and imm). In flight note the black flight feathers with large white patch on outer primaries. ✳ Semi-desert and neighbouring cultivation. Singly or in groups. ▽ Normally silent. **B*W4**

8 **Indian Bustard** *Ardeotis nigriceps* (354) 110cm. Largest bustard. ♂ easily distinguished by the crested black crown and breast-band, also noticeable in flight. ♀ is like ♂ but smaller and appears duller due to fine black vermiculations on the neck and the fact that the dark breast-band is usually absent or faint. ✳ Semi-desert, open arid grasslands. In pairs or groups. ▽ Barking *hook* alarm. **E●4**

9 **Lesser Florican** *Sypheotides indica* (357) 48cm. **Br♂** from ♂12 by distinctive long plumes with rackets projecting back from the sides of the head; white throat and thinner neck. **♀/imm** from ♀/imm 12 by bold spotting on upper breast and pale rufous-buff tinge to underparts. In flight ♂ has white restricted to inner wing (vs entire upperwing in 12); ♀ has white upperwing-coverts; **imm** has buffy upperwing-coverts and only the three outer primaries dark. Range largely disjunct from that of 12 apart from occasional stragglers. ✳ Plains (up to 1000). Tall open grassland with scattered bushes; standing crops. Polygamous. ▽ Low chuckle; whistling; rattle in display jump. **E●M4**

10 **Great Bustard** *Otis tarda* (352) 102cm. Note the grey head and neck without black markings; rufous tinge to upperparts; rufous tail with narrow black bars (young birds less rufous, more sandy); **br♂** acquires long white whiskers and a diagnostic broad rufous collar. In flight wing appears largely pale with very broad black trailing edge. ♀ smaller. ✳ Dry open grassland, crops, stubble. ▽ Usually silent in winter. **V(W)**

11 **Little Bustard** *Tetrax tetrax* (353) 46cm. **Br♂** has diagnostic neck pattern. **Nbr♂** and **imm** are similar to ♀ and appear rather like a galliform but for the somewhat different jizz with relatively long neck and strong legs; told from ♀ floricans by absence of black lateral crown-stripes. In flight note the wing pattern. ✳ Open short grassland, crops. Small groups. ▽ Usually silent; dry *krik*. **W*** (irregular) **5**

12 **Bengal Florican** *Houbaropsis bengalensis* (356) 66cm. In flight ♂ has entire upperwings white, edged with black (only inner wing is white in 9); ♀/imm like 9 but much larger with white belly and completely dark primaries. ✳ Tall damp grassland with scattered bushes, often feeding in adjacent burnt- or grazed-over grassland and crops. Solitary outside breeding season. ▽ Usually silent; shrill *chik* or *tsik*. **R*4**

PLATE 29

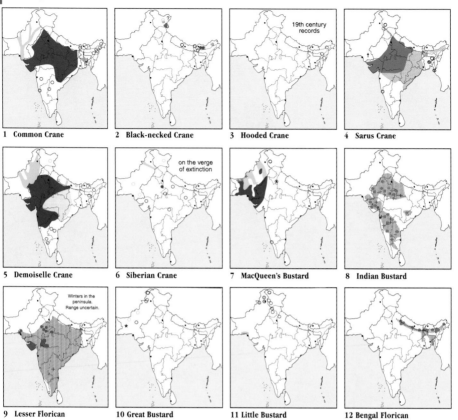

1 Common Crane

2 Black-necked Crane

3 Hooded Crane

19th century records

4 Sarus Crane

5 Demoiselle Crane

6 Siberian Crane

on the verge of extinction

7 MacQueen's Bustard

8 Indian Bustard

9 Lesser Florican

Winters in the peninsula. Range uncertain.

10 Great Bustard

11 Little Bustard

12 Bengal Florican

PLATE 30

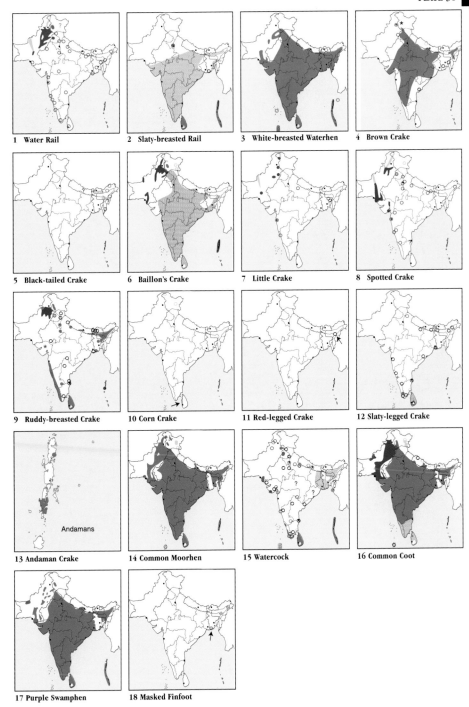

1 Water Rail

2 Slaty-breasted Rail

3 White-breasted Waterhen

4 Brown Crake

5 Black-tailed Crake

6 Baillon's Crake

7 Little Crake

8 Spotted Crake

9 Ruddy-breasted Crake

10 Corn Crake

11 Red-legged Crake

12 Slaty-legged Crake

13 Andaman Crake

Andamans

14 Common Moorhen

15 Watercock

16 Common Coot

17 Purple Swamphen

18 Masked Finfoot

107

PLATE 30: RAILS, CRAKES, GALLINULES AND FINFOOT

1 Water Rail *Rallus aquaticus* (327-8) 28cm. Long red bill separates from other rails and crakes except 2 which has barred upperparts. **Juv** (not shown) has brownish underparts and horny bill. ✳ Marshes. ∇ Squealing *queeek...*; *krik*. **B*W3**

2 Slaty-breasted Rail *Gallirallus striatus* (329-30) 27cm. From all other rails and crakes by barred upperparts. Note also medium-long red bill; chestnut cap and nape. **Juv** (not illustrated) is browner below. ✳ <1300. Marshy areas, paddyfields, mangroves. ∇ Sharp *cerrk*. **R•4**

3 White-breasted Waterhen *Amaurornis phoenicurus* (343-5) 32cm. Races **(a)** nom **(b)** *insularis*. Birds on Car Nicobar have all-white head and neck. **Juv** (not shown) has brown upperparts, lower breast and upper belly; greyish throat, cheeks and upper breast; lacks red at base of bill. Separated from similar birds by cinnamon rear flanks, vent and undertail-coverts. ✳ <1500(2200). Marshes, paddyfields, pools, ditches, etc. ∇ Varied raucous calls; *k'waak*; *krrrr-kwaak-kwaak...*; *kook...kook...kook....* **R1**

4 Brown Crake *Amaurornis akool* (342) 28cm. From other crakes except 5 (which see) by olive-brown and grey plumage and absence of barring. ✳ <800. Marshy habitats. ∇ Long high trill *trrrrrrrrrrrrrrrr* like Little Grebe but not as high. **R•4**

5 Black-tailed Crake *Porzana bicolor* (341) 22cm. From 4 by rufous-brown (vs olive-brown) upperparts; black (vs brown) upper- and undertail; dark ashy (vs ashy-grey) underparts. Red at base of bill may be absent. ✳ 880-3500. Jungle in and around paddies; grass-bordered streams; pools and marshes near forest and second growth. ∇ *keck*; *kik*; quiet *waak-waak* followed by long descending trill. **R5**

6 Baillon's Crake *Porzana pusilla* (337) 19cm. From 7 by dark green bill; extensive white spotting on rich brown upperparts; barring of underparts extending distinctly onto flanks in front of legs; short primary projection. ✳ Marshes, jheels, paddyfields, etc. ∇ Dry rattling trill *trrrrriii*. **R*W3**

7 Little Crake *Porzana parva* (335-6) 20cm. From 6 by greenish-yellow bill with red at base (absent in imm); dull brown upperparts with little or no white; obvious pale line down the scapulars and inner edge of tertials; indistinct barring on vent and undertail-coverts; long primary projection. ✳ Marshes. ∇ Measured *kweck-kweck-kweck...*; 5-10 *py-ook* then *piou-pi-pi-pi-pi-pi-pe-pe*. **W5**

8 Spotted Crake *Porzana porzana* (338) 23cm. Spotting on breast, sides of breast and mantle; white barring on wings; buffy undertail-coverts. In flight identified by obvious white leading edge to wing. ✳ Marshes. ∇ Rhythmical whiplash *hwitt* (at a distance like dripping tap); usually silent in winter. **W5**

9 Ruddy-breasted Crake *Porzana fusca* (339-40) 22cm. From 11-13 by dark rufous breast and belly; barring faint and confined to rear flanks and undertail. **Juv** has greyish underparts faintly barred with whitish and could be confused with 6, 7 or 8 but for the unmarked brown upperparts. ✳ Marshy areas. ∇ Soft *crake*; metallic *tewk*; squeaky trill. **R•2**

10 Corn Crake *Crex crex* (334) 25cm. Chestnut-brown wings; barring on flanks and undertail-coverts; pinkish bill and legs. ✳ Crops, grassland, drier parts of marshes. ∇ Loud rasping *crex-crex*. **V**

11 Red-legged Crake *Rallina fasciata* (331) 23cm. From 12 by coral-red legs; barring on folded outer wing; reddish-brown upperparts; throat normally washed rufous; white and dark bars on underparts usually same width. ✳ Marshy areas; dense stream- and pool-side undergrowth. ∇ Nasal *pek* (2/sec); long descending trill. **R*?5**

12 Slaty-legged Crake *Rallina eurizonoides* (332) 25cm. From 11 by slaty legs; absence of whitish bars on wings; dark brown upperparts; white throat; white bars on underparts usually much narrower than dark ones. **Juv** browner (not illustrated); separated from juv 11 by dark grey legs and unbarred wings. ✳ <1600. Marshes; tangled wet areas in forest, second growth and gardens. May perch in tree when flushed. ∇ Quiet *krrrr*; nasal *kaak*; *kek-kek, kek-kek, kek-kek...*; *krrrrrrrrr-ar-kraa-kraa-kraa*. **R*WM4**

13 Andaman Crake *Rallina canningi* (333) 34cm. From 9, 11 & 12 by deep chestnut head, breast and upperparts; pale green bill; large size. Lacks 12's white throat. ✳ Forest, swampy jungle. ∇ Deep *kroop kroop* as though under water; sharp *chick, chick*. **E*5**

14 Common Moorhen *Gallinula chloropus* (347-7a) 32cm. ✳ Lakes and jheels with open water and fringing marshy vegetation. ∇ Loud *peeruck*; *kirrik-krek-rek-rek*; *kek...kek....*; *pwuk...pwuk...*etc. **RW1**

15 Watercock *Gallicrex cinerea* (346) ♂43cm ♀36cm. ✳ Swamps; wet cultivation and adjoining fields. ∇ *kok kok...*, *utumb utumb...*; *kluck kluck...*; *toom*. **R•3**

16 Common Coot *Fulica atra* (350) 42cm. ✳ <2500. Lakes, jheels, tanks. ∇ Varied and loud. Ringing *pitt*; *kok*; *peeow*; *kyow, kyow, kyow...* etc. **RW1**

17 Purple Swamphen *Porphyrio porphyrio* (348-9) 43cm. ✳ Marshy and grassy areas around jheels. ∇ Varied deep hooting and clucking, including: *keh*; *kuwah*; *kah-kah-kah...*; *keerk, keerk...*; *koorrah* etc. **R•2**

18 Masked Finfoot *Heliopais personata* (351) 56cm. ✳ Pools and rivers in forest; mangroves. ∇ High-pitched bubbling as through water; grunting quack. **R*?5**

PLATE 31: WADERS I (JACANAS, THICK-KNEES, OYSTERCATCHER, CRAB-PLOVER, AVOCET, IBISBILL, STILT, PRATINCOLES, COURSERS)

1 **Pheasant-tailed Jacana** *Hydrophasianus chirurgus* (358) 31cm without tail-streamers. **Br** unmistakable. **Nbr** from 2 by yellow hind-neck and largely white wings. **Imm** possibly confusable with imm 2 but white in wing, usually some yellow on sides of head and at least an indication of a dark breast-band. ⌘ <1500(3800). Jheels, marshes and ponds with plenty of floating vegetation, particularly lilies; paddyfields. Gregarious in winter. ∇ *kyoo-kyoo-kyoo; mee-ooph-(ooph-ooph-ooph); ki-ki-ki-ki-ki*; nasal *tewn, tewn.* **R•2**

2 **Bronze-winged Jacana** *Metopidius indicus* (359) 30cm. **Ad** distinctive; in flight upperwing all dark (vs white in 1). **Imm** rather like imm 1 but has thicker bill, no dark breast-band, no white in wing, rusty-buff throat and upper breast and bronzed upperparts. ⌘ As 1 but more restricted to the lowlands. ∇ Harsh grunt; shrill *seek-seek-seek.* **R•2**

3 **Eurasian Thick-knee** *Burhinus oedicnemus* (435-6) 41cm. ⌘ Dry open scrub, sandy semi-desert, dry riverbeds, open woodland (overgrown gardens). Largely crepuscular and nocturnal. ∇ *pick-pick-pick-pick-pick-(pick-wick, pick-wick, pick-wick)*; loud *qurleee; kerreerree.* **R•3**

4 **Beach Thick-knee** *Esacus neglectus* (438) 55cm. From 5 by straighter, heavier bill; mainly black forecrown and lores; white supercilium completely enclosed by black; in flight by grey secondaries and white inner primaries (on upperwing). Note range. ⌘ Strictly coastal: beaches, reefs, mudflats, mangroves. In pairs or small groups. ∇ Harsh, mournful *wee-loo*; quiet *peet-peet.* **R*4**

5 **Great Thick-knee** *Esacus recurvirostris* (437) 51cm. From 4 by upcurved bill, whitish forecrown, white supercilium not completely enclosed by black; in flight by black secondaries and black inner primaries with white patch and tips (on upperwing). ⌘ Mainly islands and banks of freshwater rivers and lakes; also shores of lagoons and estuaries. In pairs or groups. ∇ Harsh *craak*; wailing *kree-kree-kree*; deep whistling *keee-keee...; kill-ick-kill-ick-kill-ick.* **R•3**

6 **Eurasian Oystercatcher** *Haematopus ostralegus* (360-1) 42cm. **Nbr/imm** has a white half-collar. ⌘ Seashores (inland on migration). Small scattered groups. ∇ Plaintive *teweep; peep-peep-peep...; teyou-teyou-teyou....* **W(R*)3**

7 **Crab-plover** *Dromas ardeola* (434) 41cm. ⌘ Coasts, tidal mudflats, reefs. Gregarious at roost. ∇ *tchuk-tchuk-...; kiep; chee-ruk*; whistling *kew-ki-ki.* **W(B*?)3**

8 **Pied Avocet** *Recurvirostra avosetta* (432) 46cm. ⌘ Jheels, marshes, lagoons, creeks, coasts. Gregarious. ∇ *klooit; kweet-kweet-kweet....* **WB•3**

9 **Ibisbill** *Ibidorhyncha struthersii* (433) 41cm. Plumage distinctive but suprisingly cryptic. ⌘ Shingle banks of broad Himalayan rivers. **S** 1700-4400. In pairs. **W** Many descend to the foothills and adjacent plains. Singly, in pairs or loose groups. ∇ Ringing *tee-ti-ti-ti-ti-tee; kleep; ki-kew-kew.* **RA4**

10 **Black-winged Stilt** *Himantopus himantopus* (430-1) 25cm. Ad can show variable amount of black on crown/nape/hindneck. ⌘ <1500(3600). Jheels, marshes, pools, lagoons, saltpans. Gregarious. ∇ Nasal *kyeh*; shrill *kep, kep; chek-chek-chek-....* **R•1-2**

11 **Small Pratincole** *Glareola lactea* (444) 17cm. ⌘ <1800. Sandbanks of broad slow-flowing rivers; large jheels, flooded fields, coastal swamps, saltpans. Gregarious. ∇ *tuck-tuck-tuck; tiririt, tiririt, tiririt....* **R•2**

12 **Collared Pratincole** *Glareola pratincola* (442) 23cm. From 13 by long tail reaching to wing-tip, colder-coloured breast and flanks, in flight by white trailing edge to secondaries; long tail-fork; paler mantle and wing-coverts contrasting with darker flight feathers. ⌘ Dry beds and margins of lakes and rivers. Gregarious. Somewhat crepuscular. ∇ Tern-like *kik-kirri; kit-kit-kit...kerrichtik-kerrichtik.* **B*W2**

13 **Oriental Pratincole** *Glareola maldivarum* (443) 24cm. From 12 by short tail reaching half-way along the exposed primaries, warmer breast and flanks, darker upperparts; in flight no white trailing edge to secondaries; shallow tail-fork; mantle and wing-coverts concolorous with flight feathers. ⌘ Dry margins of waterbodies, mudflats, marshes, fields. Gregarious. Most active, feeding on swarms of insects, at dawn and dusk. ∇ Similar to 12. **R•SW(?)3**

14 **Cream-coloured Courser** *Cursorius cursor* (439) 23cm. From 15 by pale buffy underparts, sandy upperparts, grey hind-crown; in flight no white uppertail. **Juv** head pattern indistinct. ⌘ Desert, semi-desert, nearby fields. Loose flocks. ∇ *wheck-wheck-(wheck) cowrr*; liquid *whit-whit; quiddle* like Chestnut-bellied Sandgrouse 42.6. **R•W3**

15 **Indian Courser** *Cursorius coromandelicus* (440) 26cm. From 14 by cinnamon breast, dark chestnut belly and crown, black lores, brown upperparts, white uppertail. **Juv** is duller, more mottled than ad, with indistinctly patterned head. ⌘ Like 14, but also margins of lakes and dry riverbeds. Loose flocks. ∇ Usually silent; low grunt; low clucking. **E•*3**

16 **Jerdon's Courser** *Rhinoptilus bitorquatus* (441). 27cm. Considered to be extinct until its rediscovery in 1986. ⌘ Dry scrub jungle. Nocturnal. Solitary or in pairs. ∇ Not very vocal; plaintive cry; *he-he-he-he-he.* **E*5**

110

PLATE 31

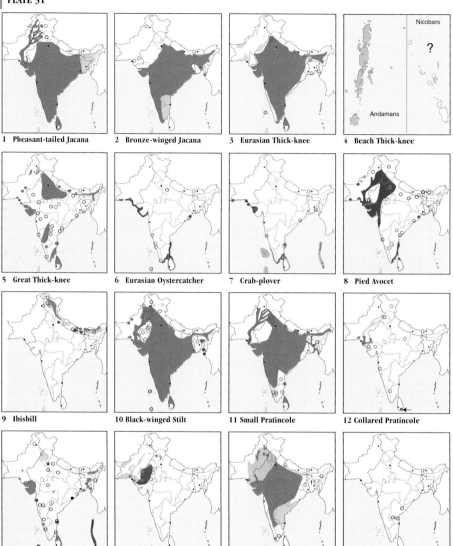

1 Pheasant-tailed Jacana

2 Bronze-winged Jacana

3 Eurasian Thick-knee

4 Beach Thick-knee

5 Great Thick-knee

6 Eurasian Oystercatcher

7 Crab-plover

8 Pied Avocet

9 Ibisbill

10 Black-winged Stilt

11 Small Pratincole

12 Collared Pratincole

13 Oriental Pratincole

14 Cream-coloured Courser

15 Indian Courser

16 Jerdon's Courser

PLATE 32

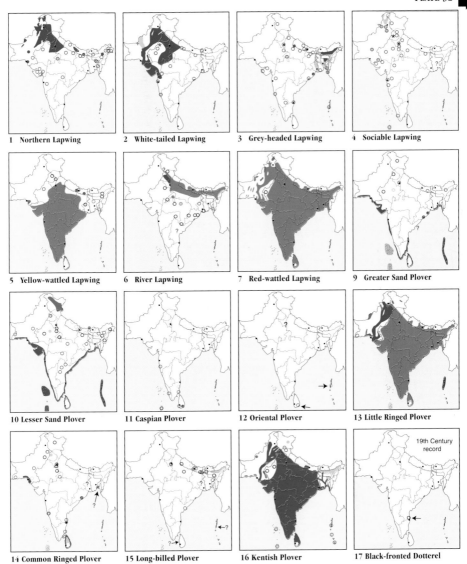

1 Northern Lapwing

2 White-tailed Lapwing

3 Grey-headed Lapwing

4 Sociable Lapwing

5 Yellow-wattled Lapwing

6 River Lapwing

7 Red-wattled Lapwing

9 Greater Sand Plover

10 Lesser Sand Plover

11 Caspian Plover

12 Oriental Plover

13 Little Ringed Plover

14 Common Ringed Plover

15 Long-billed Plover

16 Kentish Plover

17 Black-fronted Dotterel

19th Century record

PLATE 32: WADERS II (LAPWINGS, DOTTERELS AND PLOVERS)

1 **Northern Lapwing** *Vanellus vanellus* (364) 31cm. ✿ Jheels, marshes, grassy areas near water, fields, river banks. ▽ Not very vocal in winter; plaintive *pweeo-*(*wit*). **W3**

2 **White-tailed Lapwing** *Vanellus leucurus* (362) 28cm. From 3 by white tail; pale brown head and neck with all-black bill; absence of black breast-band. ✿ Jheels, marshes and adjacent wet grassland. Gregarious. ▽ Usually silent in winter; *chee-viz*; *pi-wick.* **W3**

3 **Grey-headed Lapwing** *Vanellus cinereus* (365) 37cm. From 2 by grey head; black and yellow bill; black breast-band and black tail-band. ✿ Muddy riverbanks, edges of jheels, wet fields. ▽ Rather quiet in winter; *chee*; *chee-it.* **W3-4**

4 **Sociable Lapwing** *Vanellus gregarius* (363) 33cm. Distinctive head pattern: black cap, pale supercilium meeting both above bill and on nape; in flight from above the black tail-band and white secondaries contrast with black primaries and brown wing-coverts, separating this from all but 3 which lacks black cap. ✿ Short dry grass, wasteland, stubble, ploughed fields. Only sometimes near water. Gregarious. ▽ Usually silent in winter; *kyek*; *krreh-krreh-krreh.* **W5**

5 **Yellow-wattled Lapwing** *Vanellus malabaricus* (370) 27cm. Yellow face-wattles diagnostic. **Juv** (not shown) has grey cap. ✿ Drier areas than 7; open scrub, short grass, wasteland, fallow fields. ▽ Plaintive screaming *tyi-ee*; *twit-twit-twit-twit....* **E•3**

6 **River Lapwing** *Vanellus duvaucelii* (369) 31cm. Distinctive head pattern. ✿ Inland riverbanks. ▽ *did-did-*(*did...*)-*do-wit.* **R•2-3**

7 **Red-wattled Lapwing** *Vanellus indicus* (366-8) 33cm. Red face-wattles diagnostic. Races **(a)** nom **(b)** *atronuchalis*. **Juv** (not shown) has grey throat and ear-coverts. ✿ <2000. Chiefly near fresh water in open country and arable land. ▽ Loud (*did-did...*)-*diid-*(*ye*)-*do-it.* **R•A1**

8 [**Eurasian Dotterel** *Charadrius morinellus.* 21cm. ✿ Semi-desert, arid steppe, fallow land. ▽ *drrreer*; *peet.* **X** (Could occur as a vagrant on passage or in winter.)]

9 **Greater Sand Plover** *Charadrius leschenaultii* (374) 22cm. Races **(a)** nom [**(b)** *crassirostris* is extralimital though could occur.] Often associates with 10, from which it is difficult to separate unless direct comparison is possible. Note the longer bill with a somewhat swollen tip; paler greyish-greenish (vs blackish) legs; longer tibia ('thighs'); slightly larger size. ✿ Chiefly coastal beaches and mudflats. ▽ *trrrt* or *p-r-r-r-l.* **(R)W2-3**

10 **Lesser Sand Plover** *Charadrius mongolus* (384-4a) 19cm. Races **(a)** *atrifrons* **(b)** *stegmanni*. Very similar but generally much more numerous than previous species, which see for differences. ✿ **S** 3900-5500. Steppe and desert near high-altitude lakes. **W** as 9. ▽ *trrr*; *twip*; *tk-tatrr-tatrrwhee.* **B*W1**

11 **Caspian Plover** *Charadrius asiaticus* (376) 19cm. **Br**♂ from 9 & 10 by rich chestnut breast-band bordered below with dark brown; absence of black on head. ♀/**nbr** from 9 & 10 by broad supercilium joined via white on lores to the white of throat; wing-tips extending clearly beyond tail-tip; broader brownish breast marking; dusky yellow legs. See also 12. ✿ Mainly short grassland inland also lake shores, ploughed fields, seashore. ▽ *tyup*; *tup*; rattling *tptptptptp*; *tik*; *kwhitt.* **V**

12 **Oriental Plover** *Charadrius veredus* (377) 24cm. **Nbr**♂/♀ similar to 11 but larger; little or no wing-bar; brownish underwing-coverts (vs mainly white); brighter yellow legs. ✿ As 11. ▽ *chip-chip-chip*; trill; piping *klink.* **V**

13 **Little Ringed Plover** *Charadrius dubius* (379-80) 17cm. From sand plovers by white collar. See 14 & 15. ✿ < c. 1500. Shingle shores and mudbanks of lakes, rivers, pools, coasts etc. ▽ Thin *peeu*; *treewu*; rapid *piu-piu-piu....* **R•W1**

14 **Common Ringed Plover** *Charadrius hiaticula* (378) 19cm. In spite of its name it is scarce in the region. From similar 13 by white wing-bar; lack of yellow eye-ring; orange (vs yellowish) legs; stouter bill more extensively orange at base; different call. ✿ Largely coastal. ▽ Mellow, rising *too-li.* **W4-5**

15 **Long-billed Plover** *Charadrius placidus* (383) 23cm. Very similar to 13 & 14 but larger; bill proportionately longer and slimmer with little or no yellow at base of lower mandible; pale yellowish legs; tail projects beyond wing-tip; eye-stripe of **br ad** is brown (vs black). ✿ Chiefly broad shingly riverbeds, especially at the foot of the central and eastern Himalaya; paddyfields, coastal mudflats. ▽ *peew*; *peewee*; *toodoolou.* **W5**

16 **Kentish Plover** *Charadrius alexandrinus* (381-2) 17cm. From 9-12 by white collar. From 13 & 14 by narrow bars at sides of breast; paler, sandier plumage; blackish legs; from 13 by white wing-bar in flight; from 14 by slender bill. Cinnamon-tinged crown of **br**♂ distinctive. ✿ Mainly seashore but occasionally inland riverbeds. ▽ Soft *prrr*; short *kirrik*; shrill *too-it.* **RW2**

17 **Black-fronted Dotterel** *Elseyornis melanops* (375) 17cm. **Ad** unmistakable. **Juv** the white band from eye to eye across nape is distinctive. ✿ Usually on mud and shingle at water's edge (but not open seashore). ▽ *tip.* **V** (The only record outside Australasia is of a bird collected by Jerdon at Pulicat Lake in South India in 1839/40.)

PLATE 33: WADERS III (GODWITS, DOWITCHERS, CURLEWS, RUFF, GOLDEN AND GREY PLOVERS, TURNSTONE AND PHALAROPES)

1 **Black-tailed Godwit** *Limosa limosa* (389-90) 46cm. Best separated from 2 in flight by white wing-bar, the single broad black tail-bar and legs trailing well behind tail; **nbr** note the fairly uniform upperparts and relatively straight bill. Races (**a**) *melanuroides* (**b**) nom. ✿ Mainly inland jheels, marshes, lake shallows and muddy shores. Gregarious. ▽ Usually silent in winter; *wit-it-it*; *wheew*. **W2**

2 **Bar-tailed Godwit** *Limosa lapponica* (391-1a) 39cm. Best separated from 1 in flight by absence of white wing-bar, barred tail and legs not projecting much beyond tail; **nbr** note the streaked upperparts and upcurved bill. Races (**a**) nom (**b**) *baueri*. ✿ Mainly coastal creeks, mudflats, saltpans. ✿ Rather silent; *kak-kak*; low *kirruk*. **W3**

3 **Asian Dowitcher** *Limnodromus semipalmatus* (403) 34cm. Rather similar to 1 & 2 but note the straight, all-black bill thick throughout (nearly always held pointing downwards), shorter neck, smaller, more compact size; **nbr** is scalier than 1; in flight note the whitish rump and uppertail-coverts diffusely barred. ✿ Coastal mudflats; brackish water shallows and shores. Distinctive stitching feeding action. Often associates with godwits. ▽ Usually silent in winter; *chaow*. **W5**

4 **Ruff** *Philomachus pugnax* (426) ♂31cm ♀25cm. Leg colour is very variable from orange or pink through to green. Orange-legged birds, in particular, can be confused with redshanks (plate 34) but note different jizz, short bill, scalloped upperparts. Some ♂♂ begin acquiring the fluffy neck-ruff of breeding plumage (not illustrated) in late winter. ♂ is markedly larger than ♀. ✿ Mudflats, flooded fields, marshes. Gregarious. ▽ Not very vocal; *chugh-chugh*; *tu-whit*. **WP2**

5 **Long-billed Dowitcher** *Limnodromus scolopaceus*. 29cm. Similar to 2 & 3 but smaller; greenish (vs black) legs; base of bill usually greenish; clear white lower back; entire underwing lightly barred (white in 3). ✿ Jheels, marshes, coastal mudflats. ▽ Thin *keek...*(*keek*)....**V**

6 **Pacific Golden Plover** *Pluvialis fulva* (373) 24cm. From 8 by yellow spangled plumage; in flight note the pale axillaries and rump concolorous with back. See also 7 which is very similar but only a winter vagrant. ✿ Jheels, mudflats, lagoons, short grassland, wet fields. Gregarious. ▽ *tlu-ip*; *teeh*; *tu-ee*; *tee-tew*. **W2**

7 **European Golden Plover** *Pluvialis apricaria* (372) 27cm. From closely similar 6 by somewhat larger, bulkier size, white (vs grey) underwing-coverts and axillaries, short wings only reaching tail-tip (vs well beyond tail tip), tertials falling well short of tail-tip (vs equal with tail-tip), relatively shorter bill and legs; **nbr** usually has less distinct supercilium, more obviously spotted breast, less clearly patterned upperparts. ✿ Similar to 6. ▽ *tloo-ee*; *teeu*. **V(W)**

8 **Grey Plover** *Pluvialis squatarola* (371) 31cm. Lacks yellow plumage tones of 6 & 7; in flight black axillaries diagnostic but note also white rump and more white in wing. ✿ Mainly coastal. Gregarious. ▽ *pweeoo'ee*. **W2**

9 **Ruddy Turnstone** *Arenaria interpres* (402) 22cm. ✿ Predominantly coastal rocky (and sandy) shores. Often forages by turning over stones in search of invertebrates. Usually in pairs or small groups. ▽ Metallic twitter. **W3**

10 **Eastern Curlew** *Numenius madagascariensis* 63cm. Most reliably told from 11 in flight by all-dark (vs mainly white) back and rump, dark (vs mainly whitish) underwing and entire underparts usually suffused with buffy-brown (vs whitish belly); note also (usually) buffier-brown upperparts and larger size. ✿ Chiefly coastal mudflats and beaches. Usually solitary or in loose parties. ▽ *ghrreee*. **V**

11 **Eurasian Curlew** *Numenius arquata* (387-8) 58cm. For differences see 10, 12 & 13. ✿ Largely coastal. Singly or in small loose parties when not at roost. ▽ *courléee*; *couhouwhiw*. **W2**

12 [**Slender-billed Curlew** *Numenius tenuirostris* 39cm. From 11 by shorter thinner bill, darker cap, slight supercilium, dark loral stripe, whiter breast with heart-shaped spotting; in flight by pale tail, dark outer primaries and primary coverts contrasting with inner wing. From 13 by whiter breast with heart spotting, less distinct head pattern (no crown-stripe), paler tail, pure white (vs partly or wholly barred) underwing-coverts. ✿ Jheels, mudflats, short grassland. May consort with other curlews. ▽ *curlee* like 11 but higher and shorter. **X** (Unconfirmed sight record from Sri Lanka.)]

13 **Whimbrel** *Numenius phaeopus* (385-6) 43cm. From 11 by supercilium and crown stripe, smaller size, short bill 1$\frac{1}{2}$ times (vs 2-3 times) head-length and voice. ✿ Similar to 11, though rather more sociable. ▽ Rapid (*kroo-kroo*)-*whi-whi-whi-whi-whi-whi-whic-whic*.... **W2-3**

14 **Red-necked Phalarope** *Phalaropus lobatus* (428) 19cm. For differences in **nbr** plumage see 15. ✿ Shallow coastal waters and mudflats, saltpans, shrimp pools, jheels. Shy at sea but tame inland. Usually in flocks. Often swims and spins, picking food items from the surface of the water. ▽ Rather silent; *twick* in flight. **W2-3**

15 **Red Phalarope** *Phalaropus fulicaria* (427) 20cm. **Nbr** from similar 14 by stout (vs thin, needle-like) bill; plain pale grey upperparts (vs pale-edged feathers); black patch straight back behind eye (vs one curving down behind ear-coverts). ✿ Largely marine in non-breeding season. ▽ High *wit* in flight. **V** Single record from 1846.

PLATE 33

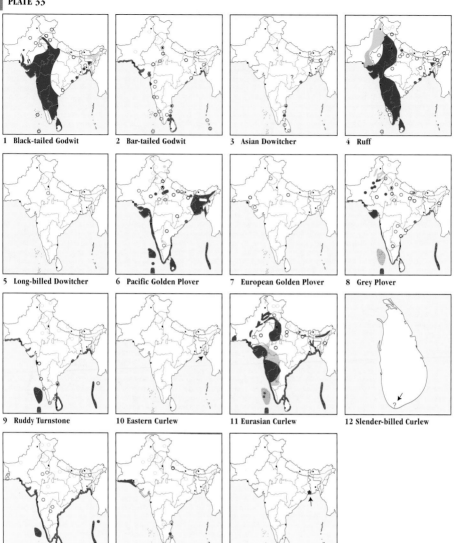

1 Black-tailed Godwit

2 Bar-tailed Godwit

3 Asian Dowitcher

4 Ruff

5 Long-billed Dowitcher

6 Pacific Golden Plover

7 European Golden Plover

8 Grey Plover

9 Ruddy Turnstone

10 Eastern Curlew

11 Eurasian Curlew

12 Slender-billed Curlew

13 Whimbrel

14 Red-necked Phalarope

15 Red Phalarope

PLATE 34

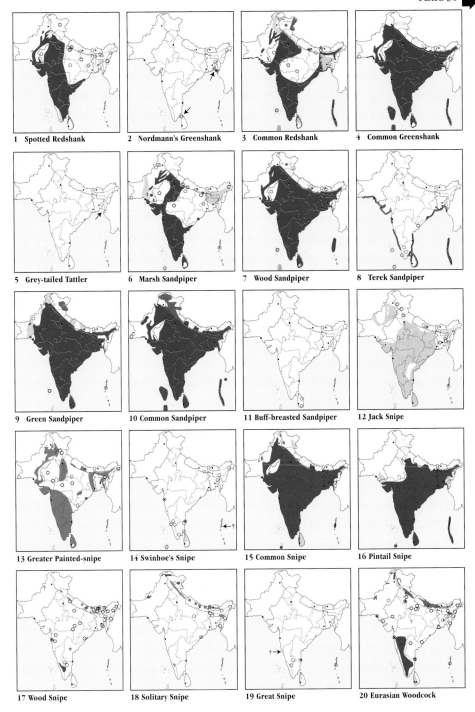

1 Spotted Redshank

2 Nordmann's Greenshank

3 Common Redshank

4 Common Greenshank

5 Grey-tailed Tattler

6 Marsh Sandpiper

7 Wood Sandpiper

8 Terek Sandpiper

9 Green Sandpiper

10 Common Sandpiper

11 Buff-breasted Sandpiper

12 Jack Snipe

13 Greater Painted-snipe

14 Swinhoe's Snipe

15 Common Snipe

16 Pintail Snipe

17 Wood Snipe

18 Solitary Snipe

19 Great Snipe

20 Eurasian Woodcock

119

PLATE 34: WADERS IV (SHANKS, TATTLER, SNIPES, PAINTED-SNIPE AND WOODCOCK)

1 **Spotted Redshank** *Tringa erythropus* (392) 33cm. **Nbr** from 3 by longer bill, red only at base of lower mandible, prominent fore-supercilium, paler grey (vs greyish-brown) upperparts; in flight lacks white in wings; legs project well beyond tail (vs toes only). ✻ Jheels, marshes, tanks, mudflats. ▽ *tew-it*; *kree-kree....* **W3**

2 **Nordmann's Greenshank** *Tringa guttifer* (399) 33cm. Like 4 but shorter yellower legs; short tibia; shorter, more obviously two-toned bill, greenish-yellow (vs greenish/bluish grey) basally; toe-webbing; tail looks all-pale; **nbr** more uniform upperparts (vs more spotted and scalloped); in flight only toe-tips project (vs entire toes); unbarred white (vs barred) underwing and axillaries; **br** large spots on breast and flanks. ✻ Mudflats, beach areas, sandbanks, short grass near water. ▽ Usually a single nasal *kwaag* (lower than 4), often in flight; *kwaeg*; *kwig kwig kwig....* **W5**

3 **Common Redshank** *Tringa totanus* (393-4) 28cm. See 1 for differences. ✻ Wetlands. ▽ *tyoo-*(*oo*); *tyew-yew-yew*; *tooleeu...tooleeu...*; *kip*; *kewp*. **B*W1**

4 **Common Greenshank** *Tringa nebularia* (396) 36cm. See 2. ✻ Wetlands. ▽ Ringing *tew tew tew* (*tew*). **W1-2**

5 **Grey-tailed Tattler** *Heteroscelus brevipes* 25cm. Note short yellow legs; straight bill approximately equal to head length; white supercilium meeting across bill; uniform grey upperparts. ✻ Coastal mudflats; seashores. ▽ *tuidee*. **V**

6 **Marsh Sandpiper** *Tringa stagnatilis* (395) 25cm. Like small light 4 with thin bill; **nbr** by white face; in flight part of tarsus (vs toes only) projects. ✻ Jheels, shallow lakes; less commonly saline wetlands. ▽ *che-weep*; *che-wee*; *kyew*. **W2**

7 **Wood Sandpiper** *Tringa glareola* (398) 21cm. **Nbr** from nbr 9 by heavier pale spotting on paler brown upperparts; supercilium extending well behind eye; in flight legs project well beyond tail. ✻ Jheels, paddyfields, lake margins, mudflats. Usually more open habitats than 9. ▽ *chiff-iff-*(*iff*). **B*W1**

8 **Terek Sandpiper** *Xenus cinereus* (400) 24cm. Upturned bill; orange-yellow legs. ✻ Coastal. ▽ *tooit-twit-twit*. **W2-3**

9 **Green Sandpiper** *Tringa ochropus* (397) 24cm. See 7; in flight more black and white. ✻ Marshes, creeks, ditches etc. Usually near cover. ▽ When flushed a ringing *ti-tui*; *twee-twee-twee*. **B*W1**

10 **Common Sandpiper** *Actitis hypoleucos* (401) 21cm. White wedge between brown breast and shoulder; white wing-bar in flicking flight low over water. ✻ Margins of lakes, rivers, jheels, etc. ▽ Piping *tee-tee-tee*. **B*W1**

11 **Buff-breasted Sandpiper** *Tryngites subruficollis* (425a) 19cm. **Nbr** streaked crown contrasts with buffy cheeks; small head; short bill; below buffy fairly uniform in flight. ✻ Short grass, dry mud flats. ▽ Low *pr-r-reet* in flight. **V**

12 **Jack Snipe** *Lymnocryptes minimus* (410) 21cm. Smaller and shorter-billed than *Gallinagos*, with no pale central crown stripe; flanks streaked. ✻ Swampy vegetated margins. Short flush. ▽ Usually silent in winter; *kurrr*. **W4**

13 **Greater Painted-snipe** *Rostratula benghalensis* (429) 25cm. Unmistakable. ✻ <1800. Well-vegetated jheels, marshes, paddyfields; often shy and crepuscular. ▽ Normally silent when flushed; hollow *pwoo pwoo....* **R3**

14 **Swinhoe's Snipe** *Gallinago megala* (407) 28cm. Very like 16 with same wing pattern but larger, bulkier, longer-billed and heavier in flight with toes projecting less; at rest usually obvious (vs little or no) primary projection; tail projects well beyond wing-tip (vs little); stout legs. ✻ Like 16. ▽ Sometimes calls when flushed like 16 but thinner. **W5**

15 **Common Snipe** *Gallinago gallinago* (409) 26cm. Commonest wintering snipe in the W and NW. 16 (which see) is commoner in S; both are common in E. ✻ Marshes, paddyfields. ▽ When flushed urgent rasping *pench*. **R*W1**

16 **Pintail Snipe** *Gallinago stenura* (406) 26cm. Most readily separated from 15 in flight by no white trailing edge to secondaries; all-dark underwing (vs panelled white); pale panel on upperwing-coverts; more rounded wings. On ground note buffy scalloping on scapulars (vs whitish diagonal stripes on outerwebs only); barred (vs spotted) median wing-coverts; slightly shorter bill; usually narrower loral stripe. Diagnostic pin-shaped outer tail feathers not normally visible. ✻ Like 15 but often in drier situations. ▽ When flushed a deeper, less rasping *squak* than 15. **W1**

17 **Wood Snipe** *Gallinago nemoricola* (405) 30cm. Dark upperparts; entirely barred underparts; rounded wings; from 20 by striped head and upperparts. Slow flight; no white edge to secondaries. ✻ S 1300-4300. W lower. Open areas with bushes; damp areas in forest; thick grass and scrub. ▽ When flushed, deep *tok-tok*; nasal *check-check-check-....* **RAM5**

18 **Solitary Snipe** *Gallinago solitaria* (404) 30cm. Only snipe with gingery breast; note also gingery upperparts, whitish central crown-stripe, scapular and mantle fringes, slow heavy flight. ✻ S 2800-4600. W <4600. Marshes, streams. ▽ Sometimes calls when flushed like 15, but deeper and fainter. **RAM4**

19 **Great Snipe** *Gallinago media* (408) 28cm. Note 2-3 white wing-bars formed by tips to coverts; bold barring on breast and flanks to vent (but not usually on centre of belly as in 17); largely white outer tail when spread (difficult to see except on landing). Slow heavy flight, less jerky than 15 & 16. ✻ Like 16. ▽ Sometimes when flushed a deep frog-like *urr*. **V**

20 **Eurasian Woodcock** *Scolopax rusticola* (411) 36cm. Head barring unique among Indian waders. Habitat indicative. ✻ Damp areas in forest. ▽ Usually silent; in display-flight a croaking *quorr-*(*quorr*)*-quorro-*(*ptick*). **MAW3-4**

PLATE 35: WADERS V (SANDPIPERS, SANDERLING, DUNLIN, KNOTS AND STINTS)

1 Broad-billed Sandpiper *Limicola falcinellus* (424-5) 17cm. 'Split supercilium' diagnostic. **Nbr** from 2 & 4 also by more obviously kinked bill and scalier upperparts. ✿ Chiefly coastal mudflats, creeks, lagoons; inland mainly on passage. Gregarious, often with stints. Feeding action slower than stints. ▽ Buzzing trill *chrrreet* in flight; *preew*. **W3**

2 Sanderling *Calidris alba* (414) 19cm. **Nbr** note very pale grey upperparts (palest calidrid); pure white underparts; straight black bill (<head-length); black legs without hind toe; often shows blackish shoulder, more obvious as dark carpal patch in flight. ✿ Seashore – characteristic habit of running rapidly back and forth with water-line, picking at items from the surf; also occurs on coastal mudflats. ▽ Liquid *plit; piyu; tuk.* **W3**

3 Dunlin *Calidris alpina* (420-1) 19.5cm. Note slightly decurved bill ≥ head-length. From 1 by larger size; lack of split supercilium; black (vs dull greenish-grey) legs; more uniform upperparts on **nbr**. See also 4. **Br** black belly-patch diagnostic. ✿ Chiefly coastal mudflats but also muddy inland wetlands and seashore. In flocks. ▽ *treep; tee.* **W3**

4 Curlew Sandpiper *Calidris ferruginea* (422) 21cm. **Nbr** from 1 & 3 by longer, more evenly decurved bill; longer legs; longer neck; in flight note pure white rump. ✿ Chiefly muddy coastal habitats; infrequent inland. Gregarious, often with other waders. Frequently feeds in deeper water than other calidrids. ▽ Soft *chirrup.* **W2**

5 Sharp-tailed Sandpiper *Calidris acuminata* (419) 19cm. From most calidrids by rufous cap but see 14. The diagnostic pointed tail feathers, which give the bird its name, are of little help in the field. ✿ Mudflats, lagoons, short grassland, dry margins of lakes. Gregarious, sometimes with other waders. ▽ In flight *wheep; pleep; trrt;* or a combination of all 3. **V**

6 Red Knot *Calidris canutus* (412) 24cm. **Nbr** like a giant stint; straight black bill; grey upperparts with slight scaling; lightly spotted breast and flanks. Most similar to 7 which see for differences. ✿ Coastal shores and mudflats. Normally highly gregarious. ▽ Usually silent; low *nwet nwet* or *knutt-knutt* or *knuup-knuup; puwee-wee.* **W4-5**

7 Great Knot *Calidris tenuirostris* (413) 27cm. Largest calidrid. **Nbr** from 6 by longer bill; more heavily spotted breast, contrasting more with white of belly; streakier upperparts, especially on crown and hind-neck; in flight by white rump with little spotting (vs barred with grey). ✿ Coastal mudflats, lagoons. Gregarious, often roosting with other waders. ▽ Low *nyut nyut* similar to 6; *chucker-chucker-chucker.* **W4**

8 Spoon-billed Sandpiper *Calidris pygmaeus* (423) 15cm. Bill-shape diagnostic but at a distance beware of other small, short-billed waders with mud stuck to bill-tip. ✿ Chiefly muddy coastal habitats. May associate with stints when its characteristic feeding action of sweeping bill from side-to-side could help pick it out; stints have a 'stitching' action like sewing-machine. ▽ soft rolling *preep;* shrill *wheet.* **W5**

9 [White-rumped Sandpiper *Calidris fuscicollis* 17cm. **Nbr** like large 10 or 11, or small 3 but with entirely white rump, most obvious in flight. Call characteristic. ✿ A vagrant could occur in any wetland. Gregarious. ▽ High mouse-like *jeeet.* **V?** (A possible sight record from Sri Lanka needs confirmation.)]

10 Red-necked Stint *Calidris ruficollis* (415) 14.5cm. From 12 & 13 by black legs. Very similar to 11 but slightly larger, shorter legs, longer wings and slightly shorter, blunter bill; **nbr** not always distinguishable but has greyer, less scaly upperparts with greyer breast-band usually confined to large patches at the sides. ✿ Chiefly coastal mudflats. Gregarious. ▽ *kreet; chreek; krep; klyt.* **W4**

11 Little Stint *Calidris minuta* (416) 13cm. From 12 & 13 by black legs. Very similar to 10 but slightly smaller, slightly longer legs, shorter wings, finer-tipped bill; **nbr** not always separable but has slightly browner, scalier upperparts with browner breast-band usually meeting in middle. ✿ More coastal than 12; mudflats, lagoons, jheels, muddy riverbanks, etc. ▽ Low *tirrr* in flight; *wit-wit-wit....* **W1**

12 Temminck's Stint *Calidris temminckii* (417) 14cm. From all other stints by white sides to tail; from 10 & 11 by yellow legs. Never shows distinct pale supercilium or 'V's on the back. **Nbr** by uniform (vs scaly) upperparts; unstreaked brownish wash on breast usually meets in the centre. ✿ Jheels, marshes, mudbanks, lagoons; more frequently inland than 11. ▽ High, thin *tirirririr* or *tirrr* in flight. **W1**

13 Long-toed Stint *Calidris subminuta* (418) 14cm. Relatively longer-legged and longer-necked, often with more upright stance than other stints. From 10 & 11 by yellow legs. **Nbr** from 12 by scalier upperparts; grey sides to tail; streaked sides of breast. The long toes are not normally a helpful feature in the field. ✿ Mainly freshwater habitats but also coastal mudflats; more partial to vegetated situations than other stints. ▽ *prrt; chrrup; chulip; tik-tik-tik.* **W4**

14 [Pectoral Sandpiper *Calidris melanotos* 21cm. From similar 5 by dark-streaked (vs less heavily streaked) breast sharply demarcated from (vs fading into) white belly; slightly longer legs usually yellowish, though sometimes greenish as is most often the case with 5. ✿ Variety of wetland habitats, usually feeding away from water's edge. ▽ Harsh *churk* or *trrit* in flight. **V?** (A recent sight record from NW India unpublished at time of writing.)]

122

PLATE 35

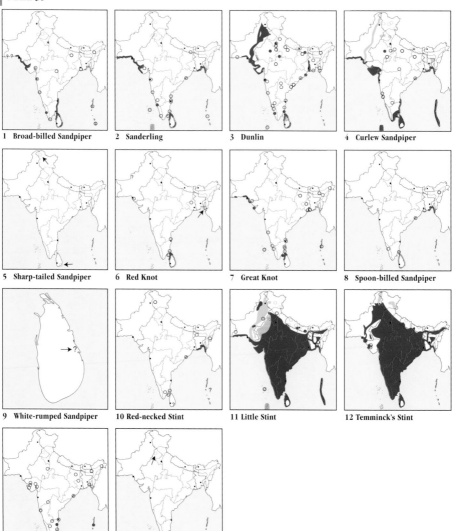

1 Broad-billed Sandpiper

2 Sanderling

3 Dunlin

4 Curlew Sandpiper

5 Sharp-tailed Sandpiper

6 Red Knot

7 Great Knot

8 Spoon-billed Sandpiper

9 White-rumped Sandpiper

10 Red-necked Stint

11 Little Stint

12 Temminck's Stint

13 Long-toed Stint

14 Pectoral Sandpiper

PLATE 36

2   Parasitic Jaeger   3   Pomarine Jaeger   4   Brown Skua   5   South Polar Skua

PLATE 36: JAEGERS AND SKUAS

1 **[Long-tailed Jaeger** *Stercorarius longicaudus* 41cm (without tail-streamers). Smallest, slimmest, most buoyant and tern-like jaeger. **Ad** is palest of the jaegers; not known to have a dark morph; very long wispy tail-streamers diagnostic if present, otherwise the uniformly dark underwing without pale flash at base of primaries is a useful identification feature; **br** also distinguished by clean white breast (without pectoral band) fading into grey belly; dark flight feathers contrast strongly with the upperwing-coverts. **Juv** is greyer, lacking the warm buffy/rusty tones of juv 2 & 3; usually shows a short tail spike rounded at the tip. **X** (A possible sight record near Lakshadweep.)]

2 **Parasitic Jaeger** *Stercorarius parasiticus* (448) 45cm (without tail-projection). Note pointed central tail feathers present in all except juvenile birds and during tail moult, but beware of 1 with half-grown tail-projection; **ad** most show a pale patch just above the bill, a feature not normally present in 1 & 3; **pale morph br** similar to pale 3 but cap is usually less well demarcated; breast-band (if present) and vent usually paler; all-dark (vs two-toned) bill; in flight the pale body cleanly demarcated from dark underwings is a clue but this is usually obscured in the non-breeding season; **dark morph br** usually has a slightly darker cap *contra* dark 3. **Juv** usually less heavily barred than juv 3; rusty nuchal band present on most birds is diagnostic. **W (Non-breeding S) 4-5**

3 **Pomarine Jaeger** *Stercorarius pomarinus* (447) 56cm (without tail-projection). **Ad** the broad twisted spatulate appearance of the central tail-projection is diagnostic if present; has the darkest upperparts of all jaegers. **Pale morph** is darker (blackish-brown) than pale 1 & 2 on upperparts, cap, vent and breast-band (in ad ♂ often reduced to dark wedges at sides of breast); ♀ often shows more broken barring on the flanks and around neck than ♂ (as in perched bird illustrated). **Imm** most show at least an indication of a tail spatula in broad rounded central tail feathers but beware of slight similar tail-projection in 5. **WP (Non-breeding S) 4**

4 **Brown Skua** *Catharacta antarctica* (445-6) 58cm. Basic colour of plumage varies from light to dark brown but there is no distinctly pale morph. Most birds separated from 5 by warmer-coloured plumage; stronger, longer bill and legs; hind-neck not contrastingly paler. Some birds show irregular whitish spotting on mantle, wings and flanks never seen in 5. In flight, unlike pale and intermediate 5, shows little or no contrast between body and underwing; the prominence of the white wing-flashes is enough to separate from adult 1-3. **Juv** (not illustrated) generally darker, more uniform than ad with some chestnut in the plumage and reduced white wing-flash. Races sometimes split into two species as: **(a)** Brown Skua *C. lonnbergi* and **(b)** Antarctic Skua *C. antarctica*. **(Non-breeding S) 4-5**

5 **South Polar Skua** *Catharacta maccormicki* (446a) 53cm. Occurs in pale and dark morphs, as well as a variety of intermediate shades. Most birds can be separated from 4 by the absence of warm tones in the plumage and presence of a pale nuchal collar, though this may be rather indistinct or absent in dark individuals, which are comparatively scarce anyway; bill and legs are shorter, not as strong as 4's; at close range an obvious pale patch, present in most birds, just above the base of bill is indicative (but may be present to a lesser extent in worn 4). **Pale morph** separated from 1-4 by entirely pale head, vent and undertail-coverts. **Dark morph** adults are distinguished from dark 1-3 by large white underwing-flash (often reduced in young birds). **V (Non-breeding S)**

126

PLATE 37: GULLS I

1 **Slender-billed Gull** *Larus genei* (456) 42cm. In all plumages separated from 3 & 4 by long slender bill; white head; long slim neck; long sloping forehead. **Ad** in fresh plumage has a pinkish tinge below. **Nbr** shows a faint grey spot on the ear-coverts as in 1st W but never as dark as on 2, 3 & 4. In flight wing pattern similar to 3 but paler; note lack of dark head markings; longer, broader wings; slower wingbeats. ⌘ Largely coastal: shallow seas, brackish lakes, lagoons, deltas. **RWB*2**

2 **Little Gull** *Larus minutus* (457) 27cm. **Ad** blackish underwing with white trailing edge diagnostic; note also small size and lack of black markings on upperwing; **br** also by pure black hood (vs chocolate-brown in 3 & 4) extending down nape; dark eye; may show a pinkish tinge to breast. **1stW** by small size and dark inverted 'W' across upperparts. ⌘ Normally maritime in winter, when most likely to occur in the region, though an accidental could turn up at any large waterbody. **V(W)**

3 **Black-headed Gull** *Larus ridibundus* (455) 38cm. Rather similar to 4 and most easily separated in flight by the primary pattern: white wedge extending almost to wing-tip. When seen perched together, the smaller size, weaker bill and dark iris (whitish in 4) may be apparent. See also 2 & 7. **Nbr/imm** of both 3 & 4 typically show a dark spot behind the eye and often a faint dark band across the top of the head. ⌘ Coasts, rivers, jheels and lakes. **W2**

4 **Brown-headed Gull** *Larus brunnicephalus* (454) 42cm. Like 3 but larger; stronger bill; white iris; **ad** has dark primaries with two white mirrors; **juv/1stW** has entirely dark primaries. See also 2 & 7. ⌘ Coasts, rivers and lakes. ∇ *kraa; kurrr*. **WB*2**

5 **Sooty Gull** *Larus hemprichii* (449) 45cm. The sooty-brown coloration extending to breast, and long tricoloured bill (bicoloured in young birds), are distinctive, but see also 6. ⌘ Strictly coastal. **SW3**

6 **White-eyed Gull** *Larus leucophthalmus* 39cm. Could be mistaken for 5 but note conspicuous white eye-ring; long, slim all-dark bill; greyer upperparts; slimmer wings; black (vs sooty-brown) hood in breeding plumage. **Juv** best separated from juv 5 by all-dark (vs bicoloured) bill. ⌘ Coastal. **V** (Vagrant, possibly annual, in the Maldives. Could stray to anywhere on the Arabian Sea coast.)

7 **Pallas's Gull** *Larus ichthyaetus* (453) 69cm. Much larger and stronger-billed than other hooded gulls. **Ad** tricoloured bill distinguishes from all but 5 which is smaller and generally sooty-brown rather than black, grey and white. **Nbr ad** often shows extensive traces of black hood; note also white-tipped primaries subterminally black. **Juv/1stW** distinguished from other young large gulls (38.2-38.5) by black tail-band cleanly demarcated from unmarked white uppertail and rump. At all ages shows white eye-crescents. ⌘ Coasts, rivers and lakes. Usually seen singly. **W3**

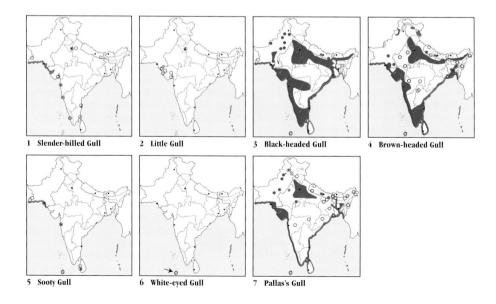

| 1 Slender-billed Gull | 2 Little Gull | 3 Black-headed Gull | 4 Brown-headed Gull |

| 5 Sooty Gull | 6 White-eyed Gull | 7 Pallas's Gull |

128

PLATE 38: GULLS II

1 Mew Gull *Larus canus* 50cm. Similar to 2 & 3 but much smaller. **Ad** characteristic slim, unmarked, greenish-yellow bill (develops a narrow blackish subterminal band in non-breeding season); greenish-yellow legs; faster wingbeats. **V**

2 Yellow-legged Gull *Larus cachinnans* (451) 60cm. Similar to 4 but upperparts paler grey. **W2**

Races

(a) *mongolicus* – mantle colour like 2b & c, with a slight bluish tinge; legs pink, orange or yellow; head streaking absent or confined to a little on hind-neck/nape and gone by mid-winter; usually a single large 'mirror' on outer primary.

(b) *cachinnans* – usually palest grey upperparts; flat forehead; bill yellow with red gonydeal spot and sometimes a subterminal black mark; eye usually further forward on head than 2c; head streaking usually confined to hind-neck/nape and gone by January; long legs mostly duller yellow than on 2c; in flight shows less black on primaries than 2c with long pale tongues on the innerwebs showing as streaks cutting into the black; usually two 'mirrors'.

(c) *barabensis* – upperpart colour averages slightly darker than 2a and a slightly paler cleaner grey than 4a, though some may be nearly as dark; rounded head with steep forehead; relatively fine bill is often rich yellow, frequently with a sub-terminal dark band and/or more vivid and extensive red spot than in other forms; eye more centrally placed on head than in 2b; head streaking usually confined to hind-neck/nape and gone by February; relatively smaller, slimmer body; shortish legs usually brighter yellow than in other similar races/species; in flight note more extensive black on primaries than 2b without pale areas on innerwebs; 1-2 'mirrors'.

3 [Vega Gull *Larus vegae* 63cm. Mantle colour intermediate between 2 & 4, often with hint of blue; similar build to 4a; head streaking usually light but may be heavier and extend onto sides of neck and upper breast – lasts into March; legs usually pink; 1-2 'mirrors'. **X** (Although there are no definite records, this east Siberian form could occur in the region.)]

4 Heuglin's Gull *Larus heuglini* (450) 60cm. Sometimes considered conspecific with *L. fuscus* (5), which see. Similar to 2 but upperparts dark grey. **W2**

Races

(a) *taimyrensis* – slightly darker upperparts than most 2, though some may be nearly as pale; upperparts often tinged brownish; relatively long, slim build; strong bill; sloping forehead; head not as long as 2b nor as round as 2c; head and hind-neck often with bold streaking lasting into February/March (usually gone by January/February in 2); legs usually yellow, occasionally pinkish; amount of black on tenth primary variable though often approaching that of 4b; 1-2 'mirrors'.

(b) *heuglini* – darkest grey mantle, usually darker than *taimyrensis* though there is some overlap; some look almost black but the contrast with the black primaries on stretched wing is marked (*contra* 5); build as 4a though averages slightly larger; head streaking as 4a; legs usually yellow, sometimes pinkish; black on the primaries more extensive than on other forms; outer primary normally 80-90% black without pale wedge below; 1-2 mirrors.

5 [Lesser Black-backed Gull *Larus fuscus* (452) 56cm. Subcontinental records of very dark-mantled herring-type gulls are probably all attributable to 4 *L. heuglini* rather than *L. fuscus*, for which the nearest known wintering ranges are in the Middle East and West Africa. Separated by the black upperparts showing no appreciable contrast (or very little) between the primaries and the rest of the upperwing, except for the white trailing edge to the secondaries, white edge to the forewing and the single white 'mirror' (occasionally two) on the outer primary (primaries). **X]**

6 [Armenian Gull *Larus armenicus* (not illustrated) 56cm. Almost indistinguishable in the field from 2c: **ad** usually shows bolder black subterminal band on the blunter bill (but beware subadults of other species with similar dark bill markings); outer primary is 80-90% black (vs grey on 30-50% of innerweb of 2c). **X** (Could possibly occur.)]

7 [Great Black-backed Gull *Larus marinus* (452a – not illustrated) 70cm. Very large size. Similar to 5 but larger; pink legs; more massive bill and head; large white tips to primaries merging with white 'mirror' on outermost, together with the presence of a 2nd largish 'mirror' (usually absent or small on 5) create the effect of an extensive white tip to the wings; white head with little or no streaking in winter; slow laboured flight; more rounded wings. **X** (Single record from Rajasthan now considered doubtful, though could conceivably occur as a winter vagrant.)]

1 Mew Gull

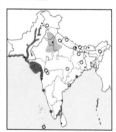

2 Yellow-legged Gull

4 Heuglin's Gull

130

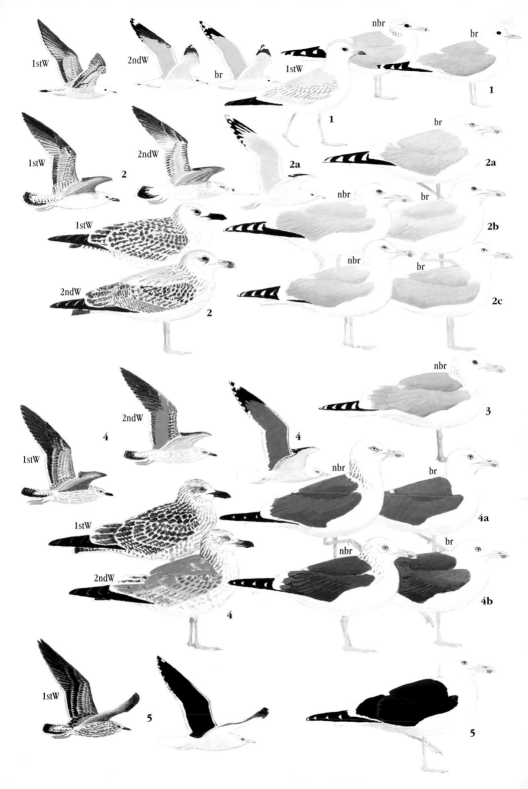

PLATE 39: TERNS I

1 **Great Crested Tern** *Sterna bergii* (478) 47cm. Note large size; white forehead; strong bill cold yellow (**br**) to greenish-yellow (**nbr**); ragged nuchal crest usually obvious on perched birds. See also 2. ⌘ Maritime and coastal. ▽ Coarse *cherrak... (cherrak).... * **R2**

2 **Lesser Crested Tern** *Sterna bengalensis* (479) 43cm. Similar to 1 but smaller, more lightly built; slimmer orange bill; paler grey upperparts; shorter legs; **br** has black (vs white) forehead, though soon becomes white in **nbr** birds. Races (**a**) *torresii* – pure forms not normally found in the region but some birds are intermediate between this and (**b**) nom. ⌘ Maritime and coastal. ▽ *kreek-kreek* higher than 1 but slightly deeper, less harsh than 3. **RW2**

3 **Sandwich Tern** *Sterna sandvicensis* (480) 43cm. At reasonably close range the diagnostic yellow tip to the relatively long, slender, straight black bill can be seen. Note the contrasting white rump and tail (vs grey and only slightly paler than back in 1 & 2). Short nuchal crest often obvious but may be depressed as in illustration of perched br. ⌘ Maritime and coastal. ▽ *kree´it; kirriw-kirriw*. **RW2**

4 **River Tern** *Sterna aurantia* (463) 42cm. Commonest *Sterna* on inland waters. From 1-3 (which are unlikely away from the coast) by lack of crest; deeply forked tail; red legs. Note also rich golden or orange-yellow bill. **Nbr** could be confused with nbr Black-bellied Tern (40.6), which see. ⌘ Mainly larger rivers, lakes and estuaries. ▽ Short high mellow *kiuk-kiuk; kierr-wick, kyerrwick, kierrwick*. **R2-3**

5 **Gull-billed Tern** *Gelochelidon nilotica* (460-1) 38cm. Told with practice by the short thick all-black bill. **Br** otherwise similar to 3 but without nuchal crest; grey (vs white) rump and tail only slightly paler than back; on underwing the outer primaries are largely pale with a dark trailing edge. **Nbr** bill shape and dark smudge through eye distinctive. ⌘ Coastal and inland waterbodies. Only occasionally plunge-dives, preferring to snatch prey from the surface of the water or ground. ▽ Generally silent; low *cher-wek-(wek)*. **B*W2**

6 **Caspian Tern** *Sterna caspia* (462) 51cm. The largest tern. The very large size (almost as big as Heuglin's Gull, 38.4) and massive red bill are normally enough to identify this tern. Note also the head pattern; flattened crown; short nuchal crest; in flight the dark outer primaries (from below); short forked tail; slow wingbeats. ⌘ Coasts, large lakes and rivers. ▽ Deeper than other terns: loud harsh *kraa-ah* reminiscent of a heron; *kuwow-kuwow*. **B*R*W2**

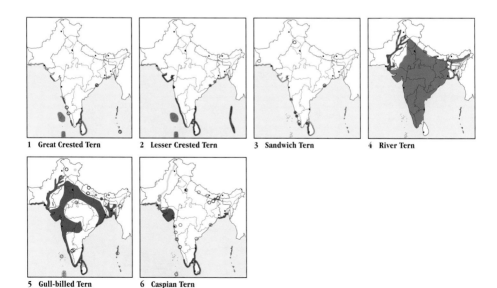

1 Great Crested Tern   2 Lesser Crested Tern   3 Sandwich Tern   4 River Tern

5 Gull-billed Tern   6 Caspian Tern

PLATE 40: TERNS II

1 Common Tern *Sterna hirundo* (464-5) 36cm. Compare the rather similar 2-4. **Br** grey mantle and upperwings; white rump; deeply forked white tail; elongated outer tail feathers not extending beyond wing-tip; outerweb of outermost tail feathers dusky; black cap extending to bill and lower rim of eye; bill blackish or coral-red tipped with black; coral-red legs; white underparts tinged with grey. **Nbr** bill and legs become blackish; forehead white; underparts lose the greyish tinge; shoulder dusky. **Juv** similar to nbr but upperparts browner and/or scalloped; rump and tail tinged with grey; dark bar on secondaries visible from above in flight. Races (**a**) *tibetana* (**b**) nom (**c**) *longipennis*. ⌘ Coastal and inland waters. In spite of its name, not as common in the subcontinent as some other species of tern. ∇ Deeper than 2; ringing *kirree`yay*; *kirri-kirri...*; *kek-kek-kek*. **MR*W3**

2 Arctic Tern *Sterna paradisaea* (466a) 36cm. Difficult to tell from 1 but slimmer with narrower wings; more rounded head; shorter neck; longer outer tail feathers; shorter legs; in all plumages the best field mark is formed by the translucent primaries (as seen in flight from below against the light) with a thin dark line along trailing edge (vs broad dusky trailing edge to outer primaries and translucency confined to wedge on inner primaries). **Br** note coral-red bill without dark tip. **Juv** lacks the dark secondary bar of juv 1. ⌘ Normally coastal but the only subcontinental record is from Kashmir. ∇ *kreer* higher and shorter than 1. **V**

3 Roseate Tern *Sterna dougallii* (466) 38cm. From 1, 2 & 4 by absence of dark trailing edge to primaries when seen from below; longer outer tail-streamers project well beyond wing-tip at rest and lack the dusky outerwebs of 1 & 2; paler upperparts; rump and tail paler grey than remaining upperparts but not contrasting. **Br** whiter below with pink tinge to underparts; largely blackish bill with red restricted to base; longer legs. **Juv** has short outer tail-streamers but is separated from young 1, 2 & 4 by same underwing feature as adult. ⌘ Coastal. ∇ Low grating *cherr`wick*. **B*3**

4 White-cheeked Tern *Sterna repressa* (467) 35cm. Darker grey upperparts than all other *Sterna*. Distinguished from 1-3 in flight by grey rump and tail concolorous with back; dark trailing edge to entire underwing. **Br** rather like Whiskered Tern (41.6) but considerably larger; deeply forked tail with long outer tail-streamers, usually equal to or projecting beyond wing-tip when perched (vs much shorter and shallower); long slender red bill with dark tip; broad white cheek-stripe contrasts more with grey underparts than on 1-3. Some br 1 are almost as dark on belly and breast but throat is whiter and undertail-coverts white (vs grey). ⌘ Marine and coastal. ∇ Said to be similar to 1 & 3; also *kee-errr*; *kerrit*; *kee-ceek*. **B*2**

5 Black-naped Tern *Sterna sumatrana* (468-9) 33cm. **Ad** has distinctive head pattern: white with clean-cut black line through eye broadening and meeting on nape. Note also black bill and legs; very pale grey (nearly white) upperparts unmarked except for dark shaft of outer primary. Br like nbr but may show slight pinkish tinge to underparts which could lead to confusion with 3, which has different head pattern and leg colour. ⌘ Strictly maritime; around islands. ∇ Sharp *kick*. **R2**

6 Black-bellied Tern *Sterna acuticauda* (470) 33cm. **Br** identified by black belly. Confusable with br Whiskered Tern (41.6) but larger; long orange/yellow (vs short red/black) bill; black (vs grey) belly; black (vs white) undertail-coverts; white (vs pale grey) throat; deeply (vs shallow) forked tail with long outer tail streamers, equal or longer than (vs much short of) wing-tip at rest. **Nbr** birds usually show some diagnostic dark mottling on the belly except immediately after the post-breeding moult; otherwise very similar to the commoner River Tern (39.4) but smaller and with a slimmer bill. ⌘ Inland rivers and jheels; not normally on the coast. ∇ Shrill, not unpleasant *krek, krek*, lower than that of River Tern; rapid *kek-kek-kek*. **R4**

7 Saunders's Tern *Sterna saundersi* (477) 23cm. Formerly regarded as a race of the extremely similar 8. **Br** differentiated by 3-4 (vs 2) dark (blacker) outer primaries; upperparts slightly paler; square-cut white forehead just reaching the front of the eye (vs sharp white wedge extending above eye); brownish tinge to slightly shorter, darker legs; shorter tail-streamers. **Nbr** may not be safely separable but usually has broader blacker wedge on outer primaries (beware of 8 with newly moulted inner primaries showing more contrast with darker unmoulted outer feathers); slightly shorter legs. Differences in rump coloration are not reliable distinguishing features in our region. **Juv** doubtfully distinguishable from juv 8. ⌘ Almost exclusively coastal. ∇ Similar to 8 but perhaps less chattering. **R•M2-3**

8 Little Tern *Sterna albifrons* (475-6) 23cm. From other *Sterna*, except 7 (which see), by small size and more rapid wingbeats. **Br** by yellow bill with black tip; black cap with white forecrown; bright yellow or reddish-orange legs. ⌘ Chiefly coastal in winter; breeds inland on islands in rivers and lakes. ∇ High chattering *kirik-(kirik)-(kirik)...*; *kewiriririk*; *kit-(kit)-(kit)*; *ke-ker-kewik*. **R•M2**

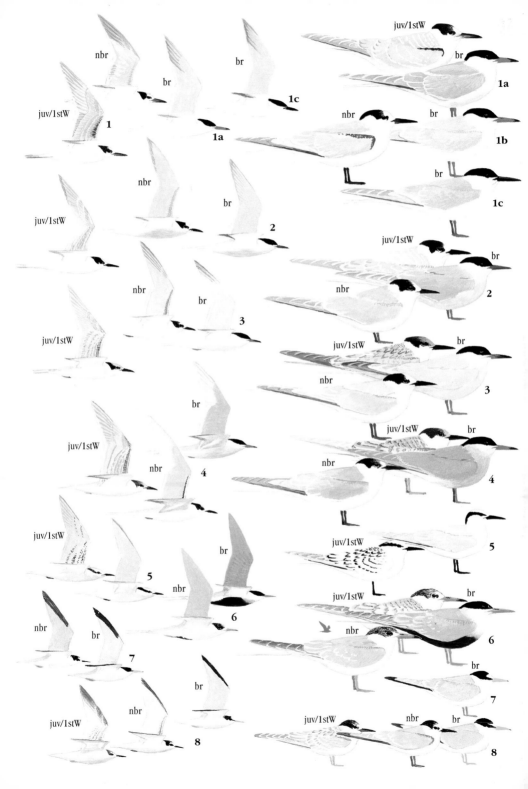

PLATE 40

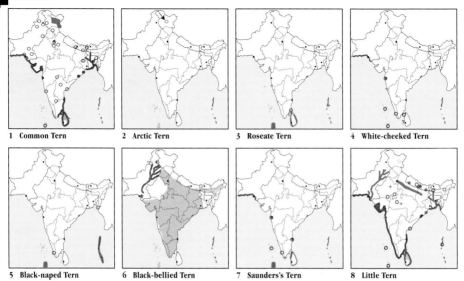

1 Common Tern
2 Arctic Tern
3 Roseate Tern
4 White-cheeked Tern
5 Black-naped Tern
6 Black-bellied Tern
7 Saunders's Tern
8 Little Tern

PLATE 41

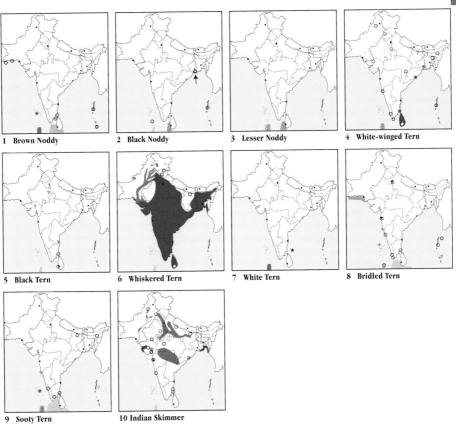

1 Brown Noddy

2 Black Noddy

3 Lesser Noddy

4 White-winged Tern

5 Black Tern

6 Whiskered Tern

7 White Tern

8 Bridled Tern

9 Sooty Tern

10 Indian Skimmer

PLATE 41: NODDIES, TERNS AND SKIMMER

1 **Brown Noddy** *Anous stolidus* (481) 41cm. From 2 & 3 by larger size; shorter bill (hardly over head-length) thicker, more decurved, with distinct gonydeal angle; browner upperparts; greyer cap; shorter tail (tail-tip level with wing-tips); from 3 by dark lores sharply demarcated from whitish forehead. In flight upperwing-coverts paler than flight feathers; centre of underwing paler than body; heavy wingbeats. **Juv** duller, more mottled, sometimes with white forecrown; best separated from juv 2 & 3 by bill shape. ❍ Marine. Rarely plunge-dives. ▽ Low croaking *karrk*; *kraa*. **B*R*2**

2 **Black Noddy** *Anous minutus* (482). 37cm. The race occurring in subcontinental waters, *worcesteri*, formerly included in Lesser Noddy (3). Similar to but blacker than 1 & 3; pure white cap bolder, more contrasting, not extending onto hindneck; lores to foreneck uniformly blackish-brown; from 1 by finer, straighter bill ¹/₃ longer than head; from 3 by distinct line of contrast between blackish lores and white cap (lores usually pale on 3); throat and foreneck concolorous with sides of face. In flight uniformly dark upperwing; underwing-coverts darker than flight feathers. **Juv** as adult but only forehead white. ❍ Marine. Rarely plunge-dives. ▽ *krikrikrik....* **V**

3 **Lesser Noddy** *Anous tenuirostris* 33cm. Differs from 1 & 2 in smaller size; pale lores not clearly demarcated from pale cap (exceptionally may have dark lores clearly defined from pale cap); throat and foreneck darker than sides of face; faster wingbeats; more uniform wing colour and thinner bill than 1; plumage browner, not as black as 2; cap grey (vs pure white in 2). In flight uniform upperwing and underwing. **Juv** paler brown; can be separated from juv 2 by same features as ad. ❍ Maritime. Does not normally plunge-dive. ▽ *karr*; *kerr*. **R*4**

4 **White-winged Tern** *Chlidonias leucopterus* (459) 23cm. **Br** has characteristic black underwing-coverts; from 5 & 6 also by contrastingly white forewing, rump and tail. **Nbr** often has diagnostic trace of black on the axillaries or underwing-coverts; whiter rump and tail than 5 & 6; from 5 by absent, or very faint, dark patch at side of breast; similar head pattern to 5 but crown paler, mottled (vs streaked) and not sharply demarcated from forehead; from 6 by head pattern – black patch extends distinctly below eye-level onto ear-coverts and white behind ear-coverts reaches up well above eye. **Juv** from juv 5 & 6 by white rump; from 5 by slightly shorter bill; darker mantle; usually little or no dark patch at side of breast; from 6 by head pattern; white collar; more uniform mantle. ❍ Lakes, jheels, rivers, coasts, paddyfields. Does not normally plunge-dive. ▽ *kwek*; *krrek*; *kurr*; *kick-kick-krrick*; *kirrek*. **W3-4**

5 **Black Tern** *Chlidonias niger* (459a) 23cm. **Br** mainly confusable with 4 which see. **Nbr** very similar to 4 & 6 but has distinct dark patch on side of breast at base of wing (but 4 & 6 can occasionally show a dark patch, usually narrower, fainter and browner); black of crown solid, sharply demarcated from forehead; shorter legs with tibia ('thighs') barely visible when perched; from 6 also by pattern on head (similar to 4). **Juv** from 4 & 6 by less mantle/wing contrast; broad dark patch at side of breast; from 4 by grey rump; slightly longer bill; from 6 by white collar; white tips to rear scapulars. ❍ Coastal and inland waterbodies. Rarely plunge-dives. ▽ Shrill nasal *kyew*; *kyek*; *key-(ye)-yek*; *kek*. **V**

6 **Whiskered Tern** *Chlidonias hybridus* (458) 25cm. Slightly larger than 4 & 5 with stouter bill. **Br** can appear very dark, almost blackish below, but not as black as 4; from 4 & 5 by white 'whiskers' between black cap and dusky underparts; from 4 by pale underwing-coverts; from 5 by uniform grey upperparts; from 40.4 & 40.6 by small size and short tail with shallow fork, tip falling well short of wing-tip when perched. **Nbr** from 4 & 5 by head pattern – white forehead, dark extending from (but not much below) eye into black streaking on crown and nape. Some birds show a similar head pattern to longer, stouter-billed Gull-billed Tern (39.5). **Juv** from 4 & 6 by head pattern (like ad but often more strongly marked); stronger bill; little or no white collar; buffy tips to rear scapulars; mantle chequered brown and black; from 4 by grey rump and tail; from 5 by pale grey wing/dark back contrast. ❍ Lakes, jheels, rivers, coasts, paddyfields. Dip-feeds; will plunge-dive. ▽ Sharp grating *kirreak...kirreak...; kerk...kerk....* **RMW1**

7 **White Tern** *Gygis alba* (483) 29cm. Only all-white tern except for black ring around eye, blue legs and base of bill. **Imm** (not shown) mottled brown on upperparts. ❍ Around marine islands. ▽ Raucous *grrich grrich grrich....* **R*3**

8 **Bridled Tern** *Sterna anaethetus* (471-3) 37cm. **Ad** from 9 by paler upperparts contrasting with black cap – usually separated by paler grey hind-collar; white of forehead more acutely angled and extending behind eye; in flight note the narrower dark trailing edge to underwing and white wedge down centre of primaries. ❍ Pelagic. ▽ Yapping *wrep-wrep*; high *kee-yharr*; hoarse *krek*. **BP*3**

9 **Sooty Tern** *Sterna fuscata* (474) 43cm. **Ad** from 8 by blacker upperparts the same colour as cap, white of forehead only extending as far as eye and not as sharply angled; in flight from below entire primaries and broad trailing edge to secondaries dusky. ❍ Pelagic. Only occasionally plunge-dives. ▽ Distinctive *wide-awake*; *ker-wack-a-wack.* **BWP*3**

10 **Indian Skimmer** *Rynchops albicollis* (484) 40cm. Unmistakable bill. At a distance note black upperparts with white collar, cheeks, forecrown, outer tail feathers and trailing edge to secondaries and inner primaries. **Imm** browner above with pale scalloping. ❍ Large rivers and lakes; occasionally coastal waters. ▽ Nasal *kap*, *kap*. **R•M4**

PLATE 42: SANDGROUSE AND PIGEONS I

1 **Pallas's Sandgrouse** *Syrrhaptes paradoxus* (485a) 48cm. ♂ in flight: black belly-patch, buffy wing-coverts, whitish flight feathers, dark spotting in armpits. ✿ Steppe, semi-desert, cultivation, waste-land. ▽ Resonant *ten-ten*; *quat*; *tryou-ryou*. **V**

2 **Black-bellied Sandgrouse** *Pterocles orientalis* (489) 39cm. ♂ in flight: dark belly and vent, white underwing with black primaries. ✿ Sandy semi-desert, fallow cultivation. ▽ Resonant bubbling *karrr-r-rl*; *whi-whi-whu*. **W3**

3 **Pin-tailed Sandgrouse** *Pterocles alchata* (486) 38cm. ♂ in flight: white belly, orange breast edged black, white underwing with dark primaries. ✿ Stony semi-desert, fallow land. ▽ Loud nasal *errrh-errrh*; *weh-eh-eh-eh-eh*. **W5**

4 **Crowned Sandgrouse** *Pterocles coronatus* (490) 28cm. ♂ in flight: all-pale underbody; whitish underwing with mainly dark primaries and white trailing edge to dark secondaries. ✿ Stony wastes and semi-desert. ▽ Soft *kla, kla, kla...*; nasal rattling *kaaa-kara-kara-karah*. **RW2**

5 **Tibetan Sandgrouse** *Syrrhaptes tibetanus* (485) 48cm. ♂ in flight: dark underwing and pale underparts. ✿ 4200-5400. Semi-desert steppe. ▽ *guk-guk*, *yak-yak* or *koonk-koonk* deeper than other sandgrouse. **RA2**

6 **Chestnut-bellied Sandgrouse** *Pterocles exustus* (487) 28cm. ♂ in flight: dark underwing and dark belly. ✿ Barren plains, fallow land, scrubby semi-desert. ▽ Throaty *wup-pu-du*. **R●2**

7 **Spotted Sandgrouse** *Pterocles senegallus* (488) 36cm. In flight: dark bar down centre of pale belly. ✿ Desert and open semi-desert. ▽ *wakù-wakù* or *kwitoo-kwitoo*. **WPR*3**

8 **Painted Sandgrouse** *Pterocles indicus* (492) 28cm. ♀ similar to ♀9 but slightly darker ground-colour; chin and upper throat plain sandy-buff; bill orange-brown. Ranges disjunct. ♂ in flight: barred underbody and pale underwing separate from all but ♂9. ✿ Dry, stony areas with sparse scrub. ▽ *chirik-chirik*; *yek-yek-yek*. **E●4**

9 **Lichtenstein's Sandgrouse** *Pterocles lichtensteinii* (491) 27cm. ♀ similar to ♀8 but paler ground-colour; chin and upper throat spotted with dark brown; bill brown. ♂ in flight barred underbody and pale underwing separate from all but ♂8. ✿ Stony low hills with sparse scrub. ▽ *kwhee-ah*; *arrk*; *whit*, *wheet*, *wheeoo*; *greg-greg-greg-greg*. **R3**

10 **Red Collared Dove** *Streptopelia tranquebarica* (535-6) 23cm. ♀ like small version of 11 but shorter tail; sandy-brown (vs pale vinous-grey) breast; whitish (vs grey) vent and undertail-coverts. ✿ <1300. Mainly lowland open scrub and cultivation with scattered trees. ▽ Repeated *groo-gurr-goo*. **R●M3**

11 **Eurasian Collared Dove** *Streptopelia decaocto* (534) 32cm. From all pigeons except 10 (which see) by thin black hind-collar. ✿ <2400(3000). Gardens; scrub and cultivation with scattered trees. ▽ *ku-koo koo*; *khaa...khaa*. **R●A1**

12 **Laughing Dove** *Streptopelia senegalensis* (541) 27cm. ✿ <1500. Semi-desert; scrub and cultivation with scattered trees. ▽ Soft *coo-roo-roo-rororoo*. **R●1**

13 **Spotted Dove** *Streptopelia chinensis* (537-40) 30cm. White spots on black hind-neck. ✿ <2400(4900). Parks, gardens, farmland, scrub, wooded areas. Usually in moister, less open biotope than 11 & 12. ▽ *krookruk-krukroo...kroo-kroo-(kroo)-(kroo)-(kroo)-(kroo)*; *kruk-krooo*. **R●A1**

14 **European Turtle Dove** *Streptopelia turtur* (529) 28cm. Very similar to 15a but 3-4 black bars on white neck-patch; nape same colour as crown; brown rump; broad orangy fringes to wing feathers; pale lilac breast. ✿ Mainly dry open scrub. ▽ Purring *toorrr-toorrr trrroo...*. **V**

15 **Oriental Turtle Dove** *Streptopelia orientalis* (530-3) 33cm. Races **(a)** *meena* very similar to 14 but **(4)**5-6 black bars on blue-grey neck-patch; vinaceous-brown nape contrasts with grey crown; bluish-grey rump; wings appear scaly due to narrow buff/orange fringes to feathers; vinous-brown breast. **(b)** *agricola* is darker, more richly coloured than a, with vinous-brown extending across belly. ✿ <4000. Open forest. ▽ *goor...gur-grugroo...* **RMW3**

16 **Barred Cuckoo Dove** *Macropygia unchall* (526) 41cm. Like 17 but barred upperparts and tail; ranges disjunct. ✿ 450-2700. Dense evergreen forest and second growth. ▽ Deep *croo-umm*. **R3**

17 **Andaman Cuckoo Dove** *Macropygia rufipennis* (527-7a) 41cm. Like 16 but unbarred upperparts and tail; ranges disjunct. ✿ Dense evergreen forest, forest edge, second growth. ▽ Deep hoarse *o-o-o-o-ah*; *whoo-úp whow*. **E*4**

18 **Nicobar Pigeon** *Caloenas nicobarica* (544b) 41cm. Unmistakable; tail white. ✿ Dense evergreen forest; mainly on small uninhabited islands. ▽ A harsh guttural *croak* but usually silent. **R*●3**

19 **Emerald Dove** *Chalcophaps indica* (542-4a) 27cm. Note broad wings and rapid flight. ✿ <1800+. Forest – mainly evergreen and moist deciduous. Usually on the ground and in low to mid-storey. ▽ Low resonant *(huk)-hwoon*. **R(M?)2**

PLATE 42

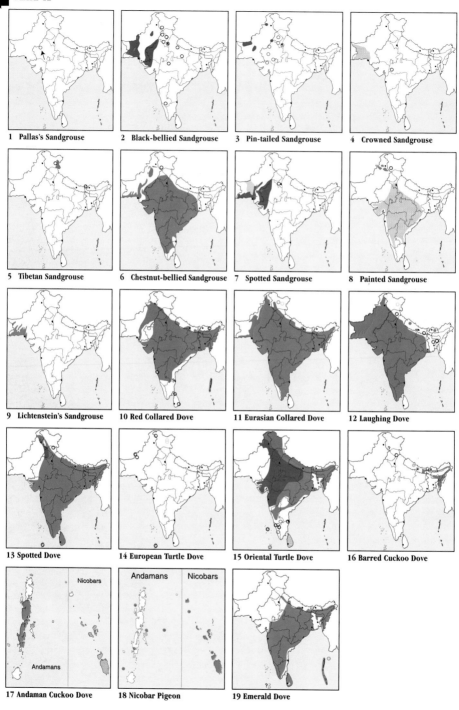

1 Pallas's Sandgrouse

2 Black-bellied Sandgrouse

3 Pin-tailed Sandgrouse

4 Crowned Sandgrouse

5 Tibetan Sandgrouse

6 Chestnut-bellied Sandgrouse

7 Spotted Sandgrouse

8 Painted Sandgrouse

9 Lichtenstein's Sandgrouse

10 Red Collared Dove

11 Eurasian Collared Dove

12 Laughing Dove

13 Spotted Dove

14 European Turtle Dove

15 Oriental Turtle Dove

16 Barred Cuckoo Dove

17 Andaman Cuckoo Dove

18 Nicobar Pigeon

19 Emerald Dove

PLATE 43

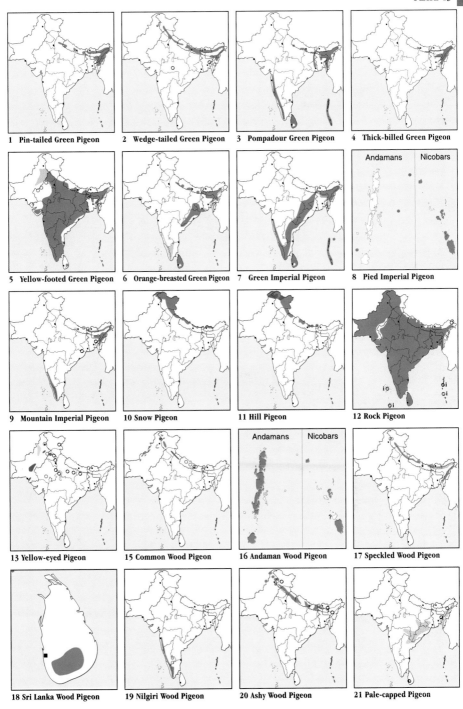

1 Pin-tailed Green Pigeon

2 Wedge-tailed Green Pigeon

3 Pompadour Green Pigeon

4 Thick-billed Green Pigeon

5 Yellow-footed Green Pigeon

6 Orange-breasted Green Pigeon

7 Green Imperial Pigeon

8 Pied Imperial Pigeon

9 Mountain Imperial Pigeon

10 Snow Pigeon

11 Hill Pigeon

12 Rock Pigeon

13 Yellow-eyed Pigeon

15 Common Wood Pigeon

16 Andaman Wood Pigeon

17 Speckled Wood Pigeon

18 Sri Lanka Wood Pigeon

19 Nilgiri Wood Pigeon

20 Ashy Wood Pigeon

21 Pale-capped Pigeon

143

PLATE 43: PIGEONS II

1 **Pin-tailed Green Pigeon** *Treron apicauda* (493) ♂40cm ♀35cm. Note long pin-tail; blue lores, base of bill and skin around eye. Undertail coverts of ♀ dark green streaked with yellow. ⌖ <1800. Mature forest. Arboreal. ▽ Mellow wandering *ko-kla-oi-oi-oi-oilli-illio-kla*. **R•3**

2 **Wedge-tailed Green Pigeon** *Treron sphenura* (494) 33cm. Broad, wedge-shaped, all-green tail unique among *Treron*. ♂ orange-rufous crown diagnostic. ♀ lacks blue lores of 1. ⌖ <2500(2800). Forest – mainly broadleaved. Arboreal. ▽ Mellow whistling *boo-whoo-huhuhu-boo-boo-oo-eee-bu*. **R•3**

3 **Pompadour Green Pigeon** *Treron pompadora* (496-500) 28cm. Forehead and crown ashy-grey. ♂ separated from 1, 5 & 6 by chestnut-maroon back. From 2 & 4 by orangy breast and grey terminal band on tail. ♀ from ♀4 by green central tail feathers. Races **(a)** *phayrei* **(b)** *chloroptera* **(c** - not shown) nom of Sri Lanka has yellow 'face'. ⌖ <1200(1500). Forest. Arboreal. ▽ Very high-pitched meandering whistling *wooweeyouweeyouweepiweepiwooweeyuweeyou*. **R•2**

4 **Thick-billed Green Pigeon** *Treron curvirostra* (495) 27cm. Only *Treron* with red at base of short thick bill; bare skin around eye vivid green. ⌖ <1500. Forest and well-wooded country. Arboreal. ▽ Mellow whistles; hoarse *goo-goo*. **R•4**

5 **Yellow-footed Green Pigeon** *Treron phoenicoptera* (503-5) 33cm. Yellow legs; grey head contrasting with orangey yellow-green collar; lilac shoulder-patch (reduced in ♀). Races **(a)** nom **(b)** *chlorigaster*. ⌖ <1500. Forest, groves, parks and gardens. Arboreal. ▽ Modulated, mellow, musical whistles, like 6 but lower pitched. **R•2**

6 **Orange-breasted Green Pigeon** *Treron bicincta* (501-2) 29cm. ♂ lilac/orange breast. ♀ from other ♀♀ by grey central tail feathers and terminal band. ⌖ <1500. Forest, well-wooded areas. Arboreal. ▽ Typical *Treron* whistling. **R•3**

7 **Green Imperial Pigeon** *Ducula aenea* (506-8a) 43cm. In poor light confusable with 9 & 16 but note chestnut undertail-coverts and green upperparts. ⌖ <300(600). Forest and second growth with fruit trees. Arboreal. ▽ Deep (*wuck*)-*wuck-wooorr*; *whoohoo*; *ghoom*; *qoo*; *qroo*; *whuck-woop-woop-woop-woop-woop*. **R•3**

8 **Pied Imperial Pigeon** *Ducula bicolor* (509) 41cm. ⌖ Littoral forest, mangroves. ▽ *cru-croo*; *hu-hu-hu*. **R•*2**

9 **Mountain Imperial Pigeon** *Ducula badia* (510-2) 51cm. ⌖ <2300. Mature evergreen forest. Arboreal. ▽ Deep booming *whoomp...whoomp*. **R•3**

10 **Snow Pigeon** *Columba leuconota* (513-4) 34cm. Dark hood contrasts with white neck and breast. ⌖ S 3000-5000 W >1500(750). Alpine cliffs, gorges, slopes. ▽ A repeated croak; high, tremulous *coo* on take-off/landing. **RA2**

11 **Hill Pigeon** *Columba rupestris* (515) 33cm. From 12,13 & 14 by white band across dark tail. ⌖ S 3000-5500 W >1500. Mountain cliffs, gorges, cultivation, mainly northern slopes of Himalayas. ▽ High *gut-gut-gut-gut*. **RA2**

12 **Rock Pigeon** *Columba livia* (516-7) 33cm. Interbreeds with feral pigeons, so numerous colour varieties. From 13 & 14 by long (vs short) wing-bars; from 11 by tail pattern. Race *neglecta* (not shown) of W Himalaya often has pale patch on lower back. ⌖ <3300. Rocky country. ▽ Low *koo-roo-koo*; *oorh-oorh*. **RA1**

13 **Yellow-eyed Pigeon** *Columba eversmanni* (518) 30cm. Like small pale 12 but wing-bars short; pale lower back contrasting with dark grey uppertail-coverts. Bare yellow skin around eye diagnostic at close range. ⌖ Groves and open cultivation. ▽ *quooh, quooh, quooh-cuw-gooh-cuw-gooh-cu-gooh*. **WP5**

14 **[Stock Pigeon** *Columba oenas* 33cm. Extralimital. Very similar to 12 & 13 but dark flight feathers and pale grey lower back concolorous with rump and uppertail-coverts. From 13 also by dark eye. ▽ Gruff *oowo oowo oowo*. **X]**

15 **Common Wood Pigeon** *Columba palumbus* (519) 43cm. Buffy patch on side of neck; whitish bend of wing forms wing-crescent in flight. ⌖ S 1500-3000 W lower. Slopes and valleys with scrub forest. ▽ *kroo-krooo-koo kroo-koo*. **R•AW5**

16 **Andaman Wood Pigeon** *Columba palumboides* (525) 41cm. From a distance surprisingly difficult to separate from the sympatric 7 but note the dark slaty upperparts with slight green and purple gloss; vinous-grey (vs greyish-white) head and ashy vent. ⌖ Evergreen forest and second growth. Arboreal. ▽ Deep *groo-groo*; *whoohoo*; *whoom*. **E•*3**

17 **Speckled Wood Pigeon** *Columba hodgsonii* (520) 38cm. ⌖ 1800-4000. Hill forest. Chiefly arboreal. ▽ Deep *whock-whr-o-o...whroo*. **R•A3**

18 **Sri Lanka Wood Pigeon** *Columba torringtonii* (522) 36cm. ⌖ >1200(300). Forest and forest edge. Arboreal. Usually singly, in pairs or small flocks. ▽ Rather silent; deep *boo-(oo)*. **E•A3**

19 **Nilgiri Wood Pigeon** *Columba elphinstonii* (521) 42cm. Check pattern on hindneck diagnostic. ⌖ Foothills-2000. Moist evergreen forest, sholas. Arboreal. Singly, in pairs, small flocks. ▽ Deep eerie *who-who-who-(who)*. **E•3**

20 **Ashy Wood Pigeon** *Columba pulchricollis* (523) 36cm. Buff collar diagnostic. ⌖ (100)1200-3200. Dense forest. Arboreal. ▽ Usually silent; deep *coo*. **R•3**

21 **Pale-capped Pigeon** *Columba punicea* (524) 36cm. ⌖ <1600. Forest, scrub, wooded ravines, cultivation. Usually solitary or in small groups. ▽ Like 7 but softer, less booming; soft mew. **R*5**

144

PLATE 44: PARAKEETS AND HANGING PARROTS

1 **Red-breasted Parakeet** *Psittacula alexandri* (551-2) 38cm. Only parakeet with rosy breast. ⌘ <1500. Open deciduous forest, orchards and cultivation. ▽ Loud squeaky *eeow; euw; web; kaink.* **R•1**

2 **Slaty-headed Parakeet** *Psittacula himalayana* (562) 41cm. The slaty head separates this from all but 6; from latter by darker, slatier head, shorter, broader central tail feathers with the distal half rich yellow. ⌘ (250)600-2500(3260). Forest, orchards, cultivation. ▽ Shrill *reep-(reep); tooi-tooi.* **R•A2**

3 [**Intermediate Parakeet** *Psittacula 'intermedia'* (561) 38cm. Only known from specimens and captive birds. Recent studies have shown that this bird is a hybrid between 2 & 4 rather than a species in its own right.]

4 **Plum-headed Parakeet** *Psittacula cyanocephala* (557-8) 36cm. ♂ easily distinguished by the plum-coloured head (but see following species). ♀ is diagnosed by the combination of lavender-grey head, greenish-yellow collar, yellow upper mandible and whitish tail-tip. ⌘ <600(1500). Open broadleaved forest, orchards, forest edge adjoining cultivation. ▽ *oink-oink,* mellower than 13; *wink; tsyeet tsyeet... .* **E•2**

5 **Blossom-headed Parakeet** *Psittacula roseata* (559-60) 36cm. Very similar to 4 but ♂ has pale rosy sides of head merging into lavender-blue crown and yellowish tip to the tail. ♀ is distinguished from ♀4 mainly by the latter feature, the head being paler lavender-grey than ♀4 and the yellow collar being indistinct; normally has a maroon shoulder-patch (unusual in ♀4). ⌘ and ▽ similar to 4. **R•4-5**

6 **Grey-headed Parakeet** *Psittacula finschii* (563) 36cm. Very similar to 2 but note the lavender-blue tinge to the somewhat paler slaty head and the lilac-yellow on the distal third of the very long, narrow central tail feathers. ⌘ <2100. Hill forest and cultivation. ▽ Like 2. **R•(A?)4-5**

7 **Malabar Parakeet** *Psittacula columboides* (564) 38cm. Grey back, breast and head together with blue primaries. ⌘ 500-1500. Evergreen and mixed-deciduous forest, second growth, cultivation. ▽ Harsh squeaky *screet-screet...; cheechi chichichi.* **E•2**

8 **Layard's Parakeet** *Psittacula calthropae* (565) 31cm. Not dissimilar to the allopatric 7 but lacks the grey breast and blue primaries. The only other parakeets within its range are 4, 11 & 13, all of which lack the grey back and emerald collar. ⌘ <1800(2000). Mainly hill forest but also adjoining lowlands. Usually in pairs or small groups, sometimes with mixed flocks. ▽ *eh-ee eh-ee...; gree-gree; greek greek....* **E•3**

9 **Long-tailed Parakeet** *Psittacula longicauda* (555-6) 47cm. Red cheeks on green head diagnostic. ⌘ Forest, cultivation, gardens, mangroves. ▽ Screech similar to 13 but deeper, less harsh. **R2**

10 **Nicobar Parakeet** *Psittacula caniceps* (553) 61cm. Endemic to the Nicobars where it is unlikely to be confused with 9, the only other parakeet found on the islands. ⌘ High forest. ▽ Wild screech; cawing *kraan.* **E*2**

11 **Alexandrine Parakeet** *Psittacula eupatria* (545-8) 53cm. The large size and huge bill distinguish this from all other parakeets within its range. The only other species with a black and pink collar is the much smaller 13 which lacks the maroon shoulder-patch. ⌘ <1600. Deciduous forest, woodland, plantations, cultivation, mangroves. ▽ Squealing *kree-arr,* usually deeper than 13. **R•3**

12 **Derbyan Parakeet** *Psittacula derbiana* (554) 46cm. Only parakeet with mauve breast and belly. ⌘ >1250. Montane forest, preferring conifers; cultivation. ▽ *creeo creeo creeo; graaa graaa.* **R*(?)5**

13 **Rose-ringed Parakeet** *Psittacula krameri* (549-50) 42cm. The most common and widespread parakeet throughout most of the region. ♂ is a largely slim green bird distinguished by the black and rose collar, absent in ♀. Both ♂ and ♀ are much smaller and smaller-billed than the similarly plumaged 11 and lack that species's obvious maroon shoulder-patch. Races **(a)** *borealis* **(b)** *manillensis.* ⌘ Mainly lowlands. Variety of (mainly broadleaved) wooded habitats including vicinity of man; cultivation. ▽ Squeaky *keew; keeow;* shrill *kee-ak.* **R1**

14 **Vernal Hanging Parrot** *Loriculus vernalis* (566-7) 14cm. Lacks red crown of 15. Seen perched less frequently than in flight when its presence is often given away by its call as it whizzes rapidly by. Often sleeps while hanging upside-down, whence the name. ⌘ <1800. Forest, open woodland, orchards, plantations, gardens. ▽ *cht-cht-cht,* usually in flight. **R•2-3**

15 **Sri Lanka Hanging Parrot** *Loriculus beryllinus* (568) 14cm. Distinguished from 14 by red crown. Displays similar habits to its congener. ⌘ As 14 but <1300(1600). ▽ Similar to 14; *chi-chi-chit.* **E•2**

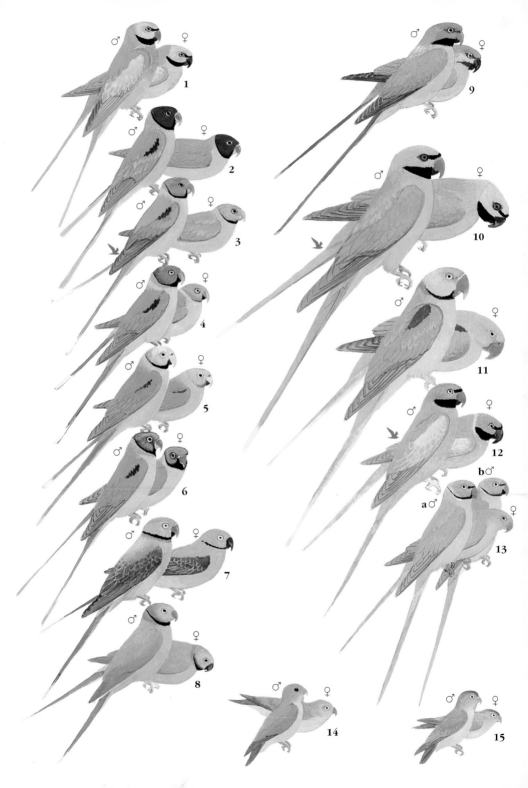

PLATE 44

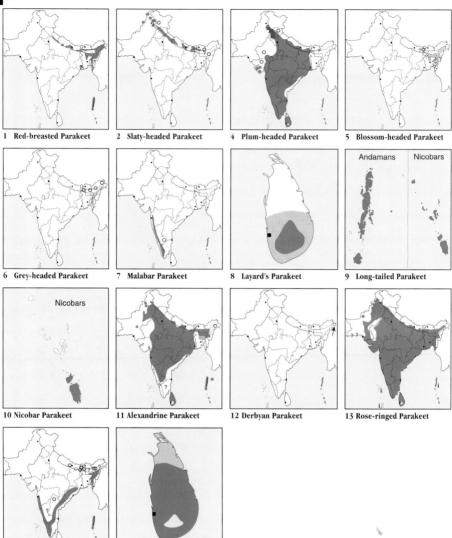

1   Red-breasted Parakeet

2   Slaty-headed Parakeet

4   Plum-headed Parakeet

5   Blossom-headed Parakeet

6   Grey-headed Parakeet

7   Malabar Parakeet

8   Layard's Parakeet

9   Long-tailed Parakeet

10 Nicobar Parakeet

11 Alexandrine Parakeet

12 Derbyan Parakeet

13 Rose-ringed Parakeet

14 Vernal Hanging Parrot

15 Sri Lanka Hanging Parrot

PLATE 45

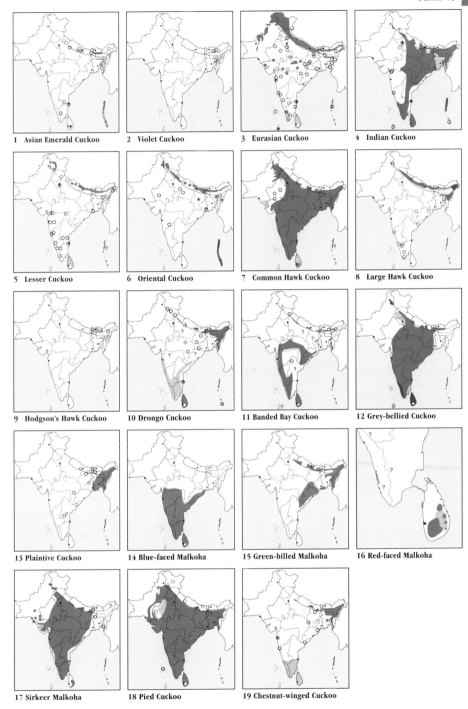

1 Asian Emerald Cuckoo

2 Violet Cuckoo

3 Eurasian Cuckoo

4 Indian Cuckoo

5 Lesser Cuckoo

6 Oriental Cuckoo

7 Common Hawk Cuckoo

8 Large Hawk Cuckoo

9 Hodgson's Hawk Cuckoo

10 Drongo Cuckoo

11 Banded Bay Cuckoo

12 Grey-bellied Cuckoo

13 Plaintive Cuckoo

14 Blue-faced Malkoha

15 Green-billed Malkoha

16 Red-faced Malkoha

17 Sirkeer Malkoha

18 Pied Cuckoo

19 Chestnut-winged Cuckoo

PLATE 45: CUCKOOS AND MALKOHAS

1 **Asian Emerald Cuckoo** *Chrysococcyx maculatus* (586) 18cm. ♀ confusable with ♀2 but head/upper mantle rufous, upperparts glossed green; orange-yellow bill usually has distal third black. **Juv** is like ♀ but throat washed pale chestnut and a little more barred above. ⌘ <1000(1830). Evergreen forest, second growth. ∇ *chweek* in flight; trill. **R●MS4**

2 **Violet Cuckoo** *Chrysococcyx xanthorhynchus* (587) 17cm. ♀ from ♀1 by less greenish upperparts, red base to bill. **Juv** like ♀ but more rufous and barred above; whiter, more sparsely barred below. ⌘ As 1 but <1500. ∇ *che-wick* in flight; high accelerating trill. **R●MS5**

3 **Eurasian Cuckoo** *Cuculus canorus* (577-9) 33cm. **Grey ad** not safely separable from 6 except by call; slightly larger, paler; barring generally narrower, mid-brown, on whiter ground-colour; at close range dark barring on white bend of wing (usually absent on 6). **Grey** ♀ often has rufous wash on breast. **Hepatic** ♀ from 6 by black bars above usually narrower than the rufous; barring on rump broken/irregular (vs broader, regular). **Juv** browner than ♀ with pale nuchal patch. ⌘ <4100(5250). Open forest, clearings. ∇ ♂ *cuck-koo*, ♀ bubbling *whiwhiwhi...* . **SM2**

4 **Indian Cuckoo** *Cuculus micropterus* (576) 33cm. From 3, 5 & 6 by one dark tailband, grey head contrasting with dark brown upperparts. ⌘ <2300(3700). Wooded areas. ∇ ♂ *toh-toh'ta`toh* (*crossword pu-zzle*); ♀ bubbling. **R●M2**

5 **Lesser Cuckoo** *Cuculus poliocephalus* (581) 26cm. Very like 3 & 6 except for call but smaller, dark slaty above, tail scarcely darker than dark grey rump (vs contrasting with medium grey), underparts usually buffier with broader, wider-spread barring. ⌘ <3200(4000). Wooded country. ∇ Rattling *that's your choky pepper...*(*choky pepper*). **M3**

6 **Oriental Cuckoo** *Cuculus saturatus* (580-0a) 31cm. **Grey ad** like 3; normally smaller, darker above, barring dark brown, wider spaced; in flight broad (vs narrow) whitish band reaches 3-4th (vs 5-6th) primary. ♀ (not shown) like 3, which see. ⌘ <3300. Open woodland. ∇ ♂ 4 (3-8) hollow *oop*. ♀ bubbling *qui qui-quiquiquiquiquip*. **S(R*?)3**

7 **Common Hawk Cuckoo** *Hierococcyx varius* (573-4) 34cm. Like 8 but smaller, paler, no breast streaking, different tail pattern. Mistakable for a Shikra (12.5) but has cuckoo-like bill, long broad tail, no mesial stripe, longer, more pointed wings. ⌘ <1000(1200). Well-wooded areas, gardens etc. ∇ Loud shrill *pee pee-ah* or *brain fe-ver* repeated in long sequence at diminishing intervals, each phrase higher in pitch, rising to a crescendo. Very like 8. **R●2**

8 **Large Hawk Cuckoo** *Hierococcyx sparverioides* (572) 38cm. Like 7 but larger; dark brown barring below; (usually) streaked breast; usually darker/browner above; different tail pattern. **Imm** larger, darker than imm 7, more obvious dark chin, different uppertail pattern. ⌘ **S** 900-3000. **W** >plains. Wooded country. ∇ Like 7 but often lower, harder, less shrill, less manic. **M3**

9 **Hodgson's Hawk Cuckoo** *Hierococcyx fugax* (575) 29cm. From 7 & 8 by slaty upperparts; no barring on underparts. ⌘ 600-1800. Wooded country. ∇ Shrill repeated *gee-whizz-(jiwiz)*. **R●A(S?)4**

10 **Drongo Cuckoo** *Surniculus lugubris* (588-9) 25cm. Superficially like drongo. For differences see 59.3. ⌘ <2000. Well-wooded country. ∇ 5-7 short whistles on ascending scale, given also in a hoarse, drawn-out version. **R●AM3**

11 **Banded Bay Cuckoo** *Cacomantis sonneratii* (582-3) 24cm. Pale supercilium and lores; broad dark band behind eye. ⌘ <2400. Forest, open woodland. ∇ *phee-wi phi-wi* repeated each time at higher pitch; *pe-ter pi-per*. **R●M3**

12 **Grey-bellied Cuckoo** *Cacomantis passerinus* (584) 23cm. ♂ and imm/hepatic ♀ shown. **Ad** is only cuckoo with un-barred grey breast and belly. **Imm/hepatic** lack contrasting pale supercilium of 11; brighter rufous than 13. ⌘ <2700. Lightly wooded country. ∇ Plaintive *pteer`pteer`pteer peepipi*; *pwee pee piwee*. **E●M3**

13 **Plaintive Cuckoo** *Cacomantis merulinus* (585) 23cm. **Ad** from other cuckoos by grey breast with rufous belly and vent. **Imm/hepatic** ♀ lack contrasting pale supercilium of 11; duller rufous than 12. ⌘ <2000. Wooded country. ∇ Clear whistled *PEE pee pee peepipipipi*, 1st note loudest, trailing off at the end. **R●M3**

14 **Blue-faced Malkoha** *Phaenicophaeus viridirostris* (595) 39cm. Smaller than 15; blue orbital skin, dark grey pale-streaked throat and breast, rufous-buffy belly wash. ⌘ <1000. Thick scrub, undergrowth. ∇ Rather silent; low *kraa*. **E3**

15 **Green-billed Malkoha** *Phaenicophaeus tristis* (593-4) 51cm. Like 14 but larger; red orbital skin; pale grey forehead; finely streaked throat/breast. ⌘ <700(1800). Tangled undergrowth. ∇ Usually silent; (*ga..ga..ga...*)*kok... kok.....* **R3**

16 **Red-faced Malkoha** *Phaenicophaeus pyrrhocephalus* (599) 46cm. Unique. ♀ has white iris. ⌘ <550(1700). Ever-green forest. Singly, in pairs or mixed flocks. ∇ Rather silent; low *kaa*; *kok*; soft, low *krrr*; petulant low *krâ*. **E*5**

17 **Sirkeer Malkoha** *Phaenicophaeus leschenaultii* (596-8) 43cm. Overall earthy-brown with yellow-tipped, cherry-red bill. ⌘ <1000(2100). Dry woodland and scrub jungle. ∇ Usually silent; *kek-kek-kek....* **E4**

18 **Pied Cuckoo** *Clamator jacobinus* (570-1) 31cm. Pied crested appearance distinctive. ⌘ <2600. Light woodland, scrub, gardens etc. ∇ *peew piu-piu-(piu)-(piu)*; *pee-ew*; *piu...(piu...pee-pee-piu...*). **R●S4**

19 **Chestnut-winged Cuckoo** *Clamator coromandus* (569) 42cm. Easily distinguished from 18 by chestnut wings. ⌘ Broad-leaved forest, scrub jungle. ∇ *peep-peep*; rasping scream; usually silent in winter. **M4**

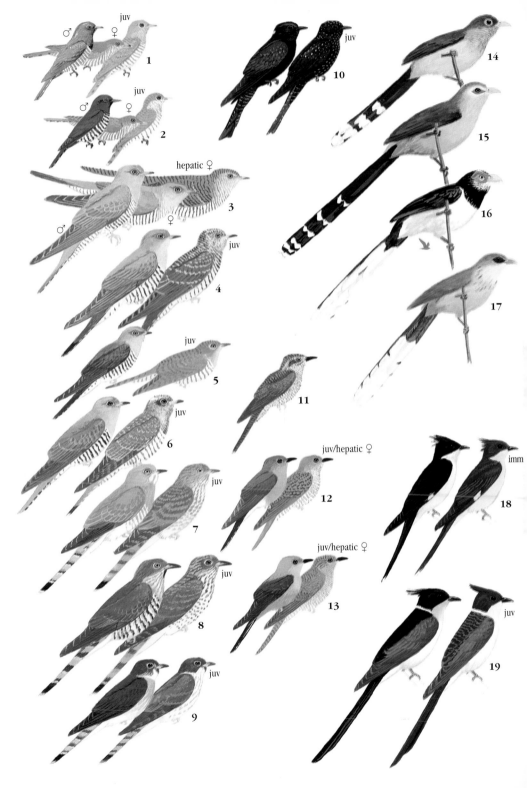

PLATE 46: KOEL, COUCALS, FROGMOUTHS AND NIGHTJARS

1 **Asian Koel** *Eudynamys scolopacea* (590-2) 43cm. ♂ resembles slender crow with pale green bill, red eye, long tail; see plate 63. ✾ <1800. Woodland, parks, gardens. ▽ Rising *ko-eu´...ko-eu´...; kruk-keookeookeoo....* **R•1**

2 **Hodgson's Frogmouth** *Batrachostomus hodgsoni* (667) 27cm. Like 3 but larger; ♂ slightly more rufous-brown; crown more heavily streaked; breast darker than remaining underparts with large white spots; ♀ has large white spots on scapulars and breast (vs small white spots on wing-coverts, breast and belly). Range indicative. ✾ 300-1800. Subtropical evergreen forest. ▽ Drawn-out whistled (*u*)*wheeeow*; *whurrree*; chuckling *whoo*; soft *gwaa*. **R5**

3 **Sri Lanka Frogmouth** *Batrachostomus monileger* (666) 23cm. ♂ like ♂2 but smaller, greyer; underparts fairly uniform with a few small whitish spots on lower throat; more on belly and flanks. ♀ for differences see ♀2. ✾ <1800. Evergreen forest, bamboo. ▽ Rapid rolling notes repeated 6-12x *warra´warra´warra...*; harsh *qruaaoh*; *kaow*. **E4**

4 **Green-billed Coucal** *Centropus chlororhynchos* (604) 43cm. Like 5 but pale green or ivory bill; black has purple gloss (vs blue/blue-green in Sri Lankan race of 5); darker ruddy-chestnut wings. ✾ < foothills. Moist primary and riverine forest. Usually in pairs. ▽ 3-4(5-6) hollow *oop* notes, deeper, slower, more rounded than 5; loud cough. **E*5**

5 **Greater Coucal** *Centropus sinensis* (600-2) 48cm. The commonest and most widespread coucal. For distinctions see 4 & 6. ✾ <2200. Overgrown and tangled shrubbery in light forest, forest edge, gardens, cultivation, tall grassland. ▽ 6 or more deep hollow (*pr*)*oop* notes usually decreasing in volume towards the end. **R1**

6 **Lesser Coucal** *Centropus bengalensis* (605) 33cm. Like 5 but smaller; chestnut (vs black) underwing-coverts. **Nbr** streaks on head and mantle (not shown by 5). **Juv** from 5 by brown- and buff-barred tail (vs black with narrow grey bars). ✾ <1830. Moist tall grassland, reeds, scrub. ▽ *oop, oop, oop, oop, oop ... kutook, kutook, kutook, kutook.* **R4**

7 **Brown Coucal** *Centropus andamanensis* (603) 48cm. Andamans. ✾ As 5, also dense forest, mangroves. ▽ Similar to 5. **E2**

8 **Large-tailed Nightjar** *Caprimulgus macrurus* (675, 678-9) 30cm. Large; brownish; fairly long broad tail; bold black-centred scapulars edged buff; unbroken white throat-band; rusty nuchal collar relatively indistinct; white tail-corners and wing-patches (buffy, less obvious on ♀); warmer (browner) than 12. ✾ <1800(2000). Open forest, forest edge, clearings, second growth. ▽ Resonant *chaunk* like heavy blow on hollow log at a rate of 1-2/sec. **RM2**

9 **Indian Nightjar** *Caprimulgus asiaticus* (680-1) 24cm. Like 8 & 11 but smaller; shorter wings and tail; rufous nuchal collar distinct; white throat-band broken; scapular markings smaller. White on wings and tail in both sexes. Less uniform than 14 with rusty collar; white on four (vs three) primaries; pale scapular-band bordered black. ✾ <1500. Thin scrub, young plantations, etc. ▽ *chuck chuck* (*chuck*) *chk-r-r-rrrrr*, like bouncing ping-pong ball; *chuck-chuck.* **R•2**

10 **Savanna Nightjar** *Caprimulgus affinis* (682) 25cm. Mottled, grey-brown above; darker/browner than 13, 14 & 15 but lacks bold black markings of 8, 9, 11 & 12; white throat-band usually broken. White outer tail of ♂ diagnostic (brown in ♀). ✾ <1200(2400). Open forest, lightly wooded grassland, scrubby hillsides. ▽ *chweez* or *sweesh.* **R•SP3**

11 **Jerdon's Nightjar** *Caprimulgus atripennis* (676-7) 26cm. Almost identical to 8 but smaller; shorter-tailed; a fairly distinct dark band across mantle; less heavily spotted on crown; smaller white wing-patches. Best distinguished by voice and range. ✾ <2000. Like 8. ▽ Similar to 8 but slower, more drawn-out and quavering: <1 call every 2secs. **E3**

12 **Grey Nightjar** *Caprimulgus indicus* (670-2a) 29cm. Darker, greyer than congeners; heavily marked black above; white throat-band sometimes broken. Narrow white subterminal band on outer tail of ♂ diagnostic. ♀ lacks ♂ white on wing. ✾ <3300. Clearings, scrub, teak, blue pines. ▽ Engine-like *chuk-chuk-chuk...* at 3-4/sec; *chuckoo-chuckoo-chuckoo...* (tailing off to hollow *wowowowowow*); deep hoarse *quor-quor-quor.* **R•AP3**

13 **Eurasian Nightjar** *Caprimulgus europaeus* (673) 25cm. Brownish-grey above; dark brown and buffy scapular-bands; overall darker, more boldly streaked than 14 & 15. ♂ white (♀ buffy) wing-patches and tail-corners (smaller than 8, 9 & 11). ✾ 1600-2800. Thinly vegetated hillsides. ▽ Prolonged churring, occasionally changing pitch; liquid *quoit.* **SP2**

14 **Sykes's Nightjar** *Caprimulgus mahrattensis* (674) 23cm. Like 15 but darker sandy-grey; white patches on three primaries visible in flight; ♂ has large white tail-corners (small, buffish in ♀). Broken white throat-band. ✾ <500. Semi-desert, low waterside tamarisk. ▽ Like 13 but softer, unvarying in pitch; soft *chuck-chuck* when flushed. **R•2-4**

15 **Egyptian Nightjar** *Caprimulgus aegyptius* (673a) 25cm. Palest in region; sandy without obvious streaking; buffy spots on scapulars and wing-coverts; no white in wings and tail though ♂ has buffy corners to undertail; broken white throat-band. Very pale underwing in flight; dark flight feathers on upperwing. ✾ Semi-desert. ▽ Fast *kowrr-kowrr-kowrr...* at 3-4/sec, slowing slightly at the end; guttural *tuk-l tuk-l; toc* notes interspersed with *churrs.* **B*5**

16 **Great Eared Nightjar** *Eurostopodus macrotis* (668-9) 39cm. Ear-tufts diagnostic when visible. Very large with no white on wing or tail; unbroken white band across blackish throat and upper breast; pale crown; long tail with broad dark bands. Slow sailing flight with wings in a V. ✾ <1000. Mainly broad-leaved evergreen foothill forest. ▽ Loud upslurred (metallic *kik*) *ki-wheeeeow*, usually in flight. **R(•)4**

See page 310 for nightjar tail patterns.

PLATE 46

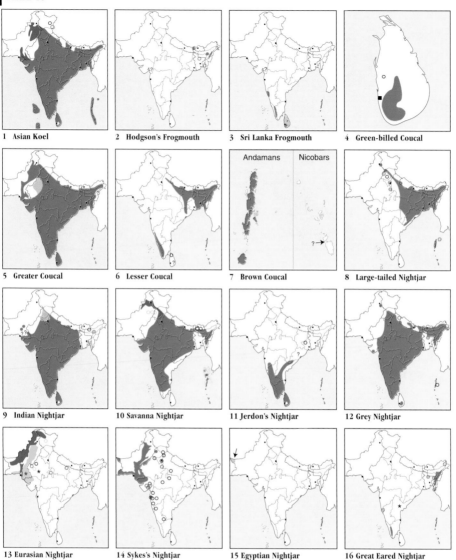

1 Asian Koel

2 Hodgson's Frogmouth

3 Sri Lanka Frogmouth

4 Green-billed Coucal

5 Greater Coucal

6 Lesser Coucal

7 Brown Coucal

8 Large-tailed Nightjar

9 Indian Nightjar

10 Savanna Nightjar

11 Jerdon's Nightjar

12 Grey Nightjar

13 Eurasian Nightjar

14 Sykes's Nightjar

15 Egyptian Nightjar

16 Great Eared Nightjar

PLATE 47

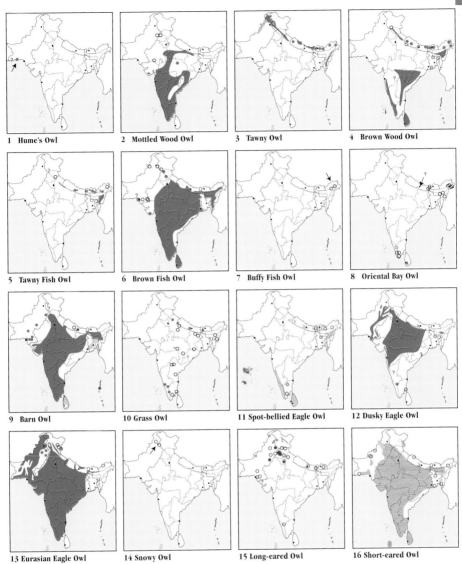

1 Hume's Owl

2 Mottled Wood Owl

3 Tawny Owl

4 Brown Wood Owl

5 Tawny Fish Owl

6 Brown Fish Owl

7 Buffy Fish Owl

8 Oriental Bay Owl

9 Barn Owl

10 Grass Owl

11 Spot-bellied Eagle Owl

12 Dusky Eagle Owl

13 Eurasian Eagle Owl

14 Snowy Owl

15 Long-eared Owl

16 Short-eared Owl

1 **Hume's Owl** *Strix butleri* (654) 36cm. Like 2, 3 & 4 but rather pale below with faint vermiculations, pale sandy-buff sides of breast, collar and facial outline, orange iris and broad dark tail banding. ✡ Stony deserts, gorges. ▽ Deep dove-like *whoooo hoo-hoh hoo-hoh*. **R*?5**

2 **Mottled Wood Owl** *Strix ocellata* (655-7) 48cm. Overall more mottled than 4 with concentric facial barring, spotted head and narrow dark streaking on vermiculated upperparts. From 3 by barring below. See also 1. ✡ Plains. Densely canopied trees in open forest, mango groves, edges of fields, gardens. ▽ Quavering *hooa-(a-a-a)*; mellow *hoot*. **E4**

3 **Tawny Owl** *Strix aluco* (661-2) 46cm. From similar 1, 2 & 4 by streaked underparts. Race *biddulphi* is shown; race *nivicola* (not illustrated) is darker, richer brown and less grey with much of the white replaced by fulvous. ✡ (600)1200-4250. Forest. ▽ Loud quavering *hoo-oo-oo...(hoo-ho-ho-hooo)*; *coo*; *kewak*. **RAW3**

4 **Brown Wood Owl** *Strix leptogrammica* (658-60) 50cm. From 1, 2 & 3 by chocolate-brown colour, face pattern with dark brown eye-patches, bold barring below and relatively uniform crown; much larger and darker than 1; not mottled like 2 and without its concentric rings on facial disk and head spotting. It has recently been suggested that Himalayan populations should be treated as a separate species Himalayan Wood Owl *Strix newarensis*. ✡ 750-2450(4000). Dense forest. ▽ (*wuh*)...*wu-whoo*; *whu whuwuwoo*; *wu úp-òo*; shrieks and chuckles. *S.(l.) newarensis* low *tu-whoo*. **R4**

5 **Tawny Fish Owl** *Ketupa flavipes* (633) 61cm. From 6 by rich rufous-buff plumage; no fine cross-bars. Larger than 7; broadly streaked with dark brown below. ✡ <1500 (2450). Wooded areas neighbouring water. Partly diurnal. ▽ Deep *whoo-hoo*; cat-like mewing. **R5**

6 **Brown Fish Owl** *Ketupa zeylonensis* (631-2) 56cm. Browner, without the rufous-buffy tones of 5 & 7 and with fine dark cross-barring on underparts. ✡ Plains and foothills (up to 1800): as 5. Semi-nocturnal. ▽ Very low *hwoum*; *hoou*. **R3**

7 **Buffy Fish Owl** *Ketupa ketupu* (633a) 50cm. Smaller than 5 & 6; buffier than 6; no fine cross bars below. From 5 by paler, warm buff (vs rich tawny) underparts with finer dark streaking (usually contrastingly broader on upper breast). ✡ Similar to 5 & 6. ▽ Monotonous *bup-bup-bup-bup-bup-bup-bup....* **V**

8 **Oriental Bay Owl** *Phodilus badius* (609-10) 29cm. Rather like 9 & 10 but flat crown with very short erectile ear-tufts, long dark vertical smudges through the eyes, rich chestnut above, vinous-tinged below. ✡ <1500. Dense evergreen hill forest. ▽ Undulating *klee hwoo hoowi hoowee hooweeoo*. **R*5**

9 **Barn Owl** *Tyto alba* (606-7) 36cm. White heart-shaped facial disc distinctive but see also 8 & 10. Races **(a)** *stertens* **(b)** *deroepstorffi* of the Andaman Is. may represent a separate species. ✡ Vicinity of human habitation and cultivation. ▽ Hisses, snorts and shrieks. **R3-4**

10 **Grass Owl** *Tyto capensis* (608) 36cm. Similar to 9 but upperparts heavily blotched with dark brown, white/pale buffy tail with narrow dark bars. Facial disk may be as shown or white. ✡ Grassland. Avoids human habitation. ▽ Similar to 9. **R5**

11 **Spot-bellied Eagle Owl** *Bubo nipalensis* (628-9) 63cm. From other large 'eared' owls by the blackish-brown, heart-shaped spots on underparts, brown eyes and yellow bill. ✡ <1800(2100). Thick forest. ▽ *hoo...hoo*; bleating *uah-uah-uah*; guttural *oo-ah-ah-ah-awa-oo*; *uah-kli-kli-kli-kli*. **R5**

12 **Dusky Eagle Owl** *Bubo coromandus* (630) 58cm. From other large 'eared' owls by greyish plumage largely without rufous or buffy tones; from fish owls by feathered tarsi; from 11 & 13 by fine dark streaks below. ✡ Lowland well-wooded areas near water and/or habitation. ▽ Booming *WO WO Wo wo-wo-wowowowuw*. **R4**

13 **Eurasian Eagle Owl** *Bubo bubo* (625-7) 56cm. Races **(a)** *turcomanus* **(b)** *bengalensis*, latter sometimes treated as a separate species under the name Rock Eagle Owl. ✡ <4500 (*bengalensis* <2400). Bare rocky areas, semi-desert, ruined forts, rocky ravines, cliffs, mature groves. ▽ Deep resonant *wu-hoo*; *bengalensis* slightly higher-pitched *wu-huoh*.. **R4**

14 **Snowy Owl** *Nyctea scandiaca* (634) 61cm. Unmistakable. ✡ Open country. Diurnal. ▽ Usually silent in winter; *grouhu*; harsh *eh-eh-eh-eh*. **V**

15 **Long-eared Owl** *Asio otus* (663) 37cm. Similar to 13 but much smaller and slimmer and without obvious cross-barring on belly. From 16 by long ear-tufts (sometimes hidden), orange eyes, black band down the face between eye and the white bordering bill, more orangy plumage, bold ('barbed') streaking on underparts, slimmer, upright stance and habitat. From 3 by orange eyes and long ear-tufts. Roosts colonially in winter. ✡ Semi-desert with low trees, woodland, plantations, tall grass. ▽ Moaning *oo...oo...oo*. **W(B*)5**

16 **Short-eared Owl** *Asio flammeus* (664) 38cm. Similar to 15 but with paler, sandier plumage, short ear-tufts (often hidden), lemon-yellow eyes surrounded by black, finer streaking (without 'barbs') on underparts and different habitat. ✡ <1400 (3320). Grassland, marsh, cultivation, scrub. Rather diurnal. ▽ Silent in winter. **WP4**

PLATE 48: SMALLER OWLS

1 **Collared Scops Owl** *Otus bakkamoena* (619-24) 23cm. Buffy hind-collar (can be hard to see), lightly streaked below (except race *plumipes*), weak scapular spots. Morphs **(a)** rufous **(b)** grey **[(c)** brown, not shown]. ⌘ <2200+. Woods. ∇ Mellow interrogative *wút* repeated every few seconds; *wúk*; *bowu* (race *lettia* of the E Himalayas and NE, which may be a separate species); chattering *ack,´ack,´ack....* **R4**

2 **Andaman Scops Owl** *Otus balli* (613) 19cm. Warm dark brown or rufous-brown with fine buffy spots on upperparts; paler and slightly greyer below with scattering of short dark streaks and diffuse pale spots; indistinct barring on greyish-brown uppertail; 4-5 white bars on primaries. ⌘ Forest; around habitation. ∇ Inflected *wuúp* similar to 1. **E*3**

3 **Pallid Scops Owl** *Otus brucei* (614) 21cm. Like grey phase 1, 5, 6 & 7 but more uniformly coloured, paler and greyer; no rufous tones; more neatly streaked black below without pale blocks of 6; lacks distinct white spots on scapulars, crown and nape of 6. ⌘ <1800. Semi-desert, stony hillsides. ∇ Low resonant metronomic *whoop*, c. 100/min; longer low *whooo* every 5-6 sec. **SM5**

4 **Nicobar Scops Owl** *Otus alius* 24cm. From 7 by larger size; finely barred above and below with little or no streaking. ⌘ Littoral forest. ∇ ♂ ?. ♀ *ooo-m; oün* – rising melancholic moan (2-2.5 sec), repeated every 3-5 sec. **E*5**

5 **Mountain Scops Owl** *Otus spilocephalus* (611-2) 19cm. Slightly smaller than other *Otus* and more-or-less unstreaked; mottled black and white on rufous-brown upperparts; brownish or rufous below with diffuse pale spots. ⌘ 600-2600. Dense evergreen forest. ∇ Metallic *poop-poop* or *plew...plew* with ¹/₂ sec between notes, repeated every 4-7 sec. **R3**

6 **Eurasian Scops Owl** *Otus scops* (615) 20cm. Like 3 but smaller, sandy-grey with dark streaks and pale rufous splashes; bolder streaks with more obvious barbs and pale horizontal blocks below, giving a more mottled impression. From 7 only safely by voice but is generally slightly paler and greyer. ⌘ 1500-3000. Rocky hillsides, juniper and holly-oak forest. ∇ *pioo*, c. 25/min. **S(M)2**

7 **Oriental Scops Owl** *Otus sunia* (616-8b) 19cm. Has rufous and grey forms. From 1 by boldly streaked underparts and no nuchal collar. From 6 by voice. Races **(a)** nom **(b)** *modestus* **(c)** *nicobaricus*. ⌘ Mainly lower elevations (1500). Forest, second growth, groves, gardens. ∇ *uk kook-krook*. Race *modestus*: tinkling *ku-turrw*. **R3**

8 **Brown Hawk Owl** *Ninox scutulata* (642-5) 32cm. Distinctive chocolate-brown head (without ear-tufts) and facial disk without spotting or barring; comparatively long, boldly-banded tail. Races **(a)** *lugubris* **(b)** *obscura* of the Andamans and Nicobars. ⌘ Wooded areas, often near water and/or habitation. ∇ *boowúp.... boowúp... boowúp...; booweb....* **R3**

9 **Andaman Hawk Owl** *Ninox affinis* (646-7) 28cm. No confusion species in range; the local race of 8 is *obscura* (largely unspotted dark brown below). ⌘ Forest clearings, second growth, mangroves. ∇ Loud, short barking *craw*. **E4**

10 **Asian Barred Owlet** *Glaucidium cuculoides* (639-41) 23cm. Lacks the contrasting wing-colour of 11; barring on upperparts more broadly spaced (i.e. dark spaces 3-4 x width of pale bars); barring on belly usually more broken, turning to streaking on lower flanks. Often waves tail from side to side. ⌘ <2700. Open forest. Quite diurnal. ∇ Rapid bubbling *wowowowowowowo...* (4-10 sec) often falling gradually in pitch but increasing in volume; also a repeated *kao-kuk* call like 11 but ending suddenly rather than trailing off. **RA2**

11 **Jungle Owlet** *Glaucidium radiatum* (636-7) 20cm. From 10 by the contrasting rusty colour of barring on primaries and secondaries; barring on upperparts narrowly spaced (i.e. dark spaces 1¹/₂-2 x width of pale bars); barring below usually extends to include flanks and belly. ⌘ Mainly lower elevations (up to 2000). Open mixed and secondary forest. Partly diurnal. ∇ *KAO KAO KAO kao-kuk (kao-kuk kaokuk kaokukkaokukaokuk...)*; single, slightly quavering *kaow*. **R2**

12 **Chestnut-backed Owlet** *Glaucidium castanonotum* (638) 19cm. From 10, 11 & 13 by chestnut wings and back. ⌘ <1950. Wet/Hill Zone forests. Quite diurnal. ∇ *prro prroo prroo-prao-prao-prao-(prao)-(prao)*. **E5**

13 **Collared Owlet** *Glaucidium brodiei* (635) 17cm. Tiny size; face-like pattern on nape; lacks 11's contrasting rufous primaries. Many birds darker than shown. ⌘ <3200. Open hill forest. Quite diurnal. ∇ *poop-papoop-poop*. **R3**

14 **Little Owl** *Athene noctua* (648-9) 23cm. Like 15 but paler; streaked (vs barred) below; white spotting in lines on crown (vs random); wings and tail with broad (vs narrow) pale barring; clearer white hind-collar. ⌘ <4600. Semi-desert, cliffs, ruined walls. Partly diurnal. ∇ Deep *pwoo* every 2-3 seconds; barking *werro; booo-oo booo-oo*. **R3**

15 **Spotted Owlet** *Athene brama* (650-2) 21cm. Most familiar owl. From 10-13 by white spotting on head. See also 14, 16 & 17. ⌘ <1530(2750). Near villages/cultivation, light forest, semi-desert. ∇ Harsh screeches and chuckles. **R1**

16 **Forest Owlet** *Heteroglaux (Athene) blewitti* (653) 23cm. From 15 by darker brown plumage, unspotted head, whiter face, distinct dark throat-band; white underparts with unbroken breast-band and broken flank barring, boldly barred tail and tertials. Wings appear boldly banded in flight. ⌘ <c. 400. Deciduous jungle, mango groves, riverine woodland. Diurnal. ∇ Sweet, medium-pitched *ou-hu*; flat buzzing *kheek; kweek...kweek*. **E*5**

17 **Boreal Owl** *Aegolius funereus* (665) 25cm. Like 15 but larger, darker brown, squarer head shape, facial disc bordered dark brown, legs and toes feathered. ⌘ Conifer forest. ∇ Fast hollow *po´po´po´po´po po-po´po*. **V**

PLATE 48

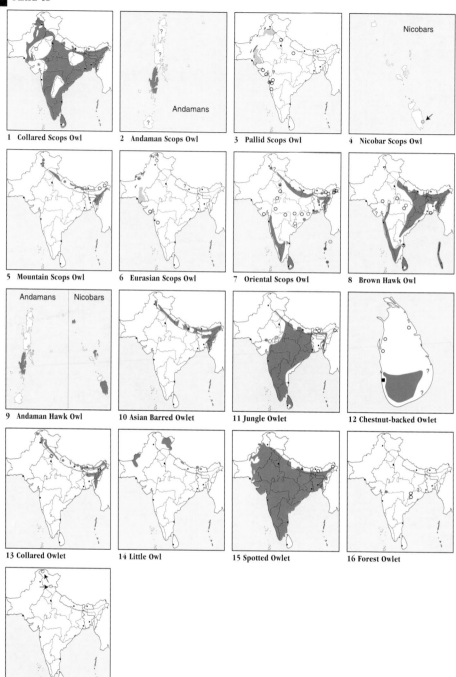

1 Collared Scops Owl

2 Andaman Scops Owl

3 Pallid Scops Owl

4 Nicobar Scops Owl

5 Mountain Scops Owl

6 Eurasian Scops Owl

7 Oriental Scops Owl

8 Brown Hawk Owl

9 Andaman Hawk Owl

10 Asian Barred Owlet

11 Jungle Owlet

12 Chestnut-backed Owlet

13 Collared Owlet

14 Little Owl

15 Spotted Owlet

16 Forest Owlet

17 Boreal Owl

PLATE 49

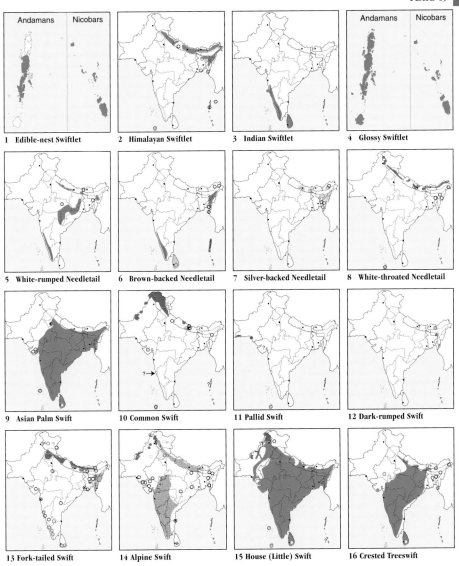

Andamans Nicobars

1 Edible-nest Swiftlet

2 Himalayan Swiftlet

3 Indian Swiftlet

4 Glossy Swiftlet

Andamans Nicobars

5 White-rumped Needletail

6 Brown-backed Needletail

7 Silver-backed Needletail

8 White-throated Needletail

9 Asian Palm Swift

10 Common Swift

11 Pallid Swift

12 Dark-rumped Swift

13 Fork-tailed Swift

14 Alpine Swift

15 House (Little) Swift

16 Crested Treeswift

161

PLATE 49: SWIFTS, SWIFTLETS, NEEDLETAILS AND TREESWIFT

1 Edible-nest Swiftlet *Collocalia fuciphaga* (686) 12cm. Doubtfully distinguishable from 2 by smaller size, shorter wings, tail usually less deeply forked (only slightly notched), slightly darker above with somewhat paler rump. Normally no overlap within our region though 2 has been recorded on the Andamans where present species is common. Unlikely to be confused with 4, the only other swiftlet within its range. ❀ Hawks over mangroves, plantations, forest and cultivation. Nest normally white, made of hardened saliva with little or no foreign matter. **R2**

2 Himalayan Swiftlet *Collocalia brevirostris* (683-4) 14cm. From 3 by rump distinctly paler than back; very similar to 1 which see. ❀ Foothills to 4580. Montane habitats, especially forested valleys. Nest combines moss and saliva. **R3**

3 Indian Swiftlet *Collocalia unicolor* (685) 12cm. Overall nondescript sooty-brown. From 1 & 2 with difficulty by rump concolorous with back or only slightly paler. Ranges disjunct. ❀ <2200. Forages chiefly over hilly and montane habitats. Whitish nest of saliva mixed with moss etc. **E3**

4 Glossy Swiftlet *Collocalia esculenta* (687) 10cm. Note small size, glossy blue-black upperparts and white belly. ❀ Forages over all island habitats including human habitation. **R1-2**

5 White-rumped Needletail *Zoonavena sylvatica* (692) 11cm. Note short rear end, conspicuous white rump, belly and vent. Much smaller than other needletails. ❀ <1700. Hawks chiefly over hill forest and clearings. **E*●3**

6 Brown-backed Needletail *Hirundapus giganteus* (691) 23cm. From 7 & 8 by brown back, paler than rest of upperparts but not white; at reasonable range the white loral spot is diagnostic. ❀ Prefers to forage in flocks over forest. **R●3**

7 Silver-backed Needletail *Hirundapus cochinchinensis* (689-90) 20cm. Contrastingly whitish back and absence of white loral spot separate from 6; throat, although paler than breast, is not strikingly white as in 8; tertial spots are buffy brown (vs white). ❀ Over forest, usually at lower altitudes than 8. **RS(?)3**

8 White-throated Needletail *Hirundapus caudacutus* (688) 20cm. Strongly contrasting, sharply demarcated white throat distinguishes from 6 & 7; if visible, the small white patch on tertials is also diagnostic; paler saddle and absence of white loral spot are additional features which separate from 6. ❀ 1250-4000. Can be seen over most montane habitats. **SR*B*3**

9 Asian Palm Swift *Cypsiurus balasiensis* (707-8) 13cm. Slim shape with long slender, often back-swept wings and very long tail (deeply forked when open, needle-like when closed); similar in build to 16 but smaller and slimmer, browner overall, often faster and lower. ❀ Mainly plains (up to 1000). Open country near palm trees. **R2**

10 Common Swift *Apus apus* (696) 17cm. Uniform dark plumage with strong tail fork and long sickle wings. The diffuse whitish throat is only noticeable at close range. See also 9, 11, 12 & 13. Birds occurring in the subcontinent are race *pekinensis*, slightly paler than nom. ❀ (Plains)1500-3800(5730?). Rugged mountains. **B*(W)1**

11 Pallid Swift *Apus pallidus* (697) 17cm. Very like 10 but paler brown; larger pale throat patch. Supporting features: paler forecrown; relatively dark eye-patch compared with rest of head; outer primaries darker than other flight feathers; slightly blunter wing-tips; at close range slight pale scalloping on the underparts. ❀ Coasts. **W*(R*?)4**

12 Dark-rumped Swift *Apus acuticauda* (698) 17cm. Distinguished from 13 by absence of white rump; from 10 by glossy black upperparts with bluish-green hue and dusky throat merging into paler breast/belly (scaly at close range). Tail longer and usually held closed. ❀ Partial to the vicinity of high cliffs (often with waterfalls). **B*(N?)4**

13 Fork-tailed Swift *Apus pacificus* (699-700) 18cm. Similar to 10, 11 & 12 but narrow white 'wrap-around' rump is diagnostic. ❀ <3700. Varied habitats. **M3** (Nomadic)

14 Alpine Swift *Tachymarptis melba* (693-5) 22cm. Note large size; brown plumage with contrasting white lower breast and upper belly; white throat and dark breast-band less obvious. ❀ <2200(3700). Chiefly forested hill country. **B*M●3**

15 House (Little) Swift *Apus affinis* (702-6) 15cm. Small size, relatively short tail not deeply forked, blackish plumage with distinctive white rump and throat. Races barely distinguishable: **(a)** *nipalensis* sometimes considered a separate species. **(b)** nom. ❀ <2000. Neighbourhood of towns, cliffs, ruins, etc. Flocks noisy in flight. **R●1**

16 Crested Treeswift *Hemiprocne coronata* (709) 23cm. Very long, slender scythe-like wings and deeply forked tail could lead to confusion with 9-13 (9 especially) but note the much longer, extremely thin tail, often held closed; bluish-grey upperparts; greyish underparts becoming paler ventrally. Crest inconspicuous in flight but distinctive when perched (plate 58, figure 16). ❀ <1280. Chiefly broadleaved hill forest. Relatively slow flight consists of much gliding interspersed with a few rapid wingbeats, often low above treetops. ∇ Squeaky chattering *ke-ke-ke-(ke)*; *kay-ko*; *ti-chuk*. **R●3**

17 [Black-nest Swiftlet *Collocalia maxima* (684a, not illustrated). 14cm. Doubtfully distinguishable from 1 & 2 except in the hand. Blackish nest of feathers mixed with dried saliva. **X** (Found in neighbouring areas of South-East Asia. Records from our region to date erroneous though could occur in the Andamans and Nicobars.)]

162

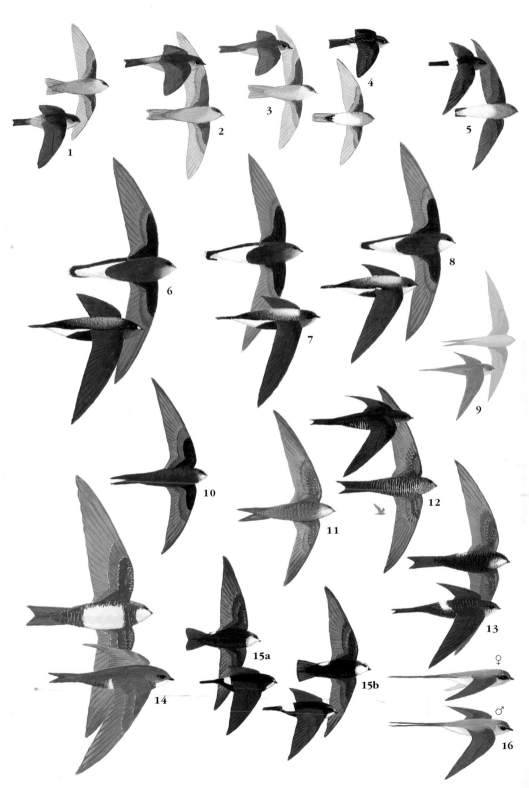

PLATE 50: ROLLERS, TROGONS AND KINGFISHERS

1 **European Roller** *Coracias garrulus* (754) 31cm. Separated from 2 by entirely pale blue head and underparts; in flight by entirely dark purple-blue flight feathers; from 2a also by (broken) dark-blue terminal band on tail. ✶ Breeding: 1700-2200(3200). Lightly wooded areas; cultivation. ∇ Harsh grating call. **BP3**

2 **Indian Roller** *Coracias benghalensis* (755-7) 31cm. Distinguished from 1 by turquoise-blue cap contrasting with remainder of head and throat; rufous-brown breast; in flight the alternating brilliant pale blue and dark blue bands in the wing are spectacularly distinctive. Races **(a)** nom **(b)** *affinis* sometimes considered separate species. ✶ <1500(3700) Open country with suitable lookout perches; light woodland. ∇ Loud, harsh *kraak*. **R•2**

3 **Dollarbird (Broad-billed Roller)** *Eurystomus orientalis* (758-62) 31cm. In flight shows a bluish-white oval patch on the primaries, said to resemble a silver dollar. ✶ <1000(2500). Tropical forest edge and clearings; cultivation. Frequently perches in exposed positions at the tops of trees. ∇ Harsh *chrack-chrack*; *chk-chk-chk-chk*. **R3**

4 **Ward's Trogon** *Harpactes wardi* (716) 40cm. Fairly distinctive but note also range. ✶ 1500-3000. Mixed broadleaved evergreen forest; bamboo. ∇ Moderately loud, slightly plaintive *kew-kew-kew-kew-kew-ke-ke-ke*; *whirr-ur*. **R5**

5 **Malabar Trogon** *Harpactes fasciatus* (710-2) 31cm. Only trogon within its range. ✶ <1800+. Tropical broadleaved forest. ∇ Measured *teuw teuw teuw* (*teuw*) (*teuw*); *kyo-kyo-kyo-*(*kyo*); *krreeu*; *krr-r-r-r*. **E3**

6 **Red-headed Trogon** *Harpactes erythrocephalus* (713-5) 35cm. ✶ <1830. Dense broadleaved evergreen forest and bamboo. ∇ *tyaup,`tyaup,`tyaup,`tyaup,`tyaup....* **R3**

7 **Crested Kingfisher** *Megaceryle lugubris* (717-8) 41cm. Separated from 8 by large size; barred upperparts; striking, shaggy black crest streaked with white. Eastern birds tend to have broken barring giving a more spotted impression. ✶ <2000(3000). Fast-flowing rivers and large streams in the mountains and adjacent plains in both open and forested areas. Frequently sits on boulders in the river. ∇ Rather silent; *kik*. **R3**

8 **Pied Kingfisher** *Ceryle rudis* (719-20) 31cm. Similar to 7 but smaller; upperparts appear blotched with black rather than barred; black band through eye with broad white supercilium above it; restricted crest. ✶ <900(1800). Standing water and slow rivers in open country. Frequently hovers. ∇ High *chirrik-chirrik*. **R2**

9 **Brown-winged Kingfisher** *Halcyon amauroptera* (729) 36cm. Differs from 10 in having dark brown wings, mantle and tail. Note restricted range and habitat. ✶ Mangroves, creeks, tidal rivers. ∇ Harsh grating call. **R*3**

10 **Stork-billed Kingfisher** *Halcyon capensis* (730-2) 38cm. Races **(a)** nom **(b)** *intermedia*. ✶ Lowland rivers, streams and lakes in well-wooded areas (up to 1200). ∇ *peew-pìu*; *ke-ke-ke-ke-KE*. **R3**

11 **Black-capped Kingfisher** *Halcyon pileata* (739) 30cm. In flight from all kingfishers except 12 by bold white wing-patch. ✶ <1000. Largely coastal; occasionally inland lakes, jheels and rivers. ∇ Shrill cackling laugh. **R•3**

12 **White-throated Kingfisher** *Halcyon smyrnensis* (735-8) 28cm. In flight from all kingfishers except 11 by bold white wing patch. ✶ <2300(3050). Wide range of open habitats; not tied to water. ∇ Loud *ke-ke-kek-kek-kek-kek* in flight; descending whinnying trill. **R•1**

13 **Ruddy Kingfisher** *Halcyon coromanda* (733-4) 26cm. **Juv** has warm brown upperparts and dark bill; could be confused with 10 but smaller; head paler warm brown not contrasting with wings (vs orange-buff and contrasting). ✶ <1800. Freshwater and brackish swamp forest; evergreen forest with streams and pools; mangroves. Very shy. ∇ 4-5 descending whistles; *quirrr-r-r-r-r*. **R•(M?)5**

14 **Collared Kingfisher** *Todiramphus chloris* (740-3) 24cm. Races **(a)** *humii* **(b)** *occipitalis*. ✶ Coastal: creeks, mudflats, mangroves etc. ∇ *krerk-krerk-krerk-krerk*. **R3-4**

15 **Common Kingfisher** *Alcedo atthis* (722-4) 17cm. Races **(a)** *benghalensis* **(b)** *taprobana*. ✶ <1850(3100). Wide variety of waterbodies; generally in more open habitats than those of the rare 16 & 17. ∇ Piping *chee*; *chichee*. **RM1**

16 **Blyth's Kingfisher** *Alcedo hercules* (721) 22cm. Much larger, darker version of 15 with deeper rufous underparts; ear-coverts concolorous with crown (vs rufous); heavier crown spotting. From 17 by size and dark greenish-blue plumage. Note range. ♀ distinguished from ♂ by red lower mandible with dusky base. ✶ <1200. Usually prefers undisturbed, steep-sided, shady streams and rivers through dense forest. ∇ Similar to 15 but louder and deeper. **R*5**

17 **Blue-eared Kingfisher** *Alcedo meninting* (725-6a) 16cm. From 15 by blue ear-coverts; darker, more intense cobalt-blue upperparts and richer rufous underparts. Beware **juv** which has rufous ear-coverts like 15 but usually shows some mottling on the throat and upper breast, a feature not normally present in the latter. See also 16. ✶ <1000(1500). Pools and streams in dense evergreen forest. ∇ Piping *chee*, higher and shorter than 15. **R5**

18 **Oriental Dwarf Kingfisher** *Ceyx erithacus* (727-8) 13cm. Races **(a)** nom **(b)** *rufidorsus*. ✶ <1000. Usually near small shady streams and pools in hill forest. Low to mid-storey. ∇ Like 17 but shriller. **R•(M?)5**

PLATE 50

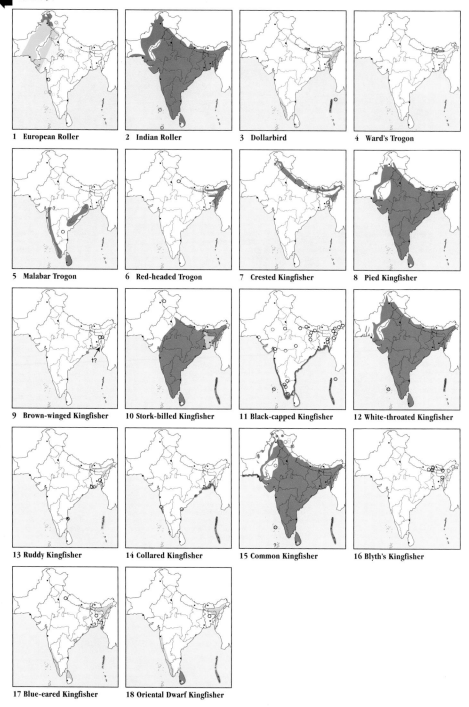

1   European Roller
2   Indian Roller
3   Dollarbird
4   Ward's Trogon

5   Malabar Trogon
6   Red-headed Trogon
7   Crested Kingfisher
8   Pied Kingfisher

9   Brown-winged Kingfisher
10 Stork-billed Kingfisher
11 Black-capped Kingfisher
12 White-throated Kingfisher

13 Ruddy Kingfisher
14 Collared Kingfisher
15 Common Kingfisher
16 Blyth's Kingfisher

17 Blue-eared Kingfisher
18 Oriental Dwarf Kingfisher

PLATE 51

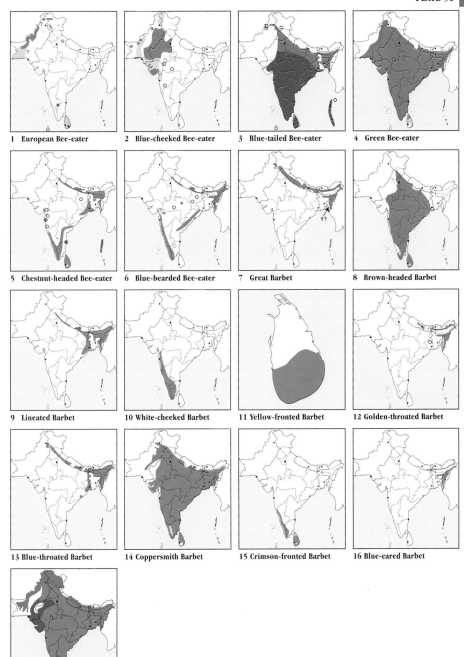

1 European Bee-eater 2 Blue-cheeked Bee-eater 3 Blue-tailed Bee-eater 4 Green Bee-eater

5 Chestnut-headed Bee-eater 6 Blue-bearded Bee-eater 7 Great Barbet 8 Brown-headed Barbet

9 Lineated Barbet 10 White-cheeked Barbet 11 Yellow-fronted Barbet 12 Golden-throated Barbet

13 Blue-throated Barbet 14 Coppersmith Barbet 15 Crimson-fronted Barbet 16 Blue-eared Barbet

17 Common Hoopoe

PLATE 51: BEE-EATERS, BARBETS AND HOOPOE

1 **European Bee-eater** *Merops apiaster* (746) 27cm. Distinguished by its vivid, contrasting melange of colours. ✴ <2100. Open country. ∇ Liquid trilling *prreep*, deeper than 4. **BP2**

2 **Blue-cheeked Bee-eater** *Merops persicus* (747) 31cm. From 3 by blue supercilium, green tail and rump. From 4 by larger size, green crown, yellow chin and chestnut throat. ✴ Chiefly plains. Vicinity of lakes, jheels and sandy shores. ∇ Liquid trilling *prrreew* louder and deeper than 4, but higher than 1. **SP2**

3 **Blue-tailed Bee-eater** *Merops philippinus* (748) 31cm. From 2 by blue tail and rump, absence of blue supercilium. From 4 by larger size, blue tail and rump, green crown, yellow chin and chestnut throat. ✴ Chiefly lowland (up to 1530). As 2, but often near wooded areas. ∇ Like 2; *pewp*. **MR•3**

4 **Green Bee-eater** *Merops orientalis* (749-52) 21cm. The most familiar and widespread bee-eater. Small size, largely green plumage, head washed with coppery tinge and pale greenish-blue throat. Races **(a)** *ferrugeiceps* **(b)** *beludschicus*. More richly coloured races could be confused with 5 but separable by blue throat and cheeks; elongated central tail feathers; usually in more open habitat. ✴ <2140. Open country, semi-desert. ∇ Liquid *trri-trri*. **R•M1**

5 **Chestnut-headed Bee-eater** *Merops leschenaulti* (744-5) 21cm. The rich chestnut cap distinguishes from all bee-eaters except 1 which is larger, bluer below, golden-yellow on scapulars and rump; and has elongated central tail feathers. ✴ <1500. Broadleaved forest, often near water. ∇ Similar to 2 & 3; *perrip perrip*. **R•3**

6 **Blue-bearded Bee-eater** *Nyctyornis athertoni* (753) 36cm. Bulkier and longer-billed than other bee-eaters. Dark blue forecrown, throat and breast are diagnostic. Tail lacks projections. ✴ <1980. Moist broadleaved forest, second growth, riverine forest, clearings. Less active than other bee-eaters. ∇ Deep *kor-r-r, kor-r-r...kawkarra-kow-kowk-ko-ko-ko*. **R*4**

7 **Great Barbet** *Megalaima virens* (777) 33cm. Large size and navy-blue head distinctive. ✴ **S** 1000-3000. **W** >foothills. Moist temperate forest. ∇ Loud, far-carrying, monotonously repeated *pee-lioo* or *kow-(oo)*; harsh *kyarr-r*; *kräe-äeb*. **A2**

8 **Brown-headed Barbet** *Megalaima zeylanica* (780-2) 27cm. From 9 or 10 by the brown head with thin pale streaks, large bare orange eye-patch and lack of white cheek-patch. ✴ <800(1500). Well-wooded areas, parks, gardens. ∇ (*KURR-R-R-RRR kurrub)...kuteroo...kuteroo...kuteroo...*; repeated *kutroo*; *kuk-uk-uk-(uk)*. **E2**

9 **Lineated Barbet** *Megalaima lineata* (783-4) 28cm. Similar to 8 & 10 but head and breast covered in broad pale streaks, large bare yellow eye-patch and lack of white cheek-patch. ✴ <1000. Moist broadleaved forest, open woodland, parks, gardens. ∇ Repeated *kurók*; *pukró*. **R2**

10 **White-cheeked Barbet** *Megalaima viridis* (785) 23cm. Short white supercilium and cheek-patch diagnostic; lacks the bare orange/yellow eye-patch of 8 & 9. ✴ <1800(2300). Wooded areas, parks, gardens. ∇ (*prrr-rrr* followed by) repeated *pucack* or *pukrak*, similar to 8 but higher-pitched. **E2**

11 **Yellow-fronted Barbet** *Megalaima flavifrons* (786) 21cm. Yellow forecrown diagnostic. ✴ <2000. Forest and well-wooded areas. ∇ (Rolling, ascending *kowowowowowo* followed by) repeated *kweear* or *puquiroo*. **E2**

12 **Golden-throated Barbet** *Megalaima franklinii* (787) 23cm. Yellow throat distinguishes from all but 14 & 15a which have crimson breast-patch and yellow cheeks. ✴ (600)1500-2400. Hill forest. ∇ (Rolling *krrr-krrr* followed by) monotonous repeated *pukuo* or *pukweo* or *puk-wowk*. **R3**

13 **Blue-throated Barbet** *Megalaima asiatica* (788) 23cm. Blue throat and cheeks separate this from all but the allopatric 11, and 16 which lacks red on crown. ✴ <1500(2000). Wooded areas. ∇ Repeated *kutoorrook* or *kutoororok*. **R2**

14 **Coppersmith Barbet** *Megalaima haemacephala* (792) 17cm. Most widespread and common barbet; distinctive head pattern. Main confusion species is 15a which has blue on sides of head and lacks streaking on underparts. ✴ <2000. Open woodland, parks, gardens. ∇ Resonant mechanical *tok...tok...tok...*like 15b but at a slower rate. **R1**

15 **Crimson-fronted Barbet** *Megalaima rubricapilla* (790-1) 17cm. The two races may be split in future: **(a)** nom is distinguished from 14 by blue on sides of head and unstreaked green breast and belly. **(b)** *malabarica* is the only barbet with a strikingly red face. ✴ **(a)** <1300. Open wooded country including parks and gardens. **(b)** <1200. Broadleaved evergreen forest. ∇ **(a)** measured *whot whot whot whot*; rapid high *poop-oop-oop-oop-(oop)-(oop)*; **(b)** Resonant, long-repeated *tok...tok...tok...*similar to 14 but at a faster tempo. **E2**

16 **Blue-eared Barbet** *Megalaima australis* (789) 17cm. Blue throat and sides of neck separate from all but 11 & 13 which lack the black forecrown. ✴ <1200. Thick broadleaved evergreen forest. ∇ Repeated *koo-turr*. **R4**

17 **Common Hoopoe** *Upupa epops* (763-6) 31cm. Unmistakable. ✴ <4600(5000). Open country, light woodland, parks, cultivation. ∇ Usually three hollow notes *oop-oop-oop*. **RBW2**

168

PLATE 52: HORNBILLS

1 **Indian Grey Hornbill** *Ocyceros birostris* (767) 61cm. Very like 2 but with a casque and a fairly extensive area of black on basal half of bill. ⌘ <1000(1400). Well-wooded open areas, parks, gardens, groves. ∇ Squealing *wheeee*; *kew*; *k-k-k-ka-e*. **E•3**

2 **Malabar Grey Hornbill** *Ocyceros griseus* (768) 59cm. Very like 1 but has no casque; basal half of bill reddish in ♂, only showing a small patch of black in ♀. Beware of juv 1 which also lacks casque but has a completely yellow bill and no white tips to the wings. ⌘ < 1600. Moist open broadleaved forest. ∇ Loud squeaky laughing *quah...quah...quah.....ka-ka-kakakaka*; *kyaeh*. **E3**

3 **Sri Lanka Grey Hornbill** *Ocyceros gingalensis* (769) 59cm. Unlikely to be confused with 9, the only other hornbill in Sri Lanka. Note that outer tail feathers become entirely white in old birds. ⌘ <1200. Forest, woodland, well-wooded gardens. Usually in pairs or small flocks. ∇ Loud, far-carrying, goat-like *kweaeh*; laughing *kwaa...kwaa...(kwa)..ka ka ka ka*...**E3**

4 **Brown Hornbill** *Anorrhinus tickelli* (770) 76cm. Separated from 1, 2 & 3 by dark brown upperparts and brownish-rufous breast and belly (note also range); from 5, 6, 7 & 8 by largely brown tail with only tips of all but central rectrices white and absence of contrastingly coloured gular pouch, among other features. ⌘ <1000. Primary broadleaved evergreen forest. ∇ Croaks, chuckles and squeals. **R4-5**

5 **[Plain-pouched Hornbill** *Aceros subruficollis* 90cm. Very similar to 7 but smaller; plain pouch without black line; base of bill lacking ridges. Beware of juv 7 which also lacks ridges on the bill and only has faint dark bars on the pouch. **X** (Record from NE India apparently erroneous but the species occurs in Myanmar.)**]**

6 **Rufous-necked Hornbill** *Aceros nipalensis* (771) 122cm. Only hornbill with white distal half to black tail. ♂ is distinctive with its rufous head, neck and breast. ♀ lacks the corrugated casque and black bar on gular pouch of ♀7 and has blue (vs orange) facial skin. ⌘ <1800. Primary broadleaved evergreen forest. ∇ Deep barking *bok* or *wouk* – at a distance similar to the sound of an axe hitting a tree. **R4**

7 **Wreathed Hornbill** *Aceros undulatus* (772) 110cm. The wholly white tail distinguishes this from all except the extralimital 5 and the allopatric 8; from 5 by colour of gular pouch and ♂ white sides to head and neck; from 8 by black bar on gular pouch and corrugations on base of bill. Separated from 6 by corrugated casque and orange facial skin. ⌘ <2400. Primary broadleaved evergreen forest. ∇ Harsh *kuk-kwehk*; noisy flight. **R3**

8 **Narcondam Hornbill** *Aceros narcondami* (773) 66cm. Endemic to Narcondam Island where it is the only hornbill. ⌘ High forest. ∇ *ka-ka-ka-ka*; *kok-kok-kok kokkok*. **E2**

9 **Malabar Pied Hornbill** *Anthracoceros coronatus* (775) 92cm. Separated from 10 by white on tail being restricted to tips of outer tail feathers; white throat-patch often tinged pink; convex shape to the casque when viewed from the front; different pattern of black on the bill and casque. ⌘ Mainly lowlands (up to 1200). Open broadleaved forests, forest edge, groves of mangoes and figs. ∇ *kleng-keng, kyek-kek kek-kek*; *kak-kak, kak-kak*; loud whistle. **E•4**

10 **Oriental Pied Hornbill** *Anthracoceros albirostris* (774) 89cm. Distinguished from 9 by wholly white outer tail feathers; bluish gular skin; flat sides of the casque when viewed from the front; different pattern of black on the bill and casque. ⌘ < foothills. Similar to 9. ∇ Similar squealing, cackling and yelping to 9 but higher-pitched and more modulated; loud squeaky *que-que-quequequeque*. **R•3**

11 **Great Hornbill** *Buceros bicornis* (776) 130cm. Largest hornbill of the region. The white tail with a broad black band across it is diagnostic, as is the white (or yellow) band through the black wings. The (yellowish-) white neck also helps distinguish it from 9 & 10. The white parts of the plumage often become stained yellow with oil from the bird's preen gland. ⌘ <2000. Primary broadleaved evergreen and moist deciduous forest. ∇ Deep rasping *wrouff(a)*; *hurrwah*; loud deep *trek*; *gok*; deep hoarse grunts; barks. **R•4**

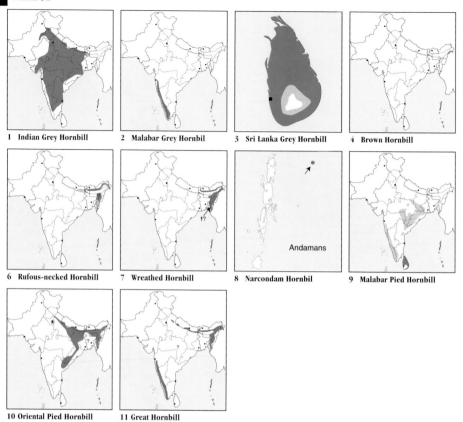

PLATE 52

1 Indian Grey Hornbill

2 Malabar Grey Hornbil

3 Sri Lanka Grey Hornbill

4 Brown Hornbill

6 Rufous-necked Hornbill

7 Wreathed Hornbill

8 Narcondam Hornbil

Andamans

9 Malabar Pied Hornbill

10 Oriental Pied Hornbill

11 Great Hornbill

PLATE 53

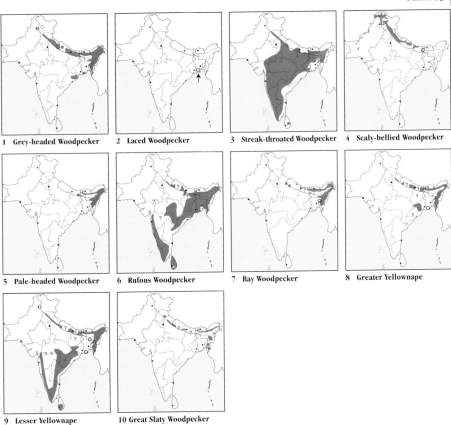

1 Grey-headed Woodpecker   2 Laced Woodpecker   3 Streak-throated Woodpecker   4 Scaly-bellied Woodpecker

5 Pale-headed Woodpecker   6 Rufous Woodpecker   7 Bay Woodpecker   8 Greater Yellownape

9 Lesser Yellownape   10 Great Slaty Woodpecker

PLATE 53: 'GREEN', PALE-HEADED, RUFOUS, BAY AND SLATY WOODPECKERS

1 **Grey-headed Woodpecker** *Picus canus* (809-11) 32cm. Grey sides of head; no scaling on green underparts. ⌘ <2000 (3500). Moist subtropical and temperate forest; open country in the vicinity of forest. ∇ *kik*; *pew-pew-pew-pew-pew*. **R3**

2 **Laced Woodpecker** *Picus vittatus* 30cm. Sides of neck, throat and upper breast unscaled buffy-yellow or yellowish-green; rest of underparts scaly; bolder moustachial stripe than 3; dark eye. ⌘ <1500. Evergreen and deciduous forest, mangroves, second growth, scrub and gardens. ∇ *keep*, *kweep* or *kee-ip*. **V** Single record from Bangladesh.

3 **Streak-throated Woodpecker** *Picus xanthopygaeus* (808) 29cm. Smaller than 4; dark scalloping on underparts becomes thinner on upper breast and continues as streaking all the way up the throat and chin; moustachial stripe ill-defined; bill appears dark overall with only the basal three-quarters of the lower mandible yellowish. ⌘ <900(1800). Semi-evergreen, moist-deciduous, bamboo, teak and sal forest, second growth and rubber plantations. ∇ Generally not very vocal; short *queemp*; *kip*. **R3**

4 **Scaly-bellied Woodpecker** *Picus squamatus* (806-7) 35cm. Larger than 3; dark scalloping on underparts extends from lower breast downwards; bolder moustachial stripe; longer overall pale bill with only the basal two-thirds of upper mandible dusky horn; montane habitat. Only green woodpecker with barred secondaries and tertials. ⌘ 1000-3300 moving down from the higher altitudes in winter. Open evergreen, mixed oak, juniper, poplar and pine forest, orchards. ∇ High-pitched *kik*; ringing (*kee*)-(*kee*)-*kee-oh* or *pea-cock*; nasal *cheenk* or *peer*. **R3**

5 **Pale-headed Woodpecker** *Gecinulus grantia* (827) 25cm. Distinctive combination of reddish upperparts and pale green head. ⌘ <1000. Moist-deciduous forest, second growth and scrub jungle. Usually found in bamboo. ∇ When agitated a chittering *kereke-kereke-kereke...* similar to treepie; a four or five note, accelerating nasal *chaik-chaik-chaik-chaik* descending in pitch. **R4**

6 **Rufous Woodpecker** *Celeus brachyurus* (802-4) 25cm. Not unlike 7 but note smaller size, small black bill. No red on nape but red patch beneath eye on ♂. ⌘ <700(1500). Moist-deciduous and sal forest, scrub and secondary growth with bamboo. Excavates its nest hollow in the active spherical nests of tree ants. ∇ Fast, high-pitched nasal *quean-quean-quean*; *ki-ki-ki-ki-ki-ki-keerr*; *whi-chee whi-chee...*. **R3**

7 **Bay Woodpecker** *Blythipicus pyrrhotis* (857) 27cm. Larger than 6 with longer pale bill. Large red nape-patch on ♂. Usually prefers higher altitudes than 6. ⌘ 1500-2500. Sometimes lower down to plains level. Dense primary forest and adjacent secondary growth with bamboo. ∇ Chittering *kikkakarikkakarik...*; four or five *chake* notes accelerating but becoming softer towards the end; when disturbed a chattering *kerere-kerere-kerere...*. **R3**

8 **Greater Yellownape** *Picus flavinucha* (812-3) 33cm. Yellow nuchal crest; no red in plumage; streaked upper breast; no barring on underparts; folded primaries chestnut barred with black. Chin and throat yellow on ♂, chestnut on ♀. ⌘ 300-1500(0-2750). Mixed evergreen, deciduous, pine, sal, teak and secondary forest. ∇ Fairly loud plaintive *pee-u* or *kyew*; metallic *chenk*; variety of *keep* notes; accelerating *kwee- kwee- kwee- kwee- kwee- kwee- kwee- kwee-kwi-kwi-kwi-kwi-wi-wi-wi-wik*. **R3**

9 **Lesser Yellownape** *Picus chlorolophus* (814-7) 27cm. Yellow nuchal crest; red markings on head; barred or spotted underparts; folded primaries unbarred or with faint pale barring. Races (**a**) nom distinguished from 8 by white moustachial stripe (**b**) *chlorigaster*. Not all races shown. ⌘ <2100. Mixed deciduous, evergreen and secondary jungle; teak, bamboo, rubber and coffee plantations. ∇ Loud plaintive nasal *pee-a*; *kiyew ke-ke-ke*. **R3**

10 **Great Slaty Woodpecker** *Mulleripicus pulverulentus* (828-9) 51cm. Unmistakable. The largest woodpecker of the region. Usually met with in pairs or parties of up to six or more birds. Quite obvious and boisterous. Rather noisy flight. ⌘ <600(2000). Scarce resident of primary forest, mature sal and teak plantations in the terai and foothills of the Himalaya. Also affects more open woodland if there are sufficient tall mature trees. ∇ Loud whinnying *whi-whi-whi-woo*; *woikwoikwoik woik*, first note higher in pitch, last note lower; *kwek-kwek*; *dwot*; *dew-it*. **R4**

174

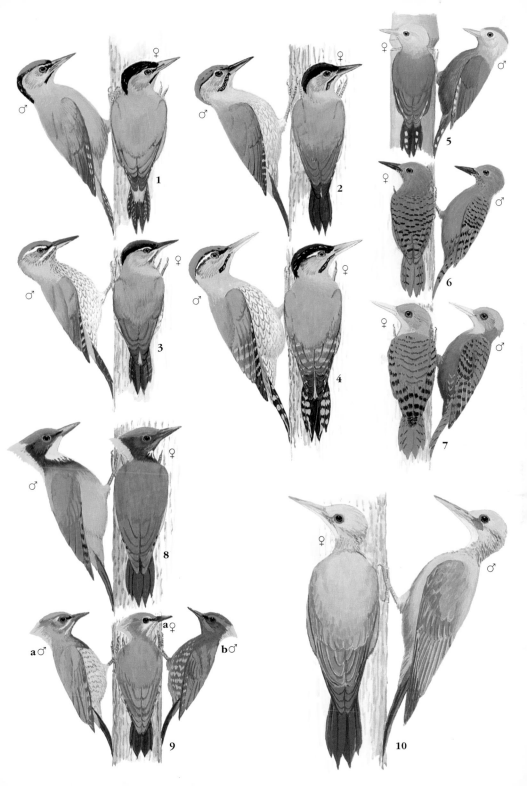

1 **Black-rumped Flameback** *Dinopium benghalense* (818-23) 29cm. White spotting on black throat, white spots on shoulders and white barring on folded black primaries separate this species from the other flamebacks. The black rump distinguishes from all but 5 but is often difficult to see on a perched individual. Has four toes. On ♀ forecrown is black streaked with white, hindcrown is red. The commonest flameback in most of the subcontinent. Race *psarodes* (**a**) of Sri Lanka south of a line from Puttalam to Trincomalee. ⌘ <1700. All types of woodland but avoiding denser forest. ∇ A rattling, trilling or laughing *kyi kyi kyi-kyi-kyikyiirrrr-r-r-r*, similar to call of White-throated Kingfisher 50.12 but tinnier; single *kierk*; in flight a scream. The 'rattling' or 'laughing' calls of all the flamebacks are similar but can be told apart with practice. **N1**

2 **Common Flameback** *Dinopium javanense* (825-6) 28cm. The single, undivided black moustachial stripe distinguishes this from other flamebacks. Note also small bill; red rump; solid black hindneck and upper mantle; unspotted golden shoulders. Only has three toes, but this feature is not often useful in the field. Crown and crest of ♀ streaked with white. In spite of its English name it is not very common in the Indian subcontinent, being restricted to the Western Ghats and parts of Bangladesh and north-east India. ⌘ <2300. Mainly lower-altitude moist-deciduous and evergreen forest. Prefers moister habitat than 1. ∇ Like 1 but higher-pitched. **R4**

3 **Himalayan Flameback** *Dinopium shorii* (824) 31cm. Separated from other similar species by combination of split black moustachial stripe (centred brownish, sometimes tinged faintly pink) and unspotted black hindneck and upper mantle. Has red rump and only three toes. Crown of ♀ black streaked with white. ⌘ <1200. Mature semi-evergreen and deciduous forest, chiefly in the lowlands and foothills. ∇ Rattling *ki-ki-ki-ki-(ki)-(ki)-(ki)*, slower and softer than 4. **N3**

4 **Greater Flameback** *Chrysocolaptes lucidus* (860-3) 33cm. Golden-backed races identified by combination of split black moustachial stripe together with white patch on black hindneck and white spotting on upper mantle. Note also large bill; red rump; four toes. **Ad** is only flameback with pale (creamy-white or lemon-yellow) eyes. Crown of ♀ with round white spots rather than streaks. Race *stricklandi* (**a**) of Sri Lanka. ⌘ <2100. Open evergreen, semi-evergreen and moist-deciduous forest, secondary forest, older plantations. ∇ Rattling *ki-ki-ki-ki-ki-ki*, weaker and higher-pitched than 1. **R3**

5 **White-naped Woodpecker** *Chrysocolaptes festivus* (858-9) 29cm. Large white area on hindneck, mantle and upper back surrounded by black identifies this species. Note also black rump, split moustachial and four toes. The ♀ is the only flameback with a yellow crown. ⌘ <1000. Widespread but not common in lowland open deciduous forest as well as scrub and cultivation with scattered trees. ∇ Similar to 4 but weaker. **E3-4**

6 **White-bellied Woodpecker** *Dryocopus javensis* (830) 48cm. ⌘ <1200. Mature evergreen and moist-deciduous forest. Sensitive to disturbance and hence declining in many areas. Flies strongly like a crow. ∇ Loud emphatic *kweb*; *quweh*. **R4**

7 **Andaman Woodpecker** *Dryocopus hodgei* (831) 38cm. Treated by some authors as race of 6 but is much smaller, has no white in plumage and different voice. Only black woodpecker in its range. ⌘ Tropical evergreen forest, where it seems to prefer more open areas and forest edge. Sometimes found in adjacent mangroves. ∇ *quweeh* higher-pitched than 6; *kuk-kuk-kuk kui*. **E3**

8 **[Black Woodpecker** *Dryocopus martius* (831a). 46cm. Unlikely to occur within the range of 6 or 7, but note pale bill, absence of crest, and in ♂ the lack of red moustache; lacks white belly of 6. ⌘ Mature forest. ∇ When perched a far-carrying *kleeoo*; in flight a *kree-kree-kree-kree-kree*. **X** (Possible sighting from Jaldapara, northern West Bengal but no definite records. Found in Tsangpo Valley of Tibet, so could occur in adjacent Arunachal Pradesh.)]

9 **Heart-spotted Woodpecker** *Hemicircus canente* (856) 16cm. Fairly unmistakable within the subcontinent. ⌘ <1300. Humid forest, bamboo, teak and coffee plantations. Peculiar rounded tailless appearance in flight. Frequently perches sideways on branches like a passerine. Often accompanies bird waves hunting through the forest. ∇ Repeated *kirrik*; high-pitched tittering *(twi)-(twi)-titititititi...* often in duet; *chi-wheew*. Rarely drums. **R3**

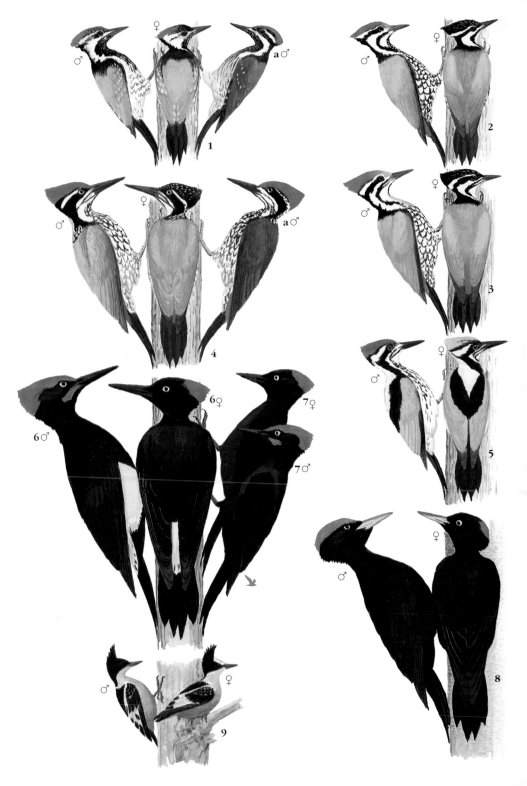

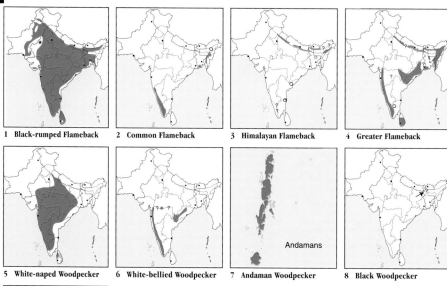

1 Black-rumped Flameback   2 Common Flameback   3 Himalayan Flameback   4 Greater Flameback

5 White-naped Woodpecker   6 White-bellied Woodpecker   7 Andaman Woodpecker   8 Black Woodpecker

9 Heart-spotted Woodpecker

Andamans

PLATE 54

PLATE 55

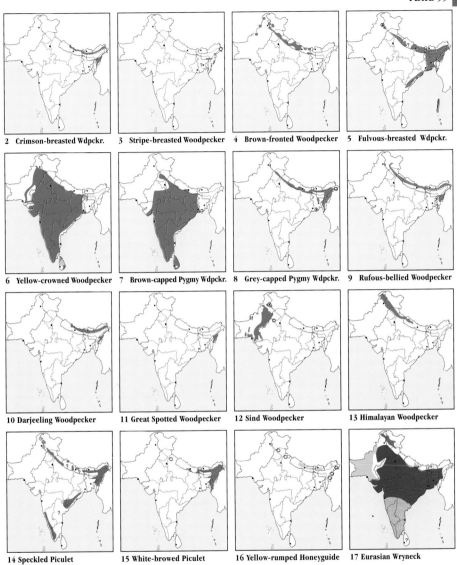

2 Crimson-breasted Wdpckr.

3 Stripe-breasted Woodpecker

4 Brown-fronted Woodpecker

5 Fulvous-breasted Wdpckr.

6 Yellow-crowned Woodpecker

7 Brown-capped Pygmy Wdpckr.

8 Grey-capped Pygmy Wdpckr.

9 Rufous-bellied Woodpecker

10 Darjeeling Woodpecker

11 Great Spotted Woodpecker

12 Sind Woodpecker

13 Himalayan Woodpecker

14 Speckled Piculet

15 White-browed Piculet

16 Yellow-rumped Honeyguide

17 Eurasian Wryneck

179

1 **[Three-toed Woodpecker** *Picoides tridactylus* (855) 23cm. **Juv** duller and browner. ⌘ 3000-3800. Coniferous and deciduous forest. ▽ Quiet *kip*; harsh *krrre*. **X** (Could occur in Arunachal Pradesh.)]

2 **Crimson-breasted Woodpecker** *Dendrocopos cathpharius* (840-1) 18cm. Fulvous heavily streaked below, usually red patch on breast; back unbarred. Like 10 but no yellow on neck. **Juv** darker/duller below with little/no red; orange-red hindcrown/nape, less on ♀. ⌘ 1800-3000. Moist montane forest. ▽ Loud *chip*, higher than 10; *ki-ki-ki-....* . **R3**

3 **Stripe-breasted Woodpecker** *Dendrocopos atratus* (844) 21cm. Similar to 5 but whitish sides of head and neck, more boldly streaked below. **Juv** duller with some red-tipped feathers on crown of ♀. ⌘ 800-2000. Pine and oak forest. ▽ Loud *chick*; whinnying and squeaking calls. **R4**

4 **Brown-fronted Woodpecker** *Dendrocopos auriceps* (842-3) 20cm. Like 6 but forehead brown, back barred (vs spotted); black moustache (vs brown sides of neck); montane habitat. **Juv** duller. ⌘ 1000-3100. Pine, oak, deodar forest. ▽ *pick*, squeakier than 13; *cheek-cheek-cheek -rrrr*; soft *tu-twit*. **NA2**

5 **Fulvous-breasted Woodpecker** *Dendrocopos macei* (845-6) 19cm. Similar to 3 but fulvous sides of head and neck, faint streaking below. In east, where range overlaps 3, usually at lower elevations. **Juv** duller with pink vent. Races **(a)** nom **(b)** *andamanensis* in Andamans. ⌘ <2000(2800). Open forest, woodland. ▽ *chick*, softer than 3. **R2**

6 **Yellow-crowned Woodpecker** *Dendrocopos mahrattensis* (847) 18cm. Back spotted with white. Upperparts browner than 4, facial markings more diffuse, forehead and crown yellow. **Juv** duller, pinker belly and some orange-red on crown. ⌘ <1000(1700). Mainly lowland; dry open woodland and scrub including semi-desert, parks, gardens and riverine habitats. Avoids dense forest. ▽ Weak *peek*; *tiririk*; *kik-kik-kik-r-r-r-r-b*. **N2**

7 **Brown-capped Pygmy Woodpecker** *Dendrocopos nanus* (851-4) 13cm. Like 8 but smaller; upperparts brown; brown crown; indistinct brownish streaks below; white bar-like spots on central tail feathers; pinkish-red eye-ring; iris usually pale. ♂ red at side of hindcrown usually obscured. **Juv** duller with orange-red on nape of ♂. ⌘ <1200. Lowland secondary growth, open woodland, gardens, mangroves, coastal scrub. ▽ Weak *clickr-r-r*; *kik kik kikikikiki*; *ti-ti-ti-ti-ti-ti*. **E2**

8 **Grey-capped Pygmy Woodpecker** *Dendrocopos canicapillus* (848-50) 14cm. Like 7 but larger; grey crown; dark (almost black) above; distinct streaks below; plain central tail; no red orbital ring; iris dark. **Juv** darker; blackish crown, heavier streaks below; orange-red nape on ♂. Races **(a)** *semicoronatus* from Murree into Nepal, **(b)** *mitchellii* E Nepal eastwards. ⌘ <1700. Open forest, gardens, etc. ▽ Soft *pick*; *pirrrrirrrri*; *tit-tit-errrrrr*. **R3**

9 **Rufous-bellied Woodpecker** *Dendrocopos hyperythrus* (832-3) 20cm. Rufous underparts. **Juv** has heavily streaked throat, barred underparts, pink vent, more spotted upperparts, brownish-black wings. ⌘ 800-4100. Subtropical pine and moist temperate forest. ▽ *chit-chit-chit-r-r-r-r-b*; *ptikitititit*. **R3**

10 **Darjeeling Woodpecker** *Dendrocopos darjellensis* (838-9) 25cm. Similar to 2 but larger, longer-billed, sides of neck yellow in both sexes and no indication of red on breast. **Juv** duller, with streaked throat but without yellow on sides of neck. ⌘ 1700-treeline. Deciduous, coniferous, oak and rhododendron forest. ▽ *tsik*. **R3**

11 **Great Spotted Woodpecker** *Dendrocopos major* (834) 24cm. Like 13 but facial markings meet black of nape; on ♂ red only on nape. **Juv** has red crown, pink vent. ⌘ 2000-3000. Oak, pine and subtropical forest. ▽ Sharp *kek*. **R*5**

12 **Sind Woodpecker** *Dendrocopos assimilis* (835) 22cm. Like 13 and 11 but ranges do not overlap; black line on face meets black of upper back but not across to nape. Whiter than 13 below. **Juv** duller; pink vent; some red on crown. ⌘ <1000 (2000). Dry scrub jungle. ▽ Weak *chir-rir-rirrh-rirrh*; *toi-whit toi-whit toi-whit*. **N3**

13 **Himalayan Woodpecker** *Dendrocopos himalayensis* (836-7) 25cm. Not unlike 11 but facial markings extend up behind ear-coverts but not down to black of back; ♂ has entire crown red. **Juv** duller, browner; white spotting on forecrown; orange-red on centre of crown; pink vent. Races **(a)** nom **(b)** *albescens*. ⌘ 1500-treeline. Montane oak, rhododendron and coniferous forest. ▽ *kit*, typical of most of genus. **NA2**

14 **Speckled Piculet** *Picumnus innominatus* (798-9) 10cm. Smaller than sparrow. ⌘ <2000(3000). Moist deciduous and semi-evergreen forest, often with bamboo. ▽ Sharp *tsit*; squeaky *pseep-pseep-pseep-pseep*; *ti-ti-ti-ti-ti*. **R3**

15 **White-browed Piculet** *Sasia ochracea* (800-1) 9cm. Smaller than sparrow. Races **(a)** *reichenowi* **(b)** nom. ⌘ <2100. Forest and secondary scrub. Partial to bamboo. ▽ *tsick*; high-pitched trilling *ti-i-i-i-i-i*. **R4**

16 **Yellow-rumped Honeyguide** *Indicator xanthonotus* (793-5) 15cm. Note orange-yellow forehead, malar area and rump (less on ♀). ⌘ 1500-3500. Vicinity of cliffs with honeycombs of rock bees in broadleaved and coniferous forest. ▽ *tzt*; *weet*. **N*A4**

17 **Eurasian Wryneck** *Jynx torquilla* (796) 19cm. ⌘ **S** 1500-3300. Orchards, light mixed forest. **W** Lower; open woodland, cultivation, semi-desert, scrub, thorn forest. Often feeds on ground. ▽ Usually silent in winter. **WPB*3**

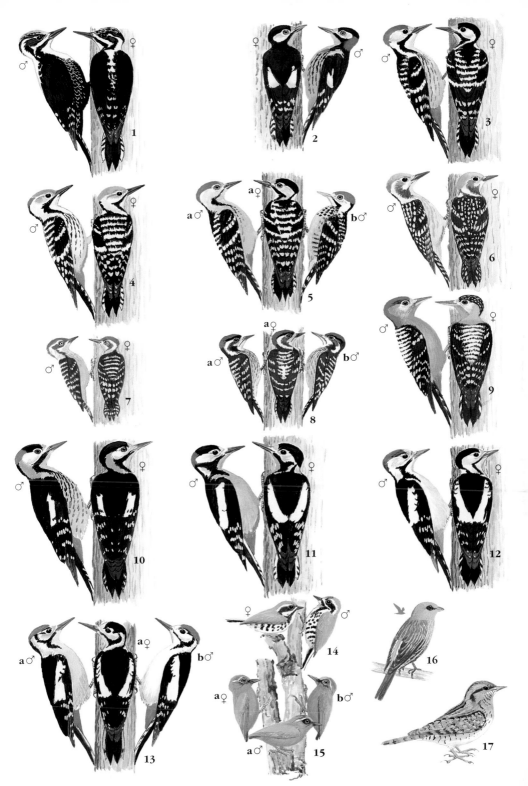

PLATE 56: BROADBILLS, IORAS, LEAFBIRDS, FAIRY BLUEBIRD, ORIOLES, WAXWING AND PITTAS

1 **Long-tailed Broadbill** *Psarisomus dalhousiae* (865) 27cm. ✿ <2000. Tropical and subtropical evergreen forest. Arboreal. Often in flocks, sometimes with other species in bird waves. ▽ Loud, whistling repeated *tseeay*. **R•3**

2 **Silver-breasted Broadbill** *Serilophus lunatus* (864) 19cm. ✿ <1700. Semi-evergreen and sal forest, secondary growth, bamboo. Arboreal. Keeps in loose parties of 5 to 20. ▽ Soft musical whistle; low *chir-r-r-r;* clicks. **R4**

3 **Marshall's Iora** *Aegithina nigrolutea* (1102) 14cm. Like 4 but more white in wings; tail black, broadly tipped white; **br** ♂ yellow collar. ✿ Scrub, thorn forest, groves. ▽ *tjee tjee-tew;* harsh *che che-che-che-che; wheeti...wheeti.* **E4**

4 **Common Iora** *Aegithina tiphia* (1097-1101) 14cm. See 3 for differences. ✿ <2000. Gardens, woodland, etc. Races **(a)** nom **(b)** *multicolor.* ▽ Variety of whistles: *peeou; wheee-choo wheeee-choo; chee-wheee?* **R•2**

5 **Orange-bellied Leafbird** *Chloropsis hardwickii* (1106) 19cm. ✿ S 600-2400. W Foothills (and adjoining plains in Assam). Forest and secondary growth. Usually at higher altitudes than its relatives. ▽ Very varied. Good mimic. **A2**

6 **Golden-fronted Leafbird** *Chloropsis aurifrons* (1103-5) 19cm. Confusable with 7 but forecrown orange; more black on face and throat. Races **(a)** *frontalis* **(b)** nom. ✿ <1200(1800). Forest, preferring lighter growth in northern part of range. ▽ *wheet; chaa kee-wheew; swich-chich-chich-wee; tzik; chup-chaw.* Imitates other species. **R•3**

7 **Blue-winged Leafbird** *Chloropsis cochinchinensis* (1107-8) 18cm. Like 6 but forecrown yellow; broader yellow border to throat; ♀ has pale blue throat; in ♂ black of throat does not extend behind eye. Race *jerdoni* shown. Only nom (not illustrated) found in the north-east has blue in wings and tail. ✿ <1000(1800). All types of more open wooded country. ▽ Various harsh notes and whistles as well as mimicry of other species. **R3**

8 **Asian Fairy Bluebird** *Irena puella* (1109-10) 27cm. ✿ <1300 (1800 in S. India). Evergreen forest. Commoner at lower altitudes. ▽ Liquid *weet-weet; whitit; whit; (whick) whick-we-wick; weeyouwit.* **R•3**

9 **Eurasian Golden Oriole** *Oriolus oriolus* (952-3) 25cm. Races **(a)** resident *kundoo* **(b)** nom, a vagrant, lacks black behind eye. ✿ <2000(3500). Open wooded country, groves. ▽ Harsh *cheeah;* fluty *wee-lo-(weeo).* **RMP2**

10 **Black-naped Oriole** *Oriolus chinensis* (954, 956-7) 25cm. Thicker-billed and with broader black nape-band than 11. ✿ Open forest, secondary growth, plantations and gardens. ▽ Rasping nasal *kyebhr;* fluty whistles. **RW3**

11 **Slender-billed Oriole** *Oriolus tenuirostris* (955) 25cm. More slender-billed with thinner black nape-band than 10. ✿ S 1500-2100. Pine forest. W Semi-evergreen forest. ▽ Woodpecker-like *kick;* mellow fluty whistled *wheeow.* **BM4-5**

12 **Black-hooded Oriole** *Oriolus xanthornus* (958-9) 25cm. ✿ <1200 (2000). Well-wooded country, parks, gardens, orchards. ▽ Descending *cheeuw; k(u)ray;* fluty *poopeelo.* **R•2**

13 **Maroon Oriole** *Oriolus traillii* (961) 28cm. ✿ <2400. Evergreen forest. ▽ Cat-like, nasal *oowewe;* fluty *pi-lo-i-lo.* **R•3**

14 **Bohemian Waxwing** *Bombycilla garrulus* (1062) 18cm. ✿ Largely frugivorous and arboreal. A few (mainly high-altitude) winter records. ▽ *sirrr.* **V(W)**

15 **Blue-naped Pitta** *Pitta nipalensis* (866) 25cm. ✿ <2150. Tropical and sub-tropical evergreen forest, bamboo jungle, overgrown clearings. ▽ Loud double whistle *whoo-wooee.* **A4**

16 **Blue Pitta** *Pitta cyanea* (871) 23cm. ✿ Plains and foothills (2000). Dense undergrowth in evergreen forest and damp ravines. ▽ Clear, liquid double whistle *pleoow-whit.* **R•5**

17 **Indian Pitta** *Pitta brachyura* (867) 19cm. See 18 for differences. ✿ Lowland scrub and undergrowth in lightly forested areas (up to 1700). ▽ *wheet-whiyou;* wheezy *wheew; chee; mew.* Calls at dawn and dusk ('Six o'clock Bird'). **EM3**

18 **Mangrove Pitta** *Pitta megarhyncha* (868) 23cm. Like 17 but crown is brown; lacks white supercilium and subocular crescent; more extensive, darker blue wing-patch. Habitat indicative. ✿ Mangrove swamps. ▽ Fluty *hhwa-hwa.* **V(R*)5**

19 **Hooded Pitta** *Pitta sordida* (869-70) 19cm. ✿ Mainly plains and foothills (up to 2000). Subtropical moist forest and secondary growth. ▽ Wheezy, fluting double-whistle *quek-quek* or *whaew-(whaew);* harsh *skyew.* **S(R?)4-5**

20 **Eared Pitta** *Pitta phayrei* (not illustrated). 23cm. **Ad** Broad buffy-white supercilia, scaled blackish, extend as ear-tufts behind nape; warm brown above; wings darker with brown and buff spotting on wing-coverts; buffy wing-patch; heavy black bill. ♂ blackish central crown-stripe, nape, eye-line and malar; underparts warm brownish-buff with a few dark spots on breast, flanks. ♀ dark head markings brown not blackish; duller below, heavily scaled dark brown. **Juv** like ad but duller, more uniform, broad buffy scaled supercilia/ear-tufts, buffy-white throat and browner bill. ✿ Evergreen and mixed broadleaved forest; bamboo; in drier areas than 16. ▽ Drawn-out whistle *wheeow-whit;* dog-like whine. **B*(?)** (A new addition to the regional avifauna: juv recently recorded in E Bangladesh.)

PLATE 56

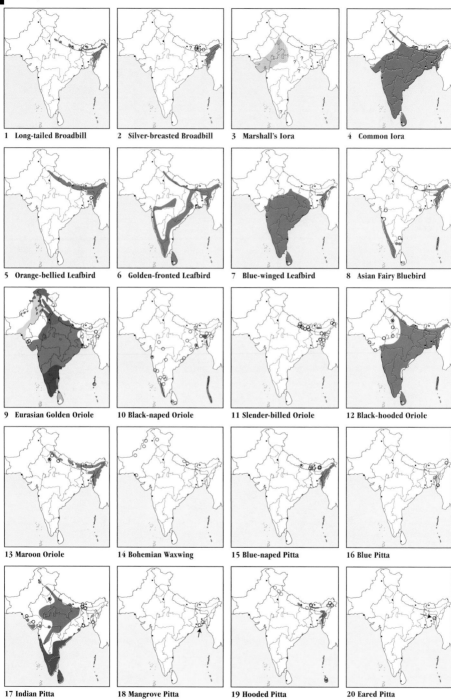

1 Long-tailed Broadbill   2 Silver-breasted Broadbill   3 Marshall's Iora   4 Common Iora

5 Orange-bellied Leafbird   6 Golden-fronted Leafbird   7 Blue-winged Leafbird   8 Asian Fairy Bluebird

9 Eurasian Golden Oriole   10 Black-naped Oriole   11 Slender-billed Oriole   12 Black-hooded Oriole

13 Maroon Oriole   14 Bohemian Waxwing   15 Blue-naped Pitta   16 Blue Pitta

17 Indian Pitta   18 Mangrove Pitta   19 Hooded Pitta   20 Eared Pitta

PLATE 57

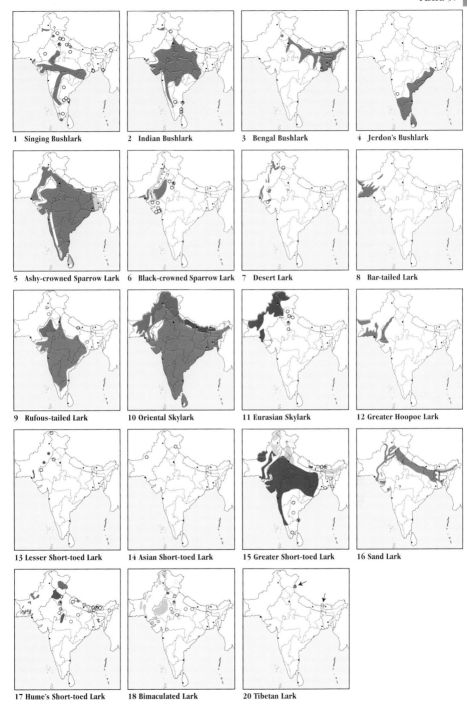

1   Singing Bushlark

2   Indian Bushlark

3   Bengal Bushlark

4   Jerdon's Bushlark

5   Ashy-crowned Sparrow Lark

6   Black-crowned Sparrow Lark

7   Desert Lark

8   Bar-tailed Lark

9   Rufous-tailed Lark

10 Oriental Skylark

11 Eurasian Skylark

12 Greater Hoopoe Lark

13 Lesser Short-toed Lark

14 Asian Short-toed Lark

15 Greater Short-toed Lark

16 Sand Lark

17 Hume's Short-toed Lark

18 Bimaculated Lark

20 Tibetan Lark

PLATE 57: LARKS

1 **Singing Bushlark** *Mirafra cantillans* (872) 14cm. Only bushlark with whitish outer tail feathers (difficult to see). Fine faint breast streaking, often confined to sides of breast; in fresh plumage a rather contrasting pattern to mantle and scapulars and a slight (rufous-)brownish breast-band. From 3 & 4 also by slimmer build, longer tail, smaller bill. ⌘ <350. Dry plains and foothills with bushes, grassland, stubble, fallow, scrubby patches in sandy semi-desert. Solitary, shy. ∇ Short sharp high-pitched notes; prolonged skylark-like song (aerial or perched) with much mimicry. **R*4**

2 **Indian Bushlark** *Mirafra erythroptera* (875-7) 14cm. More extensive rufous on primaries than other bushlarks, more obvious in flight. From 1 also by buffy not white outer tail feathers, heavier breast spotting, more prominent supercilium. Very like 4, which see. ⌘ Plains. Sparsely scrubbed semi-desert, waste/fallow land, stony scrub grazed-over grassland. Solitary. ∇ *sweee*; tinkling *trrrrrrr-weet-(weet)*; series of high-pitched, thin, clear whistles of alternating length and pitch in song-flight; *tit-tit-tit-tit...*while perched followed by *tsweeib-tsweeib-tsweeib...*in song-flight. **E2**

3 **Bengal Bushlark** *Mirafra assamica* (873) 15cm. From congeners by relatively dark brownish (rufous-)buff underparts; greyer above with less distinct streaking; less contrasting head pattern. ⌘ Plains; open short, often damp, grassland; cultivation. Solitary. ∇ *yu-eez* (*dzreee*); *p'zeeeoo*; thin high *tzrep-tzit-tzee-tzee-tzuene*; jingle of high notes. **R2**

4 **Jerdon's Bushlark** *Mirafra affinis* (874) 15cm. Formerly treated as conspecific with 3, which see. Difficult to separate from 2 but more heavily streaked above; buffier underparts; bigger bill; shorter tail; rufous on outerwebs of primaries only, so that wings appear less rufous in flight; less contrastingly patterned tail; less distinct head pattern; at close range arrow-head (vs round) shape of breast spotting. ⌘ Plains. Dry, open scrubby areas with scattered trees and bushes; cultivation. Unlike other bushlarks also occurs in scrubby glades in well-wooded areas and frequently perches high, even in tall trees. Solitary. ∇ Thin, high *zir-ri-ri-ri-rit*; *drreeet eeet*; *ueeet-ueeet-dzip-dzuep*; *dzeep-dzuep, dzeep-dzuep-tzi-tzi-eee*; rattling *zizizizezezezeze*. **E2**

5 **Ashy-crowned Sparrow Lark** *Eremopterix grisea* (878) 13cm. See 6 for differences. ⌘ <1000. Stony areas with sparse scrub, dry cultivation, sandy riverbeds, dry tidal mudflats. Gregarious in winter. ∇ *chulp*; *tweele-deedle-deedle-(deedle)* and *wheeeh* in undulating song flight. **E•2**

6 **Black-crowned Sparrow Lark** *Eremopterix nigriceps* (879) 13cm. ♂ from 5 by black crown. ♀ scarcely differs from 5 but slightly paler, sandier, with whiter belly and slightly larger bill. ⌘ Desert and semi-desert; vicinity of desert cultivation; sandy hills. Gregarious. ∇ *rrrrp*; *tchep*; *dwee-di-ul-twee-e-h* and *deeeeeeh* in undulating song flight. **R•3**

7 **Desert Lark** *Ammomanes deserti* (880) 16cm. See 8 for differences. ⌘ <1800(2500). Stony semi-desert, barren foothills, fallow fields. Solitary or in pairs. ∇ *phew*; *chewee(t)*; whistling *peef-poof* interspersed with warbles in song-flight. **R2**

8 **Bar-tailed Lark** *Ammomanes cincturus* (881) 15cm. Like 7 but clearly demarcated dark brown terminal bar on rufous tail, most prominent (as an inverted T-shape) when spread on landing (vs more evenly brown merging into rufous uppertail-coverts); shorter, slimmer, pinkish-brown bill; white (vs buffy) belly. ⌘ Sandy desert; stony barren areas. Solitary; pairs. ∇ *chrriet*; *pwee-oo* flight call; weak, fluty *dee-dee-doo*; distinctive 'creaky-gate' *dyuu-wee* song. **R2**

9 **Rufous-tailed Lark** *Ammomanes phoenicurus* (882-3) 16cm. Note rufous rump, uppertail-coverts and underparts. ⌘ Open stony scrub, fallow fields, edges of cultivation. Usually in pairs. ∇ Mellow *qu-i-qu*; whistles; chirrups. **EM3**

10 **Oriental Skylark** *Alauda gulgula* (904-9) 16cm. See 11 for differences. Rufous tinge to primaries is less contrasting than in bushlarks (1-4) and the bill much finer. Darker, more rufous (unillustrated) races *australis* and *lhamarum* confusable with 22 & 23, but note shorter crest; smaller bill; heavier breast streaking; buffy-white (vs pale rufous) outer tail feathers; call. Compare also 21. ⌘ <4300. Open grassland and cultivation. Solitary. ∇ Short explosive *pzhr* or *baz* or *pzeebz*; *pyup*; *twip*; *trrp*; a long sustained continuous warbling in song-flight, often containing excellent mimicry. **R•W2**

11 **Eurasian Skylark** *Alauda arvensis* (903-3a) 19cm. Similar to 10 but larger; thicker bill usually horny (vs pinkish); longer tail; white trailing edge to wing and outer tail feathers (usually buffy in 10 but can bleach to whitish); longer primary projection (c. half of visible tertials); lacks 10's lightly rufous wing-panel. ⌘ Plains–1500(3000+). Grassland and cultivation. Gregarious in winter. ∇ Liquid *chirrup* unlike 10; sustained song like that of 10, not usually heard in winter. **W3**

12 **Greater Hoopoe Lark** *Alaemon alaudipes* (884) 23cm. Distinctive. In flight note blackish flight feathers with white trailing edge and wing-bar. ⌘ Desert biotope. Solitary or in pairs. ∇ Characteristic, high-pitched whistling song *tyooo...tyeee...tyeee...tee...tee...tyee...tee...hoo*. **R4**

13 **Lesser Short-toed Lark** *Calandrella rufescens* (888a) 14cm. See 14 for differences. ⌘ Arid habitats. ∇ Dry rippling *pirrrit*; *prrir-irr-irr*; *drrie*; *sik*. **W*P3-4**

14 **Asian Short-toed Lark** *Calandrella cheleensis* (888b) 14cm. Extremely similar to 13, with which often considered conspecific. Doubtfully separable in the field but upperparts paler, more lightly streaked; proportionally slightly longer tail; slightly less streaking on breast; outermost tail feather entirely white (vs dark on part of innerweb) but only apparent when tail fully spread. ⌘ Arid biotope. ∇ Similar to 13. **V**

15 Greater Short-toed Lark *Calandrella brachydactyla* (885-6) 15cm. This and 17 separated from other *Calandrella* species by almost unstreaked breast; normally a small dark patch, or trace thereof, at side of breast; on closed wing tertials virtually cover the primaries. See 17 for differences. Races **(a)** *longipennis* **(b)** *dukhunensis*. ✖ <5000. Dry open country; cultivation; semi-desert. Gregarious in winter. ▽ Flight call short dry *chirrip* or *tchriup* or *trrip*; *dyu*; *trriep-dyu*. **W(MP)2**

16 Sand Lark *Calandrella raytal* (889-91) 13cm. Small size; fine streaking on breast and sandy-grey upperparts; (very short primary projection); fine bill; short tail. ✖ Lowlands. Sandbanks by water, saltpans, dry fields, coastal dunes, mudflats. Small flocks in winter. ▽ *prrr...prrr*; undulating warble in song flight. **N2**

17 Hume's Short-toed Lark *Calandrella acutirostris* (887-8) 14cm. Hard to distinguish in the field from 15 but usually has less distinct supercilium (almost none in front of eye in eastern birds); crown almost unstreaked; dark loral stripe (not always apparent in eastern birds); greyer (vs tawny), less heavily streaked upperparts; unstreaked greyish-brown (vs buffy) breast-band; longer, thinner yellow-tinged (vs pinkish) bill with darker culmen; greyer than 15a. Separated from other *Calandrella* species by same features as 15. ✖ <5000. Open arid tracts. Flocks in winter. ▽ Flight call a full rolling *tiyrr* somewhat different to 15; *djirr-de*; feeble monotonous song. **M2**

18 Bimaculated Lark *Melanocorypha bimaculata* (892) 18cm. From 19 & 20 by lack of white trailing edge to wing; brownish outer tail feathers. From 19 by white-tipped tail (except for innermost pair of tail feathers); from 20 by buffy-grey underwing. ✖ <2000 except on passage. Open arid habitats; dry margins of lakes. Gregarious. ▽ Dry *cherrup*; *trr-trr-treel*; churring, harsh *klee-trra*; similar notes to 15. **WP3** (erratic)

19 [Calandra Lark *Melanocorypha calandra* 19cm. Very similar to 18 but shows white outer tail feathers; white trailing edge to wing and blackish underwing. ✖ Stony barren land, open dry cultivation, steppes. ▽ High dry nasal *kleetra* like 18; *tshrreeet*. **X** (Could occur as a vagrant to Pakistan and NW India.)**]**

20 Tibetan Lark *Melanocorypha maxima* (893-4) 22cm. Distinctly larger and darker than 18; longer, slightly decurved bill; relatively plain head pattern/unstreaked crown; neck-spot usually smaller; white on outer tail; conspicuous white trailing edge to inner wing. ✖ >3600. Barren steppe; hummocky marshes near lakes. ▽ Song includes mimicry. **S*2**

21 Crested Lark *Galerida cristata* (898-900) 18cm. Crest usually obvious, long and pointed. For differences see 22 & 23. Note range. ✖ Mainly lowlands (up to 2400). Sandy desert and semi-desert, vicinity of cultivation, dry coastal mudflats. Solitary or scattered individuals. ▽ Fluty, melancholy *dju-ee*, *ti-ee* or *tee-urr*; song of disjointed phrases includes call notes and some mimicry in flight, from ground or low perch. **R●M2**

22 Malabar (Crested) Lark *Galerida malabarica* (901) 15cm. Like 21 but smaller; darker, more heavily streaked above; rufous-buff tinge below, especially on breast and flanks; outer tail feathers rufousy (buffy-white in 21). See also 10 & 23. Note range. ✖ <2000. Sparse scrub, dry fields, stony hillsides. ▽ *chu-chichuwi*; similar to 21. **E3**

23 Sykes's (Crested) Lark *Galerida deva* (902) 13cm. Like small 21 & 22 but with entirely rufous-buff underparts; very little streaking on upper breast; smaller bill. See also 10. Note range. ✖ <1000. Stony, sparsely scrubbed plateaus; dry short grass around lake margins; arable land. Seems to prefers darker soils. ▽ Nasal *dzewy* or *juury*; song like 21. **E●4**

24 Horned Lark *Eremophila alpestris* (895-7) 20cm. ♀/nbr (not shown) duller; black parts of plumage partly obscured by pale feather fringes though breast-band usually still evident; horns shorter or absent; upperparts often streaked. Races **(a)** *longirostris* **(b)** *albigula*. ✖ S 3500-snowline. W >1500. Barren steppes, grassy pastures, riverbanks. Gregarious. ▽ Thin mournful *tze-le*; *peo*; *ee-up*; *tsip*; short squeaky song usually from perch. **AM2**

21 Crested Lark

22 Malabar (Crested) Lark

23 Sykes's (Crested) Lark

24 Horned Lark

PLATE 58

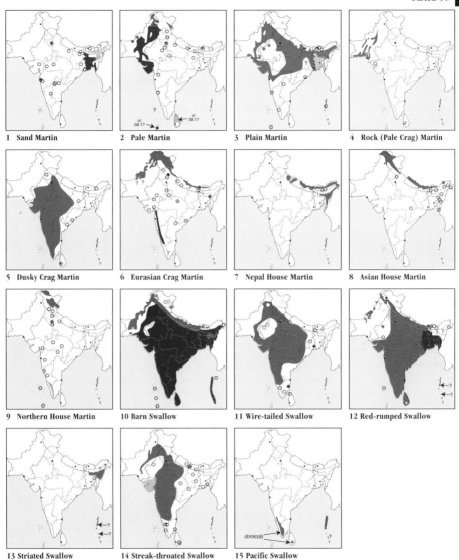

1 Sand Martin

2 Pale Martin

3 Plain Martin

4 Rock (Pale Crag) Martin

5 Dusky Crag Martin

6 Eurasian Crag Martin

7 Nepal House Martin

8 Asian House Martin

9 Northern House Martin

10 Barn Swallow

11 Wire-tailed Swallow

12 Red-rumped Swallow

13 Striated Swallow

14 Streak-throated Swallow

15 Pacific Swallow

PLATE 58: SWALLOWS AND MARTINS

1 **Sand Martin** *Riparia riparia* (911) 13cm. From other martins by distinct dark breast-band contrasting with white throat; from 2 also by the border between clear white throat and dark brown ear-coverts being distinct. ⌘ Vicinity of rivers with sheer banks. **RM(W?)3**

2 **Pale Martin** *Riparia diluta* (910) 13cm. From 1 by breast-band being ill-defined; border between pale greyish-brown ear-coverts and greyish-white throat indistinct. ⌘ <4500. Near large streams and rivers with perpendicular banks. **RM(W?)3**

3 **Plain Martin** *Riparia paludicola* (912) 12cm. From 1 & 2 by dusky throat fading into white upper breast, which lacks a contrasting breast-band. ⌘ similar to 1 & 2. **R•1**

4 **Rock (Pale Crag) Martin** *Hirundo fuligula* (915) 13cm. From 5 by pale brownish-grey upperparts and pale underparts contrasting with darker tail feathers. From 6 by unstreaked white throat; pale smoky-brown belly concolorous with vent. ⌘ Rocky mountains, at high and low altitudes. **R•5**

5 **Dusky Crag Martin** *Hirundo concolor* (914) 13cm. Separated from other martins by the very dusky underparts, lack of contrast between the flight feathers and the underwing-coverts, as well as between the underparts and tail feathers. ⌘ <1800+. Rocky hills, old forts etc. **R•2**

6 **Eurasian Crag Martin** *Hirundo rupestris* (913) 14cm. From 5 by flight feathers distinctly paler than underwing-coverts. From 4 & 5 by paler brownish belly becoming darker brown on vent which is almost concolorous with undertail; at close range the dark streaking on fulvous-white throat is also a distinguishing feature. ⌘ **S** 1600-5000. **W** <2150. Mountain crags and cliffs, old hill forts. **RM3**

7 **Nepal House Martin** *Delichon nipalensis* (932) 13cm. From 8 & 9 by dark vent (and throat), square tail, smaller white rump-patch. ⌘ **S** 2000-4000. **W** >350(160). Mountain cliffs, river valleys. **RA3**

8 **Asian House Martin** *Delichon dasypus* (931) 14cm. From 7 by lightly forked tail, whitish throat and vent. From 9 by contrast between dark underwing-coverts and pale flight feathers, dusky suffusion on underparts darkest on breast, shallow tail-fork. ⌘ **S** 1500-5000. **W** >plains. Mountain cliffs and villages, grassy slopes, along waterways, cultivation. **RMS3**

9 **Northern House Martin** *Delichon urbica* (930) 15cm. From 7 by forked tail, entirely white underbody and larger white rump-patch. From 8 by larger size (when seen together), lack of contrast on greyish underwing, whiter underbody, deep tail-fork and white rump-patch usually larger. ⌘ **S** 3000-4500. **W** >plains. Open valleys, grassy slopes, cliffs. **BM3**

10 **Barn Swallow** *Hirundo rustica* (916-8) 18cm. From other swallows by chestnut throat bordered below by a blue-black band. In flight the very deeply forked tail separates from all but 12 & 13. From latter two by white spots in tail; lacks their dark vent and rufous rump. Races **(a)** nom **(b)** *tytleri*. ⌘ <3000(6400). Open country. **RMW1**

11 **Wire-tailed Swallow** *Hirundo smithii* (921) 14cm. The wire-like streamers on the outer tail feathers are diagnostic, but only visible at close range. Note also the clean-cut pure white underparts and chestnut cap. In flight the tail appears conspicuously short and square-cut with the outer tail-wires only visible at close range. ⌘ <1500(2700). Open country, usually near water. **RM2**

12 **Red-rumped Swallow** *Hirundo daurica* (923-8) 19cm. The rufous rump (varies from almost white to rich chestnut) separates from all swallows except 13 which see. From 10 by pale throat, dark vent and lack of white tail-spots. The contrasting rumps of the house martins are never rufous and their tails are much less deeply forked. Races **(a)** *rufula* **(b)** *hyperythra* **(c)** *japonica*. ⌘ <3300. Open country. **RAMW1-2**

13 **Striated Swallow** *Hirundo striolata* (929) 19cm. Very similar to 12c but slightly bulkier; underparts heavily streaked (streaking longer and broader); small blackish patch at side of rump diagnostic when present/visible; rump usually darker/redder. From 10 by underpart streaking, rufous rump and absence of white spots in tail. 14 is much smaller with a reddish cap and unstreaked white belly and vent. ⌘ Open hilly country. **RW3**

14 **Streak-throated Swallow** *Hirundo fluvicola* (922) 12cm. The combination of chestnut-red cap and heavy blackish streaking on throat, sides of neck and upper breast is diagnostic. ⌘ Open country near water. **RM3**

15 **Pacific Swallow** *Hirundo tahitica* (919-20) 13cm. Very similar to 10 but lacks the blue-black breast-band, the underparts are dusky white and the tail is much less deeply forked. Races **(a)** *javanica* **(b)** *domicola* sometimes treated as a separate species. ⌘ **(a)** vicinity of coasts **(b)** (300)700-2400. Grassy hillsides, tea plantations. **R3**

16 (**Crested Treeswift** *Hemiprocne coronata* illustrated here for comparison as it is likely to be seen perched. For main entry see plate 49, figure 16.)

190

PLATE 59: WOODSWALLOWS AND DRONGOS

1 **Ashy Woodswallow** *Artamus fuscus* (982) 19cm. Similar to 2 but separated by vinous-grey (vs white) underparts and broader white tail-band; in flight also by the greyish (vs white) underwing-coverts. Pale birds can appear confusingly white below in strong light but range does not overlap with that of 2. ✻ <1700(2100). Open wooded country, often in the neighbourhood of palms. Usually in small groups or loose flocks. ▽ Harsh nasal *chek-chek-chek*. **R•3**

2 **White-breasted Woodswallow** *Artamus leucorynchus* (983) 18cm. Like the allopatric 1 (which see) but distinguished by white breast, belly and rump (1 only shows white on the tips of the uppertail-coverts). ✻ Open wooded country, clearings, plantations. ▽ Similar to 1. **R3**

3 [**Drongo Cuckoo** *Surniculus lugubris* 25cm. Though not a drongo, illustrated here for comparison. Similar to 4 and 10b but has the typical small, thin, slightly decurved, cuckoo-type bill; lacks the white rictal spot of 4; usually shows white barring on vent and undertail (note that juv drongos may show diffuse white barring on belly); tail is usually square-cut, though may sometimes appear slightly forked as in bird illustrated. Rather quiet and retiring in its habits (in contrast to the boldness of the drongos) except when calling in the breeding season. For main entry see plate 45, figure 10.]

4 **Black Drongo** *Dicrurus macrocercus* (962-4) 31cm. The only drongo commonly found in open country. White rictal spot (visible at close range) is diagnostic. Most likely to be confused with 9 but note black (vs dark grey) plumage below; dark (vs bright) red iris of adult. 11 is smaller with a stronger, bluer gloss and less deeply forked tail. See also 12. **Imm** may have rictal spot reduced or absent. ✻ <2100. Open country, cultivation, open woodland, marshes; avoids dense forest. Usually solitary. ▽ *ti-tiu*; harsh *cheeche-chichichichichuk*; squeaking and chattering. **R•A1**

5 **Greater Racket-tailed Drongo** *Dicrurus paradiseus* (976-81) 33cm. From all other drongos except 8 by the long tail-streamers. From 8 by the deeply forked tail, longer crest, the 'rackets' at ends of the tail only on one side of the exposed shaft (and usually twisted). Races **(a)** nom **(b)** *lophorinus* of SW Sri Lanka. Latter lacks the long tail-streamers of nom, but has a short crest-tuft making head appear more like 8, but has deeply forked tail with broad outer tail feathers twisted slightly out and up. ✻ <1700. Forest and secondary jungle. ▽ Extremely varied: from harsh and metallic calls to rich mellow songs; excellent mimic. Normally singly or in pairs, often in mixed flocks. **R2**

6 **Spangled Drongo** *Dicrurus hottentottus* (973) 31cm. Identified by the tail shape (square-ended but with the outer tail feathers curved out and round) and crest of long, wire-like feathers (only visible at reasonably close range). Note also the relatively long, decurved pale bill. ✻ <1400(2000). Largely associated with flowering forest trees. ▽ Metallic clanging *klaa'tlok*; creaking *tooi*; clear whistles; mimicry. **R•3**

7 **Andaman Drongo** *Dicrurus andamanensis* (974-5) 35cm. Similar to 4 but overall browner-tinged; broader tail with shallower fork and outer tail feathers curled inwards; less glossy upperparts; underparts matt brownish-black; larger bill; tuft of hair-like feathers on forecrown. ✻ Inhabits forests on Andamans where the only other drongos are (possibly 4), 5 and the vagrant 9b. Often in large flocks, also with other species. ▽ *chyiew*; sharp metallic calls. **E3**

8 **Lesser Racket-tailed Drongo** *Dicrurus remifer* (972) 28cm. Separated from the similar 5 by lack of tail-fork, tail 'rackets' usually untwisted and symmetrical about tail-shafts, flat head (with only a short tuft on forecrown). ✻ Humid broadleaved forests. In ones, twos and threes, regularly associating with mixed hunting parties. ▽ Similar to 5. **RM3**

9 **Ashy Drongo** *Dicrurus leucophaeus* (965-6b) 30cm. Similar to 4 but dark ashy-grey rather than black, the difference being most obvious on the underparts; lacks 4's white rictal spot; adult's eye bright (vs dark) red. Normally seen in forest (except on passage) whereas 4 is a bird of more open country and cultivation. Races **(a)** nom **(b)** *salangensis* (vagrant to the Andamans). ✻ <3300. Forest and well-wooded country. Singly, in pairs and small parties. ▽ *chaa ke-wip*; *kit-whew*; *chah-kíp...(chrah)*; harsh *cheece-cheece-chichuk...tililili*; mimicry. **RAM2**

10 **White-bellied Drongo** *Dicrurus caerulescens* (967-9) 24cm. The white belly and vent separate this from all other drongos. Races **(a)** nom **(b)** *leucopygialis* of the Sri Lankan low-country Wet Zone with white restricted to vent; the only other drongos present in this region are 5, which is distinctive, and 9, which is greyer; both the latter lack white vent. ✻ <2000. Broadleaved forest; forest edge; well-wooded areas. Singly, in twos and threes, often in mixed flocks. ▽ Pleasant whistles and liquip chirps; mimicry. **E•3**

11 **Bronzed Drongo** *Dicrurus aeneus* (971) 24cm. Small size and strong bluish gloss distinctive. From 4 also by shallower tail-fork and forest habitat. ✻ <2000. Evergreen forest, forest edge, bamboo, plantations. Singly, in twos and threes, often in mixed hunting parties. ▽ Various musical whistles and harsh notes; *dreet cheechew*; mimicry. **R•2**

12 **Crow-billed Drongo** *Dicrurus annectans* (970) 27cm. Hard to distinguish from 4 but larger bill; tuft on forecrown; shorter, broader tail with shallower fork and outer feathers curving round more. Habitat indicative. ✻ <700. Moist, dense broadleaved forest; well-wooded areas. ▽ Loud mellow whistles; churrs; descending series of harp-like notes. **MR•?4**

PLATE 59

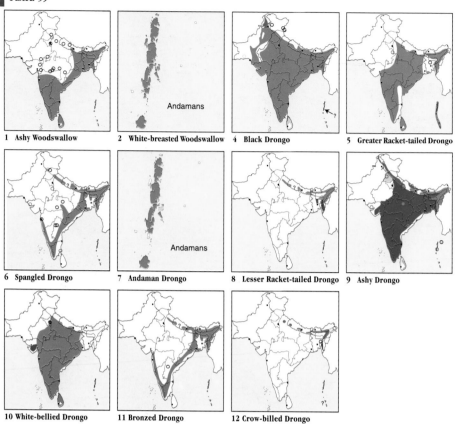

1 Ashy Woodswallow

2 White-breasted Woodswallow

4 Black Drongo

5 Greater Racket-tailed Drongo

6 Spangled Drongo

7 Andaman Drongo

8 Lesser Racket-tailed Drongo

9 Ashy Drongo

10 White-bellied Drongo

11 Bronzed Drongo

12 Crow-billed Drongo

Andamans

Andamans

PLATE 60

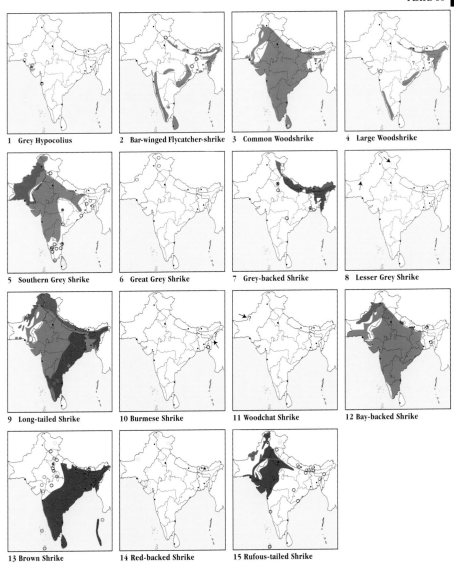

1 Grey Hypocolius

2 Bar-winged Flycatcher-shrike

3 Common Woodshrike

4 Large Woodshrike

5 Southern Grey Shrike

6 Great Grey Shrike

7 Grey-backed Shrike

8 Lesser Grey Shrike

9 Long-tailed Shrike

10 Burmese Shrike

11 Woodchat Shrike

12 Bay-backed Shrike

13 Brown Shrike

14 Red-backed Shrike

15 Rufous-tailed Shrike

PLATE 60: HYPOCOLIUS, FLYCATCHER-SHRIKE, WOODSHRIKES AND SHRIKES

1 Grey Hypocolius *Hypocolius ampelinus* (1063) 25cm. Recalls shrike but shape of mask and terminal tail-band on ♂ distinctive; in flight contrasting black primaries tipped white. ♀/imm ♂ separated by jizz and terminal tail-band. Crest not usually raised. ❄ Semi-desert scrub, acacias and *Salvadora persica* (Tooth-brush Tree). ∇ Mewing *piew-piew*; *que-ee*; *chirrup*; trilling. **W*4**

2 Bar-winged Flycatcher-shrike *Hemipus picatus* (1064-6) 14cm. From comparable shrikes by small size, black cap and long white band through wing. Could be confused with 64.5, 64.6 & 73.13 but lacks white supercilium and forecrown. Races **(a)** *leggei* **(b)** *capitalis* **(c)** *picatus*. ❄ S <2100. W <1500. Forest. Often in loose flocks and mixed hunting parties. ∇ *chip*; *tsit-it-it-tsit-it-it...*; squeaky *whiriri-whiriri-whiriri*. **RA2**

3 Common Woodshrike *Tephrodornis pondicerianus* (1069-71) 16cm. From 4 by small size, white supercilium, white on outer tail feathers. ❄ <900(1400). Acacia and scrub jungle, open woodland, overgrown gardens. ∇ *chew*; *weet-weet-(wheet) whi-whi-whi-whee-wheea*; soft trills. **R2**

4 Large Woodshrike *Tephrodornis gularis* (1067-8) 23cm. Like 3 but larger, no white supercilium or in tail. ❄ <1800. Broadleaved forest; well-wooded areas. In loose parties, mixed feeding flocks. ∇ Musical *kew-kiw-kew-kiw-(kew)-(kiw)*; *whit-whit-wheet-wheet-whi-wee-wee-wewe-wee*; mellow *tra-a-a*; harsh *chack*; *chrr*. **R●3**

5 Southern Grey Shrike *Lanius meridionalis* (933-5) 25cm. Most grey shrikes in region are this species. See 8 for differences. Races **(a)** *pallidirostris* a possible future split. From 6 by white patch at base of primaries not extending to base of secondaries, largely pale bill, lores and forecrown (some br ad show black bill and lores). **(b)** *lahtora* from 6 by darker grey upperparts; no white supercilium or forecrown; relatively broad, black facial band enclosing eye, distinct on forecrown and curving onto sides of neck; grey (vs white) uppertail-coverts. **(c)** *aucheri* (not shown) like b but washed grey below, paler above, narrower frontal band, less white in wings. ❄ <2100. Open semi-desert, scrub, thorn forest, field-margins; drier areas than 9. **R●MW2**

6 Great Grey Shrike *Lanius excubitor* (936) 25cm. Race recorded in our region is *homeyeri*, very similar to 5 but with white band at base of primaries extending onto base of inner secondaries, black bill and lores. **1stW** birds can show reduced black on lores and paler base of bill making them more difficult to separate from 5. ❄ As 5. **V(W)**

7 Grey-backed Shrike *Lanius tephronotus* (944-5) 25cm. From other 'grey' shrikes except 9 by rufous flanks; from latter by no white wing-patch, darker grey upperparts, shorter, less graduated tail. Race *lahulensis* (not illustrated) of W Himalayas is like 9a of S India in its small white wing-patch, but upperparts dark grey, contrasting less with the dark brown (vs black) wings, and rufous usually restricted to rump area. High altitude and range are often clues. ❄ S 2700-4500. W >plains. Scrub, clearings, second growth, edges of fields. **RA2**

8 Lesser Grey Shrike *Lanius minor* (937) 23cm. **Ad** from 5 & 6 by broad black mask across forecrown; pinkish wash below. From 7 & 9 by no rufous in plumage; pinkish wash below. **1stW** birds lack black forecrown-band but note the short, bullfinch-like bill, little or no white between closed black wing and grey mantle, no white supercilium, long primary projection, more upright stance. ❄ Open semi-desert, cultivation. **V**

9 Long-tailed Shrike *Lanius schach* (946-8) 25cm. The commonest shrike throughout most of its range. Separated from most other grey-mantled shrikes by the rufous flanks and long tail. See 7 for differences with that species. Races **(a)** *caniceps* **(b)** *erythronotus* **(c)** *tricolor*. ❄ <3000. Variety of open habitats. **R●M2**

10 Burmese Shrike *Lanius collurioides* (938) 23cm. From 12 by chestnut (vs whitish) rump; narrower, more diffuse black band on forecrown. From ♂14 by black forecrown, darker crown, white primary patch, entire outer tail feathers white (vs basal two-thirds) and disjunct range. ❄ Clearings, forest edge, second growth, gardens, field margins. **P*W*(B*?)4**

11 [Woodchat Shrike *Lanius senator* (951) 17cm. ❄ Dry open country, scrub etc. **X** (No reliable records.)]

12 Bay-backed Shrike *Lanius vittatus* (939-40) 18cm. Distinctive combination of grey crown, chestnut back and black forecrown, but see also 10 & 14. On ad in flight the white wing patch is more striking than in other similar species. ❄ <2000. Dry thorn forest, open scrub, hedges; usually in drier areas than 9 but not as arid as 5 & 6. **RM2**

13 Brown Shrike *Lanius cristatus* (949-50a) 19cm. Brown upperparts with black band through eye. Races **(a)** nom **(b)** *luconensis*. ❄ Open country, clearings etc. **W2**

14 Red-backed Shrike *Lanius collurio* (941) 17cm. See 10 for differences. Confusion also possible with 12 but lacks the black forecrown (black restricted to narrow line above the bill), rump grey, wings are brown mixed with rufous, white patch at base of primaries absent or much reduced (prominent in ad 12). ❄ Open scrub, margins of cultivation. **P5** (mainly autumn)

15 Rufous-tailed Shrike *Lanius isabellinus* (942-3) 17cm. From 13 by rufous rump/tail; sandier/greyer-brown mantle. Races **(a)** *phoenicuroides* **(b)** nom. ❄ Sparse dry thorn jungle, semi-desert, tamarisks, edges of fields. **MPW3**

PLATE 61: STARLINGS AND MYNAS

1 **Spot-winged Starling** *Saroglossa spiloptera* (984) 19cm. ❀ **S** Foothills-2000. **W** <1000. Tall open broadleaved forest. Mainly arboreal. ▽ Noisy chatter; *chek-chek-chek*; soft *chik-chik.* **MP3**

2 **Chestnut-tailed Starling** *Sturnus malabaricus* (987-9) 21cm. Races **(a)** nom **(b)** *blythii* may prove to be a separate species. ❀ <1500(2000). Open woodland, second growth, young plantations, gardens, cultivation. Chiefly arboreal. ▽ Sharp disyllabic metallic note; rattling *krrep*; single whistle, etc. **R●M2**

3 **White-headed Starling** *Sturnus erythropygius* (990-2) 21cm. Similar to 2 but ranges do not overlap. Races **(a)** nom **(b)** *andamanensis.* ❀ Forest, second growth, gardens and cultivation. ▽ Loud *cheew*; *chree-chri-chri-chree*; cheery *chi-choo-wee, tooweerly* etc. **E3**

4 **White-faced Starling** *Sturnus albofrontatus* (993) 22cm. ❀ <1300. Well-forested hill country in Sri Lankan Wet Zone. Arboreal. In pairs and small groups. ▽ Sharp, high-pitched *cheow*; chirp. **E4**

5 **Brahminy Starling** *Sturnus pagodarum* (994) 22cm. Crest not obvious unless raised. ❀ <1600(2400). Open broadleaved forest, gardens, second growth, cultivation. ▽ Creaking and chattering notes; rambling warble mixed with mimicry. **R●M3**

6 **Purple-backed Starling** *Sturnus sturninus* (995) 19cm. **Ad** from 7 by glossy purple upperparts and nape-patch, two white wing-bars, no white tail-tip. **Imm** from imm 7 by same features except that upperparts are brown and rump is pale. ❀ Cultivation, forest edge and secondary growth. Arboreal. ▽ Soft *prrp*; whistling and whickering notes. **V**

7 **White-shouldered Starling** *Sturnus sinensis* (1005) 20cm. See also 6. ❀ Mainly lowland open country with scattered trees, bamboo thickets, cultivation, mangroves. Arboreal. ▽ Soft *preep;* harsh *kaar.* **V**

8 **Rosy Starling** *Sturnus roseus* (996) 23cm. **Juv** from juv 9 by pale underparts and bill. ❀ Lowland open country, cultivation, scrub, grassland. ▽ Like 9 but song less discordant. **PW1-2** (erratic)

9 **Common Starling** *Sturnus vulgaris* (997-1001) 19cm. **Juv** from juv 8 by dark underparts and bill. ❀ Cultivation, grassland, lake margins. ▽ *prrp*; continuous chattering; whistles; long varied song with mimicry. **WPMR*1**

10 **Asian Glossy Starling** *Aplonis panayensis* (985-6a) 22cm. ❀ Open forest, second growth, cultivation, gardens. Arboreal. ▽ Metallic ringing whistle. **RS*1**

11 **Asian Pied Starling** *Sturnus contra* (1002-4) 23cm. Pied plumage with large white patch behind eye distinctive. **Imm** is browner. ❀ Damp lowland grassy habitats, cultivation, towns. ▽ Chuckles; warbles; whistles; more liquid than 13. **R●2**

12 **Bank Myna** *Acridotheres ginginianus* (1008) 21cm. Like 13 but orange or brick-red facial skin and bill, pale orange-brown tail-tip and wing-patch; **ad** by bluish-grey underparts, neck and mantle. **Imm** browner. In flight note colour of the wing-patch. ❀ <800(1200). Around human habitation and cultivation. ▽ Like 13 but softer. **E●2**

13 **Common Myna** *Acridotheres tristis* (1006-7) 23cm. Note vinous-brown overall colour, black head with bare yellow eye-patch. ❀ <3050. Around human habitation. ▽ Ringing *kew kew kreew-kreew-kreew;* harsh *chake-chake; kweerh.* **R1**

14 **Jungle Myna** *Acridotheres fuscus* (1009-11) 23cm. Greyer and blacker than 13 with black tuft of feathers on forecrown; no bare skin around eye. Similar to 15 but blue base of bill (looks short from a distance), short crest-tuft. Races **(a)** nom **(b)** *mahrattensis.* ❀ <2400. Well-wooded areas near habitation/cultivation. ▽ Like 13 but higher; *tinck-tinck-tinck.* **R●1**

15 **Great Myna** *Acridotheres grandis* (1012) 23cm. From 14 by black plumage, orange-yellow bill, reddish or orange-brown iris, longer crest. ❀ Well-watered open country, paddyfields, gardens. Often follows cattle. ▽ Harsher than 13. **R3**

16 **Collared Myna** *Acridotheres albocinctus* (1013) 23cm. Buffy-white neck patches. ❀ mainly 800-1200. Damp grassy areas often near habitation. Frequently associates with cattle. ▽ Undescribed. **R●5**

17 **Golden-crested Myna** *Ampeliceps coronatus* (1014) 21cm. ♀ yellow on crown and throat much reduced. **Imm** dark brown crown, yellowish-white throat and lores. ❀ <1000. Open forest. Arboreal. ▽ Higher than 18; bell-like note. **R?5**

18 **Common Hill Myna** *Gracula religiosa* (1015, 1017-8) 29cm. From 19 & 20 by pattern of wattles on head. ❀ <2000. Broadleaved semi-evergreen forest. Arboreal. ▽ Variety of loud whistles, screeches and croaks; *cheong; chip.* Excellent mimic in captivity. **R●3**

19 **Southern Hill Myna** *Gracula indica* (1016) 25cm. Treated by some authors as a subspecies of 18 but distinguished from it and 20 by the nape-wattles extending up the sides of the hindcrown; gap between eye and nape-wattles; and by voice. ❀ <1300(1700). Evergreen forest, clearings, plantations. Arboreal. ▽ *squeeoo* or *skew* similar to 20 but less varied, squeakier and higher-pitched. Good mimic in captivity. **E●3**

20 **Sri Lanka (Hill) Myna** *Gracula ptilogenys* (1019) 25cm. From 19 by wattles being restricted to nape, blackish base of bill and pale (vs brown) iris. ❀ <2100+. Well-forested areas and adjoining plantations and gardens in Sri Lankan Wet Zone. Arboreal. In pairs and small flocks. ▽ *h'you* like 19 but louder and deeper. Good mimic in captivity. **E3**

198

PLATE 61

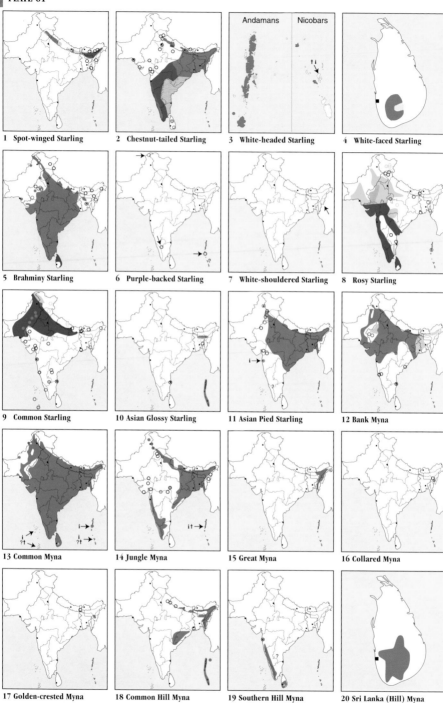

1 Spot-winged Starling

2 Chestnut-tailed Starling

3 White-headed Starling

Andamans | Nicobars

4 White-faced Starling

5 Brahminy Starling

6 Purple-backed Starling

7 White-shouldered Starling

8 Rosy Starling

9 Common Starling

10 Asian Glossy Starling

11 Asian Pied Starling

12 Bank Myna

13 Common Myna

14 Jungle Myna

15 Great Myna

16 Collared Myna

17 Golden-crested Myna

18 Common Hill Myna

19 Southern Hill Myna

20 Sri Lanka (Hill) Myna

PLATE 62

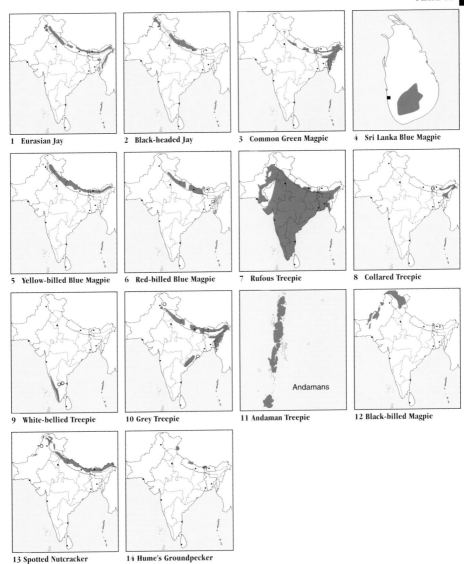

1 Eurasian Jay

2 Black-headed Jay

3 Common Green Magpie

4 Sri Lanka Blue Magpie

5 Yellow-billed Blue Magpie

6 Red-billed Blue Magpie

7 Rufous Treepie

8 Collared Treepie

9 White-bellied Treepie

10 Grey Treepie

11 Andaman Treepie

Andamans

12 Black-billed Magpie

13 Spotted Nutcracker

14 Hume's Groundpecker

201

PLATE 62: CORVIDS (JAYS, MAGPIES, TREEPIES, NUTCRACKER AND GROUNDPECKER)

1 **Eurasian Jay** *Garrulus glandarius* (1020-1) 33cm. Unmistakable. ⌖ (1000)1500-3000(3600). Moist mixed forest. Equally at home on the ground and in trees. Singly, in pairs or flocks; sometimes joining mixed feeding flocks. ▽ Harsh *shak*; *qui-eh*; *ko-kaw-wee-eh*; mimicry. **RA3**

2 **Black-headed Jay** *Garrulus lanceolatus* (1022) 33cm. Distinctive. ⌖ 900-2500(3000). Open mixed forest, often near habitation. Similar habits to 1. ▽ *krraa-(a)-(a)-(a)*; *jay-jay-jay*. **RA3**

3 **Common Green Magpie** *Cissa chinensis* (1023) 47cm. Unmistakable. **(a)** wild bird **(b)** cagebird (in captivity the green fades to pale blue). ⌖ <1200(1600). Moist forest, bamboo, scrubby understorey. Sometimes in bird waves. Shy. ▽ Loud *peep-peep*; *klee-whew*; wailing *ayeuw*; melodious squealing whistles; some mimicry. **R3**

4 **Sri Lanka Blue Magpie** *Urocissa ornata* (1024) 47cm. Only blue magpie in range. ⌖ 150-2100. Dense primary evergreen forest. Forages on ground, in bushes and trees. Singly, in pairs or small parties, regularly in mixed flocks. ▽ Loud *chink chink chink*; rasping *crakrakrakrak*; loud *whee whee*. **E4**

5 **Yellow-billed Blue Magpie** *Urocissa flavirostris* (1025-6) 66cm. From 6 by golden-yellow bill and small white nape-patch surrounded by black. **Juv** duller with larger white nape-patch making it hard to distinguish from 6. ⌖ **S** 1600-2700(3660). **W** >800. Mixed forest, normally at higher altitudes than 6. Chiefly arboreal. In loose parties, sometimes associating with other species. ▽ Loud harsh and creaking calls; sharp squealing whistles; mimicry. **RA2**

6 **Red-billed Blue Magpie** *Urocissa erythrorhyncha* (1027-8) 70cm. Differentiated from 5 by the red bill and large white nape-patch extending from crown to mantle. **Juv** duller with greyish bill; confusingly similar to imm 6 though the two species are usually separated altitudinally. ⌖ Foothills-1600(3050). Mixed forest. Habits as 5 but not as shy. ▽ Loud sharp *pit*; various calls similar to 5; piercing *quirer-pig-pig*. **RA2**

7 **Rufous Treepie** *Dendrocitta vagabunda* (1030a-4) 50cm. The most common and widespread treepie, distinguished by dark greyish-brown hood contrasting with rufous back, black and white wings and buffy underparts. ⌖ <1400(2100). Well-wooded areas, open forest, parks etc. Chiefly arboreal. Sociable. ▽ Ringing *ko-ki-lee*; harsh *kitter kitter kitter*; *ta-chuck chuck chack chack*; *mee-aao*. **R2**

8 **Collared Treepie** *Dendrocitta frontalis* (1035) 38cm. Identified by the black face sharply demarcated from grey head and breast. Chiefly arboreal. Singly and in small parties. ⌖ <2100. Humid evergreen broadleaved and bamboo forest. ▽ Bell-like *kok-lu*; variety of harsh and metallic calls. **R4**

9 **White-bellied Treepie** *Dendrocitta leucogastra* (1036) 50cm. Only treepie with white belly and contrasting black face on white head. ⌖ <1500. Broadleaved evergreen forest, overgrown plantations, cardamom sholas; in moister areas than 7. Mainly arboreal. Singly, in groups or flocks, often joining mixed feeding flocks. ▽ *kwreah*; ticking *tidiktuk-tidiktuk*; variety of loud, harsh, metallic and rattling notes similar to 7. **E3**

10 **Grey Treepie** *Dendrocitta formosae* (1037-9) 42cm. Most similar to 7 but note the brownish-grey underparts, black wings with a white patch at the base of the primaries, brownish back, chestnut vent contrasting with greyish belly. In flight from 7 & 8 by the white patch on black wings; grey (vs rufous) rump. ⌖ <2100(2300). Broadleaved forest, secondary jungle, overgrown plantations. Mainly arboreal. Small parties and loose flocks, often with other species. ▽ *kraeh-kraeh-kre-kre-(kre)*; *kokil-ko-ko-ko*; *wokuWAK-awk*; *tutuli-kakak*; creaky *kree-ee-chok*. **RA2**

11 **Andaman Treepie** *Dendrocitta bayleyi* (1040) 36cm. Only treepie in range. ⌖ Rainforest, littoral forest. In pairs or flocks, sometimes with Andaman Drongos. ▽ Metallic and hoarse notes; *k'chew*; *chee*. **E3**

12 **Black-billed Magpie** *Pica pica* (1029-30) 52cm. Unmistakable. Races **(a)** *bactriana* **(b)** *bottanensis*. ⌖ 1500-4600. Villages, orchards, groves, cultivation. Utilises all strata of its habitats. Singles, family groups and flocks. ▽ Harsh rattling *kekekekekek*; *querk*; *ker-plonk*. **RA2**

13 **Spotted Nutcracker** *Nucifraga caryocatactes* (1042-4) 32cm. Races **(a)** *hemispila* **(b)** *multipunctata* possibly a distinct species. From Striated Laughingthrush (71.17) by crow-like proportions and lack of crest. In flight note contrasting white rump, vent and terminal band to the undertail. ⌖ (300)2000-3300(4000). Oak, rhododendron and coniferous forest. More arboreal than terrestrial, frequently on treetops. Sometimes in parties or small flocks. ▽ Far-carrying, harsh rattling *kraak-kraak*; *krrreh*. **RA3**

14 **Hume's Groundpecker** *Pseudopodoces humilis* (1041) 20cm. Sandy plumage and upright stance recall a wheatear, but the longish decurved bill is distinctive. ⌖ 4000-5340. Tibetan steppe, villages. Largely terrestrial. Singly, in pairs or small loose groups. Moves by long bouncing hops or short flights. Feeds by digging for invertebrates. Often rather tame. ▽ Feeble *cheep*; *chip...cheep-cheep-cheep-cheep*. **R*4**

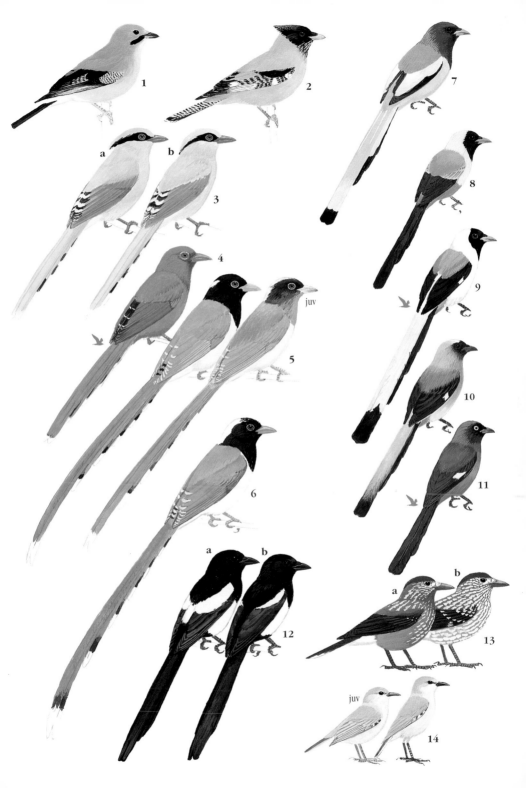

PLATE 63: BLACK CORVIDS (CROWS, ROOK, RAVENS, JACKDAWS AND CHOUGHS)

1 **(Asian Koel** *Eudynamys scolopacea* – ♂ illustrated here for comparison, as it is sometimes mistaken for a crow. Note slim build, long tail, green bill and red eye. For main entry see plate 46, figure 1.**)**

2 **Red-billed Chough** *Pyrrhocorax pyrrhocorax* (1046-7) 45cm. Distinguished from all other crows by long decurved red bill and from all but 3 by red legs. In flight from 3 by squarer tail with angular corners; longer head; longer, relatively slimmer, more angled wings with longer primary 'fingers'. **Juv** can be mistaken for 3 because of its shorter yellowish bill though this is usually tinged with orange or flesh rather than the pure yellow of 3. Such birds are usually accompanied by adults of their own species. ⌘ **S** 2400-4800(7950) **W** >(1450)1600 Open montane habitats. Usually at slightly lower elevations than 3 but sometimes found together. ▽ Plaintive *chiao; khew; jack; keea; chee-o-kah; kor-quick.* **RA1**

3 **Yellow-billed Chough** *Pyrrhocorax graculus* (1045) 38cm. Separated from all crows by short decurved yellow bill and from all but 2 by red legs. In flight from 2 by rounded tail; shorter head; shorter, straighter, relatively broader and more rounded wings with shorter primary 'fingers'. **Juv** has duller bill and brownish legs. ⌘ **S** (2700)3500-5000(8600). **W** >(1800)2400. Open montane habitats. Usually at somewhat higher elevations than 2. ▽ High musical *kwee-yu; quee-ah.* **RA1**

4 **[Daurian Jackdaw** *Corvus dauuricus* 33cm. ⌘ Grassy steppe, open meadows. ▽ As 5. **X** (Could occur as a vagrant.)**]**

5 **Eurasian Jackdaw** *Corvus monedula* (1053) 33cm. Somewhat resembling a small 6 but more compact, small bill, rounded head, short neck, pearly white eye, black face shading into grey on rear of head, wing-tips almost reaching tail-tip. In flight smaller than other crows; faster wing beats. ⌘ 1700-3500. Alpine pastures, meadows, cultivation, around human habitation. Gregarious. ▽ Characteristic short *kow* or *kya; jack; kwai;* hoarse *kraa.* **RWP3**

6 **House Crow** *Corvus splendens* (1048-51) 43cm. Familiar bird around human settlements through most of the subcontinent. The black and grey pattern distinguishes from all but the much smaller 5 (which see) and 9b. From latter by steep forehead, relatively longer, deeper bill, black of head not extending to breast or hindcrown, wing-tip usually only reaching two-thirds down tail (vs almost to tail-tip). Races **(a)** nom **(b)** *zugmayeri.* ⌘ <1600(2100). Towns and larger villages. Gregarious. ▽ *quah quah* softer than 10. **RA*1**

7 **Brown-necked Raven** *Corvus ruficollis* (1061) 58cm. Told with difficulty from 8, except at close range by the bronze-brown tinge to neck and nape; in flight by the relatively longer, slimmer wings and longer head. The brown tinge is absent on **juv**. Range indicative. ⌘ Sandy or gravelly desert; tame around encampments. In pairs and flocks. ▽ Deep *aarragh* but higher-pitched than 8. **R*W*3**

8 **Common Raven** *Corvus corax* (1059-60) 69cm. Distinguished from most crows by large size; heavy bill and shaggy throat feathers; in flight by the long wedge-shaped tail; protruding head; long 'fingers'. From 7 by absence of brown tinge (only appreciable at close range); stouter head and bill; in flight note the broader wings and head. Range indicative. See also 10. ⌘ Race *subcorax* <600. Desert and semi-desert. Race *tibetanus* (2500)3500-5000(8240). Dry stony Trans-Himalayan desert. Usually in pairs; sometimes in small flocks. ▽ Deeper and more metallic than any other corvid: *krraah; gonk-gonk; pru-uk pru-uk.* **RW3**

9 **Carrion Crow** *Corvus corone* (1058-8a) 47cm. Races **(a)** *orientalis* from 10 by flat head and slimmer bill. **(b)** *sharpii* could be confused with 6 but the grey parts are much paler and include the back and mantle. This race is sometimes regarded as belonging to a separate species Hooded Crow *Corvis cornix.* ⌘ 2000-3600. Open barren areas with patches of cultivation and forest; often around habitation. Gregarious. ▽ Harsher *kah kah* than 6. **R*W*2**

10 **Large-billed Crow** *Corvus macrorhynchos* (1054-7) 48cm. Easily told from 6 by larger size and glossy black plumage. Size and bill shape distinguish from 2, 3, 5 & 11. From 9 by more domed head; heavier bill, more strongly curved on the culmen. Most likely to be confused with 8 but more domed head; lack of shaggy throat feathers; wing-tip reaching only $^{1}/_{2}$-$^{3}/_{4}$ down tail (vs more-or-less to tail-tip); in flight less diamond-shaped tail and less protruding head. Races **(a)** *levaillantii* sometimes treated as a separate species, Jungle Crow (including *culminatus*). **(b)** *intermedius.* ⌘ **(a)** <1000(2300). Forest, well-wooded compounds on the outskirts of towns and villages. **(b)** 1800-4500(6400) Mixed forest, alpine meadows, vicinity of habitation. Mostly in pairs and small groups, though may roost in larger numbers. ▽ **(a)** Deeper *kraa kraa* than 6. **(b)** deeper still, but not as deep as 8. **RA2**

11 **Rook** *Corvus frugilegus* (1052) 48cm. Best separated from other crows by the relatively thin, tapering bill, pale greyish at its base and on the adjoining facial skin; steep angular forehead often apparent. **Juv** lacks the grey colour and has black feathers covering nostrils; has to be identified by shape of bill and head (from 9 also by shaggy 'thighs'). ⌘ Arable land, outskirts of towns and villages. Gregarious. ▽ *kaa kaa* like 6 but less harsh; *kwow.* **W*P3**

PLATE 63

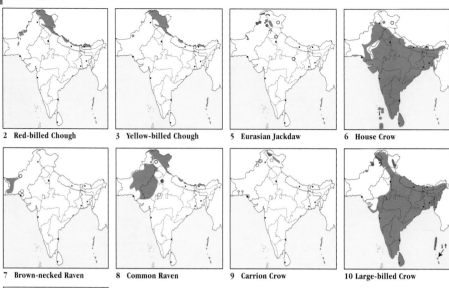

2 Red-billed Chough   3 Yellow-billed Chough   5 Eurasian Jackdaw   6 House Crow

7 Brown-necked Raven   8 Common Raven   9 Carrion Crow   10 Large-billed Crow

11 Rook

PLATE 64

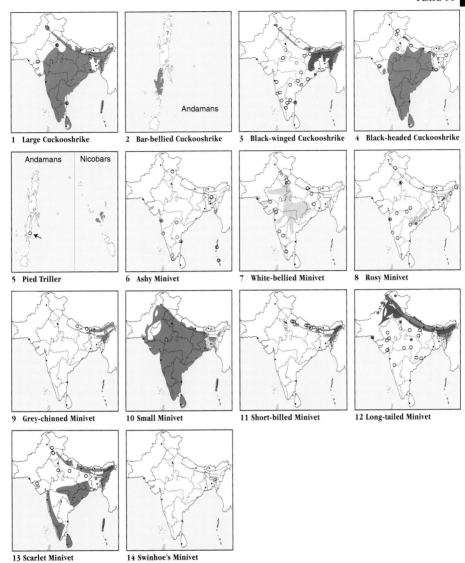

1 Large Cuckooshrike 2 Bar-bellied Cuckooshrike 3 Black-winged Cuckooshrike 4 Black-headed Cuckooshrike

Andamans

Andamans Nicobars

5 Pied Triller 6 Ashy Minivet 7 White-bellied Minivet 8 Rosy Minivet

9 Grey-chinned Minivet 10 Small Minivet 11 Short-billed Minivet 12 Long-tailed Minivet

13 Scarlet Minivet 14 Swinhoe's Minivet

PLATE 64: CUCKOOSHRIKES, TRILLER AND MINIVETS

1 **Large Cuckooshrike** *Coracina macei* (1072-5) 28cm. Large size. ♂ conspicuous dark band through eye. See also 3. Races **(a)** *nipalensis* ♂ from other cuckooshrikes (except 3) by grey throat and breast fading into unbarred white belly and vent; much paler and larger then 3. ♀/imm from other ♀♀ by grey throat and upper breast. **(b)** nom. Race *andamana* (not illustrated) of the Andaman Islands is like *nipalensis* but paler. ✺ **S** <2400. **W** <1500(2400). Open wooded country, groves, scrub jungle. ▽ Loud squealing *chiyeuw*(*ee*) or *ooeea*. **R•A3**

2 **Bar-bellied Cuckooshrike** *Coracina striata* (1076) 26cm. Restricted to the Andaman Islands. Very dark grey colour distinguishes this from the local race of 1 which is pale grey. Note also habitat. ✺ Dense primary forest. Usually in pairs, often in mixed flocks. ▽ [In Thailand a whinnying *kliu-kliu-kliu-kliu*; harsh grating *gree-ew...gree-ew.*] **R*4**

3 **Black-winged Cuckooshrike** *Coracina melaschistos* (1077) 22cm. Black wings. ♂ much darker and smaller than ♂1. ♀ from other cuckooshrikes by grey underparts usually with some barring. ✺ **S**<2200. **W**<1000. Open forest, groves, secondary jungle. ▽ Loud plaintive (*tweet*)-*tweet-tweet-tweeor* or *peeoo-peeoo-peeoo*. **RAM3**

4 **Black-headed Cuckooshrike** *Coracina melanoptera* (1078-9) 20cm. Black hood of ♂ diagnostic. ♀ from 1 by small size, browner upperparts and white supercilium (not always present); from ♀3 by white underparts with dark barring (and white supercilium if present). ✺ <2100. Open forest, secondary jungle, orchards, groves, mangroves. ▽ Clear whistles followed by *pit-pit-pit*; *twit-wit-wit-wee-twee-twee-twee-twee*; chirp. **R•3-4**

5 **Pied Triller** *Lalage nigra* (1079a) 16cm. ♂ could be confused with 6 but note white supercilium and large amount of white in wings. See also Bar-winged Flycatcher-shrike (60.2) and Little Pied Flycatcher (73.13). ♀ like juv but greyer. ✺ Forest edge; secondary jungle. ▽ [In E Asia a disyllabic whistle and nasal *tre`tre`tre....*] **R*4**

6 **Ashy Minivet** *Pericrocotus divaricatus* (1089a) 19cm. No red or yellow in plumage. Small white wing-patch can be seen in flight. For differences see 14. ✺ Chiefly <1000. Forest, wooded compounds, mangroves. ▽ Musical trill. **W5**

7 **White-bellied Minivet** *Pericrocotus erythropygius* (1096) 15cm. ♂ pied with orange-red rump and breast patch. ♀ from other ♀♀ by white in wing. ✺ Mainly plains level and lower hills. Dry open forest, semi-desert scrub, open grassy forest. Less arboreal than other minivets, often perching on low bushes. ▽ *tseep*(*it*)-*tseep*; *chit-chit*. **R*4**

8 **Rosy Minivet** *Pericrocotus roseus* (1089) 18cm. ♂ washed with pink below. ♀ only slightly olive rump, weakly yellowish below with greyish-white throat. ✺ <1800. Forest, lightly wooded areas, gardens. **R*M*?4**

9 **Grey-chinned Minivet** *Pericrocotus solaris* (1088) 17cm. ♂ grey chin; pale orange throat. ♀ from 11 and 12 by greyish-white chin (very little or no yellow on forehead). ✺ <3000. Open moist hill forest. ▽ Rasping *tsee-sip* reminiscent of Vernal Hanging Parrot (44.14). **A3**

10 **Small Minivet** *Pericrocotus cinnamomeus* (1090-5) 15cm. ♂ grey crown, nape, back and mantle, black throat and mask, orange breast and rump. ♀ orange rump. Races **(a)** nom **(b)** *pallidus*. ✺ Mainly lowlands (up to 1650). Open forest, semi-desert, thorn forest, scrub, groves, gardens. ▽ High feeble *swee-swee....* **R1**

11 **Short-billed Minivet** *Pericrocotus brevirostris* (1084) 17cm. ♂ red chevron on wing does not extend down tertials to form a 'U' as in ♂12. ♀ very similar to ♀12 showing the same wing pattern but richer yellow below, yellow wash on ear-coverts, yellow of forehead extends up above the eye to the middle of the crown where it fades into the olive-grey of the upperparts. ✺ **S** 1800-2400(2750). **W** >foothills. Broadleaved open forest, forest edge, second growth. ▽ Loud, high whistle *tseee*; *tup*. **A3**

12 **Long-tailed Minivet** *Pericrocotus ethologus* (1085-7) 18cm. ♂ inverted red 'U' on wing. ♀ similar to ♀11 but not strongly yellow below, grey ear-coverts, yellow of forehead confined to small patch just above the bill. In western races, where 11 is absent, yellow is more extensive. ✺ **S** 1200-3400(3970). **W** <1000(2140). Open forest, groves, wooded compounds, forest edge. ▽ *swiswisweet*; *swisweet-sweet-sweet*; *see-see-tew-ke-wit*. **RAM2**

13 **Scarlet Minivet** *Pericrocotus flammeus* (1080-3) 20cm. Large size; red wing-chevron with (one or) two additional 'drops' on the secondaries (yellow in ♀). Races **(a)** *speciosus* **(b)** nom. ✺ <2700. Forest, mango groves. ▽ Sweet *twee-twee*; *tweetywee-tweetywee-tywee*. **RA2**

14 [**Swinhoe's Minivet** *Pericrocotus cantonensis* (not illustrated). 18cm. Formerly treated as a race of 8. Very similar to ♀6 but has brownish upperparts with contrasting paler rump and uppertail-coverts and a yellowish-tinged wing-bar. Whitish forecrown of ♂ extends back to above eye as in ♂6 but hindcrown is brown (vs black). **V?** (Recent records from Bangladesh not yet fully documented.)]

PLATE 65: BULBULS

1 **Black Bulbul** *Hypsipetes leucocephalus* (1148-51) 23cm. Races (**a**) *psaroides* (**b**) *ganeesa*. ⌘ <3000. Mature forest, plantations, gardens. Gregarious. ▽ Cat-like nasal *weenh*; *eeagh*; *whew whé*; *wur-kíyu*; chattering. **R•A1**

2 **Nicobar Bulbul** *Hypsipetes nicobariensis* (1142) 20cm. ⌘ Forest, gardens. Gregarious. ▽ Chattering like 1. **E*4**

3 **Mountain Bulbul** *Hypsipetes mcclellandii* (1146) 23cm. Bushy rusty-brown crest. ⌘ S 900-2700. W >plains. Forest, second growth. Sometimes in bird waves. ▽ *cheep-har-lee*; *pseeuw*; squeaky *tsyi-tsyi*; *kui-krrit...kuikuikuikui*. **A3**

4 **Striated Bulbul** *Pycnonotus striatus* (1133-4) 20cm. Yellow throat and streaked plumage. ⌘ S 1200-2400(3000). W > foothills. Moist broadleaved forest. ▽ *tyiwut*; *pyik.....pyik*; mellow *chee-tu-(ti-ti-ti-twee-oo)*; chattering. **RA3**

5 **Yellow-throated Bulbul** *Pycnonotus xantholaemus* (1135) 20cm. ⌘ 600-1200. Rocky hillsides covered in scrub with scattered trees and/or groves. Usually singly, in pairs or small groups. ▽ Cheery *whichit-woo-ichit-wheweew* etc. **E*4**

6 **White-throated Bulbul** *Alophoixus flaveolus* (1140) 23cm. ⌘ <1800. Primary and secondary evergreen forest with thick undergrowth. Usually in flocks. ▽ Harsh nasal *kake kake*; loud clear *teek*, *da-te-ek*, *da-té-ek*. **RA1-2**

7 **Yellow-browed Bulbul** *Iole indica* (1143-5) 20cm. ⌘ (Plains)900-1500(1950). Moist evergreen forest, sholas, forest edge, coffee plantations. Often in mixed hunting parties. ▽ Mellow *whit-whee*; harsh alarm note. **E1-2**

8 **Olive Bulbul** *Iole virescens* (1141) 19cm. Fairly nondescript. From 18 by olive-toned upperparts, warmer brown crown, olive-yellow wash on underparts. ⌘ <900. Well-wooded ravines, moist evergreen forest, second growth; usually in canopy, singly or small groups; may form large flocks. ▽ Nasal *chwaa*; *jer-wee*; soft whistling. **R*5**

9 **Ashy Bulbul** *Hemixos flavala* (1147) 20cm. ⌘ S 700-1600. W >plains. Forest, forest edge, second growth. Gregarious. ▽ Musical *dew de-di-do-it*; (*daddy*) (*daddy*) *daddy*, *leave it*. **RA1-2**

10 **Crested Finchbill** *Spizixos canifrons* (1111) 20cm. ⌘ S 1400-2500. W >900. Forest, scrub, second growth. Gregarious. ▽ Rattling *whi-whi whi-whi* (*whi-whi*); *whi-whi whi-whi-whi-wheee*; *proo-dee-do-dee-do-dee-dit*. **RA3-4**

11 **Red-vented Bulbul** *Pycnonotus cafer* (1126-32) 20cm. The commonest and most widespread bulbul. Races (**a**) nom (**b**) *bengalensis*. ⌘ <1500(2140). Open scrub, parks, gardens, open deciduous forest, secondary jungle. In pairs and small parties. ▽ *be care-ful*; sharp *peep*; *chwee*; *jit-jew*. **R1**

12 **Red-whiskered Bulbul** *Pycnonotus jocosus* (1118-22) 20cm. From all bulbuls except 11 by red vent. From latter by jaunty crest, white ear-coverts with red post-ocular 'whiskers' (reduced or absent in some birds of the extreme north-east and in immatures). ⌘ <1800. Parks, gardens, scrub, light forest, second growth. Usually in moister habitats than 11 & 13. Normally in pairs or small parties; occasionally in flocks. ▽ Cheery (*kick*)-*pettigrew*; *pleased-to-meet-you*. **R1**

13 **White-eared Bulbul** *Pycnonotus leucotis* (1123-4) 20cm. See 14 for differences. ⌘ <1800. Semi-desert, scrub, gardens, cultivation, mangroves. Chiefly in pairs and small parties; sometimes in flocks. ▽ Similar to 14. **R•2**

14 **Himalayan Bulbul** *Pycnonotus leucogenys* (1125) 20cm. From 13 by long jaunty crest, brown (vs black) head, smaller white cheek-patch with a different shape, short indistinct white supraloral stripe, earth-brown (vs grey-brown) upperparts; pure yellow (vs orangy-yellow) vent. ⌘ 300-2400. Open scrub, second growth, hedges, cultivation. Chiefly in pairs and small parties; sometimes in flocks. ▽ *tea for two*; *whichyou-whichyou-whreeu*. **R•2**

15 **Yellow-eared Bulbul** *Pycnonotus penicillatus* (1136) 20cm. Head pattern distinctive. ⌘ >900. Hill forest, wooded parks and gardens. Usually in bushes and low trees. In pairs, small parties and mixed flocks. ▽ *wheet-wit-wit*; *crr-crr*. **E2**

16 **Black-headed Bulbul** *Pycnonotus atriceps* (1112-3) 18cm. Where ranges overlap, separated from 17 by tail pattern and absence of crest. Races (**a**) nom (**b**) *fuscoflavescens*. ⌘ <700. Broadleaved forest, second growth, gardens. Generally in pairs. ▽ Sharp *chirp*; mournful double whistle; *whi`whi-tyee*. **R3-4**

17 **Black-crested Bulbul** *Pycnonotus melanicterus* (1115-7) 18cm. For differences see 16. Races (**a**) nom (**b**) *gularis* (**c**) *flaviventris* considered as separate species by some authors. ⌘ <1500(2400). Thick forest with good undergrowth, secondary jungle, well-wooded country, scrub adjoining arable land, orchards. Normally singly or in pairs; sometimes in small groups. ▽ (**a**) *whit-it-it...*; *troo-troo tilloodeetyoo* (**b**) *weet-tre-trippy-weet* (**c**) *weet-trippy-weet*. **R3**

18 **Flavescent Bulbul** *Pycnonotus flavescens* (1137) 20cm. From 8 by the contrasting yellow vent and whitish supraloral stripe. ⌘ S 900-2100. W >450. Forest with dense undergrowth, thick scrub, second growth, dense bushes. Shy. In small groups or flocks. ▽ Harsh churring; two bold notes followed by short trill. **RA4**

19 **Grey-headed Bulbul** *Pycnonotus priocephalus* (1114) 19cm. ⌘ (plains)600-1000(1800). Moist habitats with dense bamboo, lantana scrub, fruiting trees. Usually singly or in pairs. ▽ Buzzy ringing *dzee*; high *tweep*; wheezy *chaik*. **E4**

20 **White-browed Bulbul** *Pycnonotus luteolus* (1138-9) 20cm. From all similar bulbuls by white supercilium. ⌘ Dense bushes in dry, fairly open scrubby country. Shy. Usually in pairs or small groups. ▽ Bursts of bubbly rattling notes. **E3**

PLATE 65

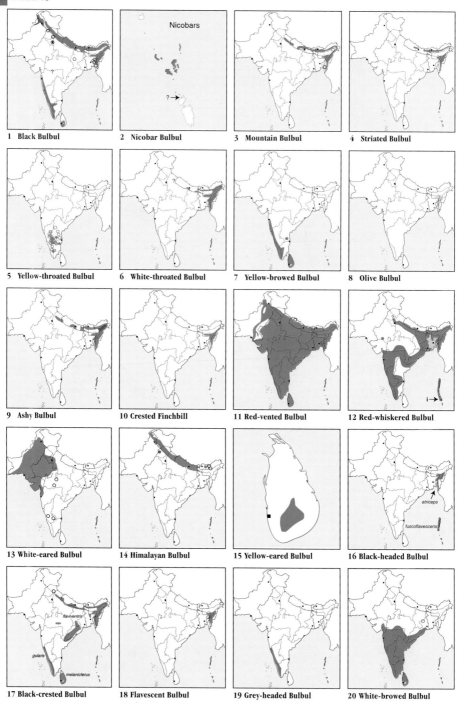

1 Black Bulbul

2 Nicobar Bulbul

3 Mountain Bulbul

4 Striated Bulbul

5 Yellow-throated Bulbul

6 White-throated Bulbul

7 Yellow-browed Bulbul

8 Olive Bulbul

9 Ashy Bulbul

10 Crested Finchbill

11 Red-vented Bulbul

12 Red-whiskered Bulbul

13 White-eared Bulbul

14 Himalayan Bulbul

15 Yellow-eared Bulbul

16 Black-headed Bulbul

17 Black-crested Bulbul

18 Flavescent Bulbul

19 Grey-headed Bulbul

20 White-browed Bulbul

PLATE 66

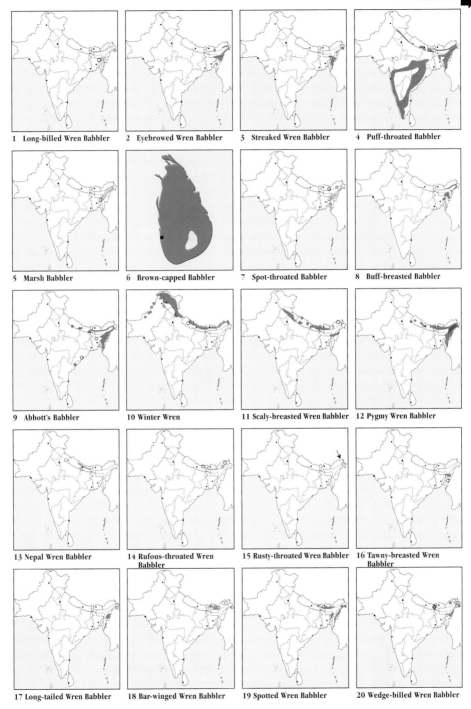

1 Long-billed Wren Babbler

2 Eyebrowed Wren Babbler

3 Streaked Wren Babbler

4 Puff-throated Babbler

5 Marsh Babbler

6 Brown-capped Babbler

7 Spot-throated Babbler

8 Buff-breasted Babbler

9 Abbott's Babbler

10 Winter Wren

11 Scaly-breasted Wren Babbler

12 Pygmy Wren Babbler

13 Nepal Wren Babbler

14 Rufous-throated Wren Babbler

15 Rusty-throated Wren Babbler

16 Tawny-breasted Wren Babbler

17 Long-tailed Wren Babbler

18 Bar-winged Wren Babbler

19 Spotted Wren Babbler

20 Wedge-billed Wren Babbler

PLATE 66: BABBLERS I (JUNGLE AND WREN BABBLERS) AND WINTER WREN

1 **Long-billed Wren Babbler** *Rimator malacoptilus* (1193) 12cm. Small size with long downcurved bill and long pale streaks on plumage distinctive. ✿ 900-2700. Forest undergrowth, dense scrub. ▽ Sweet chirping whistle. **R*(A?)5**

2 **Eyebrowed Wren Babbler** *Napothera epilepidota* (1195-6) 10.5cm. Long pale supercilium; streaking on throat/breast. ✿ S 1000-1800. W >plains. Boulders and treefalls in forest. ▽ Descending *keeeeee*; shrill *chir-r-r*; low whistles. **A4**

3 **Streaked Wren Babbler** *Napothera brevicaudata* (1194) 12cm. Diffuse streaking on white throat. Cf. 2. ✿ 350-2100. Rocky forested slopes. ▽ *tsik*; *wit-(tu)*; loud *pwee-pwee...*; *wee-wi-wi-(wi)*; plaintive *piou*; *pseeou*; churring. **A*3-4**

4 **Puff-throated Babbler** *Pellorneum ruficeps* (1152-9) 16cm. Note pale supercilium; rufous-brown cap contrasting with brown back; broad brown streaking on breast and flanks. Races **(a)** nom **(b)** *mandelli*. ✿ <1800. Forest undergrowth, woodland scrub. ▽ *(be'll) beat you*; *kraa*; mellow *tee-tee tee`too tee-tee tee`too too too-too*. **R2**

5 **Marsh Babbler** *Pellorneum palustre* (1160) 15cm. Like 4 but cap concolorous with back; rusty flanks, vent, cheeks and breast; breast streaking to base of throat; no supercilium, lores pale. ✿ Reeds, tall grass and tangled scrub near water. ▽ *(prrk)-(prrk) whee-chee-chee-chee-chi-cheew-choo*, etc.; churring alarm. **E*5**

6 **Brown-capped Babbler** *Pellorneum fuscocapillum* (1161-3) 15cm. ✿ <1650. Undergrowth. ▽ *prit`tee `dear*; *wit*. **E3**

7 **Spot-throated Babbler** *Pellorneum albiventre* (1164-5) 14cm. From 8 & 9 by spotting on clear white throat (hard to see); grey lores and supercilium; more rounded tail than 8. ✿ S 500-1500. Bamboo, heavy scrub, second growth. W >plains. Forest undergrowth. ▽ *chick*; low chuckling and rippling notes; clear whistle; mellifluous thrush-like song. **A4**

8 **Buff-breasted Babbler** *Pellorneum tickelli* (1166) 14cm. Nondescript skulker; from 7 & 9 by pale shaft-streaks on crown and upper mantle; unspotted buffy white throat; squarer tail than 7; smaller bill than 9. ✿ **(Plains)** 1000-1400(2100). Scrub, forest undergrowth, bamboo. ▽ *tsip*; *chirr-chirr*; *pit-you...pit-you*; churring alarm. **A3**

9 **Abbott's Babbler** *Malacocincla abbotti* (1167) 16cm. From 7 & 8 by large bill; greyish-white supercilium and throat; rusty vent; longer-tailed appearance. Lacks 7's throat spotting. ✿ <600. Tangled undergrowth in primary forest, forest edge, streamside vegetation; partial to palm-ferns. ▽ *twee`choo`twee*; *poor ol bear dear dear*. **R3**

10 **Winter Wren** *Troglodytes troglodytes* (1769-71) 9cm. Barring on rear half; stub tail held cocked. Races **(a)** *neglectus* **(b)** *nipalensis*. ✿ S (2400)2700-5000(5300). W 1200-3600(4700). Tangles, piles of rocks; forest undergrowth. ▽ *tzick*; *tzrrr*; *trrrk*; loud rapid song. **A2**

11 **Scaly-breasted Wren Babbler** *Pnoepyga albiventer* (1197-8) 10.5cm. Larger than 12; usually more spotted including head/sides of neck. From 13 by warm dark brown upperparts; spotted (vs streaked) underparts; spotting on head, mantle, wing-coverts. Colour forms **(a)** white **(b)** fulvous. ✿ S 1000-4000, usually higher than 12. W >(270)1000. Moist undergrowth; mossy boulders. ▽ High *tsik*; *tsup*; rapid *tzee-tsu-wi-tu-ti-ti-wi-ti-ti-tit*. **A3**

12 **Pygmy Wren Babbler** *Pnoepyga pusilla* (1199) 9cm. See 11 and 13 for differences; colour forms as 11. ✿ S (1000)2100-2400(3500). W >plains. Wet evergreen forest undergrowth. ▽ *tsee.....tsu* like squeaky swing; *tzit*; *tzook*. **A3**

13 **Nepal Wren Babbler** *Pnoepyga immaculata* 10cm. Unspotted above; more olive-tinged than warmer 11 & 12; longer-billed; scaly feathers of underparts longer/narrower, streaked rather than spotted. ✿ S 2000-3100. W >plains. Dense undergrowth and clearings in mixed forest. ▽ High rapid *ti-ti-ti-ti-ti-ti-ti-ti-ti* descending slightly in tone. **E*4**

14 **Rufous-throated Wren Babbler** *Spelaeornis caudatus* (1200) 9.5cm. From all but 15 (which see) by rusty throat, upper breast and flanks; grey sides of head. ✿ S >2400. W 1800-3100. Undergrowth and mossy rocks in dense broadleaved forest. ▽ High-pitched *tzit*; quiet, hard rasping *tip-tip-tip-tip-(tip)*; *wheewchy-wheechy-wheechy-wheech*. **EA*4-5**

15 **Rusty-throated Wren Babbler** *Spelaeornis badeigularis* (1201) 9cm. Similar to 14 but white chin; rufous restricted to throat and upper breast, streaked dark brown; longer legs. ✿ 1600m in wet forest, Mishmi Hills. **E*5** Single record.

16 **Tawny-breasted Wren Babbler** *Spelaeornis longicaudatus* (1202) 11cm. Rufous below except whitish chin and centre of belly; greyish-brown ear-coverts; long unbarred tail. ✿ 1000-2000. Gullies and undergrowth in wet evergreen forest on rocky hillsides. ▽ Loud clear whistle; chirring alarm. **E*5**

17 **Long-tailed Wren Babbler** *Spelaeornis chocolatinus* (1203-4) 11cm. Relatively long unbarred tail; mainly white below, spotted black. As 12. ▽ Explosive *wheeuw*; soft *chir*; *tuc*; *turruc*; *tititjui...*; *ticki-ticki-ticki-ticki*. **R*5**

18 **Bar-winged Wren Babbler** *Spelaeornis troglodytoides* (1205) 11cm. Relatively long barred tail and wings; contrasting white throat/upper breast; black and white spotting on head and mantle; distinctive pale spot behind eye. ✿ 3000-3300. Dense undergrowth/bamboo in wet temperate evergreen forest. ▽ *cheep*; *churr*; loud *chu wulu-wulu-wulu-wulu*. **R*5**

19 **Spotted Wren Babbler** *Spelaeornis formosus* (1206) 10cm. Entire underparts 'starred': white on throat, black and white on breast and belly. ✿ >300. Mossy rocks and undergrowth in broadleaved evergreen forest, often near streams. Shy. ▽ *tsik*; *p-r-r-r-r-t*; distinctive, very high thin *teet`teet-tititidee`tititidee-tititidee*. **A*4**

20 **Wedge-billed Wren Babbler** *Sphenocichla humei* (1207-8) 18cm. Wedge-shaped bill. Races **(a)** nom **(b)** *roberti* may be separate species. ✿ >(800)1200. Evergreen forest understorey; bamboo. Gregarious. ▽ *brrrh brrrh...*. **NA*5**

PLATE 67: BABBLERS II (SCIMITAR, TREE AND TIT BABBLERS)

1 **Indian Scimitar Babbler** *Pomatorhinus horsfieldii* (1172-7) 23cm. Races **(a)** nom **(b)** *travancoreensis* **(c)** *melanurus*. ✳ Forest, thorn scrub, bamboo, cardamom. ∇ Hollow *oop pu-pu-(pu)-(pu)* (♂)...*krukru-(wree)*(♀); *churr*. **E2**

2 **White-browed Scimitar Babbler** *Pomatorhinus schisticeps* (1168-71) 23cm. From 1 by rusty border to white throat and breast. ✳ Edge of plains–1500(2000+). Forest undergrowth, bamboo, second growth and scrub. ∇ *woot-oot-oot- (oot)-(oot)-(oot)*; *woot-wowowowowowoh*; *woot-a-ah-hoot*; *woot-ah-wree*; *tjoo-tjoo*. **R3**

3 **Red-billed Scimitar Babbler** *Pomatorhinus ochraceiceps* (1189-90) 23cm. Similar to 6 but longer bill orange-red (vs coral-red); eye-stripe brown and usually narrow (vs black and broad) behind the eye; underparts largely white (vs orange or deep rufous) with rufous-buff on flanks and vent only; from 6a by brown (vs blackish) crown. ✳ **S** >1500. **W** >foothills. Dense forest and bamboo. ∇ Liquid *tu-lip*; hollow *hoop-hoop*; whistling chuckle. **A4**

4 **Streak-breasted Scimitar Babbler** *Pomatorhinus ruficollis* (1178-80) 19cm. ✳ 700-3300. Forest and scrubby hill-sides. ∇ *off-an-on*(♂)..*quee-quee*(♀); *peeo*. **A3**

5 **Large Scimitar Babbler** *Pomatorhinus hypoleucos* (1185) 28cm. ✳ <1200. Forest undergrowth; bamboo, scrub, grass. ∇ Deep mellow *koot-koot-koot*(♂)...*hoot-ha-hoot*(♀); *hoo-hoo-peh*(♂)..*hoo-pi-hoo*(♀); chuckling. **R*4**

6 **Coral-billed Scimitar Babbler** *Pomatorhinus ferruginosus* (1186-8) 22cm. Like 3 which see. Races **(a)** nom **(b)** *formosus*. ✳ (600)1200-3800. Thick undergrowth/bamboo, especially near streams. ∇ *ou-pu-pu-(pu)*; *churrr*. **R3**

7 **Rusty-cheeked Scimitar Babbler** *Pomatorhinus erythrogenys* (1181-3) 24cm. ✳ 450-2200(2700). Thick scrub at forest edge; overgrown nullahs; bushy slopes. ∇ *cue-pee*(♂)-*quip*(♀); *raow-kuw*(♂)-*kip*(♀); *kokuko*(♂)-*kit*(♀); *quoik*; *chur*; *kew*; *che-che-che*. **R2**

8 **Spot-breasted Scimitar Babbler** *Pomatorhinus erythrocnemis* (1184) 22cm. ✳ 750-1800+. Forest, scrub jungle, second growth. ∇ *callow-cree*(♂)-*quip*(♀). **R5**

9 **Slender-billed Scimitar Babbler** *Xiphirhynchus superciliaris* (1191-2) 20cm. ✳ Foothills-3300(3400). Bamboo and dense undergrowth in moist forest. ∇ Mellow tremulous (*hwo*)-*hwowowowowowowo* trailing off at end; *doo...whee-whee-whee-(whee)*. **A4**

10 **Rufous-fronted Babbler** *Stachyris rufifrons* (1209) 12cm. Chestnut cap does not extend beyond hind-crown; white throat and centre of belly. See 11. ✳ <1200. Forest, grassland, bamboo, scrub. ∇ Piping *pu pu-pu-pu-pu-pu-(pu)*. **R3**

11 **Rufous-capped Babbler** *Stachyris ruficeps* (1210) 12cm. Like 10 but chestnut cap extends back to nape merging into greyish-olive back; whitish throat tinged yellow; pale yellow belly. ✳ **S** (1000)1500-1400(2700). **W** >600. Usually higher than 10. Undergrowth in evergreen forest, second growth and bamboo. ∇ Piping *pee pee-pee-pee-pee-pee*. **R3**

12 **Black-chinned Babbler** *Stachyris pyrrhops* (1211) 10cm. ✳ (300)750-2000(2400). Light forest, scrub, bamboo, overgrown streams, hedges. ∇ *chir*; *preew-vee-(vee)*; mellow *wit-wit-wit-wit-wit-wit-(wit)*. **E3**

13 **Golden Babbler** *Stachyris chrysaea* (1212-3) 10cm. Races **(a)** nom **(b)** *binghami*. ✳ 300-2600. Dense undergrowth in moist evergreen forest and second growth. ∇ *chirik-chirik*; *pee pee-pee-pee-pee-pee* similar to 11 but slower, more measured and usually with a more obvious gap after the first note; *tzu-tzu-tzu*. **R3**

14 **Grey-throated Babbler** *Stachyris nigriceps* (1214-7) 12cm. Races **(a)** nom **(b)** *coltarti*. ✳ Plains edge-1800. Undergrowth in evergreen forest, bamboo and thick scrub. ∇ Explosive *churri*; *tweeye-t'twa*; high *tsee-tsee t-r-r-rrrrrrri*. **R3**

15 **Snowy-throated Babbler** *Stachyris oglei* (1218) 13cm. ✳ <1800+(?). Primary forest, bamboo, moist dense scrub in rocky ravines. In flocks. ∇ Hard ticking chittering; *chirr-chirr*; *chit*; *chirrik*. **E*4**

16 **Tawny-bellied Babbler** *Dumetia hyperythra* (1219-23) 13cm. Races **(a)** nom **(b)** *albogularis*. ✳ <1800. Grassland, scrub, bamboo, deciduous forest. ∇ Weak *sweech...sweech*; *check-check*; clear whistling song. **E3**

17 **Dark-fronted Babbler** *Rhopocichla atriceps* (1224-7) 13cm. Races **(a)** nom **(b)** *siccatus*. ✳ <2100+. Undergrowth in evergreen forest, scrub and bamboo. ∇ Dry rattling *chirr-irr*; squeaks. **E3**

18 **Striped Tit Babbler** *Macronous gularis* (1228) 11cm. From 10 & 11 by wholly yellow underparts; yellow supercilium; narrow black streaks on breast visible at close range; yellow eye; distinctive voice. ✳ <600(900). Forest undergrowth, bamboo, long grass and brushwood. ∇ Emphatic resonant *chew-chew-chew...*or *chonk-chonk-chonk...* in runs of up to 50 or more (sometimes mistaken for a barbet); *chichoo*; *chr-r-r*; *pick pick*. **R1-2**

19 **Yellow-eyed Babbler** *Chrysomma sinense* (1230-2) 18cm. ✳ <1200(1800). Variety of scrubby and coarse grassy habitats. ∇ Clear plaintive *cheep-cheep-cheep*; *chip-chew*; *churrr*; *twee-twee-twee-ta-whit-chu*. **R3**

20 **Jerdon's Babbler** *Chrysomma altirostre* (1233-4) 17cm. Races **(a)** *scindicum* **(b)** *griseigulare*. ✳ Plains. Broad expanses of long (elephant-) grass and reeds. ∇ *tsik*; *trik*; *chew chew chi`chi`chyeuw...*; *sweet oot sweet oot sweetee eedle*. **N*5**

216

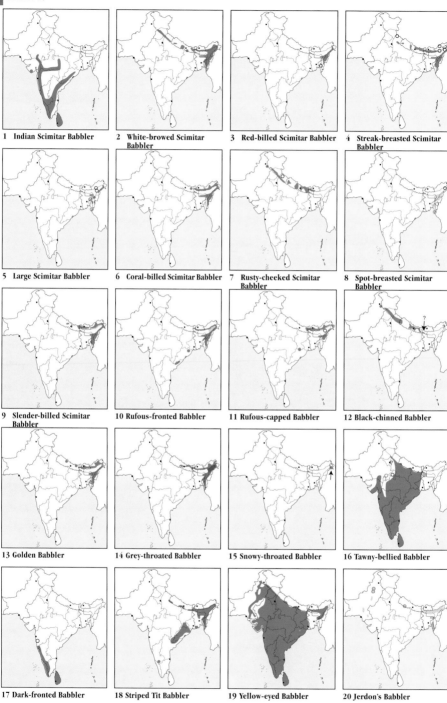

PLATE 67

1   Indian Scimitar Babbler

2   White-browed Scimitar Babbler

3   Red-billed Scimitar Babbler

4   Streak-breasted Scimitar Babbler

5   Large Scimitar Babbler

6   Coral-billed Scimitar Babbler

7   Rusty-cheeked Scimitar Babbler

8   Spot-breasted Scimitar Babbler

9   Slender-billed Scimitar Babbler

10 Rufous-fronted Babbler

11 Rufous-capped Babbler

12 Black-chinned Babbler

13 Golden Babbler

14 Grey-throated Babbler

15 Snowy-throated Babbler

16 Tawny-bellied Babbler

17 Dark-fronted Babbler

18 Striped Tit Babbler

19 Yellow-eyed Babbler

20 Jerdon's Babbler

PLATE 68

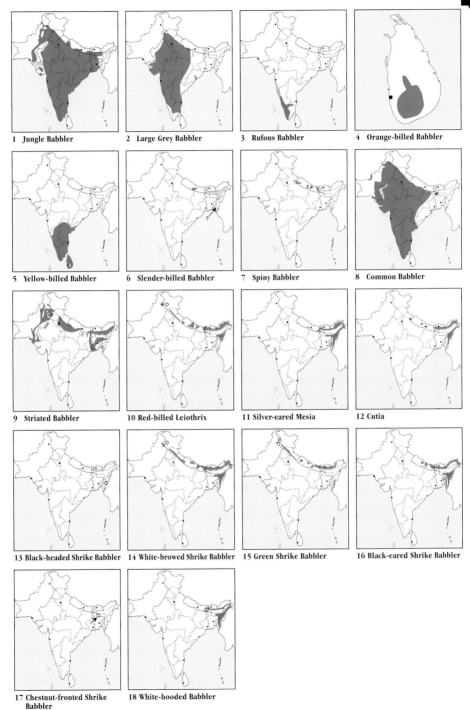

1 Jungle Babbler

2 Large Grey Babbler

3 Rufous Babbler

4 Orange-billed Babbler

5 Yellow-billed Babbler

6 Slender-billed Babbler

7 Spiny Babbler

8 Common Babbler

9 Striated Babbler

10 Red-billed Leiothrix

11 Silver-eared Mesia

12 Cutia

13 Black-headed Shrike Babbler

14 White-browed Shrike Babbler

15 Green Shrike Babbler

16 Black-eared Shrike Babbler

17 Chestnut-fronted Shrike Babbler

18 White-hooded Babbler

219

PLATE 68: BABBLERS III (*TURDOIDES*, LEIOTHRIX, MESIA, CUTIA, SHRIKE BABBLERS)

1 **Jungle Babbler** *Turdoides striatus* (1261-5) 25cm. From 2 by pale lores; yellow bill; shorter tail without pale outer feathers. Races (**a**) nom (**b**) *somervillei*. ✿ <1200(1800). Mainly plains cultivation, gardens, scrub, deciduous forest, second growth. ▽ Harsh *ke-ke-ke*; discordant squeaking and chattering. **E1**

2 **Large Grey Babbler** *Turdoides malcolmi* (1258) 28cm. From 1 by dark lores and upper mandible; grey forecrown; in flight by pale outer feathers on long graduated tail; distinctive voice. ✿ <1200. Dry, open areas with sparse scrub. ▽ Persistent nasal *naeh-naeh-naeh...* often for minutes at a time. **E2**

3 **Rufous Babbler** *Turdoides subrufus* (1259-60) 25cm. ✿ <1000. Thick understorey of evergreen and moist-deciduous forest, forest edge and second growth. ▽ Persistent shrill trilling *tree-tree-treet...*(*chik*); squeaks. **E3**

4 **Orange-billed Babbler** *Turdoides rufescens* (1266) 25cm. Similar to 3 but ranges disjunct. Lacks ashy-grey crown and ear-coverts of 72.2; orange-yellow bill. ✿ <2100+. Damp primary hill forest. In flocks. ▽ Squeaky babbling. **E3**

5 **Yellow-billed Babbler** *Turdoides affinis* (1267-8) 23cm. Races (**a**) nom from other *Turdoides* by the pale cap and dark mottling on throat and breast (can be less striking than illustrated). (**b**) *taprobanus* quite similar to 1 but restricted to Sri Lanka where latter absent. ✿ <300(1000)(up to 1500 in Sri Lanka). Mainly lowland scrub, cultivation, gardens, open country. ▽ Musical tinkling *trr-ri-ri-ri...*; *keek*; low *kre-kre*. **E2-3**

6 **Slender-billed Babbler** *Turdoides longirostris* (1257) 23cm. Note dark slender decurved bill; whitish cheeks and lores. ✿ <1200. Long grass and dense scrub near water. ▽ Varied musical/harsh; *sweet surdit turdit teeiw*. **N*5**

7 **Spiny Babbler** *Turdoides nipalensis* (1269) 25cm. Note streaked breast and white on face. Throat varies from white to brownish. ✿ **S** 1500-2140. **W** 920-1830. Dense secondary scrub. ▽ Clear *el-el-el-el-ele*; *churrrr*; *wick-er-wick-er-wick-er*; *tew-tew keer kerchee-kerchee-kercheewee*. **EA3**

8 **Common Babbler** *Turdoides caudatus* (1253-4) 22cm. Best distinguished from 9 by white throat and unstreaked breast. Note dull brownish or dark iris *contra* 1, 2 & 9. ✿ <1200(2100). Dry open scrub, semi-desert. ▽ *t-R-R-R-R-R-r-r-r-r..*; *which-which-whichi-ri-ri-ri-ri-ri*; *keeoo pew-pew*; *pit pit tee-tee-tee-tee-tee*; squeaks. **R2**

9 **Striated Babbler** *Turdoides earlei* (1255-6) 25cm. Note streaked throat (tinged rufous), breast, head and back. Habitat suggestive. ✿ Tall grassland, reeds and acacia scrub in lowland river plains. ▽ *pyew...pyew...*(*pyew*)...; *keep quiet*; *cheer cheer cheer.* **N*3**

10 **Red-billed Leiothrix** *Leiothrix lutea* (1335-7) 13cm. Races (**a**) *kumaiensis* (**b**) *calipyga*. ✿ **S** 1000-2400(2750). **W** (350)600-2100. Forest undergrowth, scrub, second growth, wooded gullies. ▽ Rattling babble; *pue-pue-pue-pue-pue*; *che-che-che*; *whiwit-tya-yiyo-tyu-chi-chiwe....* **A3**

11 **Silver-eared Mesia** *Leiothrix argentauris* (1333-4) 15cm. ♀ (not shown) has olive-yellow uppertail-coverts and orangy undertail-coverts. ✿ 200-2100. Bushes and low trees in evergreen and secondary forest, scrub, margins of cultivation. ▽ Babbling rattle; *weet chewit-chewit-chewee-cheweeu*; *seesee-siweewee*; *u-cherit*, *cheroi-cherit*. **A2**

12 **Cutia** *Cutia nipalensis* (1339) 20cm. ✿ **S** (1350)1600-2300(2500). **W** 900-2100. Mossy oak and evergreen forest. Behaves somewhat like a nuthatch. ▽ Loud *cheet-cheet-cheet...*; *chichip-chip-chichip...*; rising *cheeeet*. **A4**

13 **Black-headed Shrike Babbler** *Pteruthius rufiventer* (1340) 17cm. ✿ 1500-2500. Mossy oak and evergreen forest. ▽ Usually silent; *whick pew-whew*; *whew-pew-wew*; *pew-pew-peee-tu*. **R4**

14 **White-browed Shrike Babbler** *Pteruthius flaviscapis* (1341) 16cm. Supercilium of ♀ often obscure. ✿ **S** 1500-2500. **W** (300)1200-2000+. Mature forest. ▽ Churring; distinctive loud *pik kew'weew*; (*kik*) *kewkew-kewkew...*; loud *cha-chew*, *cha-cha-chip*. **A3**

15 **Green Shrike Babbler** *Pteruthius xanthochlorus* (1342-4) 13cm. Could be mistaken for a warbler but note the thick bill; heavy build; relatively sluggish movements. Races (**a**) nom ♂ (**b**) *occidentalis* ♂ (**c**) *hybridus* (not illustrated) has distinct white eye-ring. ♀ is like *occidentalis* ♂. ✿ **S** (1800)2100-2700(3600). **W** 1200-3050. Forest. Arboreal. Usually in mixed flocks. ▽ Usually silent; *whit*; grating *chaa*; *whee-tee* rapidly repeated. **A3**

16 **Black-eared Shrike Babbler** *Pteruthius melanotis* (1345) 11cm. ✿ **S** (1800)2100-2400(2700). **W** (300)700-2000. Open areas of cool evergreen forest. ▽ Usually silent; *too-weet, too-weet*. **A3**

17 **Chestnut-fronted Shrike Babbler** *Pteruthius aenobarbus* (1346) 11cm. ✿ Fairly open forest and evergreen forest edge. ▽ *chr-r-r-r-uk*; sharp *pwit*; rhythmic *ka-chip, ka-chip, ka-chip*. **V** (The only record from the subcontinent is of a specimen collected in the Garo Hills of Meghalaya.)

18 **White-hooded Babbler** *Gampsorhynchus rufulus* (1347) 23cm. ✿ Plains edge-1200. Evergreen and secondary forest, bamboo, bush and grass jungle. ▽ Grating *kaw-ka-yawk*; chattering and squeaking. **R3**

PLATE 69: BABBLERS IV (FULVETTAS, MINLAS AND SIBIAS)

1 **Streak-throated Fulvetta** *Alcippe cinereiceps* (1385) 11cm. From 2 by brownish-grey crown with diffuse dark brown supercilium and smaller, fainter rusty-brown streaks on smoky-grey throat. ✿ 1500-2500. Secondary scrub, dense bamboo. ∇ *cheep*; short rattling song. **R*5**

2 **Brown-throated Fulvetta** *Alcippe ludlowi* (1384) 11cm. From 5 by the heavier rusty-brown streaks on white throat. From 1 by reddish-brown crown without supercilium. ✿ 2200-3500. Bamboo and rhododendron forest. ∇ Rattling alarm; song unknown. **A3**

3 **Rufous-winged Fulvetta** *Alcippe castaneceps* (1379) 10cm. ✿ S (1500)1800-3000(3500). **W** (300)700-2750. Undergrowth of evergreen forest edge. ∇ *tu-twee-twee*; *cheep*; *purr*. **A2**

4 **White-browed Fulvetta** *Alcippe vinipectus* (1380-3) 11cm. Races (**a**) nom (**b**) *chumbiensis*. ✿ S (2400)2700-4200. **W** 1500-3000. Montane scrub, forest undergrowth, ringal bamboo. ∇ *chip, chip*; *tsuid, tsuid*; *churr*; thin *tsee-tsee-(tsee)-tir-tee*; *pees-psee-kew*. **A1**

5 [**Chinese Fulvetta** *Alcippe striaticollis* (1385a) 11cm. Separated from most other fulvettas by throat streaking; from 1 by dark streaks on upper back and brown (vs rusty) rump; from 2 by fine blackish (vs broad rusty) streaks; lacks white supercilium of 4b. ✿ S 2800-4200. **W** Lower? Holly-oak, rhododendron and other Himalayan shrubbery. ∇ *tserrr-tserrr*. **X** (Resident in SE Tibet. Could occur in northern Arunachal Pradesh.)]

6 **Rufous-throated Fulvetta** *Alcippe rufogularis* (1386-7) 12cm. ✿ <900. Evergreen and secondary forest undergrowth, bamboo, scrub. Usually in pairs or small groups. ∇ *chirrirrirri*; *chip-churr*; cheeping *chree-chree*; buzzing metallic *dzoi*; *twoi tee twoi tee twee tee twoi tee twee*. **R3**

7 **Rusty-capped Fulvetta** *Alcippe dubia* (1388) 13cm. ✿ 900-2400. Dense bushes in light forest, forest edge, scrub, second growth. ∇ *chu-chi-chiu* and variations; *chir-r-r*; sharp *chit*; chattering; *chee-chee-chee-chee-chee-hpwit*. **R*4**

8 **Brown-cheeked Fulvetta** *Alcippe poioicephala* (1389-91) 15cm. Similar to 9 but lacks the supercilium and white eye-ring. ✿ <2500. Forest undergrowth, scrub, bamboo (gardens). ∇ Churring; *chewy-chewy-chwée-chèwey-chew*. **R2**

9 **Nepal Fulvetta** *Alcippe nipalensis* (1392-4) 12cm. From 8 by long dusky supercilium and obvious white eye-ring. ✿ S Foothills-2400. **W** <1800. Forest undergrowth, bamboo and second growth. ∇ Twittering; *p-p-p-p-jet*; *dzi-dzi-dzi-dzi-dzi*; *pi-pi-pi-pi-pi-(pi)*. **A1**

10 **Golden-breasted Fulvetta** *Alcippe chrysotis* (1376-7) 11cm. Races (**a**) nom (**b**) *albilineatus*. ✿ 2000-3050. Undergrowth on hillsides; partial to bamboo. ∇ Continual low twitter; high-pitched buzz. **A4**

11 **Yellow-throated Fulvetta** *Alcippe cinerea* (1378) 10cm. ✿ 900-2100. Undergrowth in evergreen forest; bamboo, roadside scrub. ∇ Soft *prrrrp*; low *chip-chip*; *sisisisisi*. **R4**

12 **Red-tailed Minla** *Minla ignotincta* (1357) 14cm. ✿ S (1350)1800-3400. **W** Foothills 1800(2400). Forest. Arboreal. ∇ *wi-wi-wi*; *chik* x 7; *tsi...tsi*; *chitititit*; *whi-whee-tee-tew*; *whi-whi-te-sik-sik*; *twiyi-twiyuwi*. **A3**

13 **Blue-winged Minla** *Minla cyanouroptera* (1362) 15cm. The blue on this species can appear rather grey in the field and is not always obvious except at fairly close range, but note the long distinctive square-cut tail. ✿ S 1400-2500(2750). **W** (200)1000-1830(2290). Forest. ∇ *cheep*; *cree-cree*; 3-note whistle. **A3**

14 **Chestnut-tailed Minla** *Minla strigula* (1358-61) 14cm. ✿ S 1800-3750. Oak and rhododendron. **W** (1030)1300-2750(3700). Forest, low bushes and scrub. ∇ *pseep*; *tsee-tsi-tsay-tsee*; mellow *peera-tzip*; *pe-oo*. **A2**

15 **Long-tailed Sibia** *Heterophasia picaoides* (1401) 30cm. ✿ S <2000? **W** <900. Forest, scrub with large trees. ∇ *tsip-tsip-tsip-tsip*; musical piping; dry rattle. **A3**

16 **Beautiful Sibia** *Heterophasia pulchella* (1400) 22cm. ✿ S 2100-3000. **W** 1200-2700. Mossy forest. ∇ Often silent; jingling notes. **A*3-4**

17 **Grey Sibia** *Heterophasia gracilis* (1399) 21cm. ✿ S >1200. **W** >900. Forest. ∇ Similar to 18; *tee-weeo`wee-weeo`weeo`do*; scolding *pik-pik-pik*; harsh babbling. **A2**

18 **Rufous Sibia** *Heterophasia capistrata* (1396-8) 21cm. ✿ S (1600)1800-3500. **W** (100)1000-2750. Forest, especially mixed evergreen. ∇ Loud ringing *teedee`deedee`dee`olu*; harsh *chre-chre.....* **NA1**

19 **Rufous-backed Sibia** *Heterophasia annectens* (1395) 18cm. ✿ S 1200-2300(2650). **W** >foothills. Moist evergreen forest. Often creeps over trunks and branches. ∇ *chirr-r-r*; *chip, chu chu-ii*; *tee deedeedeedeedeedee*. **A*4**

222

PLATE 69

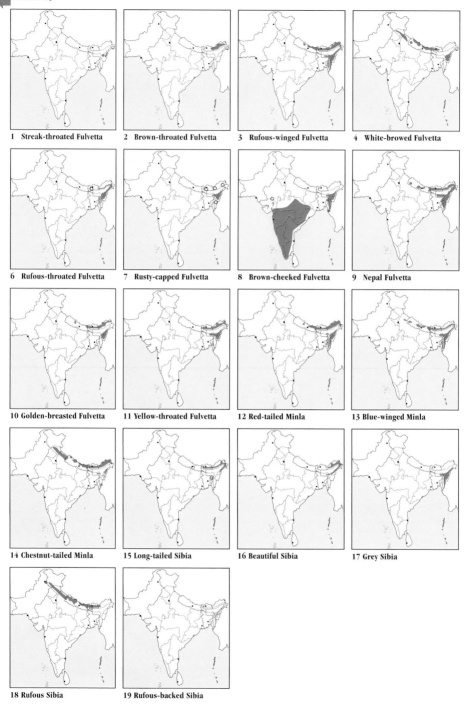

1 Streak-throated Fulvetta

2 Brown-throated Fulvetta

3 Rufous-winged Fulvetta

4 White-browed Fulvetta

6 Rufous-throated Fulvetta

7 Rusty-capped Fulvetta

8 Brown-cheeked Fulvetta

9 Nepal Fulvetta

10 Golden-breasted Fulvetta

11 Yellow-throated Fulvetta

12 Red-tailed Minla

13 Blue-winged Minla

14 Chestnut-tailed Minla

15 Long-tailed Sibia

16 Beautiful Sibia

17 Grey Sibia

18 Rufous Sibia

19 Rufous-backed Sibia

PLATE 70

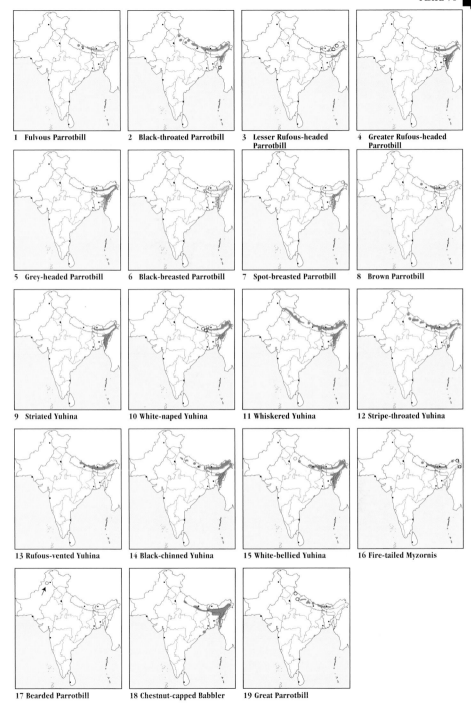

1 Fulvous Parrotbill

2 Black-throated Parrotbill

3 Lesser Rufous-headed Parrotbill

4 Greater Rufous-headed Parrotbill

5 Grey-headed Parrotbill

6 Black-breasted Parrotbill

7 Spot-breasted Parrotbill

8 Brown Parrotbill

9 Striated Yuhina

10 White-naped Yuhina

11 Whiskered Yuhina

12 Stripe-throated Yuhina

13 Rufous-vented Yuhina

14 Black-chinned Yuhina

15 White-bellied Yuhina

16 Fire-tailed Myzornis

17 Bearded Parrotbill

18 Chestnut-capped Babbler

19 Great Parrotbill

PLATE 70: BABBLERS V (PARROTBILLS, YUHINAS, MYZORNIS AND *TIMALIA*)

1 **Fulvous Parrotbill** *Paradoxornis fulvifrons* (1238-9) 12cm. ✺ 2700-3400. Bamboo. ▽ Continual twittering; *cheep.* **R*4**

2 **Black-throated Parrotbill** *Paradoxornis nipalensis* (1239a-44) 10cm. Races **(a)** nom **(b)** *humei* **(c)** *poliotis* **(d)** *patriciae.* ✺ 530-3300 but altitudinal limits vary widely from one part of the range to another. Ringal bamboo, rhododendron, forest undergrowth. ▽ High thin *tsi-tsi-tsi; tsup*; high twitter. **R3**

3 **Lesser Rufous-headed Parrotbill** *Paradoxornis atrosuperciliaris* (1245-6) 15cm. Very like 4 but smaller; small stubby bill; ear-coverts distinctly paler than rest of head; strongly graduated tail. Races **(a)** nom from 4 by short black supercilium. **(b)** *oatesi.* ✺ 600-1500. Reed-bamboo, tall grass, scrub jungle. ▽ Wheezy twang; chittering. **R*4**

4 **Greater Rufous-headed Parrotbill** *Paradoxornis ruficeps* (1247-8) 18cm. From 3 by larger size; large bill; ear-coverts concolorous with head; less graduated tail; lacks black supercilium of 3a. Races **(a)** nom **(b)** *bakeri.* ✺ <1800. Bamboo, scrub, reeds, tall grass. ▽ Squirrel-like chittering interspersed with *tee-ur; chir-chirrup*; bleating; bill snapping. **R3**

5 **Grey-headed Parrotbill** *Paradoxornis gularis* (1249-50) 16cm. Races **(a)** nom **(b)** *transfluvialis.* ✺ **S** 600-2100 (2400). **W** >plains. Bamboo, bushes, low trees. ▽ Four loud notes on same pitch; chattering. **A*3**

6 **Black-breasted Parrotbill** *Paradoxornis flavirostris* (1251) 19cm. ✺ <2400, mainly lower. Reeds, tall grass, bamboo. ▽ *gweh-gweh-gweh*; rapid *chee-chee-chee-chi-chit; phewy phewy phewy phewit*; bleating; mellow 3-note warble. **R*5**

7 **Spot-breasted Parrotbill** *Paradoxornis guttaticollis* (1252) 19cm. Spotting on breast often much reduced and hard to see in the field. A blackish throat-patch shows when bird is calling. ✺ (900)1500-1800(2100+). Scrub, grass, bushes, bamboo. ▽ *chu-jewy-jewy-jewy-jewy-(jewy)-(jewy)*; chittering. Noisy. **R*5**

8 **Brown Parrotbill** *Paradoxornis unicolor* (1237) 21cm. ✺ **S** 2700-3400. **W** >2000. Maling bamboo, dwarf rhododendron. ▽ Chirruping; churring; bleating *(chit-wit)-weab-weab-weoob* and variations. **RA*4**

9 **Striated Yuhina** *Yuhina castaniceps* (1363-5) 13cm. From other yuhinas by chestnut ear-coverts (streaked white) and long graduated tail tipped white. Races **(a)** nom **(b)** *plumbeiceps.* ✺ Foothills-1500. Undergrowth and low trees in forest and second growth. ▽ *prrrr; tsees*; twittering *chir-chit...chir-chit.* **R3**

10 **White-naped Yuhina** *Yuhina bakeri* (1366) 13cm. White nape on chestnut crest is diagnostic. From below note the white throat contrasting with darker breast and belly. ✺ Foothills-2000. Moist evergreen and secondary forest. ▽ *chip*; chatter; nasal *chueh-chueh.* **A3**

11 **Whiskered Yuhina** *Yuhina flavicollis* (1367-70) 13cm. Note flank streaking and whitish nape above rusty nuchal collar. Western race *albicollis* (not illustrated) has narrower rufous collar with white below it. ✺ **S** 1700-3000. **W** Plains edge-2750. Broadleaved forest, second growth. ▽ Thin twitter interspersed with harsh *chi-chiu; twe-tyurwi-tyawi-tyawa; tse-kling.* **A1**

12 **Stripe-throated Yuhina** *Yuhina gularis* (1371-2) 14cm. Diagnostic features are the streaked throat, black and orange wing. Could be confused with Rufous-winged Fulvetta (69.3) but easily separated by the crest, streaked throat and lack of white supercilium. ✺ **S** (2400)2700-3700. **W** (foothills)1700-3050. Forest, (scrub, bamboo). ▽ Nasal *kway* or *chay*; *shr...shr...; kweeeee; cheep; zaei zaei.* **A1**

13 **Rufous-vented Yuhina** *Yuhina occipitalis* (1373) 13cm. Rufous vent and rusty orange nape above grey nuchal collar diagnostic. ✺ **S** 2400-3900. **W** 1500-2750+. Evergreen forest. ▽ Rattling *trrr-trrr-trrr.* **A1**

14 **Black-chinned Yuhina** *Yuhina nigrimenta* (1374) 11cm. Small black chin and black crest scaled with grey diagnostic. ✺ 300-1800. Evergreen forest, second growth. ▽ Twittering; buzzing; high *de-de-de-de; whee-to-whee-de-der-n-whee-yer.* **A3**

15 **White-bellied Yuhina** *Yuhina zantholeuca* (1375) 11cm. Like a warbler but for crest and absence of supercilium. ✺ (Plains)360-1650(2290). Forest and second growth, especially clearings. ▽ Rather silent; *chit; cheaan.* **R●2-3**

16 **Fire-tailed Myzornis** *Myzornis pyrrhoura* (1338) 12cm. ✺ **S** 2700?-3950. **W** 1600-2750+. Shrubbery, forest, bamboo (on sunny slopes). Occurs singly, in pairs or small groups. Often feeds at flowering rhododendrons. ▽ Usually silent; high-pitched *tsi-tsit.* **A4**

17 **Bearded Parrotbill** *Panurus biarmicus* (1235) 15cm. ✺ Plains. Reeds, grass and tamarisk scrub. ▽ *chip; tzew; dzwee; ping; chirr.* **V**

18 **Chestnut-capped Babbler** *Timalia pileata* (1229) 17cm. ✺ <1200, mainly floodplains. Damp tall grassy and scrubby areas. ▽ *tit, tit; korchuk; prrew; raa-ch-ch-ch-ch; chew-aye, chit, chit, chit, chit.* **R3**

19 **Great Parrotbill** *Conostoma oemodium* (1236) 28cm. Note large size, pale forehead over dark loral area, grey primaries. ✺ **S** 2700-3600. **W** >2100. Ringal bamboo, rhododendron. ▽ *krrarchah, krarch krarchah; wheou wheou*; churring and chattering. Noisy. **RA4**

226

PLATE 71: BABBLERS VI (BABAXES, BARWINGS AND LAUGHINGTHRUSHES I)

1 Chinese Babax *Babax lanceolatus* (1270) 28cm. ✦ >1500. Light forest, open scrubby hillsides. ▽ *ou-phee* repeated 6-8 times; *aua qua qua quo, qui wa wa wa*; *zerr-zerr-zerr-zerr.* **R*5**

2 [Giant Babax *Babax waddelli* (1271) 31cm. Larger and greyer than 1. ✦ 2800-4500. Dry scrub. ▽ Rapid series of quavering whistles; thrush-like song. **X** (Possible in extreme NE Sikkim and N Arunachal Pradesh.)]

3 Rusty-fronted Barwing *Actinodura egertoni* (1348-51) 23cm. Note rufous face. ✦ **S** 1200-2000(2400). **W** (Foothills)1000-1800. As 4; secondary growth. ▽ *cheep*; *(dee)-dee-dee-dee`dyoo*; *ti-ti-ta.* **A2**

4 Hoary-throated Barwing *Actinodura nipalensis* (1352-3) 20cm. Streaked crown/mantle. ✦ (1500)1800-3300 (3500). Evergreen forest with good undergrowth. ▽ *tui whee-er*; rattling *je-je-je...*; *doo-dewdy-dewdy-dewdy.* **R2**

5 Streak-throated Barwing *Actinodura waldeni* (1354-6) 20cm. Scalloping on crown. Races **(a)** nom, rufous underparts. **(b)** *daflaensis*, streaked breast. ✦ **S** 2200-3300. **W** >1500. Mossy forest. ▽ *chup, chup*; mewing; *churr.* **R*3-4**

6 Rufous-chinned Laughingthrush *Garrulax rufogularis* (1292-6) 22cm. Rufous chin often much reduced and not a very obvious field mark. Races **(a)** nom **(b)** *occidentalis.* ✦ (600)1000-1800(3500?). Forest undergrowth, scrub, second growth. In pairs or small groups. ▽ Chatters, squeals and chuckles; *whee whoo wheewoowee.* **A3**

7 Chestnut-crowned Laughingthrush *Garrulax erythrocephalus* (1324-30) 28cm. Races **(a)** nom **(b)** *nigrimentum* **(c)** *chrysopterus.* ✦ **S** (1800)2100-3000(3300). **W** (600)1200-2000(2750). Dense undergrowth and scrub. ▽ Twitters; chuckles; *m-u-r-r-r-r*; *yo-whéeo*; *perl-lee*; *to-real-yer*; *pheeou*; *wee-ou-wee-whip*; *twi-ee-you.* **A1-2**

8 Scaly Laughingthrush *Garrulax subunicolor* (1320) 23cm. From 9 by absence of black supercilium; straw-coloured wing-patch; white-tipped outer tail feathers. ✦ **S** 1500-3600+. **W** 800-3400. Forest undergrowth, shrubbery, bamboo. ▽ *wheet-wheeoo*; *wheeooeeoo*; 4-note whistle; squeaks; churring babble. **A3**

9 Blue-winged Laughingthrush *Garrulax squamatus* (1319) 25cm. From 8 by black eyebrow; pale blue wing-patch; rufous-tipped tail. ✦ 900-2400(3400?). As 8. ▽ *chuck*; *whew wee-ee*; *free-for-you*; *chrreee chrewy-chrewy-chrewy.* **R4**

10 Brown-capped Laughingthrush *Garrulax austeni* (1318) 22cm. ✦ (1200)1800-2700. Oak and rhododendron forest, bushes, bamboo. ▽ *to meet you*; soft *tick*; *ti-ti-ti-tia-tui-ti*; *krrü-krrü*; *krüpp...krüpp...krüpp.* **R*5**

11 Striped Laughingthrush *Garrulax virgatus* (1317) 25cm. From 17 & 18 by white supercilium. ✦ 900-2400. Undergrowth in humid forest, second growth. ▽ Peculiar soft single note; *(whi)-chit-wheeeow*; conversational notes. **N*4**

12 Spot-breasted Laughingthrush *Garrulax merulinus* (1304-5) 22cm. ✦ 900-2400. Dense undergrowth and scrub in moist evergreen forest. ▽ Noisy. Clear beautiful notes; coughing chuckle. **R*5**

13 Spotted Laughingthrush *Garrulax ocellatus* (1298-9) 32cm. From 14 by dark throat, blackish ear-coverts and heavier scalloping on upper breast. ✦ 2100-3660. Undergrowth in mixed evergreen forest, bushes, rhododendron scrub. ▽ Beautiful, far-carrying *tu wee, tu wee, tu witty-o*; *chuwu chwee-eh*; subdued *pie, pie, pie, pie*; *cacreee-creee-creee-creee-rrrr-cacreee-creee.* **R3**

14 [Giant Laughingthrush *Garrulax maximus* (1297) 35cm. From 13 by rusty-brown throat and ear-coverts. ✦ 2200-2900+. Undergrowth and bushes in dry subalpine forest. ▽ *gno gnoit gno gnoit*; churring. **X** (Found in SE Tibet. Could occur in Arunachal Pradesh.)]

15 Greater Necklaced Laughingthrush *Garrulax pectoralis* (1277-8) 29cm. Like 16 but broad black necklace extending lower down breast; entire area inside the necklace white or washed rufous-buff; dark patch at base of primaries diagnostic when visible; ear-coverts variable (entirely black to almost wholly white) but usually the lower black edge connects to bill (not in 16). ✦ 80-1700. Forest, second growth, bamboo, scrub. Often in flocks with 16 and other laughingthrushes. ▽ Nasal *week, week, week*; piping; high whistles; grating calls. **R3**

16 Lesser Necklaced Laughingthrush *Garrulax monileger* (1275-6) 27cm. Like 15 but black breast-band not as broad, lined inside with rusty-buff and edged below with white; white throat. ✦ Plains edge-1000(1400). Habitat as 15 with which it often flocks. ▽ Similar to 15. **R3**

17 Striated Laughingthrush *Garrulax striatus* (1279-82) 28cm. Could conceivably be mistaken for 11 or 18 but note the distinctive bushy crest. Races **(a)** nom **(b)** *cranbrooki.* ✦ **S** (1200)1500-2750(2850). **W** >foothills. Dense forest, scrub. ▽ Squeaky *psit* or *pseet*; cackles; chattering; *oh see-saw-oh-whitey oh-white*; *whit-whichyou-whit-whee-wheeo chiwee*; *wit-wit wheetyou whityouwit*; *hwe-ho*; *doo-da-dee-da-diew*; *woick-woick-woick-woick.* **A2**

18 Streaked Laughingthrush *Garrulax lineatus* (1312-6) 20cm. Races **(a)** nom **(b)** *imbricatus* **(c)** *setafer* **(d)** *gilgit.* ✦ **S** (1200)1800-3000(3900). **W** (600)1000-1800(2750). Scrub, bushes, undergrowth, gardens. ▽ *chit-chit-chitrr*; *crrer-r*; *whit-wheeoow*; *t-t-t-t-t-TEE-TEE-TEW*; *twee-twee-twee*; *sweet-pea-pea-pea*; *trit-tew, tewit*; *ju-wi-ye.* **A1**

228

PLATE 71

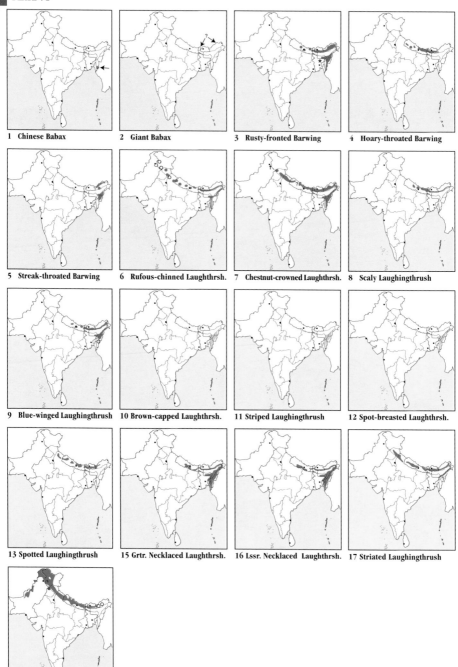

1 Chinese Babax

2 Giant Babax

3 Rusty-fronted Barwing

4 Hoary-throated Barwing

5 Streak-throated Barwing

6 Rufous-chinned Laughthrsh.

7 Chestnut-crowned Laughthrsh.

8 Scaly Laughingthrush

9 Blue-winged Laughingthrush

10 Brown-capped Laughthrsh.

11 Striped Laughingthrush

12 Spot-breasted Laughthrsh.

13 Spotted Laughingthrush

15 Grtr. Necklaced Laughthrsh.

16 Lssr. Necklaced Laughthrsh.

17 Striated Laughingthrush

18 Streaked Laughingthrush

PLATE 72

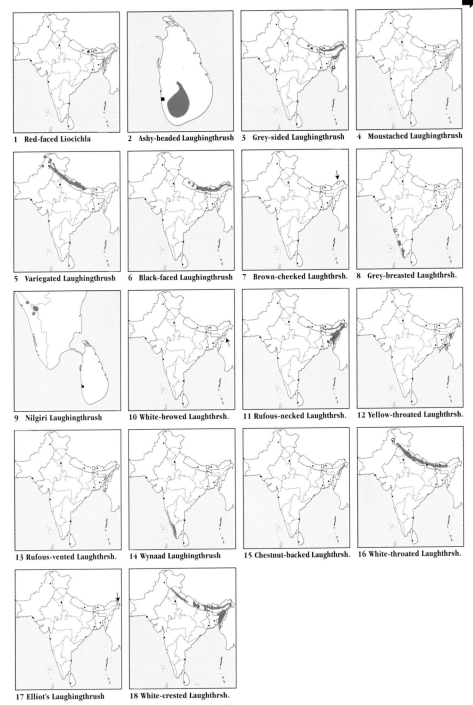

1 Red-faced Liocichla

2 Ashy-headed Laughingthrush

3 Grey-sided Laughingthrush

4 Moustached Laughingthrush

5 Variegated Laughingthrush

6 Black-faced Laughingthrush

7 Brown-cheeked Laughthrsh.

8 Grey-breasted Laughthrsh.

9 Nilgiri Laughingthrush

10 White-browed Laughthrsh.

11 Rufous-necked Laughthrsh.

12 Yellow-throated Laughthrsh.

13 Rufous-vented Laughthrsh.

14 Wynaad Laughingthrush

15 Chestnut-backed Laughthrsh.

16 White-throated Laughthrsh.

17 Elliot's Laughingthrush

18 White-crested Laughthrsh.

PLATE 72: BABBLERS VII (LIOCICHLA AND LAUGHINGTHRUSHES II)

1 **Red-faced Liocichla** *Liocichla phoenicea* (1331-2) 23cm. Singly, in pairs or small groups. ✚ **S** 900-2400. **W** >600. Dense understorey in forest and second growth. ∇ *tu-reew-reew* (*ree-reew*); *tu-reew-ri*; rattles; squeaks. **A4-5**

2 **Ashy-headed Laughingthrush** *Garrulax cinereifrons* (1272) 23cm. The only laughingthrush in Sri Lanka. Could be confused with 68.4 but note the ashy-grey crown and ear-coverts; dark bill. ✚ <1200. Dense damp hill forest. Often in bird waves. ∇ Usually silent; chattering; laughing; screams; squeaks. **E4**

3 **Grey-sided Laughingthrush** *Garrulax caerulatus* (1300-2) 25cm. ✚ **S** (1000)1200-2750. **W** >600. Forest undergrowth, bamboo, scrubby hillsides. ∇ *ovik-chorr*; *new jericho*; *oh dear dear*; chittering. **A4**

4 **Moustached Laughingthrush** *Garrulax cineraceus* (1291) 22cm. In pairs and small groups. ✚ **S** (1500)1800-2400. **W** >1200. Forest bushes, scrub, second growth. ∇ *dü-düuid*; low musical calls. **RA*5**

5 **Variegated Laughingthrush** *Garrulax variegatus* (1289-90) 24cm. Races **(a)** nom **(b)** *similis*. ✚ **S** (1800)2400-treeline. **W** 1000-2100(2700). Dense undergrowth, ringal bamboo, rhododendron. ∇ *weet-a-weer*; *choky william*; *pte-weer*; muttering; squealing. **EA2**

6 **Black-faced Laughingthrush** *Garrulax affinis* (1322-3) 25cm. ✚ **S** (2400)2800-4200(4600). **W** 1500-3600+. Forest bushes, montane shrubbery. ∇ Chuckles; churring; (*chu*)*wheeit-wheeoo-oo*; *whirr-whirrer*; *to-wee*(*-you*). **A2**

7 **Brown-cheeked Laughingthrush** *Garrulax henrici* (1321) 25cm. Sometimes shows fine white supercilium. ✚ 2000-4500. Scrub. ∇ *whoh-hee*; chattering. **V(R*?)** (Single winter record from 1500m in NE Arunachal Pradesh.)

8 **Grey-breasted Laughingthrush** *Garrulax jerdoni* (1309-11) 20cm. Races **(a)** nom **(b)** *meridionale* **(c)** *fairbanki*. ✚ >1100. Streamside undergrowth, shola edge, gardens. Partial to wild raspberry. ∇ Mellow *puwee puwee pokee*; *pee-koko*, *pee-koko*; *ku-hi-yu*; shrieks; squeaks; whistles; 'laughter'; *har-har-har*; *wit-wit-wit*. **E*2**

9 **Nilgiri Laughingthrush** *Garrulax cachinnans* (1307-8) 20cm. ✚ >1200. Forest undergrowth, sholas, scrub, gardens. ∇ Squeals; 'laughter'; *pee-ko-ko*; (*qa*) *pee-ko*; *ke-ke-ke*; *chirrr*. **E*2**

10 **White-browed Laughingthrush** *Garrulax sannio* (1306) 23cm. Singly, in pairs or small groups. ✚ 1000-1800. Dense forest, second growth, scrub. ∇ Noisy. Notes more complaining and less hilarious than those of 18; buzzing; ringing. **R*5**

11 **Rufous-necked Laughingthrush** *Garrulax ruficollis* (1303) 23cm. ✚ <1500, usually lower. Undergrowth, bushes, scrub, forest edge, bamboo, tea. ∇ Squealed *quioo*; *wiweeit-witoo*; (*whi-whi*) *whit te-dee-woo* (*deewit*); *weeeoo-wihoo-wick*. **N3**

12 **Yellow-throated Laughingthrush** *Garrulax galbanus* (1286) 23cm. From 13 by broad, clearly defined black mask including chin; ochre-grey wings and mantle; yellowish lower belly and vent; tail with broad dark terminal band and outer tail feathers distally white. ✚ 800-1800. Open jungle, evergreen forest edge, grassland with trees and bushes. ∇ Feeble chirping. **R*4**

13 **Rufous-vented Laughingthrush** *Garrulax gularis* (1288) 23cm. Similar to 12 but narrow black mask not including chin; rufous-brown mantle and wings; rufous belly and vent; dark rufous-brown tail. ✚ 1000-1800. Dense undergrowth in evergreen and secondary forest, (scrub, bamboo). ∇ Loud sweet whistle; chattering; squeaking; cackling. **R*4**

14 **Wynaad Laughingthrush** *Garrulax delesserti* (1287) 23cm. ✚ Base of hills up to summits. Dense damp rainforest undergrowth. ∇ Rattle; chirps; *kee-kee-kyew*. **E*4**

15 **Chestnut-backed Laughingthrush** *Garrulax nuchalis* (1285) 23cm. ✚ Base of hills-900. Thick undergrowth, scrub, high grass on rocky slopes and ravines. ∇ *churr*; rich 4-5 note whistle; soft *chip*. **N*4**

16 **White-throated Laughingthrush** *Garrulax albogularis* (1273-4) 28cm. ✚ **S** 1800-3300(treeline). **W** >(450)900. Dense forest, scrubby hillsides, (gardens). ∇ Noisy. Musical chattering *chip-chip-chip-chip*; *wheeoo-wheet*; *quoik*; *tsueeeeee*. **A1**

17 **Elliot's Laughingthrush** *Garrulax elliotii* 25cm. ✚ Mixed forest, scrub, bamboo, rhododendron. ∇ Interrogative whistled *tu weir..tee-u*. **V(R*?)** (2 records from 3200m in NE Arunachal Pradesh.)

18 **White-crested Laughingthrush** *Garrulax leucolophus* (1283-4) 28cm. ✚ <1700(2140). Forest undergrowth, secondary scrub, bamboo. ∇ Noisy cackling laughter; chuckles; *pick*; *pick-wo*; *re-re-re*, *marigio*, *marigio*, *marigio*.... **R(A?)1**

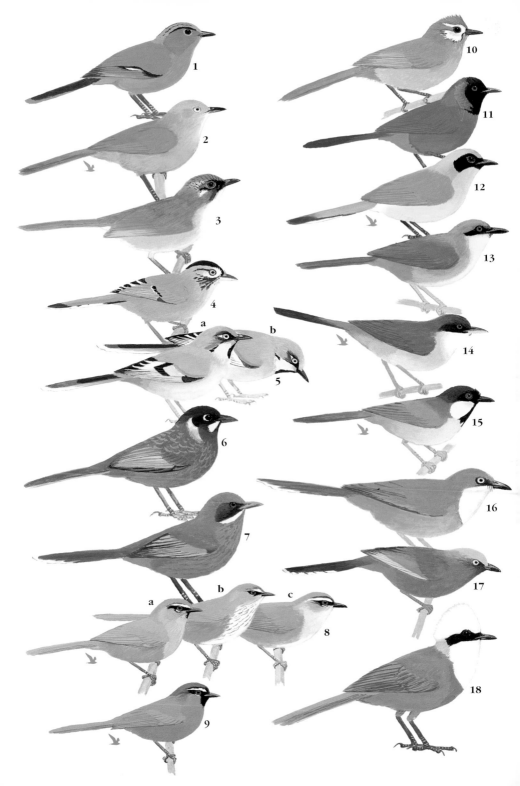

1 **Mangrove Whistler** *Pachycephala grisola* (1470) 17cm. Like woodshrike (60.3,4) without face markings. From flycatchers by stocky build and thick, hook-tipped bill. ⌘ Mangroves. ▽ Rapid ringing *(pwee)´pwee´pwee´pwee pwit.* **R*3-4**

2 **Brown-chested Jungle Flycatcher** *Rhinomyias brunneata* (1402) 14cm. Note brown breast-band; whitish throat with faint scaling; long hook-tipped bill; entire lower mandible fleshy-yellow; pale brownish lores; warm brown tail; fleshy legs. ⌘ Forest undergrowth, garden shrubbery. ▽ Tinkling whistles rising and falling. **W*(?)3-4**

3 **Spotted Flycatcher** *Muscicapa striata* (1403-4) 13cm. Streaked crown and breast. Some 4 may show breast streaking but never on crown. ⌘ (plains)2100-3300(4200). Open forest. ▽ Often silent; *tzee(p); tzee-jit.* **B*P3**

4 **Dark-sided Flycatcher** *Muscicapa sibirica* (1405-6) 13cm. Dusky breast and flanks, white centre to belly and vent. From 2, 5 & 6 also by little/no yellow at base of lower mandible; eye-ring shape; lores less contrastingly pale than in 5. ⌘ S (1500)2100-3300(3900). W >foothills. Forest; clearings. ▽ Usually silent; thin *tsee`see`see.* **A1-2**

5 **Brown-breasted Flycatcher** *Muscicapa muttui* (1408) 13cm. Rather like 6 but white throat contrasts with brown breast-band; yellow (vs brownish) legs; lower mandible fleshy/yellowish sometimes with dusky terminal ¹/₄. 4 has much darker flanks and breast. ⌘ S >1000. W <1500(2000). Evergreen hill forest. ▽ Pleasant feeble song. **M4**

6 **Asian Brown Flycatcher** *Muscicapa dauurica* (1407) 14cm. Faint greyish wash on breast; eye-ring; pale lores; largish bill with basal ¹/₂ of lower mandible distinctly yellow/fleshy, contrasting with dusky tip. ⌘ <2000. Open forest, groves, forest edge, plantations. ▽ Thin high *zee;* rapid *(chi)-chir-ri-ri-ri; chik, chik-r-r.* **RMW3**

7 **Rusty-tailed Flycatcher** *Muscicapa ruficauda* (1409) 14cm. Rufous rump and tail; brownish-white throat. ⌘ S 2100-3660. Forest. W <1000. Forest edge. ▽ Plaintive *peeu; peup;* mellow rattles; 3-4 variable clear notes. **M3**

8 **Ferruginous Flycatcher** *Muscicapa ferruginea* (1410) 10cm. ⌘ S 1200-3300. W Lowland humid forest. ▽ Quiet trill. **S(A?)4**

9 **Yellow-rumped Flycatcher** *Ficedula zanthopygia* 13cm. ⌘ Lower wooded areas. ▽ Grating *tr-r-r-rt.* **V**

10 **Red-throated Flycatcher** *Ficedula parva* (1411-2) 13cm. Note white base to outer tail, often cocked. See 16. ♀ (not shown) like 1stW without wing-bar. Races **(a)** *albicilla* has wholly black bill; black (vs dark brown) central uppertail coverts; greyish wash on breast. **(b)** nom. ⌘ Open forest, groves etc. ▽ Dry *trrrr, tszeet-tszeet.* **WP1**

11 **White-gorgeted Flycatcher** *Ficedula monileger* (1415-6) 11cm. Races **(a)** nom **(b)** *leucops.* ⌘ Foothills-2000. Forest undergrowth, scrubby ravines. ▽ Metallic *dik;* rattle; short plaintive whistle; very high wheezy song. **R4**

12 **Ultramarine Flycatcher** *Ficedula superciliaris* (1421-2) 10cm. ♂ from 18 by extensive dark-blue sides of throat, neck and breast with white central band; (white on tail hard to see, absent in b). ♀ by greyish sides of breast with buffy-white central band; some have blue tail. Races **(a)** nom **(b)** *aestigma.* ⌘ S 1500-3200. W >foothills. Open forest, bushy areas, groves, gardens. ▽ Soft *tick;* short rattling *tr-r-r-r-r, che-chi-purr.* **MA2**

13 **Little Pied Flycatcher** *Ficedula westermanni* (1419-20) 10cm. Races **(a)** *collini* **(b)** *australorientis.* ⌘ S (80)1200-3000. W <1800. Forest, woodland, orchards. ▽ Mellow *tweet; swit trrrt;* high *pi-pi-pi-pi-churr-r-r-r-r.* **AM3**

14 **Snowy-browed Flycatcher** *Ficedula hyperythra* (1417) 11cm. ♂ by short white brow. ♀ by short fulvous brow, breast and flanks. ⌘ S 1200-3000. W <1700. Primary forest undergrowth. ▽ Thin *sip;* wheezy *tsit-sit`si´sii.* **AM3**

15 **Rufous-gorgeted Flycatcher** *Ficedula strophiata* (1414) 13cm. Rufous-orange gorget diagnostic but not always obvious. ⌘ S 1800-3700(3950). W <2400. Forest. ▽ *tik-tik;* metallic *pink; churr; tin-twee(t); tin-ti-ti.* **RAM2**

16 **Kashmir Flycatcher** *Ficedula subrubra* (1413) 13cm. ♂ from ♂10 by more red on throat and breast bordered black and grey on face. ♀ from ♀10 by slight rufous wash on breast. ⌘ S 1800-2700. Mixed forest. W >750. Forest, forest edge, gardens. Often on or near ground. ▽ Sharp *chack; purr; chip-chip-chip*+rattle; loud sweet song. **EM*3**

17 **Black-and-orange Flycatcher** *Ficedula nigrorufa* (1427) 13cm. ⌘ >(700)1500. Undergrowth of sholas, cardamom and coffee plantations; damp overgrown ravines. ▽ Buzzy *zit; dzirrit-irit;* low *pee;* high metallic *chiki-riki-chiki.* **E3**

18 **Slaty-blue Flycatcher** *Ficedula tricolor* (1423-5) 10cm. ♂ from 12 by no blue patches at breast sides; slatier-blue upperparts; white base of outer tail. ♀ by rufescent rump and tail; from 8 & 12 by warm brownish-buff flanks; from 7 by small size; tail-flicking habit. Races **(a)** western **(b)** eastern. ⌘ S 1500-4000. W <2100. Forest understorey, reeds, bushes, tall grass. ▽ *ee-tick-(tick)-(tick)-(tick); zieh-ti-zietz.* **AR2**

19 **Sapphire Flycatcher** *Ficedula sapphira* (1426) 12cm. ♂ by blue breast-band broken by orange-rufous throat and breast-centre. Imm♂ has rufous breast and throat with blue only on scapulars, lower back, rump and tail. ♀ by rufous centre of throat and upper breast bordered brownish. ⌘ S (1400)1800-2600. W <800(1700). Low to mid storey in moist evergreen forest. ▽ *trrrrr; tick-tick.* **A4**

20 **Slaty-backed Flycatcher** *Ficedula hodgsonii* (1418) 13cm. ♂ bluish-slaty upperparts without contrasting bright blue elements, but with velvety black lores. ♀ nondescript with olive-brown breast, slightly paler on throat, whitish on belly. ⌘ S (1200)2400-3600(3900). W <2000. Forest; dense scrub. ▽ Deep *terrbt;* meandering *per-ip-it-u-or-per-ip-it-tu.* **A4-5**

PLATE 73

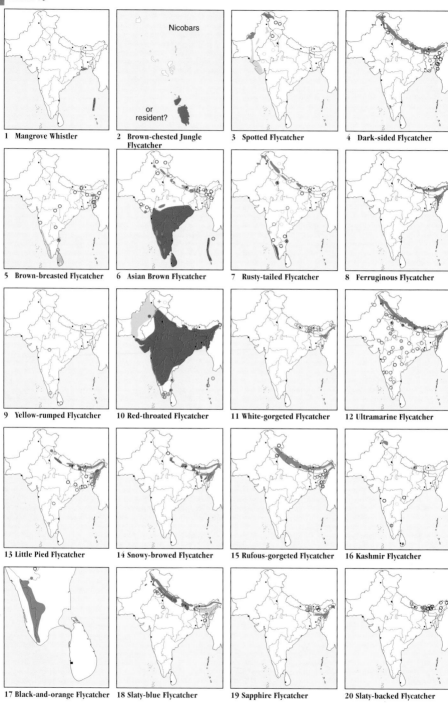

1 Mangrove Whistler

2 Brown-chested Jungle Flycatcher

3 Spotted Flycatcher

4 Dark-sided Flycatcher

5 Brown-breasted Flycatcher

6 Asian Brown Flycatcher

7 Rusty-tailed Flycatcher

8 Ferruginous Flycatcher

9 Yellow-rumped Flycatcher

10 Red-throated Flycatcher

11 White-gorgeted Flycatcher

12 Ultramarine Flycatcher

13 Little Pied Flycatcher

14 Snowy-browed Flycatcher

15 Rufous-gorgeted Flycatcher

16 Kashmir Flycatcher

17 Black-and-orange Flycatcher

18 Slaty-blue Flycatcher

19 Sapphire Flycatcher

20 Slaty-backed Flycatcher

PLATE 74

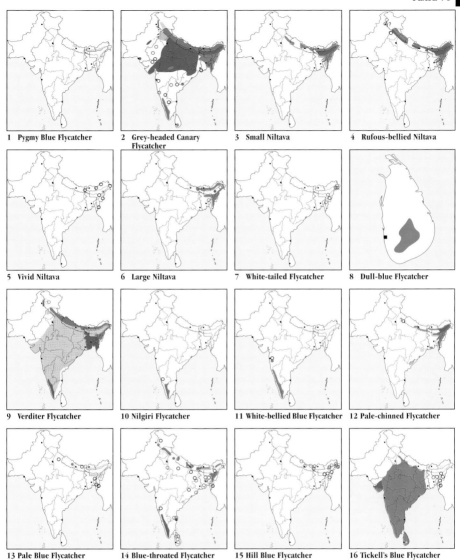

1 Pygmy Blue Flycatcher

2 Grey-headed Canary Flycatcher

3 Small Niltava

4 Rufous-bellied Niltava

5 Vivid Niltava

6 Large Niltava

7 White-tailed Flycatcher

8 Dull-blue Flycatcher

9 Verditer Flycatcher

10 Nilgiri Flycatcher

11 White-bellied Blue Flycatcher

12 Pale-chinned Flycatcher

13 Pale Blue Flycatcher

14 Blue-throated Flycatcher

15 Hill Blue Flycatcher

16 Tickell's Blue Flycatcher

PLATE 74: FLYCATCHERS II

1 Pygmy Blue Flycatcher *Muscicapella hodgsoni* (1447) 8cm. From similar species by tiny size, small bill and short tail. ♂ lacks the blue sides of breast and shining blue rump and tail of 73.19; ♀ by entire underparts washed with pale orange (vs rufous-orange centre of throat and breast with olive-brown sides). ✶ S 2100-3500. W Foothills-1800. Dense forest; second growth. ▽ Feeble *tsip*; dry rattling *trrrrk*; soft tinkling *tit-too-tiririree*; high *tzit tzit che che cheeee*. **A4**

2 Grey-headed Canary Flycatcher *Culicicapa ceylonensis* (1448-9) 9cm. Not like any other flycatcher. Similarly plumaged warblers all have obvious supercilium or eye-ring. Note head shape and upright stance. ✶ <2700(3100). Forest, open wooded country. ▽ Loud *chit...cht-cht-cht...*; *tyit...tyit...*; *(chik)...whichee-chee-whichee*; *sissee-si-see*. **RAM1**

3 Small Niltava *Niltava macgrigoriae* (1429-30) 11cm. ♂ from ♂6 by small size, grey lower breast and belly. ♀ miniature version of ♀6 but lacks the warm tones to underparts, lores and forecrown. ✶ S 900-2200. W <1400. Broadleaved evergreen forest understorey. ▽ *tsrr*; thin, high wheezing *see`see*; *twee`twee`ee`(twee)*. **A3**

4 Rufous-bellied Niltava *Niltava sundara* (1431-2) 15cm. ♂ like ♂5 (which see) but entire throat blue. ♀ from ♀5 by white gorget, blue patch at side of neck (can be hard to see). ✶ S 900-3200. W <2300. Forest undergrowth/lower storey, damp overgrown gullies, second growth. ▽ Hard *tik*; *tr-r-r-tchik*; *swee-chrik*; *sweeee-ch-tri-tr tik*. **RA2**

5 Vivid Niltava *Niltava vivida* (1433) 18cm. Lacks vivid blue neck patches of other niltavas. ♂ from ♂4 by rufous wedge up centre of throat; little or no blue on shoulder. ✶ 1500?-2700. Evergreen forest. ▽ Mellow whistles interspersed with scratchy notes. **A?5**

6 Large Niltava *Niltava grandis* (1428) 20cm. ♂ can appear black at a distance but shining blue crown, neck-stripe and shoulder striking in light. From most blue flycatchers by black throat and breast but see 3. ♀ may show bluish wash on nape; see 3 for differences. ✶ S 900-2850. W <2000. Low to mid-storey in evergreen forest. ▽ Attractive whistled *do´re´mi*; *dolo-teh-teetee*. **RA3**

7 White-tailed Flycatcher *Cyornis concretus* (1434) 18cm. From 3 & 6 by white belly, white on spread tail, lack of vivid blue neck-patch. From allopatric 11 by large size and white in tail; ♀ by white in tail and triangular white throat-patch. Compare also 82.4. ✶ Dense forest. ▽ Sibilant whistled *tii-tuu-(tii)*; *scree*; twitter. **A*?5**

8 Dull-blue Flycatcher *Eumyias sordida* (1444) 14cm. Much greyer than 9, with a conspicuous cerulean-blue forehead. ✶ (450)900-2100. Forest, wooded gullies, parks and gardens. ▽ Soft *chip-chip*; soft sweet 5-6 note song. **E3**

9 Verditer Flycatcher *Eumyias thalassina* (1445) 15cm. In good light the blue-green colour is diagnostic, but see 13. ✶ S 1200-2700(3000). W >plains. Light forest. ▽ *tze-ju-jui*; hurried, high-pitched warbling *petititi-wu-pititi-weu*. **MA2**

10 Nilgiri Flycatcher *Eumyias albicaudata* (1446) 15cm. Diagnostic white patch at base of tail not visible unless tail spread. ♂ much darker greenish-blue than 9 with bright blue forecrown and darker belly; lacks white belly of ♂11. ♀ unique in its very dark grey plumage with slight greenish-blue tinge. ✶ >(600)1200. Sholas, plantations, gardens. ▽ *tsik-tsik*; *chip*; sweet 6-10 note song *chee-chew chewy chi-chwee chwee choo chi-choo chee*. **E3**

11 White-bellied Blue Flycatcher *Cyornis pallipes* (1435) 15cm. ♂ from 10 by white belly. See also 85.5b. ♀ distinctive in range. ✶ <1700. Undergrowth in evergreen hill forest. ▽ *tsk-tsk*; sweet squeaky warbling song. **E3**

12 Pale-chinned Flycatcher *Cyornis poliogenys* (1436-8) 14cm. Brownish-grey head and whitish throat. From ♀81.5 by dark grey (vs olive-brown) sides of head, shorter legs, less terrestrial habits. From ♀16 by whitish throat. Races **(a)** *vernayi* **(b)** nom. ✶ <1500. Forest undergrowth. ▽ Harsh clicks; *chirrit*; *see-see too-teetoodootootewit*. **RA3-4**

13 Pale Blue Flycatcher *Cyornis unicolor* (1439) 16cm. ♂ from ♂9 by overall pale blue (vs verditer) colour, greyish (vs verditer) belly and vent, brownish (vs verditer) scalloping on undertail-coverts. ✶ Foothills-1800. Light broadleaved evergreen forest. ▽ *tr-r-r*; rich loud *chuchichu`chuchichu`chuchichu (twick-twick)*. **R(A?)4**

14 Blue-throated Flycatcher *Cyornis rubeculoides* (1440) 14cm. ♂ from ♂♂15 & 16 by blue throat; from 4 & 5 by white belly; lacks shining blue neck-patch of 4. ✶ <1800(2100). Forest undergrowth, well-wooded areas. Usually in moister facies than 16. ▽ *chick-chick*; *chr-r*; *tsee-choo-tee-tee-too-too-di* and similar warblings. **RAM3-4**

15 Hill Blue Flycatcher *Cyornis banyumas* (1441) 15cm. ♂ extremely similar to the far commoner ♂16 but slightly larger, larger bill and usually some olive-brown on lower flanks. Extent of orange-rufous on underparts variable. Range indicative. Some ♂♂ have small area of blue-black on chin. ✶ Moist evergreen forest with dense undergrowth. ▽ Hard *tac*; *trrt-trrt-trrt*; sweet melancholy warble, more complex and rapid than 16. **SA*5**

16 Tickell's Blue Flycatcher *Cyornis tickelliae* (1442-3) 14cm. ♂ extremely similar to ♂15 but slightly smaller; smaller bill, white lower flanks sometimes tinged rufous. Extent of orange-rufous on underparts variable. Some ♂♂ have small area of blue-black on chin but this never extends down on throat as in ♂14. ✶ <1500. Forest, groves, parks, gardens, overgrown gullies, orchards. ▽ *tick-tick*; metallic trill of 6-10 notes *si-si-si-wee-si-woo-si*. **R●M2**

238

PLATE 75: MONARCH FLYCATCHERS, FANTAILS, FLYCATCHER-WARBLERS, GOLDCREST, TESIAS AND TIT WARBLERS

1 **Asian Paradise-flycatcher** *Terpsiphone paradisi* (1460-4) 20cm (♂ overall 50cm). **(a)** young/rufous phase ♂ **(b)** old/white phase ♂; intermediates occur. ✿ <1800(3100). Low to mid-storey in open forest, groves, gardens, bamboo, scrub jungle. ▽ Grating *chreet; chechwe; queenk; tst; weep poor willie weep-poor willie; peety-to-whit....* **R●MP3**

2 **Black-naped Monarch** *Hypothymis azurea* (1465-9) 16cm. Gorget faint/absent in Sri Lanka. ✿ <900(1500). Mid-storey in well-wooded areas. ▽ Grating *which-which-(which)-(which); wheet-wheet-wheet-wheet-wheet.* **R●(M)3**

3 **White-throated Fantail** *Rhipidura albicollis* (1454-9) 17cm. Races **(a)** nom **(b)** *albogularis* sometimes treated as a separate (endemic) species, White-spotted Fantail. ✿ S <1700(3000). **W** Plains, foothills (2140). Forest, groves, gardens, scrub. ▽ Harsh *chuck(-r);* squeaky *cheek;* descending *tri-riri-riri.* **(b)** *kikirrichuck wee-si-weet weet siweet.* **R●A2**

4 **White-browed Fantail** *Rhipidura aureola* (1451-3) 17cm. Broad white brow; spotted coverts. ✿ <1000(1500). Mainly lowlands. Drier forest, groves, scrub, gardens. ▽ *chuck-chuck; ch'wch;* thin tinkling *chee-chee-cheweechee-vi.* **R●2**

5 **Yellow-bellied Fantail** *Rhipidura hypoxantha* (1450) 8cm. Like 10 but yellow below, wing-bar, broad black tail tipped white. ✿ S (1000)1800-treeline+. **W** >adjacent plains. Evergreen habitats. ▽ Repeated *tsip; weetooweetowi.* **RA2**

6 **Goldcrest** *Regulus regulus* (1628-31) 8cm. ✿ S 2200-3600(4000) Mainly conifers. **W** 1500-3050. Firs, (other forest, orchards, groves, gardens). ▽ Thin *tsi-tsi-tsi-tsi;* up and down *see-sisisiyee-sisisiyee-siseewit.* **A3**

7 **Broad-billed Warbler** *Tickellia hodgsoni* (1627) 10cm. See 14, 79.3. ✿ 1100-2700. Forest edge; dense scrub; bamboo. ▽ Thin twitter *tseeseetititseesititit;* shrill whistle. **R(A?)4-5**

8 **Rufous-faced Warbler** *Abroscopus albogularis* (1626) 8cm. ✿ (300)600-1200(1800). Bamboo, second growth, moist-deciduous forest. ▽ Soft *tit;* shrill *trrrrr.* **R*3**

9 **Yellow-bellied Warbler** *Abroscopus superciliaris* (1622-3) 9cm. ✿ S 500-1800. **W** >plains. Prefers bamboo in mixed forest and second growth. ▽ *trrit;* 3-6 thin tinkling notes. **A3**

10 **Black-faced Warbler** *Abroscopus schisticeps* (1624-5) 9cm. See 5 for differences. Races **(a)** nom **(b)** *flavimentalis.* ✿ (600)1500-2700. Forest glades, bamboo, second growth, scrub. ▽ Chattering. **RA?3**

11 **Grey-hooded Warbler** *Seicercus xanthoschistos* (1617) 10cm. Races **(a)** nom **(b)** *tephrodiras.* ✿ S (300)1000-2300(2750). **W** Foothills (2000+). Forest, orchards etc. ▽ *psit-psit; tyee-tyee; pit weety-(swee)-sweesweeet.* **A1**

12 **Golden-spectacled Warbler** *Seicercus burkii* (1616-9) 10cm. Distinctive yellow eye-ring. From 15 also by olive-green (vs grey) head. Wing-bar often faint/absent. It has recently been suggested that this should be split into several species of which three occur in our region. For details see family introduction on page 28. ✿ S (1000)1800-3800. **W** <2140. Forest undergrowth, scrub. ▽ *chichit; whit* or *psit; (ch)weechoo weechoo; weechoochi-weechoo; whichit-whichit-whichit.* **AM1**

13 **Grey-cheeked Warbler** *Seicercus poliogenys* (1620) 10cm. From 15 by pale grey chin and upper throat, crown pattern indistinct; grey on sides of head, including ear-coverts and lores, extending well below eye. ✿ S 1200-3200. **W** Foothills-1800. Open evergreen forest, bamboo. ▽ *tsweet; titsi-titsi-chi-(chi).* **A*4**

14 **Chestnut-crowned Warbler** *Seicercus castaniceps* (1621) 10cm. From 7 by grey (vs olive) nape, wing-bars, dark lateral crown-stripes, yellow (vs white) outer tail feathers, white (vs yellow) centre of belly, whitish (vs grey) throat. ✿ Foothills-2750. Dense forest. ▽ *chi-chi; tsik;* high, thin *ti tsitsititsit.* **A3**

15 **White-spectacled Warbler** *Seicercus affinis* (1613) 10cm. From 12 by white eye-ring, 13 by yellow chin, throat and lores, distinct crown pattern. ✿ S 1400-2300. **W** Plains-foothills. ▽ *che-weet.* **A4**

16 **[Crested Tit Warbler** *Leptopoecile elegans* (1632) 10cm. ✿ S 3400-4300 **W** 2800-3900. Coniferous forest, juniper. ▽ Soft peeping *tsee-tsee.* **X** (Resident in SE Tibet. Could occur in Arunachal Pradesh.)]

17 **White-browed Tit Warbler** *Leptopoecile sophiae* (1633-4) 10cm. Races **(a)** nom **(b)** *obscura.* ✿ S 2700-4580. **W** >1800. Shrubbery above treeline, streamside willows and bushes. ▽ Soft *teet;* hard *tzrit;* sweet loud chirping. **A3**

18 **Grey-bellied Tesia** *Tesia cyaniventer* (1471) 9cm. Like 19 but paler grey below, whitish centre of belly, goldish super-cilium and dull green crown, distinct black eye-stripe, (orange-)yellow lower mandible. ✿ S 1500-2550. **W** (Plains) foothills-1830. Damp forest undergrowth. ▽ *tchirik; tsik...; churrr...; ti-ti-ti-tu Tu-CHIYOU* (or *CHEWIT*). **AM3**

19 **Slaty-bellied Tesia** *Tesia olivea* (1472) 9cm. Like 18 but uniformly dark grey below, crown bright greenish-gold, diffuse eye-stripe, orange(-red) lower mandible. ✿ S 1000-2000? **W** <1000. Moist forest undergrowth. ▽ Spluttering, bubbling *prrrr-rrr-rrr; tchirik-tchirik;* 4-6 whistles, then sudden explosive jumble of notes. **AM3**

20 **Chestnut-headed Tesia** *Tesia castaneocoronata* (1473) 8cm. ✿ S (1800)2400-3300(4000). **W** <1830. Undergrowth, especially near streams. ▽ Loud *tziet* or *tsit; tissit; chiruk-chiruk; wee; seep (sit) tsee-tsu-wit.* **A3**

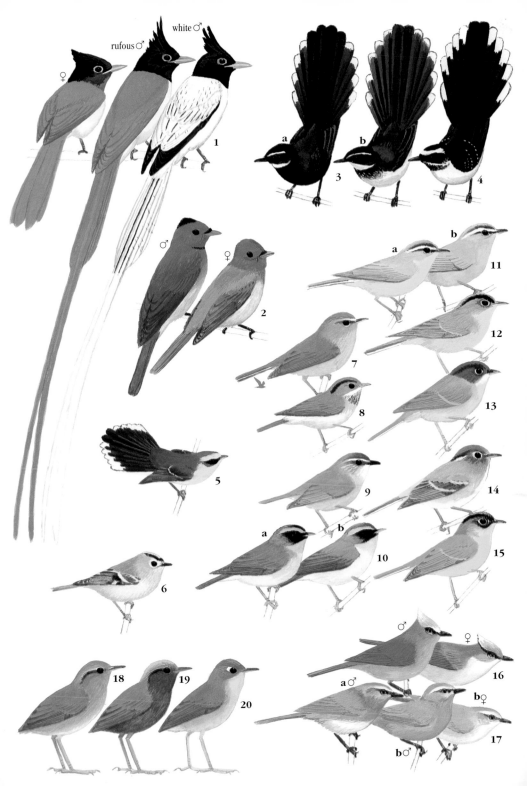

PLATE 75

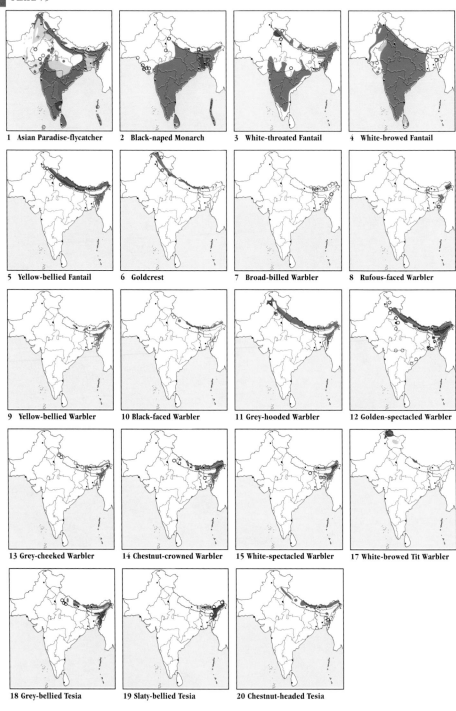

1 Asian Paradise-flycatcher

2 Black-naped Monarch

3 White-throated Fantail

4 White-browed Fantail

5 Yellow-bellied Fantail

6 Goldcrest

7 Broad-billed Warbler

8 Rufous-faced Warbler

9 Yellow-bellied Warbler

10 Black-faced Warbler

11 Grey-hooded Warbler

12 Golden-spectacled Warbler

13 Grey-cheeked Warbler

14 Chestnut-crowned Warbler

15 White-spectacled Warbler

17 White-browed Tit Warbler

18 Grey-bellied Tesia

19 Slaty-bellied Tesia

20 Chestnut-headed Tesia

PLATE 76

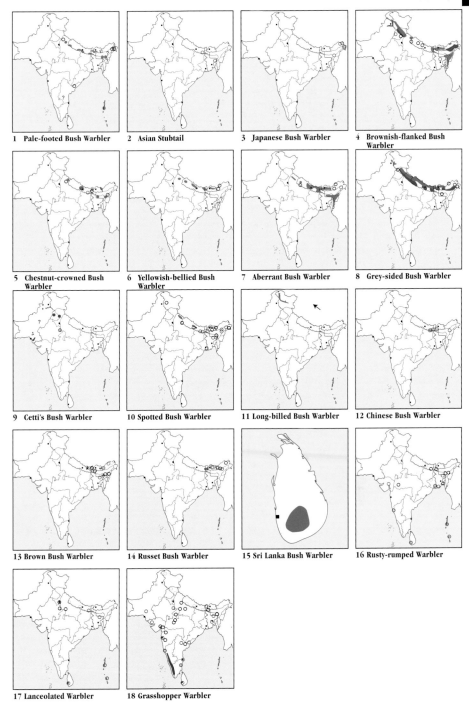

1 Pale-footed Bush Warbler

2 Asian Stubtail

3 Japanese Bush Warbler

4 Brownish-flanked Bush Warbler

5 Chestnut-crowned Bush Warbler

6 Yellowish-bellied Bush Warbler

7 Aberrant Bush Warbler

8 Grey-sided Bush Warbler

9 Cetti's Bush Warbler

10 Spotted Bush Warbler

11 Long-billed Bush Warbler

12 Chinese Bush Warbler

13 Brown Bush Warbler

14 Russet Bush Warbler

15 Sri Lanka Bush Warbler

16 Rusty-rumped Warbler

17 Lanceolated Warbler

18 Grasshopper Warbler

PLATE 76: BUSH AND GRASSHOPPER WARBLERS

1 **Pale-footed Bush Warbler** *Cettia pallidipes* (1474-5) 13cm. Pale flesh/yellowish-white legs; shortish square tail; long buffy supercilium; (rufous-)brown above; white below but for buffy-brown flanks/vent. See 2. ⌘ **S** Foothills. **W** >Plains. Undergrowth at forest edge, tall grass, second growth. ▽ *chick-chick; rip...pikwa-chick-a-chick.* A*4

2 **Asian Stubtail** *Urosphena squameiceps* 11cm. Very short rounded tail, pale fleshy legs. From 1 also by creamy-white supercilium; less contrasting underparts; dark crown-scales and ear-covert mottling (close range only). ⌘ <2000. Forest undergrowth. ▽ *stit; syit;* soft *chip-chip;* high weak *see-see-see-see-see-see-see-SEE-SEE.* V

3 **Japanese Bush Warbler** *Cettia diphone* (1476) (race in our region, *canturians,* sometimes split as Manchurian Bush Warbler.) ♂17cm ♀14cm. Large; rufescent olive-brown upperparts; brighter forecrown; rather stout bill; long notched tail. ⌘ Thick brushwood, reeds. ▽ *chak-chak;* harsh *charr; tu-u-u-teedle-ee-tee.* V

4 **Brownish-flanked Bush Warbler** *Cettia fortipes* (1477-8) 11cm. Brownish flanks, greyer on sides of breast and throat; buffy supercilium; dark legs. Upperparts more olive-brown than 1, 3 & 6. Lacks chestnut crown of 5 & 8. Some yellowish imm from 6 & 7 by dark flanks. Races **(a)** nom **(b)** *pallidus.* ⌘ **S** 1800-3200. **W** (Plains) foothills-2140. Undergrowth; scrubby slopes. ▽ *pick; chuk;* very distinctive *wheeeEEE...sweechy-chou* or *weeeeeeee'll...beat-you.* A2

5 **Chestnut-crowned Bush Warbler** *Cettia major* (1479-80) 13cm. Chestnut crown contrasts with dark olive-brown upperparts. Like 8 but larger; longer bill; chestnut extends over lores and well onto nape (vs blackish loral stripe, whitish supercilium); whiter below; olive-brown (vs grey) flanks. ⌘ **S** (1800)3300-4100. Rhododendron. **W** >plains. Reedbeds. ▽ *tzip.* A4

6 **Yellowish-bellied Bush Warbler** *Cettia acanthizoides* (1484) 11cm. Yellowish belly and vent contrasting with greyish-white throat and breast; buffy supercilium; brown upperparts washed rufous (vs olive on 7). ⌘ **S** 2400-3660. **W** >1350. Ringal bamboo; scrub. ▽ *brrr; tik tik tik;* 3 or 4 long-drawn-out, thin whistles each lasting about 2 secs followed by several quick repeated up and down *cheechy chew* or *oowy-chee* notes. A4

7 **Aberrant Bush Warbler** *Cettia flavolivacea* (1481-3) 13cm. Note greenish-yellow underparts; yellowish supercilium; olive tinged upperparts. From 80.10 & 11 by size; stockier build; longer bill; long rounded tail; voice. ⌘ **S** 2400-3600. **W** 700-2700. Long grass, scrub, undergrowth, bamboo. ▽ *trrk; tsick; titi-weety-weeeòu; chou whichy-wee.* A2

8 **Grey-sided Bush Warbler** *Cettia brunnifrons* (1485-7) 10cm. Chestnut crown but see 5. ⌘ **S** 2700-4000. Shrubbery. **W** <2200. Dense grass, bushes. ▽ Soft *tsik; tzek; tsik wichichichit whooweeou-whooweeou.* A1

9 **Cetti's Bush Warbler** *Cettia cetti* (1488) 12cm. Stout build; rufous-brown above, broad rounded tail; short whitish supercilium. ⌘ Plains. Tall grass, reeds, tamarisk. ▽ Hard chatter; *tett;* loud *tsit-tsiuit tsutsuittsvi-tsviit.* W*3-4

10 **Spotted Bush Warbler** *Bradypterus thoracicus* (1489-90) 13cm. Note spotting on throat and upper breast (often indistinct); brown-and-white scaled undertail-coverts. See 11 for differences. Races **(a)** nom **(b)** *shanensis.* ⌘ **S** 3000-4350. Shrubbery above treeline. **W** >plains. Coarse grass, reeds, scrub. ▽ *see-see; pwit; dzzzee dzzzee dzzzee....* A*4

11 **Long-billed Bush Warbler** *Bradypterus major* (1491) 15cm. Like 10 but larger; longer bill; whiter below; plain undertail. ⌘ **S** 2400-3600. **W** >1200. Coarse grass, scrub, bracken. ▽ Grating *trr;* persistent *trritik-trritik-....* N*A3

12 **Chinese Bush Warbler** *Bradypterus tacsanowskius* (1492) 14cm. From 11 by shorter bill; pale tips to undertail-coverts; unmarked throat and breast, though some may show faint spotting and/or yellowish tinge to underparts. ⌘ Plains. Grass, bushes, reeds, rice and stubblefields. ▽ *chirr chirr; dzzzzrrrrrr...dzzzzrrrrrr...dzzzzrrrrrr....* V(W)

13 **Brown Bush Warbler** *Bradypterus luteoventris* (1493) 14cm. Warmer above than 12, undertail-covert tips weak. ⌘ **S** 2100-3300(1200-1600). **W** Foothills. ▽ *teck; pink;* harsh grating *churr;* reeling grasshopper-like *tic-tic-tic....* A4-5

14 **Russet Bush Warbler** *Bradypterus mandelli* (*seebohmi*) 14cm. Note rufescent-brown upperparts; brown flanks; diffuse pale fringes to undertail-coverts; black bill. ⌘ Grassy hillsides. ▽ *chack; zeerit* repeated at almost 2/sec. A*3-4

15 **Sri Lanka Bush Warbler** *Bradypterus palliseri* (1494) 16cm. From other Sri Lankan warblers by large size; dark appearance; grey/olive-brown underparts; orangy-buff throat (lacking in juv); broad rounded tail. ⌘ >(900)1300. Thick forest undergrowth and scrub. ▽ Usually silent; *pwit; qtz; queek;* short squeaky song. E*4

16 **Rusty-rumped Warbler** *Locustella certhiola* (1542-3) 13cm. From 17 & 18 by rufous rump and uppertail-coverts; dark tail tipped white; lacks 17's flank streaking. **Juv/1stW** may be tinged yellow below with some streaking on the breast only. ⌘ Lowland marshes, reeds, paddies, waterside vegetation. ▽ *chi-chirrr, pit; ryit-yit-tyit-tyit...;* excited chacking. W5

17 **Lanceolated Warbler** *Locustella lanceolata* (1544) 13cm. Streaked breast and flanks, but see 16 & 18. ⌘ <1800. Grass, scrub, cane. ▽ *teck; chirr-chirrr* louder than 16; explosive *rink-tink-tink; rit-tit-tit-tit;* excited chacking. W5

18 **Grasshopper Warbler** *Locustella naevia* (1545) 13cm. Underparts variable **(a)** whitish **(b)** yellowish. Like 17 but unstreaked below; more diffuse streaking above; 17 rarely yellowish below. Occasionally individuals may be as heavily streaked as poorly marked 17 and not safely separable. See also 16. ⌘ <1800. Waterside grass, bushes, reeds, grassy hillsides, shola fringes. ▽ *sit; chek-chek; churr-churr; cht-cht-cht.* W*4

PLATE 77: PRINIAS, SCRUB WARBLER, GRASSBIRDS AND CISTICOLAS

1 Rufescent Prinia *Prinia rufescens* (1501) 11cm. **Br** lacks 2's breast-band; separated from 3 by all white supercilium; grey of head merging into brown mantle (vs clearly demarcated grey cap); grey (vs blackish) ear-coverts; from nbr 4 by paler grey head; longer supercilium; whiter underparts. **Nbr** similar to nbr 2 & 6 which see for differences. Note range. ✿ Foothills-1200(1800). Grass in open forest, forest edge. ▽ Buzzing *bzzee, bzzee*; *chip*; strong *chweep-chweep-chweep*; *chip-wee chip-wee*. **R2**

2 Grey-breasted Prinia *Prinia hodgsonii* (1502-5) 11cm. Grey breast-band diagnostic. **Nbr** in the northern part of its range loses breast-band, though some may retain a trace; upperparts vary from brown to rufous-brown; told from 1 by brownish-grey (vs rufescent) tail; supercilium in front of eye only; browner upperparts. Note range. See also 5 & 6. ✿ <1200(1900). Bushes, scrub, (grass, bamboo, mangrove, reeds, coffee). ▽ *zee-zee-zee*; *chew-chew-chew*; *twirrr-twirrr*; *chitit yousee-yousee-which-which-which-which*. **R•2**

3 Grey-crowned Prinia *Prinia cinereocapilla* (1507) 11cm. Note blue-grey cap and rufous-buff supercilium (sometimes white behind eye). From 1 by blue-grey (vs grey-brown) crown contrasting sharply with rufous upperparts; richer underparts. From nbr 2 & 4 by strongly rufous upperparts; colour and length of supercilium. ✿ <1350(1600). Clearings in dense jungle, second growth. Relatively arboreal. ▽ *tsirrrr*; *tweetoo-weetoo-weetoo-weetoo tr-ti-ti-tit-ti*. **E4**

4 Ashy Prinia *Prinia socialis* (1515-8) 13cm. **Br** dark ashy back diagnostic. **Nbr** combination of dark grey head and rich tawny underparts. Only some birds show the short white supercilium. Compare 1, 2 & 3. **Juv** (not illustrated) similar to 8 but less strongly coloured. Races **(a)** nom **(b)** *stewarti*. ✿ <1200. Grass, scrub, sparse jungle, crops, gardens. More humid areas than 6. ▽ Nasal *nyer nyer nyer*; *jimmy-jimmy-jimmy*; (*trik*) *eetchit-eetchit-eetchit*. **E2**

5 Rufous-fronted Prinia *Prinia buchanani* (1506) 12cm. Note rufescent crown (not always conspicuous, especially on nbr birds); whitish lores and supercilium extending well back behind the eye; pale fleshy lower mandible; white underparts with fulvous tinge restricted to lower flanks and vent; prominent whitish tips to all but central tail feathers. ✿ <1220 Coarse grass, scrub jungle, bushes in stony semi-desert, (crops). Drier areas than 2. ▽ Shrill *chirrup*; trill + tinkling *sirriget-sirriget-sirriget*. **E•3**

6 Plain Prinia *Prinia inornata* (1510-4) 13cm. Very like 7, which see. **Nbr/juv** (not shown) more rufous above and often mistaken for 1 but note longer tail (> two-thirds x body-length); uppertail brown (vs rufescent) concolorous with upperparts; richer buff underparts; range. From nbr 2 by larger size; longer tail; richer buff underparts. ✿ <1200(1800). Scrub, rank grass, crops, second growth, (mangroves). Constantly waves tail around. ▽ Plaintive *tee-tee-tee...*; reeling *tlick-tlick-tlick...*; *kink, kink...*; *chi-up*; wing-snapping. **R•2**

7 Jungle Prinia *Prinia sylvatica* (1519-23) 15cm. Very like 6 but larger; longer, stouter bill; supercilium usually shorter and diffuse; underparts usually paler; proportionately longer tail; voice. ✿ <1500(1800). Dry stony scrub, bush jungle, euphorbia. Usually drier habitats than 6. ▽ *prit-pee-tee-(wee-chi-chi-chi)*; *prit peeteew*; *pit pit pit...*; *thirrilip, thirrilip, thirrilip....* **E3**

8 Yellow-bellied Prinia *Prinia flaviventris* (1524-5) 13cm. Olive-green mantle and bright lemon-yellow belly diagnostic but beware of juv 4 which is similar but less strongly coloured. Supercilium sometimes obscure/absent. Races **(a)** nom **(b)** *sindiana*. ✿ <800(1200). Grassland, reeds and bushes near water. ▽ Plaintive *twee*; descending *twee-dulu-lu-lee*; rasping *dzeeeee*; chirp + trill; *chink, chink...*; wing-snapping. **R3**

9 Hill Prinia *Prinia atrogularis* (1529-30) 17cm. **Br** distinctive. Black of breast and throat may be lacking on **nbr** though often shows some blackish mottling. Races **(a)** nom **(b)** *khasiana* (nbr, not shown, like nbr nom but retains rufescent-brown crown). ✿ (300)900-2500. As 11; forest edge. ▽ Soft sputtered *tp-tp-tp-tp...*; *prri...prri...prri...*; *tulíp...tulíp... tulíp...*; *tjik-tjik....* **R3**

10 Graceful Prinia *Prinia gracilis* (1508-9) 13cm. Note small size; fine upperpart streaking; pale face with lores and supercilium not contrasting strongly; unstreaked buffish underparts. ♀ like ♂ but bill brown. ✿ Lowlands (up to 1000). Long grass, scrub, tamarisks; often near water. ▽ *trek*; *breep*; *tr-r-r-rrrr*; *tik*; *chrrr*; *trrit-trrit-trrit*; *teerreet-teerreet-teerreet...*; wing-snapping. **R3**

11 Striated Prinia *Prinia criniger* (1526-8) 16cm. Birds normally show some streaking on the upperparts for most of the year. Mottling on breast of nbr variable. Faint tail-barring not normally visible in the field. Note montane habitat (similar 12b restricted to lowland floodplains). ✿ S 900-2300(3100). W <2140. Rank grass, steep scrubby hillsides, grassy open pine forest, terraced fields. ▽ Wheezy, grating metronomic *chitzweet-chitzweet-chitzweet...*; *tchak-tchak*. **A2**

12 Rufous-vented Prinia *Prinia burnesii* (1531-2) 16cm. Races **(a)** nom **(b)** *cinerascens* are disjunct and may represent separate species. ✿ Floodplains, tall riverine grassland, *sarkhan* grass. ▽ Wheezy *feez*; *chit*; nasal *skeeow-skeeow-skeeow*; *szik-szik-szik*; (a) song clear, up-and-down, high-pitched warbling *tuweet-tiwittoo-tuweeet-tuwittoo-weeto-witoo...*; (b) song similar but includes trilling notes. **E*3-5**

246

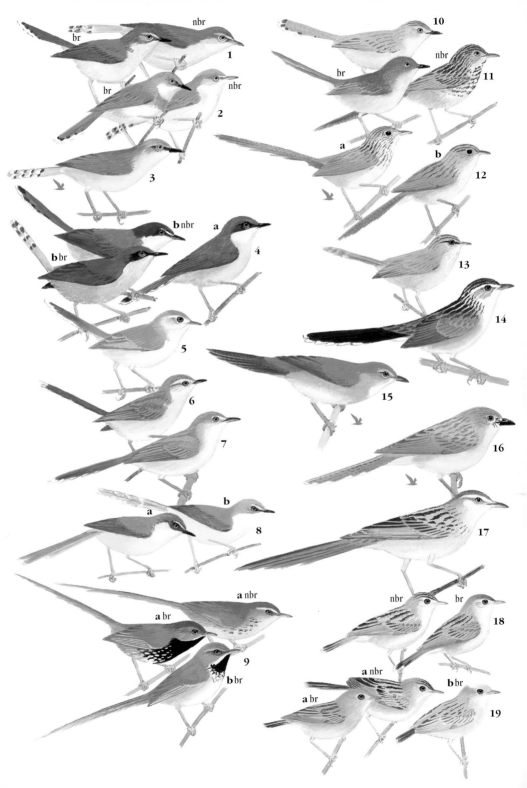

13 Streaked Scrub Warbler *Scotocerca inquieta* (1533) 10cm. From similar streaked prinias by black eye-line. Much bolder supercilium than 10. Note also blackish tail; fine streaking on whitish throat; range and habitat. ✻ Foothills-3000. Largely terrestrial in dry scrub. ▽ Plaintive *tee-chuu*; *peerururu*; trilling descending *twit-tit-tu-tu-tu-tuh*; low *pitcheeear pt-tcheeear*; *pit-pit-pit-....* **R3**

14 Rufous-rumped Grassbird *Graminicola bengalensis* (1534) 16cm. From 15-17 by dark cap; black and white streaked mantle; very dark tail. ✻ Plains. Tall grass, reeds. ▽ Mewing; harsh loud song. **R*4**

15 Broad-tailed Grassbird *Schoenicola platyura* (1546) 18cm. Very broad, rounded tail (with narrow dark barring) distinctive. Note also warm (to greyish) brown, unmarked upperparts and strong bill. ✻ 900-2000. Matted grass and reeds in marshy depressions, grassy hillsides. ▽ Nasal *tsee*; *tsip*; *chit*; *tilt*; *pink*; *psit-psit-psit-psit-psit-psit churr churr*, *pseeu*. **E*(A?)4**

16 Bristled Grassbird *Chaetornis striatus* (1547) 20cm. Sometimes shows diffuse pale supercilium. **Br** (not shown) upperparts colder brown. From 17 by smaller size; short stubby bill; lack of streaking on sides of breast; shorter rounded tail dark below with broad pale feather tips. See also 14. ✻ Plains. Coarse grassland with bushes, especially near water. ▽ Harsh *cha*; soft *zip*; *ji jee...jee ji...*in song flight or from exposed perch; *cht cht cheewheeew* etc. **E*•4**

17 Striated Grassbird *Megalurus palustris* (1548) 25cm. The largest warbler in the region. ✻ Tall grass, reeds and scrub, usually near water. Often perches openly with an upright stance. ▽ Harsh *chat*; *tzic*; subdued whistle + loud *wheeechoo*; powerful *chot-chot-chot-chot which-u-quieee-chot-trrrrt-kwit-kwit-kwit-cheee-chwot.* **R2**

18 Zitting Cisticola *Cisticola juncidis* (1498-1500a) 10cm. For differences see 19. ✻ <1350(2100). Mainly damp grassland, reeds, crops. ▽ Short sharp *plit...plit...*usually in low erratic undulating flight. **R•2**

19 Bright-headed Cisticola *Cisticola exilis* (1496-7) 10cm. In winter told from 18 by narrow buffy-brown tips to tail feathers (broad, white and contrasting in 18); strongly rufous-brown rump and hind-neck. Races **(a)** *erythrocephala* of southern India. ✻ >900. Tall grass (hillside scrub). **(b)** *tytleri* of the north and north-east. ✻ <800(1200). Tall grass. ▽ Nasal *nyaae*; *wheeez*; *bzzeeee...joo-ee.* **R3**

PLATE 77

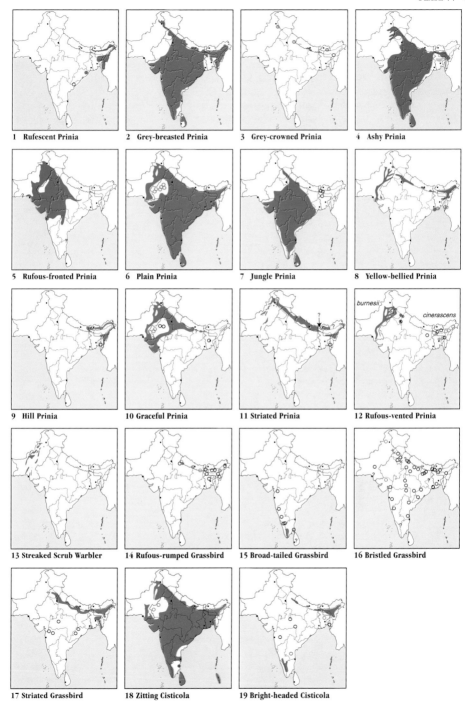

1   Rufescent Prinia

2   Grey-breasted Prinia

3   Grey-crowned Prinia

4   Ashy Prinia

5   Rufous-fronted Prinia

6   Plain Prinia

7   Jungle Prinia

8   Yellow-bellied Prinia

9   Hill Prinia

10 Graceful Prinia

11 Striated Prinia

12 Rufous-vented Prinia

13 Streaked Scrub Warbler

14 Rufous-rumped Grassbird

15 Broad-tailed Grassbird

16 Bristled Grassbird

17 Striated Grassbird

18 Zitting Cisticola

19 Bright-headed Cisticola

PLATE 78: REED AND 'TREE' WARBLERS

1 **Black-browed Reed Warbler** *Acrocephalus bistrigiceps* (1555) 13cm. Distinguished by distinctly blackish lateral crown-stripe bordering pale crown, prominent white supercilium and unstreaked upperparts. Could be confused with 2 & 3 but ranges disjunct. ✤ Lowlands. Reeds, wet grassland and paddy, waterside cover (drier areas on passage). ∇ *chak* reminiscent of 80.6, much softer than 5; *chrrr*; song like 2 but less harsh (a variety of churrings). **WP5**

2 **Sedge Warbler** *Acrocephalus schoenobaenus* 13cm. Most birds show streaking on crown (and mantle) distinguishing them from 1 & 3. Worn adults may be almost unstreaked and very similar to 3 but note paler ear-coverts; absence of rufous tinge to mantle; longer primary projection (80%); rump warmer than back. ✤ Waterside vegetation, crops. ∇ *tchuc*; *karr-r-r*; song similar to 6 but livelier, more varied. **V**

3 **Moustached Warbler** *Acrocephalus melanopogon* (1495) 13cm. From 1 & 2 by distinct blackish eye-stripe; dark crown (slightly paler than lateral crown-stripes) and ear-coverts; rusty tinge to mantle. From 2 by white supercilium (vs buffish), square-cut at the end; shorter primary projection (50%); rump not warmer than mantle. Often cocks and flicks tail. ✤ Plains (up to 1400). Reeds, rushes and tamarisk near water. ∇ *trek*; song like 2 but less harsh. **W(B*?)2**

4 **Thick-billed Warbler** *Acrocephalus aedon* (1549) 19cm. From other large *Acrocephalus* by rather plain face lacking supercilium; pale lores; relatively short thick bill; lower mandible pale without dark tip. ✤ <1500 Bushes, low trees, scrub, undergrowth in open forest. Not tied to waterside vegetation. ∇ *tschuk, tschuck*; metallic *chok-chok*; *chrr-r*; metallic *tack-tack*. Melodic varied song includes shrike-like mimicry and usually begins with several *chok* notes. **W3**

5 **Clamorous Reed Warbler** *Acrocephalus stentoreus* (1550-2) 19cm. Note large size. From 4 by whitish supercilium. Very similar to 13 & 14 but note long thin bill; longer tail more rounded at tip; supercilium less distinct behind eye. From 13 also by short primary projection (70%). ✤ <1600. Usually in waterside reeds, bushes and trees except on passage. ∇ Loud throaty *chak*; *ke*; hard *trrrrr* or *chur-r*; harsh (*tek-tek-tek*) *karra-karra-kareet-kareet-kareet...*; *gurchak-guk-guk-gurchak-geet-geet-geet-geet-kriti-kriti-kriti-keet-keet-gork-gork-gurchak....* **RPWM2**

6 [**Eurasian Reed Warbler** *Acrocephalus scirpaceus* (1555a) 13cm. Very like 10 & 11 but note supercilium faint or absent; long wing and primary projection (75-95%); 7-8 primary tips visible; distinct broken whitish eye-ring. ✤ Lowland reedbeds, (bushes). ∇ *chrrr*; *jag-jag-jag, tirri-tirri-tirri, kerr-kerr, kek-kek....* **X(B*?)** (No definite records from the subcontinent but likely to occur in Pakistan.)]

7 [**Olivaceous Warbler** *Hippolais pallida*. 12.5cm. Very similar to other *Hippolais*, especially 8b from which told by flatter (vs rounded) crown; less distinct, shorter supercilium not bordered darker above and ending just above or behind eye; greyer upperparts; slightly longer, stronger bill with all-pale lower mandible (vs usually dark-tipped); whitish underparts without buffy wash to flanks; legs usually grey (vs pinkish-brown); lores same colour as crown. From 9 by smaller size; somewhat smaller bill; browner upperparts; shorter tail not as dark; less obvious pale tips and fringes to outer tail feathers; evenly (vs unevenly) spaced tertials. ✤ As 9. Habitually pumps tail downwards as it calls; never waves it from side to side like 9. Usually feeds higher up. ∇ Similar calls to 9. Scratchy repetitive song. **X** (No confirmed records but birds of race *elaeica* could stray to NW part of region.)]

8 **Booted Warbler** *Hippolais caligata* (1562-3) 12cm. Structure more like a *Phylloscopus* warbler (plate 80) than a typical *Hippolais* or *Acrocephalus*. Very like 7 & 9 but smaller; more rounded head; slightly shorter finer bill with lower mandible normally tipped black; square-ended supercilium extending distinctly behind eye, accentuated by slightly darker border above; buffy wash on flanks; pinkish- or greyish-brown legs. Forages anywhere from ground-level to the canopy. See also 10. Races **(a)** nom ✤ Scrub, clumps of grass, bushes, trees, crops, (reeds). **(b)** *rama* sometimes regarded as a separate species, Sykes's Warbler. ✤ **S** Waterside tamarisks, reeds and bushes. **W** Acacias, bushes, scrub, gardens. Drier areas than (a). ∇ *tic* like 10 but softer; *tret*; *chit-chit-chit-chee-chee-chee-see-see-see-tit-tit-tit.* **WPB*2**

9 **Upcher's Warbler** *Hippolais languida* (1564) 14cm. Grey above with contrasting darker brown tail, flight feathers and wing-coverts. Whitish supercilium extends a short distance behind eye. Distinctly larger, greyer and more slender than 8 with longer, heavier bill; long shallow forehead reaching a peak just behind the eye (vs more rounded head); longer tail. See also 7. ✤ 2300-2400. Stony hillsides and ravines with low bushes, thorny trees, scrub. Characteristic habit of swinging tail from side to side (as well as up and down). Often flicks wings (contra 7). Frequently perches on rocks and forages close to the ground. ∇ Sharp *chak, chak...*; *chirr*; melodic stuttering and bubbling. **S*(P)4**

10 **Blyth's Reed Warbler** *Acrocephalus dumetorum* (1556) 13cm. Note fairly uniform greyish-olive upperparts (in fresh plumage paler and browner than shown) without contrasting rump; diffuse supercilium fairly obvious in front of eye but short and diffuse behind eye, without dark border above; longer primary projection than 11 & 12; greyish legs. Confusable with 8b but more olive-brown; rounded tail lacks the white tips to outer tail feathers. ✤ <2100. Dense bushes, (trees). Commonly in drier bushy habitats than other *Acrocephalus* in winter, except 4 which is much larger. ∇ Harsh *tzuck*; grating *chyairr*; *chek-chek-chek-che-chwee-too-too-chek-chek....* **WP(B*?)1**

250

11 Blunt-winged Warbler *Acrocephalus concinens* (1559-60) 13cm. Like 12 but short supercilium fades out just behind eye; lacks dark brow; less distinct eye-stripe; longer, stouter bill. ⌘ **S** 2700-3000. **W** >plains. Reeds, grassland usually near water. ∇ Quiet *tcheck*; soft *churrr*; song similar to 10, like 5 but more melodious, less harsh (uninterrupted warbles, trills and squeaks). **RL(M?)4-5**

12 Paddyfield Warbler *Acrocephalus agricola* (1557-8) 13cm. Note distinct supercilium bordered above by dark brow (but not broad and black as in 1); usually a rufous tinge to upperparts, sides of breast and flanks; short bill; very short primary projection. ⌘ Lowlands. Reeds, marsh vegetation, paddies. ∇ *chr...chuck*; *chik*; song like 10 but more varied, trilling and with some mimicry. **WPB*3**

13 Great Reed Warbler *Acrocephalus arundinaceus* (1553) 19cm. Very like 5 but note longer, more distinct supercilium; long primary projection (100%); shorter tail; shorter thicker bill. ⌘ Lowland reedbeds. ∇ Similar to 5 but song faster, less harsh, more varied. **V**

14 Oriental Reed Warbler *Acrocephalus orientalis* (1554). 19cm. Formerly considered conspecific with 5 and/or 13. From 5 & 13 by finely streaked lower throat and upper breast (white tips to outer tail feathers in fresh plumage). Shorter primary projection (70%) than 13. ⌘ Lowland reedbeds. ∇ Similar to 5 but song softer, less rhythmic. **V(W5)**

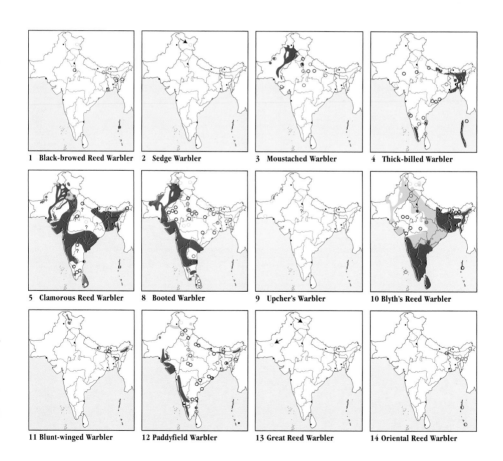

1 Black-browed Reed Warbler 2 Sedge Warbler 3 Moustached Warbler 4 Thick-billed Warbler

5 Clamorous Reed Warbler 8 Booted Warbler 9 Upcher's Warbler 10 Blyth's Reed Warbler

11 Blunt-winged Warbler 12 Paddyfield Warbler 13 Great Reed Warbler 14 Oriental Reed Warbler

PLATE 79

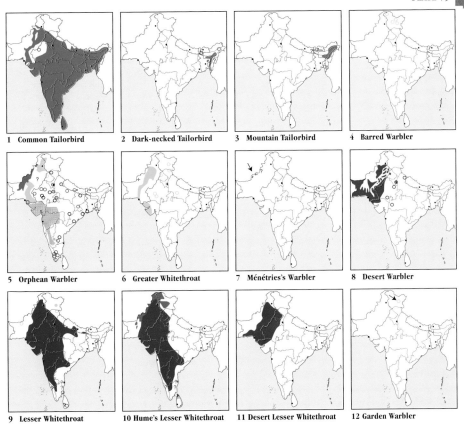

1 Common Tailorbird

2 Dark-necked Tailorbird

3 Mountain Tailorbird

4 Barred Warbler

5 Orphean Warbler

6 Greater Whitethroat

7 Ménétries's Warbler

8 Desert Warbler

9 Lesser Whitethroat

10 Hume's Lesser Whitethroat

11 Desert Lesser Whitethroat

12 Garden Warbler

PLATE 79: TAILORBIRDS AND *SYLVIA* WARBLERS

1 **Common Tailorbird** *Orthotomus sutorius* (1535-9) 13cm. A common and familiar garden bird. When singing shows a black patch at the side of the throat which could lead to it being mistaken for 2 but has a buffy-white (vs yellow) vent. ⌘ <1800(2000). Parks, gardens, scrub, hedgerows, undergrowth at edge of wooded areas. Noisy. ∇ Loud *pit-pit-pit-pit-pit-* ...; *tew-tew-*...; monotonous *chee-up...*; *pitchik-pitchik-pitchik....* **R1**

2 **Dark-necked Tailorbird** *Orthotomus atrogularis* (1540) 13cm. From 1 by more extensive rufous on crown; yellow vent and bend of wing; ♂ also by black throat; rufous lores. ⌘ <1400(1800). Understorey in dense forest. ∇ Loud trilling *krrri-krrri-krrri....* **R3-4**

3 **Mountain Tailorbird** *Orthotomus cuculatus* (1541) 12cm. From 1 & 2 by yellow belly, bright orange-rufous forehead, grey throat and breast. From Broad-billed Warbler (75.7) by thin yellow (vs grey) supercilium; long thin bill; white (vs grey) centre of throat and breast; grey (vs olive) hindneck; bright rufous (vs chestnut) cap; yellowish-green (vs yellow) rump; tailorbird jizz. ⌘ <1800. Evergreen forest undergrowth, bamboo, thick secondary growth. ∇ Buzzing *kiz-kiz-kiz*; *tue-ta-ti*; melodious sliding song *see-pipipi-tsee*. **R3**

4 **Barred Warbler** *Sylvia nisoria* (1564a) 15cm. Br♂ is distinctive. ♀ & **imm** usually show traces of scaling on the flanks, vent and undertail-coverts at close range. From 10 also by pale edges to wing feathers and tail-corners. ⌘ Bushes, hedges, thorny scrub. ∇ *tchek*; rattling, spluttering *trrr-r-r-r.* **V**

5 **Orphean Warbler** *Sylvia hortensis* (1565) 15cm. ♂ from most warblers of the region by black cap but see 7. ♀/**imm** rather like a large slow 9 with heavier bill and dark mottling on undertail-coverts. ⌘ **S** Shrubbery not far from water. **W** Dry scrub, thorn forest. ∇ *chack* like 9 but harder; *tchk*; *churr-r-r*; powerful, repetitive, thrush-like song. **WPB*3**

6 **Greater Whitethroat** *Sylvia communis* (1566) 14cm. From most warblers by the contrasting white throat. ♂ similar to 9, 10 & 11 but note the orange legs and lack of contrastingly dark ear-coverts (*icterops*, the race in our region, does not have such contrastingly warm-coloured wings as European birds). ⌘ **S** 2100-2300(<4500? on passage). Scrub, bushes, hedges. ∇ Rasping *charr*; sharp *tak, tak*; *chewee whit-whit-whit-whit*. **P(B*?)4**

7 **Ménétries's Warbler** *Sylvia mystacea* (1571a) 12cm. ♂ like 5 but much smaller; blackish tail contrasting strongly with pale upperparts (vs slightly); pink or red eye-ring; throat and breast variably flushed pinkish leaving contrasting white submoustachial stripe; contrasting yellow base of lower mandible; fleshy red legs. ⌘ Scrub, thickets. ∇ *chak*; *tret*; harsh *tzerr-r-rk*; *che-che-che-che-che.* **B*5**

8 **Desert Warbler** *Sylvia nana* (1571) 11cm. From similar warblers by small size; rufous rump and uppertail; white outer tail feathers; lack of supercilium; straw-coloured legs. ⌘ Bushes in semi-desert. Often on the ground. ∇ weak *drrrr*; high *che-che-che-che*; ringing *teere-teetyou-tyou-tyou-tyouyou.* **W2**

9 **Lesser Whitethroat** *Sylvia curruca* (1567-8) 13.5cm. Note white throat contrasting with head; brownish-grey head with darker ear-coverts; grey-brown upperparts with browner wings; blackish legs. See 10 & 11. ⌘ <900 (3300 on passage). Scrub, undergrowth, semi-desert, acacias. ∇ Hard *tak*; *chek*; rattling warble. **W1**

10 **Hume's Lesser Whitethroat** *Sylvia (curruca) althaea* (1570). 14cm. Slightly larger than 9 with darker bluish-grey upperparts and darker slaty crown; ear-coverts only slightly darker than crown (less contrasting); dusky sides of breast and flanks. ⌘ **S** 1500-3700. Bushy, stony slopes. **W** >plains. Bushes, scrub, acacias. ∇ *tek, tek*; *churrr*; *wheet-wheet-wheet*. **MW2**

11 **Desert Lesser Whitethroat** *Sylvia (curruca) minula* (1569). 13cm. Slightly smaller than 9 with paler sandier upperparts and less contrasting crown, more buffy-grey; less contrastingly dark ear-coverts; underparts white, only slightly washed with buff on flanks and breast. More lively than 9 & 10; often flicks tail. ⌘ Semi-desert, thorn scrub, acacias. ∇ Scolding rattle; churring *che-che-che-che-che.* **W2**

12 **Garden Warbler** *Sylvia borin* 14cm. Relatively featureless with greyish-brown upperparts, greyish-white underparts and poor supercilium; short, rather heavy, greyish bill; often a grey wash at sides of neck. Lacks white in tail and pale wing-feather fringes of 4. ⌘ Bushes, undergrowth in open woodland. ∇ *chek*; nasal *chet-chet-chet...*; melodious warbling. **V**

PLATE 80: LEAF WARBLERS

Leaf warblers without wing-bars, crown-stripe or yellow rump:

1 **Common Chiffchaff** *Phylloscopus collybita* (1574-5). 11cm. Race in our region is *tristis*. Rather nondescript but note all-black bill and legs; short buffy/whitish supercilium; greyish(-brown) upperparts; slight olive tinge to rump, tail and flight feathers (may be absent in worn plumage); yellow sometimes visible at bend of wing; whitish underparts with buffy/greyish wash on flanks and breast. Confusable with 2, 3, 4, 6, 9 & 16, which see. Race *collybita* (not illustrated) has occurred once: more greenish-olive above; supercilium and underparts (particularly breast and vent) washed with yellow. ✂ <2100 (higher on passage). Bushes, trees, open forest, scrub, reeds, crops. Not particularly shy. ∇ Melancholy flat piping *peet* or *peep* or *heep*; plaintive *teù*; *zit* (eastern birds); *wee-choo-choo-chivy weechoo-wee-choo-chivy-choo....* **W1**

2 **Mountain Chiffchaff** *Phylloscopus sindianus* (1576) 11.5cm. Extremely similar to 1 (*tristis*) and often indistinguishable; usually no green/olive tinge on rump, tail and flight feathers; flanks often contrast more with remaining underparts. Best separated by call. See also 3, 4, 6, 9 & 16. ✂ S 2500-4400. Willows, poplars, buckthorn, gardens, orchards. W Plains and foothills. Tamarisks, open scrub, acacia jungle. ∇ High *tiss-yip*; *tiss-yuitt*; *swe-eet*; song very similar to nominate *P. collybita* (1): *chit-chiss-chyi-chiss-chit-chiss-chyi-chip-chit-chyi.* **MP3**

3 **Plain Leaf Warbler** *Phylloscopus neglectus* (1577) 9.5cm. From 1 & 2 by small size; short tail; tiny bill; relatively larger, more rounded head; short primary projection; call. ✂ S 2000-3000. Low bushes, juniper. W Plains and foothills. Tamarisks, acacias, sheesham. ∇ Hard *chirip*; *chip*; *chi-ip*; *chit*; *tak-tak*; *churr*; short twittering warble *zilitzwit*; *chit-chuwich-chissa.* **MW3**

4 [**Willow Warbler** *Phylloscopus trochilus* (1572-3). 11.5cm. Records to date considered erroneous, doubtful or insufficiently documented, but the species could occur as a passage/winter vagrant. Very like 1 but slimmer; long primary projection (≥ ³/₄ tertial length vs ¹/₃-¹/₂); pale lower mandible with dark tip; legs usually fleshy-brown, though can be dark, (western birds in fresh plumage usually show yellow tones to underparts and supercilium, and greenish tinge to upperparts); different call. ✂ Bushes, forest edge, parks, gardens. ∇ Disyllabic *hoo-eet*; song a pleasant warble descending to a final flourish. **X(V?)** (A possible winter record in Kerala identified by song.)]

5 [**Yellow-streaked Warbler** *Phylloscopus armandii*. 12cm. Like 7 but slightly smaller; finer bill and legs; more uniform underparts without breast-band or buff wash to flanks and undertail-coverts; rather pale throat; more uniform supercilium; more arboreal habits; diagnostic yellow underpart streaking visible at close range. ✂ <3500. Prefers riverside trees in winter. ∇ Sharp, bunting-like *tic* or *tzic* or *click*; song like 7 but weaker. **X** (Could occur in NE India in winter.)]

6 **Dusky Warbler** *Phylloscopus fuscatus* (1584-6) 11cm. Like 1 but stouter; pale base to lower mandible; pale legs; longer, broader supercilium contrasts more with darker eye-stripe; tail slightly shorter and broader; different call; never shows any olive or yellow in plumage; skulks in low vegetation. From 7 by smaller size; slimmer build; finer bill; buff tinge to hind-supercilium (white and well-defined in front of eye); generally paler brownish wash to sides of breast, flanks and undertail-coverts; thinner legs normally darker. ✂ Plains and foothills (higher on passage). Low trees, bushes and long grass near water, damp cultivation, mangroves. ∇ Sharp *tak* or *tcheck*, harder than 7 and reminiscent of Blyth's Reed Warbler (78.10); *chiw-chiw-chiw-chiw-chiw* slower than 7. **W3**

7 **Radde's Warbler** *Phylloscopus schwarzi* 12.5cm. From 6 by large size; generally longer, broader supercilium with rufous-brownish tinge in front of and above the eye becoming whiter towards the rear; short, stout bill; thicker legs usually pale; longer tail; call; contrastingly rufous-buff undertail-coverts indicative but not diagnostic. See also 5. ✂ Bushes, undergrowth in open forest, forest edge, scrub; usually near ground. ∇ Soft, nasal, nervously repeated *prit* or *quip*; liquid rattling (*tyuk*)-(*tyuk*) *chwee-chwee-chwee-chwee-chwee.* **V**

8 **Smoky Warbler** *Phylloscopus fuliginiventer* (1582-3) 10cm. The only leaf warbler with such dark upperparts and smoky underparts. Races **(a)** nom **(b)** *tibetanus*. ✂ S 3600-4300(5000). Low shrubbery above treeline; alpine meadows. W Plains and foothills (3200). Waterside bushes, moist scrub and grass. ∇ Distinctive low *tsrrk*; *cht...cht*; soft *stup*; song a *tsli-tsli-tsli...* or *tsuli....* **A4**

9 **Tytler's Leaf Warbler** *Phylloscopus tytleri* (1578) 10cm. Note longish, thin, finely tapering bill – all dark except for slightly paler base of lower mandible and sometimes commisure; long whitish supercilium; broad dark eye-stripe; relatively short tail; olive-grey upperparts (greener in fresh plumage, greyer when worn); lack of pale tertial fringes; underparts washed slightly yellowish in fresh plumage (though never on throat), whitish/greyish in worn plumage; distinctive call. ✂ S 2300 to treeline+. Forest edge, conifers, hedges, dwarf willows, birches. Above treeline post-breeding. W Lower. Dwarf broadleaved forest. ∇ Plaintive drawn-out (*p*)*ssoooeet*; hoarse squeaky *huweest*; song *let's kiss him*; *ti wish i*. **NM3**

10 **Buff-throated Warbler** *Phylloscopus subaffinis*. (1580) 10.5cm. Very like 11 but note yellowy-buff (vs lemon-yellow) underparts; shorter uniformly yellowish-buff supercilium (vs lemon-yellow, often whitish towards rear); lacks 10's hint of

256

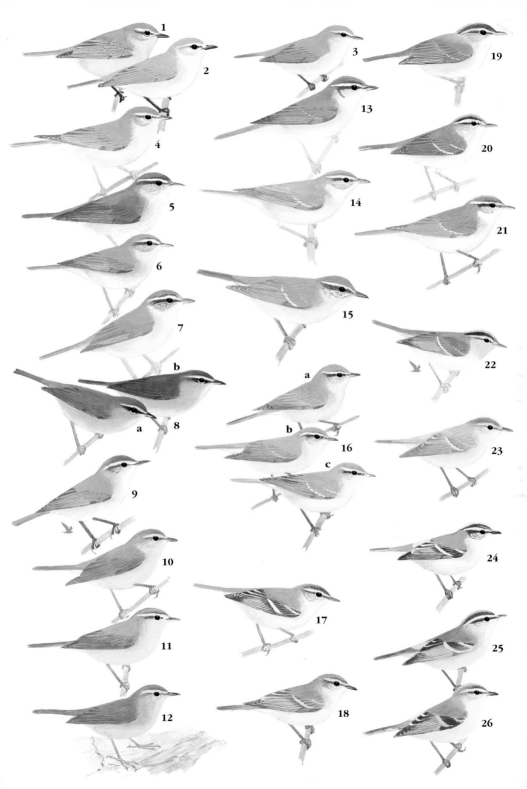

dark border above supercilium; largely dark (vs mainly pale) lower mandible; less contrasting eye-line; duskier (vs yellowish) ear-coverts; proportionately longer tail; call. See also 76.7. ⌘ >1200. Bushes and open scrub. ▽ Soft, cricket-like *chirrip*, *tripp* or *trrup*; weaker, slower, weaker version of 11's song (*trr*)-(*trr*) *tuee-tuee-tuee-tuee-tuee*. **V** (Misidentification of Aberrant Bush Warbler (76.7) previously led to an incorrect assessment of its status.)

11 Tickell's Leaf Warbler *Phylloscopus affinis* (1579) 11cm. Note greenish-olive upperparts; bold lemon-yellow super-cilium and underparts; dark eye-stripe contrasting with yellowish ear-coverts; largely pale lower mandible; slim dark legs; greyish wing-panel. See also 10, 12 & 76.7. ⌘ **S** (2700)3300-4500(4900). Juniper, low shrubbery, bushes and trees, forest edge. **W** (Plains) foothills-2100. Low bushes and trees, sometimes in flocks. ▽ Hard *chip*; *tsip*; *tret tret*; *pick*-(*pick*) *whi-whi-whi-whi-whi-*(*whi*)-(*whi*); *ze zizizizizi*. **M1**

12 Sulphur-bellied Warbler *Phylloscopus griseolus* (1581) 11.5cm. Most similar to 11 but stouter; (greyish-)browner upperparts; duskier (oily) yellow underparts; bright yellow supercilium, often more orange in front of eye, contrasts with dull underparts; pale legs; different call and habits. See also 10 & 76.7. ⌘ **S** 2400-4500. Stony slopes with scattered vegetation, juniper, willows along river beds. **W** <1000. Rocky areas, old forts and ruins, deciduous forest. Usually on or near ground, or creeping over tree trunks, branches, rocks and old walls. Often flicks wings. ▽ Soft, somewhat liquid *quip*; *tzilp*; *pick*; *chiw-chiw-chiw-chiw-chiw* slower and weaker than 6. **M3**

Leaf warblers with wing-bars but without crown-stripe or yellow rump:

13 Pale-legged Leaf Warbler *Phylloscopus tenellipes* (1605a) 11cm. 2 thin whitish or brownish-buff wing-bars (often wear away). Note very pale flesh-coloured legs; brown crown becomes contrastingly grey as plumage wears; strong white supercilium washed with buff on the front half extends back to nape; broad dark line through eye; dull flesh-coloured lower mandible with dark tip; dark upper mandible often with small pale tip; pale mottled ear-coverts; white underparts with brownish-buff wash on sides of breast and flanks, slightly yellower on vent. From similar 14 & 16 by browner upperparts; contrastingly warm brown rump; darker wash on the flanks; call; from 16 also by leg colour. ⌘ Mixed and secondary forest undergrowth and lower tree storey; mangroves. Usually on or near ground, often close to streams. Frequently pumps tail. ▽ High metallic *tink* or *peet.* **V(W5?)**

14 Arctic Warbler *Phylloscopus borealis* (1600) 12cm. 1 fine whitish wing-bar (occasionally 2). Similar to 13 but slightly larger and stouter; upperparts usually greener without the contrastingly warmer rump; thicker bill; short-tailed appearance; thinner supercilium; paler flanks, legs usually not quite as pale. From 16 by larger size and build; stouter bill; dark tip to lower mandible (vs all pale); long primary projection, almost equal to tertial length (vs $^3/_4$); thinner supercilium falling well short of forecrown (vs broader and usually meeting above bill or nearly so); complete loral stripe from eye to bill-base; paler legs (orangy/fleshy vs dusky-brownish). Best feature is call. ⌘ Lowland mixed and secondary forest, gardens, mangroves. Usually high in tall bushes and trees. ▽ Distinctive loud hard bunting-like *dzik* or *dzrit*-(*it*). **V(W5?)**

15 Large-billed Leaf Warbler *Phylloscopus magnirostris* (1601) 12.5cm. 2 wing-bars, upper indistinct and often absent. Rather similar to 16a but note large size; larger dark bill with pale only at base of lower mandible; crown darker than mantle; bolder supercilium; broader dark eye-line; distinctive voice. ⌘ **S** (1800)2100-3600. Himalayan streamside trees (and bushes). **W** <1200(2750). Evergreen and riverine forest. Chiefly mid-storey. Usually solitary. ▽ (*yaw*) *´dir´tee*; *see`si-si`si-si.* **M3**

16 Greenish Warbler *Phylloscopus trochiloides* (1602-5) 11cm. Normally shows one thin (yellowish-)white wing-bar, occasionally two, which can both wear away inviting confusion with 9-11 (which see). See 14 & 15 for differences with those species. ⌘ **S** (1800)2700-4000(4600). Conifers; mixed fir, rhododendron and birch forest. **W** <2600. All kinds of wooded areas. Largely arboreal, preferring the canopy. Usually solitary. Sometimes treated as three separate species **(a)** Greenish Warbler *P. trochiloides* with three races, (i) nom (ii) *ludlowi* (iii) *viridanus*. ▽ Disyllabic *tisswit* or *chiswee*; high warbling *chi chiwi-tchiwi-chit-chiwiwit-cheewi-chicheewit.* **(b)** Green Warbler *P.* (*t.*) *nitidus*. Brighter and greener above; yellower below. ▽ More trisyllabic: *tissuwit* or *chisuwee.* **[(c)** Two-barred Greenish Warbler *P.* (*t.*) *plumbeitarsus* is extralimital but could occur. ▽ *chi-wee*-(*ri*). **WMP1]**

17 Yellow-browed Warbler *Phylloscopus inornatus* (1592) 10cm. Two broad yellowish-white wing-bars. From 13-16 by pale tips to dark tertials; dark borders to the broader wing-bars. Sometimes shows a faint crown-stripe, though never as strongly marked as 19-26. Very similar to 18 but greener above; supercilium, wing-bars and ear-coverts often tinged yellowish; whiter underparts usually with some yellowish wash; pale lower mandible with dark distal third; paler legs; different voice. ⌘ <1880. All kinds of wooded areas. Usually solitary. ▽ Loud ascending *tseweest*; shrill *weest*; *tsooeet*; buzzy (*t*)*zwee*; high thin *tsitsoo-chiwuwi-tsisee*; *tsee tseeoo-ts-tsee.* **W3**

18 Hume's Warbler *Phylloscopus humei* (1590-1) 10cm. Formerly considered conspecific with 17. Double whitish wing-bar sometimes wearing away to one or none. Very like 17 but greyer above; browner crown; wing-bars never tinged yellowish; dark bill and legs; different voice. May show an indistinct crown-stripe. ⌘ **S** (2100)2700-3650. Mixed fir and birch. **W** <2150(2550). Dry deciduous forest, acacias, gardens, orchards. Usually solitary. ▽ Repeated, disyllabic ringing *tiss-yip* or *tseelo* or *tze-weet* or *tissoo*; *dioo dioo* reminiscent of 16; buzzing wheezy falling *tzzzeeeeeu*, often given together with calls. **MW1**

Leaf warblers with wing-bars and crown-stripe but without yellow rump:

19 Western Crowned Warbler *Phylloscopus occipitalis* (1606) 11.5cm. Two (yellowish-)white wing-bars, the upper often indistinct or absent. Larger than 20 with longer thicker bill; frostier, greyer above; little or no yellow below; thinner wing-bars. Very like 21, which see. Crown-stripe and large bill with entirely bright orange(-yellow) lower mandible help distinguish this and 21 from 13-18. ♂ **S** (1800)2000-2500(3350). Coniferous, deciduous and mixed forest; willows. Often flicks wings alternately, a habit only shared with 20. **W** (Plains) foothills-2100. Humid forest. Relatively arboreal. Sometimes in flocks. ∇ Often silent; *chiwee* or *chit-weei*; *stic-(swick)*; *stic-chwi-chwi-chwi-chwi-chwi-(chwa)*; *tityu-tiu-tiu-tiu-tiu-tiu*. **M1-3**

20 Blyth's Leaf Warbler *Phylloscopus reguloides* (1608-11) 11cm. Two broad yellow(ish) wing-bars, inner webs of outer tail feathers edged white. For differences see 19 & 21. ♂ **S** (1400)2450-3300(3800). Fir, oak and rhododendron forest. Like 19, often flicks wings open alternately, which habit helps separate it from other *Phylloscopus*. **W** Plains-1500(2750). Open forest, forest edge, bushes. Sometimes in flocks. ∇ *tsi-pit* or *chee-pit*; *kee-kew-i*; *tisshoo-eet*; *stic sweechy-sweechy-sweechy-sweech*; *pit-chew-a-pit-chew-a-pit-chew-a*. **AMW1**

21 Eastern Crowned Warbler *Phylloscopus coronatus* (1607) 11.5cm. Single thin yellowish-white wing-bar. Very like 19 but brighter, more contrastingly patterned; greener above, contrastingly darker lateral crown-stripes; clearly demarcated, darker eye-stripe; supercilium normally yellow in front of eye, white behind; yellow wash on undertail-coverts (can be difficult to see). From 20 by larger size; bigger bill; thinner wing-bar with upper absent; dull, more diffuse median crown-stripe; whiter underparts; yellow wash on undertail-coverts. ♂ (Lowlands) foothills (up to 2000). Broadleaved forest, (gardens, mangroves). Low to mid-storey. ∇ Often silent; buzzing nasal *zweet* or *dwee*; Great Tit-like *pitschu-pitschu-wii*; *djip-djip*, *djip-djip*, *djee*. **W5**

22 Yellow-vented Warbler *Phylloscopus cantator* (1612) 9.5cm. Two yellow wing-bars. The bright yellow throat and vent contrasting with the whitish breast and belly easily distinguish this from all other leaf warblers. ♂ **S** 1200-2000+. Dense evergreen forest. **W** >plains. Forest. ∇ *pio, pio...*; *pist-psit-psit-(psit) pseewoo*. **MA*3**

23 Brooks's Leaf Warbler *Phylloscopus subviridis* (1593) 10cm. Two yellowish-white wing-bars, the upper one faint. Note upperparts somewhat brighter golden-olive than other leaf warblers; rump subtly paler than remaining upperparts; yellowish supercilium and ear-coverts; crown concolorous with mantle (or only slightly darker) but with pale yellowish stripe down centre (seldom lacking); underparts with variable yellowish wash; dark legs and bill with pale base to lower mandible. ♂ **S** 2100-3600. Coniferous and mixed forest. **W** Plains-1800. Acacias, bushes, olives. ∇ High piercing *chwee* or *pseo*; *tissuwee*; *chif-chif-(chif) chu-chu-(chu)*; *tsi-tsi-tsi-ti-tchsrrrrr....* **M*3-4**

Leaf warblers with wing-bars, crown-stripes and yellow rump:

24 Lemon-rumped Warbler *Phylloscopus chloronotus* (1594-6) 9.5cm. Two yellowish-white wing-bars. Often hovers after insects showing off the pale lemon-yellow rump, which separates this from 13-18. Note also yellowish supercilium and crown-stripe; dark eye-stripe broadening behind the eye and hooking down behind ear-coverts; absence of white in tail. See also 25 & 26. ♂ **S** (2200)2700-4000(4200). Fir, oak and rhododendron forests. **W** (Foothills)1200-2000(2750). Woods, bushy hillsides. ∇ High *tisp* or *uist*; *tsirrrrrrrrrrrr-tsi-tsi-tsi...*; *tsi-tsi tsi-tsi tsu-tsu tsi-tsi tsu-tsu....* **AM1**

25 Ashy-throated Warbler *Phylloscopus maculipennis* (1597-9) 9cm. Two yellow wing-bars. Only leaf warbler with grey ear-coverts, throat and upper breast (contrasting with rest of yellow underparts). Note also greyish-white supercilium and crown-stripe; white in tail. ♂ **S** 2450-3500. Primary forest. **W** (Foothills)1400-2300(2900). Broadleaved forest, second growth. Largely arboreal. ∇ Harsh *zit-(it)*, sharper than 26; *sit sit sit*; *sweechoo sweechoo sweechoo*; *titsu titsu*. **A2**

26 Buff-barred Warbler *Phylloscopus pulcher* (1587-9) 10cm. The only leaf warbler with distinctly (buffy-)orange wing-bars, the upper one sometimes faint or absent. Note also yellowish supercilium; mainly white outer tail feathers, the tail appearing all-white from below; pale crown-stripe indistinct, often only apparent as a short greyish nuchal stripe; flesh-coloured basal ½ of lower mandible; lacks contrasting grey upper breast of 25. ♂ **S** (2450)3400-4100(4300). Mixed fir, rhododendron and birch forests; shrubbery above treeline. Often flicks tail open to show white in outer rectrices. **W** (Plains)500-3050+. Dense forest. ∇ High *tsip* or *swit*; (*tick tick tick*) + trill; *tsi-i-i-i*; musical repeated *dioo....* **RA2**

27 [Chinese Leaf Warbler *Phylloscopus sichuanensis* (not illustrated). 10cm. Very like 24 but slightly larger; more elongated; slightly longer bill; faint central crown stripe, often only apparent as pale spot on hind-crown; dark eye-stripe lacks hook at back; lacks dark base to secondaries. Best separated by voice. ♂ Preferred wintering habitat unknown. ∇ Irregularly repeated, clear whistled *tueet*; song like Striated Prinia 77.11 and unlike other leaf warblers – monotonous dry *tsiridi-tsiridi-tsiridi....* **V?** (Recently recorded in Bhutan)]

PLATE 80

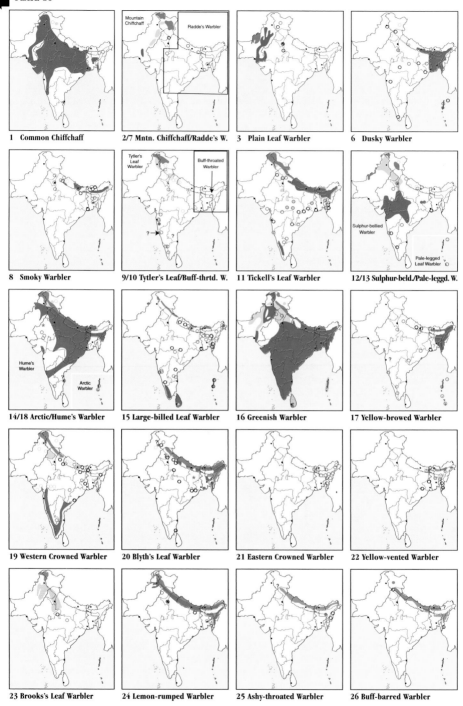

1 Common Chiffchaff

2/7 Mntn. Chiffchaff/Radde's W.

3 Plain Leaf Warbler

6 Dusky Warbler

8 Smoky Warbler

9/10 Tytler's Leaf/Buff-thrtd. W.

11 Tickell's Leaf Warbler

12/13 Sulphur-beld./Pale-leggd. W.

14/18 Arctic/Hume's Warbler

15 Large-billed Leaf Warbler

16 Greenish Warbler

17 Yellow-browed Warbler

19 Western Crowned Warbler

20 Blyth's Leaf Warbler

21 Eastern Crowned Warbler

22 Yellow-vented Warbler

23 Brooks's Leaf Warbler

24 Lemon-rumped Warbler

25 Ashy-throated Warbler

26 Buff-barred Warbler

PLATE 81

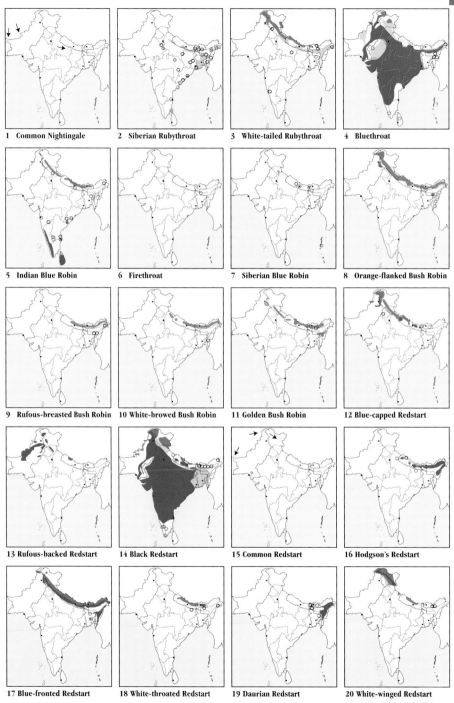

1 Common Nightingale

2 Siberian Rubythroat

3 White-tailed Rubythroat

4 Bluethroat

5 Indian Blue Robin

6 Firethroat

7 Siberian Blue Robin

8 Orange-flanked Bush Robin

9 Rufous-breasted Bush Robin

10 White-browed Bush Robin

11 Golden Bush Robin

12 Blue-capped Redstart

13 Rufous-backed Redstart

14 Black Redstart

15 Common Redstart

16 Hodgson's Redstart

17 Blue-fronted Redstart

18 White-throated Redstart

19 Daurian Redstart

20 White-winged Redstart

PLATE 81: ROBINS AND REDSTARTS I

1 **Common Nightingale** *Luscinia megarhynchos* (1642) 18cm. From ♀ redstarts by tail: longer, no 'shiver', no dark central tail feathers. ✶ Bushes in parks, gardens, woods. ▽ Usually silent on passage; *hooeet*; rattling *krrr*. **P5**

2 **Siberian Rubythroat** *Luscinia calliope* (1643) 15cm. ♀ from 1 by whitish supercilium; brown tail and uppertail-coverts; from ♀3 by fulvous-brown breast and lack of white tail-tips. ✶ <1500. Dense bushes in woodland, gardens and scrub; long grass, cane and reeds. ▽ *chak*; *ee-liu*; a rattle; pleasant scratchy warble. **W3**

3 **White-tailed Rubythroat** *Luscinia pectoralis* (1647-9) 15cm. Races **(a)** nom **(b)** *tschebaiewi*. ♀ from ♀2 by grey breast and white tail-tip (only visible when spread). ✶ S 2700-4900. Mostly in shrubbery above treeline. **W** Foothills and adjacent plains. Marshes, dense scrub, long grass. ▽ Harsh *ke*; *chruk*; *it...it...*; clear warbling song, richer than 2. **A3-4**

4 **Bluethroat** *Luscinia svecica* (1644-6a) 15cm. Forms **(a)** 'white-spotted' **(b)** 'red-spotted'. ✶ Breeds 2600-3600. Down to plains in winter. Bushes, reeds and grass near water. ▽ *chak*; *tsee-chak*; *churrr*; *wheet*. **B*WP2**

5 **Indian Blue Robin** *Luscinia brunnea* (1650-1) 15cm. ♂ from ♂10 by white vent and centre of belly; blackish ear-coverts, contrasting with blue upperparts. ♀ olive-brown above; uppertail-coverts, ear-coverts, lores and forecrown band washed rufous. Breast/flanks rufous-buff; white throat and centre of belly. See 74.12. ✶ S 1600-3300. **W** <2100. Dense forest undergrowth. ▽ *tack-tack* (knocking pebbles); *tsrr*; *(tsee) tsee tsee jerri-jerri-quick-wick-aquickick.* **M3**

6 **Firethroat** *Luscinia pectardens* (1652) 15cm. ✶ Dense bushes. Very shy. ▽ Call like 8. **V**

7 **Siberian Blue Robin** *Luscinia cyane* (1653) 15cm. ✶ Forest undergrowth and regrowth. ▽ *tuk-tuk-tuk...*; *se-ic.* **V**

8 **Orange-flanked Bush Robin** *Tarsiger cyanurus* (1654-6) 15cm. Races **(a)** nom **(b)** *rufolatus.* ✶ S 3700-4000(4400). **W** (750)1200-2600(3800). Forest undergrowth. ▽ *tek tek*; *trek-trek*; *hweet*; *pray did he then?* **A1**

9 **Rufous-breasted Bush Robin** *Tarsiger hyperythrus* (1660) 13cm. ♀ slaty-blue tail; rich buff underparts with white belly-centre and undertail-coverts. ✶ S 3400-3800. Dwarf rhododendron. **W** foothills-3500. Undergrowth along streams, trails and forest edge. ▽ *duk-duk-duk-squeak*; *zeew...zee...zwee...zwee.* **A3**

10 **White-browed Bush Robin** *Tarsiger indicus* (1659) 15cm. ♂ from ♂5 by entirely orange underparts; slaty-blue upperparts. ♀ long, thin whitish supercilium; orangy-buff below. ✶ S 3000-4200. Mixed forest. **W** (foothills)2000-3000(3700). Undergrowth in dense forest. ▽ *trrr*; *tuit-tuit*; *whreedeedee dee-doo-dee.* **A3**

11 **Golden Bush Robin** *Tarsiger chrysaeus* (1657-8) 15cm. ✶ S (1800)3000-4200(4600). **W** (foothills)1200-2000(3000). Evergreen forest undergrowth, treeline scrub. ▽ *t-r-r-r-r-(r)*; *fit fit*; *chik*; *chirik-chirik*; *tse-du-tee-tse churrr.* **A3**

12 **Blue-capped Redstart** *Phoenicurus coeruleocephalus* (1670) 15cm. ♀ by rufous rump without rufous in tail. ✶ S (1400)2700-3600(3900). **W** (foothills)1200-2600(3500). Steep rocky hillsides, junipers, open pine forest, olive groves and gardens. ▽ *tik tik...*; quiet dry warble *trrlee-trrlee-trrlee-....* **A2**

13 **Rufous-backed Redstart** *Phoenicurus erythronota* (1669) 15cm. ✶ <2100/2800. Arid country. ▽ *trr*; *few-eet.* **W4**

14 **Black Redstart** *Phoenicurus ochruros* (1671-2) 15cm. Races **(a)** *phoenicuroides* **(b)** *rufiventris.* ♂ **(a)** from 15 by black breast, no white forecrown. ♀ darker than ♀15; rufous-buff on lower belly, vent. ✶ S (2100)3000-4000(5200). **W** <1400. Stony open country, villages, open woodland. ▽ *ee-tik*; *tucc tucc titititic*; *whit...whit...whit.* **AM2**

15 **Common Redstart** *Phoenicurus phoenicurus* (1673) 15cm. ♂ from ♂14 by white forecrown, red breast. ♀ paler than ♀14 with whitish belly, vent (sometimes washed rufous at sides); doubtfully from ♀16 by browner upperparts, breast. Races **(a)** nom **[(b)** *samamisicus* – single record of uncertain origin]. ✶ Trees, bushes. ▽ *hweet-(tic)-(tic).* **P5**

16 **Hodgson's Redstart** *Phoenicurus hodgsoni* (1674) 15cm. ♂ from ♂19 by grey back. ♀ from other ♀ without white in wings by grey-brown breast contrasting with whitish centre of belly; from ♀15 by grey-brown upperparts and breast. ✶ Foothills-2800. Dry riverbeds in forest and cultivation; scrub, grassland and open parkland. ▽ *prit*; *trrr.* **W3**

17 **Blue-fronted Redstart** *Phoenicurus frontalis* (1675) 15cm. ♀ by rufous belly, vent. ✶ S (2000)3000-4500(5300). **W** (1000)1500-2400(2700). Alpine scrub, gardens, open forest. ▽ *tik*; high rapid *trrrrr*; *tt-tt-tt-tt.* **A2**

18 **White-throated Redstart** *Phoenicurus schisticeps* (1676) 15cm. Note dark inverted T on tail. ♀ by distinct white throat and wing-patch. ✶ S 2700-4900. **W** 1400-4200. Open forest and scrub, often along streams. ▽ *zieh rrrr.* **A3**

19 **Daurian Redstart** *Phoenicurus auroreus* (1677) 15cm. ♂ from ♂16 by black back. ♀ by white wing-patch except from ♀12 & 13 which have 2 wing-bars and ♀18 which has white throat-patch. ✶ S 2800-3300(3700). **W** foothills and adjacent plains. Open forest, secondary growth, streamside bushes, cultivation, villages. ▽ *hwit*; *teck-teck.* **(A?)W3**

20 **White-winged Redstart** *Phoenicurus erythrogaster* (1678) 18cm. ♂ from 82.9 by large size, white wing-patch, no black on tail. ♀ from other ♀ redstarts by large size, large bill, pale brown upperparts without white in wings, whitish eye-ring, pale fulvous-brown underparts with warmer lower breast and flanks. ✶ S (3600)3900-4800(5200). **W** (900)1500-4800. *Hippophae* bushes, riverbeds, dry scrubby alpine habitats. ▽ *lik*; *tyeet-teek-teek.* **A2**

PLATE 82: ROBINS AND REDSTARTS II, ROCK CHAT, SHAMA, FORKTAILS AND DIPPERS

1 [**White-throated Robin** *Irania gutturalis*. 18cm. ⌘ 1000-2800. Stony hillsides and scrub. ▽ *tsee-chit*; *t-r-r-r*. **X** (No reliable records from Indian subcontinent but could stray to N Pakistan.)]

2 **Rufous-tailed Scrub Robin** *Cercotrichas galactotes* (1641) 17cm. ⌘ Dry scrub, tamarisks, stony broken country. ▽ *tek*; *tcheeip*; *shrrr*; *tewee-u*; rich varied song. **P4**

3 **Brown Rock-chat** *Cercomela fusca* (1692) 17cm. Not unlike ♀10 but underparts rufous-brown and lacks chestnut on the vent. ⌘ <1300 Rocky areas, quarries, ruins, old forts. ▽ *chee*; *check-check*; thrush-like song. Good mimic. **E*3**

4 **White-tailed Robin** *Myiomela leucura* (1681) 17cm. White patch at base of tail is diagnostic but only visible when tail spread. ♂ from ♂5 by dark indigo belly and white patch at side of neck (often concealed). ♂ White-tailed Flycatcher (74.7) has white belly and vent, and more upright stance. Large and Small Niltavas (Plate 74, 6 & 3) have shiny blue patches on the sides of the neck. ⌘ S 1200-2700. W <1500. Undergrowth in broadleaved evergreen forest; often in gullies. ▽ *tey-tlee-i-ta-wey-i*. **A3-4**

5 **Blue-fronted Robin** *Cinclidium frontale* (1682) 19cm. Both sexes separated from 4 by longer graduated tail lacking white; belly and vent paler than breast. ⌘ (800)1800-2250(3000). Dense undergrowth of damp gullies in montane evergreen forest; spinach patches in small gardens. ▽ Faint *tch-tch-tch-tch....* **A?5**

6 **White-rumped Shama** *Copsychus malabaricus* (1665-8) 25cm. Races (a) nom (b) *albiventris* of Andaman Is. ⌘ <900. Bamboo and tangled undergrowth in moist evergreen forest. Shy. ▽ *chirr-churr*; rich varied fluty song. Good mimic. **R3**

7 **Oriental Magpie Robin** *Copsychus saularis* (1661-4) 20cm. ⌘ <2000(2200). Parks, gardens, scrub, forest. Not particularly shy. ▽ *swee-ee*; *chrr*; rather variable song, e.g. *chee-which-which...chee-chee-witch-chee-chi*. **RM1**

8 **White-bellied Redstart** *Hodgsonius phaenicuroides* (1680) 19cm. Note short wings and long graduated tail often held cocked and lightly fanned. ♂ white belly; rufous only at base of outer tail feathers. ♀ from ♀5 by slender build; paler underparts; white centre of belly; slightly rufous wash to uppertail. ⌘ S 2400-4400. Juniper, birch and rhododendron at treeline. W<1500. Dense undergrowth and forest edge. ▽ *chuck*; *tsiep tsiep tk tk*; *he did so*. **A3-4**

9 **White-capped Water Redstart** *Chaimarrornis leucocephalus* (1716) 19cm. Could be mistaken for White-winged Redstart (81.20) but lacks white wing-patch; tail tipped black; habitat suggestive. ⌘ S 1800-5300. W Foothills- 1500(2600). Usually on rocks in mountain streams and rivers. ▽ *tsee*; *sit sit*; melancholy whistle. **A2**

10 **Indian Robin** *Saxicoloides fulicata* (1717-21) 16cm. Races (a) nom (b) *cambaiensis*. ♀ confusable with 3 but has grey-brown underparts, chestnut vent and rufous-tinged ear-coverts. ⌘ <1000(1800). Dry scrubby areas. Usually on the ground or in low bushes. ▽ *weet*; *sweet*; *chur-r*; 4 to 8-note warble; *chee-choo-choo-tseewit*. **E1**

11 **Plumbeous Water Redstart** *Rhyacornis fuliginosus* (1679) 12cm. ⌘ S (600) 1200-4400. W 1000-1800(2400). Mountain streams and rivers. Habitually fans tail in rhythmical fashion. ▽ *ziet*; *krreee*; five-second sharp, creaky jingle. **A2**

12 **Black-backed Forktail** *Enicurus immaculatus* (1685) 25cm. From 15 by white breast and narrow (vs broad) white band on forecrown. ⌘ <1450. Hill streams through moist forest. ▽ short whistle; *dew*; *curt-seeeee*. **R3**

13 **Slaty-backed Forktail** *Enicurus schistaceus* (1686) 25cm. Slaty-grey back and crown. ⌘ <1700. Rocky torrents and lake margins. ▽ high *tsee*; *teenk*; *cheet*. **R3**

14 **Spotted Forktail** *Enicurus maculatus* (1688-9) 25cm. Spotting on back. Races (a) nom (b) *guttatus*. ⌘ S (600)1200-3000(3600). Smaller forest watercourses. W 600-2300. Also larger rivers. ▽ Harsh *dzrrreee-(jit)-(jit)*; *cheek-chik-chik-chik-chik*. **AR2**

15 **White-crowned Forktail** *Enicurus leschenaulti* (1687) 28cm. From 12 by black breast and large (vs small) white patch on forecrown often raised as slight crest. ⌘ <600(900). Rivers and streams. ▽ *scree*; *scree chit-chit-chit*. **R•3**

16 **Little Forktail** *Enicurus scouleri* (1684) 12cm. From other forktails by small size and short tail. ⌘ S (1000)1800-3300(3700). W (300)900-2000. Rocky mountain torrents; also slower waters in winter. **A3**

17 **Brown Dipper** *Cinclus pallasii* (1775-6) 22cm. Normally easily told from 18 by the overall chocolate-brown colour without white throat and breast, but beware of the rare 18c, which see. ⌘ S 450-4000(4950). W <2700(3600). Mountain streams and rivers. ▽ *dzit-dzit*; rich short song. **A2**

18 **White-throated Dipper** *Cinclus cinclus* (1772-4) 20cm. Races (a) *leucogaster* (b) *cashmeriensis* (c) the rare '*sordidus*' morph can be separated from 17 by overall dark brown (vs warm chocolate) colour; greyish tinge to wings, rump and tail; smaller size; breast sometimes slightly paler than remaining underparts. ⌘ S 3000-4800 (5100). W >2000. Mountain streams, usually at higher altitudes than 17 though ranges overlap. ▽ *dzhit*, *dzhit*; high-pitched lively song. **A3**

PLATE 82

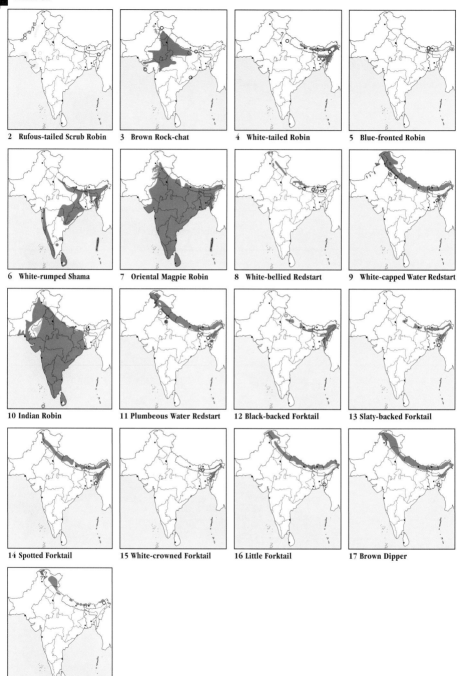

2 Rufous-tailed Scrub Robin   3 Brown Rock-chat   4 White-tailed Robin   5 Blue-fronted Robin

6 White-rumped Shama   7 Oriental Magpie Robin   8 White-bellied Redstart   9 White-capped Water Redstart

10 Indian Robin   11 Plumbeous Water Redstart   12 Black-backed Forktail   13 Slaty-backed Forktail

14 Spotted Forktail   15 White-crowned Forktail   16 Little Forktail   17 Brown Dipper

18 White-throated Dipper

PLATE 83

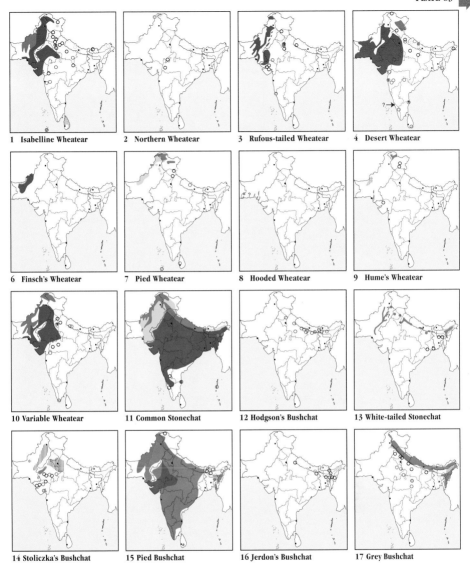

1 Isabelline Wheatear

2 Northern Wheatear

3 Rufous-tailed Wheatear

4 Desert Wheatear

6 Finsch's Wheatear

7 Pied Wheatear

8 Hooded Wheatear

9 Hume's Wheatear

10 Variable Wheatear

11 Common Stonechat

12 Hodgson's Bushchat

13 White-tailed Stonechat

14 Stoliczka's Bushchat

15 Pied Bushchat

16 Jerdon's Bushchat

17 Grey Bushchat

PLATE 83: WHEATEARS, STONECHATS AND BUSHCHATS

See page 311 for the tail patterns of the wheatears and stonechats.

1 **Isabelline Wheatear** *Oenanthe isabellina* (1706) 16cm. From ♀2 by slightly larger size; more upright stance (normally much more upright than illustrated); long legs; more uniform paler wings; contrasting black alula; broader terminal tail-bar; runs more. ✻ Plains (up to 3000). Sandy semi-desert; arid sparse scrub and fields. ▽ *chack-chack-(diu)*; grating alarm; *peeap-peeap-(chip-chip)*; slow whistles in song flight + *chok-chok-chok* in descent. **WB*2**

2 **Northern Wheatear** *Oenanthe oenanthe* (1708) 15cm. See 1. ✻ Stony country, dry fields. ▽ *(weet)-chack-(chack)*. **P5**

3 **Rufous-tailed Wheatear** *Oenanthe xanthoprymna* (1707) 16cm. Rufous base of tail and rump. ✻ **S** >2100. Dry stony slopes especially near streams. **W** <3300. Open arid country, preferring base of rocky hillsides. ▽ *(zvee)-tuk; steu-steu-steu; thrrrr thrrr thrrr*; warbling *see, wat-chew-eeper* with added mimicry; *wee, chu, chree*. **WB*3**

4 **Desert Wheatear** *Oenanthe deserti* (1709-10) 15cm. Only wheatear having all-black tail contrasting with white base and buff-tinged rump. ✻ **S** (3000)3600-4600(5100). **W** >plains. Semi-desert, dry fallow and waste land. ▽ *chuck-chrr; cht-tt-tt*; soft whistle; *teee-ti-ti-ti; tyoo-oo-oo+*(crackle). **WB*2**

5 [**Mourning Wheatear** *Oenanthe lugens* 14cm. Note white panel on open wing. ✻ Barren rocky slopes, semi-desert. ▽ *check; peet-peet*; lively twitter. **X** (Could occur as straggler to the north-west.)]

6 **Finsch's Wheatear** *Oenanthe finschii* (1711) 17cm. ♂ like 7 but buff mantle and back. ✻ Dry stony slopes; semi-desert. ▽ *tack*; mixture of scratchy and musical notes in downward zig-zag song-flight. **WB*3**

7 **Pied Wheatear** *Oenanthe pleschanka* (1715) 15cm. Note white cap and nape of Br♂. See also 10a. ✻ 1500-3100. Barren stony slopes, wasteland. ▽ Loud *tack- tack*; buzzy *trrrlt*; short lark-like song with mimicry in circling flight. **SP3-4**

8 **Hooded Wheatear** *Oenanthe monacha* (1713) 17cm. ♂ white cap; black throat and upper breast; outer tail white except for black corners. ✻ Barren regions with very little vegetation. ▽ *whit-whit; witawheat-wheet-wheet; whee-whee-whee-wheeoo*; melodious song punctuated with clicks. **R*5**

9 **Hume's Wheatear** *Oenanthe alboniger* (1714) 18cm. ♂ very like 10b which see. ✻ Stony ground in the hills. ▽ Sharp high-pitched whistle; grating alarm; *tieu-tieu-tieu*; short, loud melodious song. **WA5**

10 **Variable Wheatear** *Oenanthe picata* (1712) 16cm. Races **(a)** *capistrata* ♂ very like 7 but black upper breast, different tail pattern. **(b)** *picata* ♂ like 9 but black extends further onto upper breast and sides of breast; black sootier-brown; less white on rump. **(c)** *opistholeuca*. ✻ **S** (600)1800-2400(3300). Barren hillsides, near villages. **W** Plains-1200(2700). Semi-desert, fields. ▽ *check-check*; scratchy song from perch/song-flight includes mimicry. **WM2**

11 **Common Stonechat** *Saxicola torquata* (1695-8) 13cm. Subcontinent birds sometimes treated as Asian Stonechat *S. maura*. Br♂ black head and throat; white rump, neck and wing patches; rufous-orange breast. ♀ rufous-brown above streaked brown; white wing-patch; white rump washed rufous; buffy-white supercilium; whitish throat; washed rufous below. Races **(a)** *maura* **(b)** *przewalskii*. ✻ **S** Dry fields with bushes. **W** <2200. Scrub, grassland, cultivation, reeds. ▽ *tcheck-(tcheck)-(tcheck); pee-tack*; short lively song from perch or in song-flight. **WAM2**

12 **Hodgson's Bushchat** *Saxicola insignis* (1694) 17cm. ♂ broad white half-collar and throat; more white in wing than other bushchats. ♀ has two buffy-white wing-bars. ✻ Plains. Grassland, reeds, tamarisks, canefields. ▽ *teck teck*. **W5**

13 **White-tailed Stonechat** *Saxicola leucura* (1699) 13cm. ♂ like ♂11 but white in tail visible when flicked or fanned. ♀ uniformly grey-brown above. ✻ Plains (700+). Tall grass, reeds and tamarisks subject to seasonal flooding, usually along rivers. ▽ *pseep; kek-kek-kek; peep-chaaa*; short lark-like song (like 57.3) given from ground/low perch. **R*•3-4**

14 **Stoliczka's Bushchat** *Saxicola macrorhyncha* (1693) 15cm. Long bill. Br♂ Blackish upperparts; white supercilium, throat, wing-patch, rump and outer tail. Nbr♂ black becomes greyish-sandy streaked brown. ♀ like nbr♂ but no white on wings, tail. ✻ Lowlands. Sparse desert scrub; dry fields at desert edge. Relatively terrestrial. ▽ Sharp *chip chip*. **E*4**

15 **Pied Bushchat** *Saxicola caprata* (1700-3) 13cm. ♂ black with white wing-patch (often concealed), rump and vent. Race *bicolor* has white belly. ♀ darker than other ♀ bushchats with rufous rump. ✻ <2500 (in the south >900). Fields and grassland with bushes, scrub, tea gardens. ▽ *chep-chep-trwee; whit-whit-tit-wheee-tyeear-tiyear-tuh*. **RAM2**

16 **Jerdon's Bushchat** *Saxicola jerdoni* (1704) 15cm. ♂ entirely black above and white below. ♀ plain brown above, slightly more rufous on rump; white throat and breast merge with buffy belly and vent. Relatively shy. ✻ Riverine floodplains (700). Tall grass, reeds, bushes. ▽ Plaintive *beeeeew; chit-churr; chirrrr; swee swoo swoo* + rapid trill. **R*•5**

17 **Grey Bushchat** *Saxicola ferrea* (1705) 15cm. Dark, almost unstreaked upperparts separate ♀ from other ♀ bushchats except 16 which lacks supercilium and 15 which has rufous-brown underparts. ✻ **S** (1500)1800-3000(3350). Open scrubby slopes, forest edge, barberry, juniper. **W** <1200(2400). Cultivation, scrubby hillsides, second growth, grassland with bushes, tea gardens. ▽ *pzee; zee-chunk; tic-tic-brzeeee; tak-tak-tak-tak; titteratu-chak-tew-titatit*. **AM2**

PLATE 84: ROCK, WHISTLING AND *ZOOTHERA* THRUSHES, GRANDALA, COCHOAS

1 **Rufous-tailed Rock Thrush** *Monticola saxatilis* (1722) 19cm. From other rock thrushes by rufous tail; ♂ also by white rump and lower back. ✿ 2000-5000. Rocky hillsides. ▽ *wheet*; *tat-tak*; melodious warble. **P(B*)5**

2 **Blue-capped Rock Thrush** *Monticola cinclorhynchus* (1723) 17cm. ♂ from 1 & 3 by white wing-patch; black mask; rufous rump. ♀ from ♀4 by white throat; from ♀3 & ♀4 by white centre of belly and undertail-coverts. ✿ S (1000)1200-2200(3600). Open forest; rocky grassy slopes. W <2600. Moist-deciduous forest, second growth, plantations. ▽ *peri-peri*; *goink-goink*; mellow *ti-tew tew-ti-chew tew-ti-lo-diyu*. **M2-3**

3 **Chestnut-bellied Rock Thrush** *Monticola rufiventris* (1724) 24cm. ♂ from 1 & 2 by blue rump; darker, chestnut breast and belly; ♀ by face pattern. ✿ S (1200)1800-2400(3500). W <2300. Open forest and scattered trees on rocky hillsides. ▽ *chhhrrr*; *pseek*; *tick*; *quach*; *teetatewleedee-tweet tew*. **A3**

4 **Blue Rock Thrush** *Monticola solitarius* (1725-6) 23cm. ♀ dark barring on rump, scalloping on throat, ear-coverts and breast becoming bars on belly and vent. Races **(a)** *pandoo* **(b)** *philippensis* (vagrant) like 3 but blue is pale smoky (vs shining blue cap, blue-black throat) and usually on lower flanks; wings mostly lack blue tinge of 3. ✿ S (1200)1500-4000 (4800). Rocky hillsides. W <2100. Rocky country, ruins, villages. ▽ Usually silent; *tak-tak*; *tcher-chit*; short fluty warble. **MW2**

5 **Sri Lanka Whistling Thrush** *Myophonus blighi* (1727) 20cm. Ranges of whistling thrushes do not overlap. ✿ >(900) 1200. Heavy undergrowth, especially near torrents. Crepuscular and shy. ▽ High *srreee...ree*. **E5**

6 **Malabar Whistling Thrush** *Myophonus horsfieldii* (1728) 25cm. ✿ <2200. Evergreen growth near hill streams. ▽ penetrating *tsee-e-e-e-ee*; melodious, lazy rambling song (whistling schoolboy). **E3**

7 **Blue Whistling Thrush** *Myophonus caeruleus* (1729-30) 33cm. Races **(a)** *temminckii* **(b)** *eugenei*. ✿ S (1000)1500-2400(treeline). W Foothills-2700. Forest, especially near watercourses. ▽ Penetrating *kree*; *tzeet tze-tze-tzeet*; thin, fluty, rambling whistled song. **AM1**

8 **Grandala** *Grandala coelicolor* (1683) 23cm. ✿ S (3900)4300-5400. Rocky alpine meadows, scree slopes and hillsides above scrubline. W (2200)3000-4300. Rocky hillsides and ridges. ▽ *tju-ti*; soft *tji-u tji-u ti-tu tji-u*. **A3**

9 **Purple Cochoa** *Cochoa purpurea* (1690) 28cm. ✿ 1000-3000. Dense damp evergreen forest; dense undergrowth in ravines. ▽ Soft high *pink-pink.......trrrrrruw*; nasal *nyerrr*; low chuckle; *peeeeee*; *peeee-you-peeee*. **R5**

10 **Green Cochoa** *Cochoa viridis* (1691) 28cm. ✿ (300)700-1500(3300?). Undergrowth in dense evergreen forest, usually on steep hillsides. ▽ *pok*; high drawn-out monotone whistle *seeeeeeeeeee*; short warble. **R5**

11 **Orange-headed Thrush** *Zoothera citrina* (1733-6) 21cm. Races **(a)** *cyanotus* **(b)** nom **(c)** *andamanensis*. ✿ <2300. Well-wooded areas including groves. ▽ *kree*; variable song often interspersed with mimicry. **RM3**

12 **Pied Thrush** *Zoothera wardii* (1731) 22cm. ♀ from 14 by buff supercilium; from ♀13 by dark-brown breast with buff spots; darker brown upperparts; white-tipped tail; flanks spotted with blackish-brown. ✿ S 1200-2400. W >750. Forest, well-wooded ravines, streams, parks and gardens. ▽ *ptz-ptz-ptz-ptz*; *ple-dee*; *ple-doo-tsree*. **EM4**

13 **Siberian Thrush** *Zoothera sibirica* (1732-2a) 22cm. ♀ from ♀12 by warmer brown above; breast spotted mid-brown and buff; flanks barred mid-brown; white on tail-corners only; less spotted wing. ✿ Hill forest. ▽ *tsit*; *chack*. **V(W5?)**

14 **Spot-winged Thrush** *Zoothera spiloptera* (1737) 21cm. Two rows of white spots on wing; face pattern. ✿ 600-1200 (1800). Broadleaved evergreen and riverine forest. ▽ Feeble *tsee*; varied mellow *whee-whoo twee-twée* etc. **E3**

15 **Plain-backed Thrush** *Zoothera mollissima* (1738-9) 27cm. Like 16 but lacks wing-bars (or very thin); underpart spotting crescent-shaped; usually more heavily spotted below. ✿ S 2700-4300. Open country above treeline. W (600)1300-2400(3600). Open forest, open country with bushes near fallow land. ▽ Rattling alarm; *plee-too chup-ple-oop*. **A3**

16 **Long-tailed Thrush** *Zoothera dixoni* (1740) 27cm. From 15 by 2 buffy wing-bars; underpart spotting shaped like half-moon; blackish crescent at rear of ear-coverts. ✿ S 2100-4200. Dense birch and rhododendron forest near treeline, scrub above treeline. W (450)1500-2700. Dense forest, open country with bushes near fallow land. ▽ Fluty song. **A3**

17 **Scaly Thrush** *Zoothera dauma* (1741-4) 26cm. Only thrush with distinct scaling on upperparts. Races **(a)** nom **(b)** *neilgherriensis* **(c)** *imbricata*. The latter two may be separate species. ✿ S 2100-3300(3600). W <2100. Forest. ▽ Usually silent; *tjeee*; song of various short phrases, each usually repeated twice. **RAM3**

18 **Dark-sided Thrush** *Zoothera marginata* (1746) 25cm. Like 19 but smaller; overall mid-brown; lower breast and belly with dark scalloping; ear-coverts streaked with white. ✿ S 750-2100+. Boggy areas and streams in humid forest. W <1900. Also dense reed-jungle along slow-moving streams in evergreen forest. ▽ *tchuck*; thin whistling song. **A?5**

19 **Long-billed Thrush** *Zoothera monticola* (1745) 28cm. Like 18 but larger; longer-billed; overall dark brown; lower breast and belly with dark spots; faint buffy streaks on ear-coverts visible at close range. ✿ S 2280-3850. W (300)900-2900. Streams and boggy areas in forest. ▽ *zaaaaaaaa*; *te-e-uw*; *tew-tew-tew*. **A4**

PLATE 84

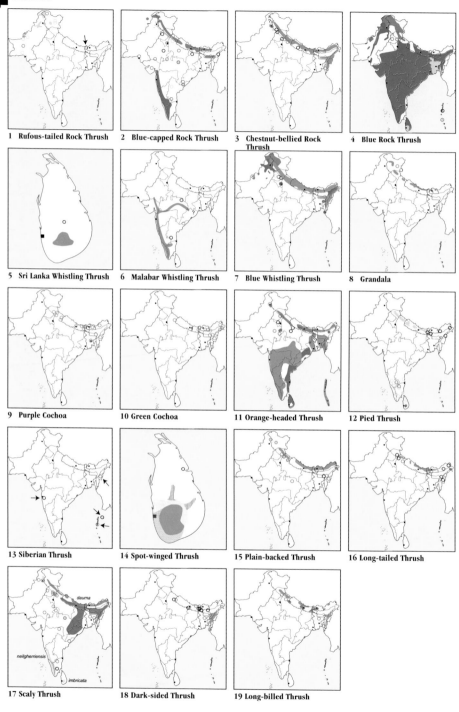

1 Rufous-tailed Rock Thrush

2 Blue-capped Rock Thrush

3 Chestnut-bellied Rock Thrush

4 Blue Rock Thrush

5 Sri Lanka Whistling Thrush

6 Malabar Whistling Thrush

7 Blue Whistling Thrush

8 Grandala

9 Purple Cochoa

10 Green Cochoa

11 Orange-headed Thrush

12 Pied Thrush

13 Siberian Thrush

14 Spot-winged Thrush

15 Plain-backed Thrush

16 Long-tailed Thrush

17 Scaly Thrush

18 Dark-sided Thrush

19 Long-billed Thrush

272

PLATE 85

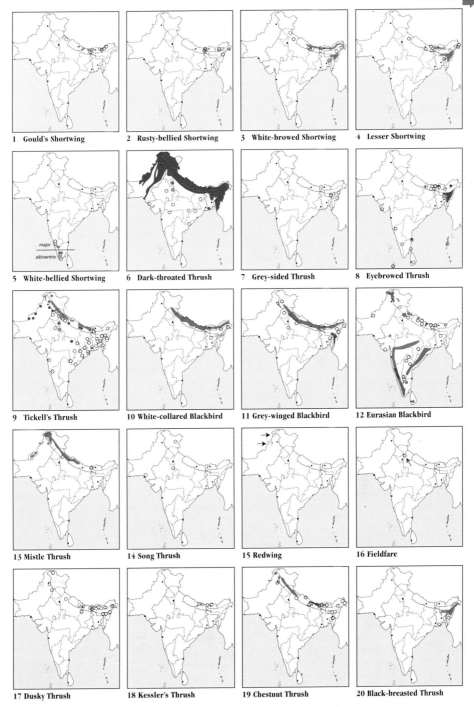

1 Gould's Shortwing

2 Rusty-bellied Shortwing

3 White-browed Shortwing

4 Lesser Shortwing

5 White-bellied Shortwing

6 Dark-throated Thrush

7 Grey-sided Thrush

8 Eyebrowed Thrush

9 Tickell's Thrush

10 White-collared Blackbird

11 Grey-winged Blackbird

12 Eurasian Blackbird

13 Mistle Thrush

14 Song Thrush

15 Redwing

16 Fieldfare

17 Dusky Thrush

18 Kessler's Thrush

19 Chestnut Thrush

20 Black-breasted Thrush

273

PLATE 85: SHORTWINGS AND *TURDUS* THRUSHES

1 **Gould's Shortwing** *Brachypteryx stellata* (1635) 13cm. ✼ S 3300-4200. W (540)2000-3400. Juniper, rhododendron, dense undergrowth, rocks and boulders above treeline. ▽ *tik-tik*; *tseee-tseee-...*; *tseeu*; chittering. **A5**

2 **Rusty-bellied Shortwing** *Brachypteryx hyperythra* (1636) 13cm. ♂ from ♂'81.10 by short supercilium and ta'' ♀ rusty underparts, white belly centre. ✼ S 1800-3000. Broadleaf evergreen forest and bamboo. W <2900. Fore ι undergrowth, scrub and reeds. ▽ Chacking; accelerating slurred hollow warble *tsoo too-deedeloodeleelelo deleeswititit.* **A5**

3 **White-browed Shortwing** *Brachypteryx montana* (1640) 13cm. White brow of ♂ may be partly concealed or puffed up in display. ♀ note rusty forehead and lores, brown underparts with pale centre of belly. **Imm**♂ like ♀ but white supercilium. Note that some ♂♂ breed in this plumage. ✼ S (1500)2000-3300. W 300-2400. Damp undergrowth along streams, ravines and in oak and rhododendron forest. ▽ *tack*; *tt-tt-tt-tt*; slightly scratchy *seei sree sree-ee....* **A3**

4 **Lesser Shortwing** *Brachypteryx leucophrys* (1639) 13cm. ♂ supercilium usually not visible. ♀ rusty-brown flanks and breast-band, short white supercilium usually concealed. Many ♂♂ retain ♀-type plumage. ✼ S 900-3900. W Lower. Moist forest undergrowth, particularly near streams. ▽ *tack*; piping note; 10-12-note accelerating warble. **A4**

5 **White-bellied Shortwing** *Brachypteryx major* (1637-8) 15cm. Only shortwing within its range. Races **(a)** nom **(b)** *albiventris* is confusable with White-bellied Blue Flycatcher (74.11) but bluish-slaty (vs indigo-blue) upperparts and breast, narrow bluish-white patch just above bill (vs bright blue forecrown and supercilium to rear of eye), white centre of belly and vent between extensively slaty flanks (vs entire belly white or lightly washed with grey), longer legs, less upright stance and more terrestrial habits. ✼ >900. Sholas and damp wooded ravines. ▽ High whistled *wheeèw*; loud chattering; thrush-like *whee-choo-chewy-chee...* and variations. **E3-4**

6 **Dark-throated Thrush** *Turdus ruficollis* (1763-4) 25cm. Races **(a)** nom **(b)** *atrogularis*. See also 9. ✼ <4200. Forest edge, scrub, cultivation. ▽ Thin *see*; Blackbird-like *which-which-which...*; *wheech-wheech*. **W2**

7 **Grey-sided Thrush** *Turdus feae* (1761) 23cm. Face pattern. ♂ grey flanks. ♀ orange-buff flanks/breast. ✼ >1500. Forest. **V(W5?)**

8 **Eyebrowed Thrush** *Turdus obscurus* (1762) 23cm. ✼ Open forest. ▽ *zip-zip*; soft pleasant *tyo-lyu*; harsh chatter. **W4**

9 **Tickell's Thrush** *Turdus unicolor* (1748) 21cm. ♀ like ♀/imm 6b but dusky flanks, faint buffy streaks on ear-coverts. ✼ S 1500-1800(2700). W > plains. Groves, forest, forest edge, gardens. ▽ *juk-juk*; *wiw-wiw-wiw...keek-keek*. **EAM3**

10 **White-collared Blackbird** *Turdus albocinctus* (1749) 27cm. ✼ S 2100-4200. W 900-3000. Forest. ▽ Throaty *tuck-tuck-tuck-tuck*; descending *tew-i, tew-u, tew-o*. **A3**

11 **Grey-winged Blackbird** *Turdus boulboul* (1750) 28cm. ✼ S (1200)1800-2700(3300). Damp dense broadleaved forest. W Lower. Forest, scrub and villages. ▽ *chuk-chuk-chuk*; rich fluty song. **A2**

12 **Eurasian Blackbird** *Turdus merula* (1751-7) 26cm. Races **(a)** *maximus* of scrub and dwarf juniper and rhododendron in the Himalayas > 3000. **(b)** *kinnisii* **(c)** *simillimus* and **(d)** *nigropileus* of peninsular India and Sri Lanka often treated as a separate species Nilgiri Blackbird *Turdus simillimus*. ✼ Forest and gardens. ▽ *kree-ee*; *chuck-chuck-chuck*; rattle; melodious song. Good mimic. **RAM3**

13 **Mistle Thrush** *Turdus viscivorus* (1768) 28cm. Greyish-brown upperparts; spotted underparts; white tips to outer tail feathers. ✼ S (1800)2400-3600(3900). Coniferous forest, junipers. W >1200. Open forest. ▽ Rattling *rrrrrr*; *kreee*; fluty 5- or 6-note song. **A3**

14 **Song Thrush** *Turdus philomelos* 24cm. Like a small 13 but upperparts mid-brown not grey-brown; lacks white tips to outer tail feathers. ✼ Scrub. ▽ Sharp *tsik*; various short song phrases, each one repeated 3-4 times. **V**

15 [**Redwing** *Turdus iliacus* (1767) 22cm. ✼ Fields and open woodland. ▽ Thin *tzeeep*; *kuk*; alarm rattle. **X** (2 doubtful records from Pakistan. Could possibly occur as a winter vagrant.)]

16 **Fieldfare** *Turdus pilaris* (1766) 27cm. ✼ Open fields with nearby trees, orchards. ▽ *shak-shak-shak...*; quiet *seee*. **V**

17 **Dusky Thrush** *Turdus naumanni* (1765) 24cm. Races **(a)** *eunomus* **(b)** intermediate nom/*eunomus*. ✼ 900-3000. Sparsely wooded country, fields and grasslands. ▽ *chak-chak-chak*; *geeh*; *spirr*. **W5**

18 **Kessler's Thrush** *Turdus kessleri* (1760) 27cm. ✼ Low scrub and cultivation. ▽ Soft *dug-dug*; *tuck-tuck-tuck*. **V**

19 **Chestnut Thrush** *Turdus rubrocanus* (1758-9) 27cm. Races **(a)** nom **(b)** *gouldii* occasional in north-east. ✼ S (1500)2100-3000(3200). Forest. W (Foothills) 1200-2600. Open country, orchards. ▽ *chak-chak-chak*; *yee-bre, yee-bre, yee-bre...diddiyit, diddiyit, diddiyit...yip-bru, yip-bru*. **A3**

20 **Black-breasted Thrush** *Turdus dissimilis* (1747) 22cm. ✼ S 1200-2400. W Down to plains. Evergreen forest and scrub jungle. ▽ *tock, tock, tock, took...*; sweet song. **A4-5**

PLATE 86: TITS

1 **Great Tit** *Parus major* (1790-7) 13cm. From 2 & 3 by grey back. Races **(a)** *caschmirensis* **(b)** *tibetanus* **(c)** *stupae.* ℋ <3600. Light forest, wooded areas. ▽ Chattering; *wittychi-wittychi-wittychi-(wittychi).* **RA1**

2 **Green-backed Tit** *Parus monticolus* (1799) 13cm. From 1 & 3 by green back; yellow underparts; double wing-bar. ℋ S 1200-3600(3900). W >foothills(plains). Forest. ▽ *teacher; whitee* x4-6; *ch-ch-ch-ch-ch; tchew-chi* etc. **RA1**

3 **White-naped Tit** *Parus nuchalis* (1798) 13cm. From 1 & 2 by black back; large amount of white in wings. ℋ Acacia groves, dry thorn forest. ▽ *tee whi whi (whi)*; bold *whew whew whew whew´whew.* **E*•4-5**

4 [**Marsh Tit** *Parus palustris hypermelaena* (1801) 12cm. **X** (Myanmar, Tibet. Could occur in NE India.)]

5 **Yellow-cheeked Tit** *Parus spilonotus* (1812-2a) 14cm. From 6 by yellow lores and forehead, black streaking on back; from 2 by latter and crest. ℋ 1200-2400. Mainly light hill forest. ▽ *sit; si-si-si; churr-r-r-r-r; chee-chee-piu.* **RA3**

6 **Black-lored Tit** *Parus xanthogenys* (1809-11) 14cm. From 5 by black lores and forehead. From 2 by crest, yellow ear-coverts. ℋ <2400. Hill forest. ▽ *tyuji tyuja; towit towit; churr; wicheewee-wicheewee-wichi.* **EA2**

7 **Rufous-vented Tit** *Parus rubidiventris* (1805-8) 10cm. Races **(a)** nom distinctive **(b)** *beavani* (E of C Nepal) from 8 & 10 by absence of white-spotted wing-bars; from 9 by grey breast, smaller black bib, lack of rufous at bend of wing and nape. ℋ S 2700-4250. W >1500(foothills). Mainly conifer forest. ▽ Thin *seet; psit*; rattling song. **RA2**

8 **Spot-winged Tit** *Parus melanolophus* (1802) 11cm. From 7 & 9 by wing-bars of white spots. From 10 by grey breast and belly with contrasting rufous flanks (and pale rufous vent). ℋ S 2000-3700. W >foothills. Forest, preferring conifers. ▽ *te-tewy; zee-zee; tiu; stit; si; psip-iu...psip-iu....* **NA2**

9 **Rufous-naped Tit** *Parus rufonuchalis* (1804) 13cm. Diagnostic rufous patch on white nape difficult to see. Lacks white wing-spots of 8 & 10. From 7 by grey belly, black bib to breast. Normally allopatric with 7b. ℋ S 2700-4000. W >1500. Chiefly conifer and oak-rhododendron forest. ▽ *peep; sip; trrr*; trilling song; *gypsie-bee; si-si-si-pu.* **RA2**

10 **Coal Tit** *Parus ater* (1803) 10cm. From 7, 8 & 9 by underparts without any rufous; from latter two also by wing-bars of white spots. Hybrids with 8 occur where ranges overlap. ℋ S (2500)2800-4250. W 1800-3600(4270). Mainly conifer forest. ▽ Thin *tsi; tsuee; peechoo-peechoo-peechoo; tu-wa-chi, tu-wa-chi....* **RA2**

11 **Grey-crested Tit** *Parus dichrous* (1807-8) 12cm. ℋ S 2400-treeline. W >2000. Variety of forest types. ▽ Thin *zai*; stuttering *ti-ti-ti-ti-ti; pee-di; whee-whee-tz-tz-tz*; trills. **RA2-3**

12 **Yellow-breasted Tit** *Parus flavipectus* (1800) 13cm. ℋ Montane forest, scrub. ▽ *trrrrit; chi-chi-chi; tis-a-u.* **V**

13 **Azure Tit** *Parus cyanus* (1800a) 13cm. Some **juvs** yellowish below. ℋ Riverine scrub. ▽ *tirr; sit; tsi-tsi-tso; chrrrr-it.* **V**

14 **White-throated Tit** *Aegithalos niveogularis* (1822) 10cm. From other *Aegithalos* by white throat with greyish bib, white forecrown. ℋ S 2400-3970. W >1800. ▽ *wee; tze-tze-tze; t-r-r-r-r-t*; complex song including *tweet* notes and rapid tittering. **EA4**

15 **Black-throated Tit** *Aegithalos concinnus* (1818-20) 10cm. From 14, 16 & 17 by rufous cap. From 14 & 17 by black throat. Races **(a)** *iredalei* **(b)** *manipurensis.* ℋ S 1400-2700(3200?). W 600-3600. Open forest, second growth. ▽ *psip, psip*; soft *trr-trr-trr; prrri-prrri; tur-r-r-tait-yeat-yeat-yeat.* **R•2**

16 **White-cheeked Tit** *Aegithalos leucogenys* (1821) 10cm. From other *Aegithalos* by dull brown cap. From 14 & 17 by black bib. From 15 by black chin, lack of white supercilium. ℋ S 1500-3660. W >450. Open forest undergrowth, tamarisks, juniper. ▽ *prrrt; si-si-si-si; seeup; tup*; feeble rambling song. **NA3**

17 **Rufous-fronted Tit** *Aegithalos iouschistos* (1823) 10cm. Note cinnamon-buff crown-stripe, more rufous on forecrown, cinnamon-rufous underparts and whitish bib bordered with black. ℋ (1100)2700-3720. Forest, low scrubby trees, undergrowth. ▽ *see-see-see-see; trrup; trr-trr-trr; zeet.* **R•3**

18 [**Black-headed Penduline Tit** *Remiz macronyx* 11cm. **X** (SE Iran. Could occur in winter in Pakistan.)]

19 **White-crowned Penduline Tit** *Remiz coronatus* (1817) 10cm. ℋ Riverine scrub and forest; variety of habitats on passage. ▽ Thin *pseee; swee-swee; see; ti-ti-ti-ti-ti.* **WP4**

20 **Fire-capped Tit** *Cephalopyrus flammiceps* (1815-6) 9cm. ♀/**imm** could be confused with 21, which see. ℋ S 2000-3500. W >plains. Forest, orchards, dense jungle. ▽ *tsit; tsee-tsee-tsee-(tsit); tooseeu-tooseeu; whitoo-whitoo.* **AM3**

21 **Yellow-browed Tit** *Sylviparus modestus* (1813-4) 9cm. From ♀/**imm** 20 by little or no wing-bar; no pale edges to tertials; stubby bill; yellow carpal; slight crest (when raised); short yellow supercilium (usually hidden). ℋ S 2100-3200(4200). W 1500-2900. Forest; timberline scrub. ▽ High *psit; chup; tzee, tzee; zee-zi zee-zi zee-zi.* **RA3**

22 **Sultan Tit** *Melanochlora sultanea* (1789) 20cm. ℋ <1200(1900). Less dense broadleaved forest. ▽ *drrr drrrp; cheeo-cheeo-cheeo; pew..pew-pew-pew-pew; tew-r-r; tiriree, tiri; chick; chip-tree-trr; krikrew.* **R3**

PLATE 86

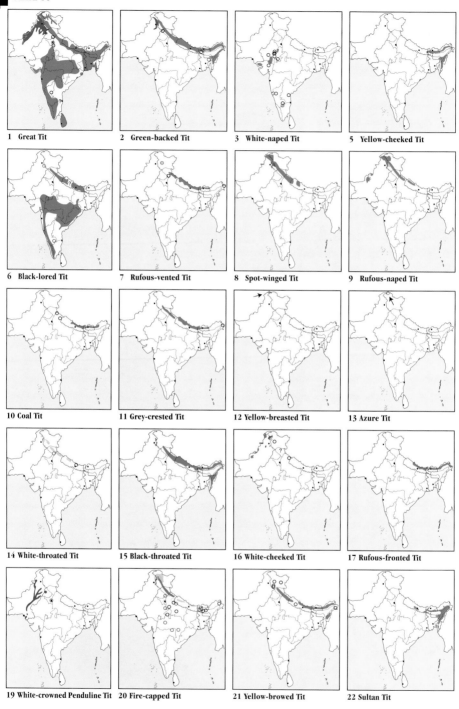

1 Great Tit

2 Green-backed Tit

3 White-naped Tit

5 Yellow-cheeked Tit

6 Black-lored Tit

7 Rufous-vented Tit

8 Spot-winged Tit

9 Rufous-naped Tit

10 Coal Tit

11 Grey-crested Tit

12 Yellow-breasted Tit

13 Azure Tit

14 White-throated Tit

15 Black-throated Tit

16 White-cheeked Tit

17 Rufous-fronted Tit

19 White-crowned Penduline Tit

20 Fire-capped Tit

21 Yellow-browed Tit

22 Sultan Tit

PLATE 87

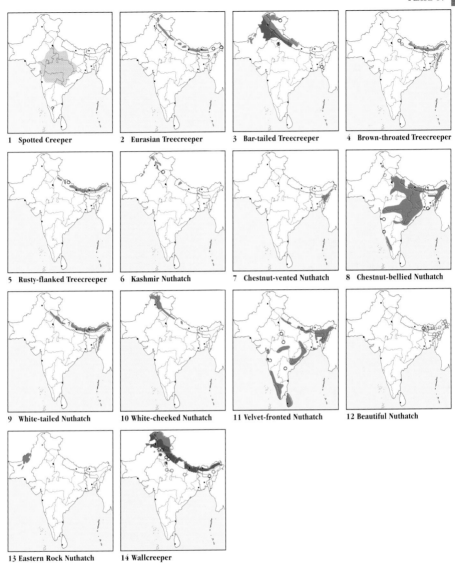

1 Spotted Creeper

2 Eurasian Treecreeper

3 Bar-tailed Treecreeper

4 Brown-throated Treecreeper

5 Rusty-flanked Treecreeper

6 Kashmir Nuthatch

7 Chestnut-vented Nuthatch

8 Chestnut-bellied Nuthatch

9 White-tailed Nuthatch

10 White-cheeked Nuthatch

11 Velvet-fronted Nuthatch

12 Beautiful Nuthatch

13 Eastern Rock Nuthatch

14 Wallcreeper

PLATE 87: CREEPERS AND NUTHATCHES

1 Spotted Creeper *Salpornis spilonotus* (1841) 15cm. Distinguished from treecreepers by larger size; variably barred and/or spotted underparts and broad white barring on tail. ✿ Open broadleaved forest, acacias, mango groves. Prefers trees with fissured bark. ▽ Faint *see-ee*; *kek-kek-kek-*...; feeble whistled *chichichiu-chi-chiu-chiu-chiu*.... **R*4-5**

2 Eurasian Treecreeper *Certhia familiaris* (1842-4) 12cm. With care can be separated from other treecreepers by the whiter underparts with dingy buff restricted to rear flanks and vent; lacks barred underparts of 1, tail barring of 3, brown throat and breast of 4, and conspicuously rusty flanks of 5. Races **(a)** *hodgsoni* **(b)** *mandellii*. ✿ 1700-treeline. Coniferous, birch, rhododendron and mixed forest. ▽ *tsee*; *tzee, tzee, tze-tzizitzi*. **RA3**

3 Bar-tailed Treecreeper *Certhia himalayana* (1845-8) 14cm. Best separated from other treecreepers by tail barring, difficult to see at a distance; longer bill; rump only slightly warmer-toned (vs distinctly rusty on other treecreepers, can also be much reduced on 2). ✿ (1500)2000-treeline. Chiefly coniferous forest. W <1800(2400). Orchards, groves, wooded compounds. ▽ Low thin *tsiu*; *tsee(et)*; *chit*; *tjeeew-tjeeew-(tjit)*; trilling *tsee-tsui-tsui-tsui-tsui-tsui-tsui-tsui-tsui-(tsui)-*.... **AM2**

4 Brown-throated Treecreeper *Certhia discolor* (1849-50) 14cm. Distinguished by the brownish wash on throat and breast (cinnamon in race *manipurensis*, not shown). ✿ (300)700-3200. Chiefly broadleaved forest, especially mossy oak and rhododendron. ▽ *chip*; *tsit*; *tirirrir*; rapid rattling *chititititit*.... **R●A3**

5 Rusty-flanked Treecreeper *Certhia nipalensis* (1851) 14cm. Extensively rusty-buff flanks (somewhat duller in juv); from 2 and 3 also by dark ear-coverts; from 3 also by unbarred tail and rusty rump. Bill shorter than on other treecreepers. ✿ S 2550-3660. W 1500-3500. Oak and mixed forests. ▽ Rather silent; thin *sit*; *(si)*-*(si)-sit-st-ttttt*. **NA3**

6 Kashmir Nuthatch *Sitta cashmirensis* (1824) 14cm. From 9 by absence of white central tail-patch; larger size; longer bill; usually has a narrower eye-stripe. From ♀8 by uniform cinnamon-buff undertail-coverts and smooth colour transition from white of cheeks into cinnamon-buff underparts, darkest on vent; normally at higher altitudes. ✿ 1800-3500. Coniferous and mixed forest; groves. ▽ Loud jay-like *shree*; *tsi-tsi*; *pee-pee-pee-pee-pee*. **RA*2**

7 Chestnut-vented Nuthatch *Sitta nagaensis* (1826) 13cm. Possibly conspecific with Eurasian Nuthatch *Sitta europea*. Chestnut flanks (and undertail scalloping) contrasting with remaining underparts differentiate from all except 10 which has white face extending above eye and black crown. Races **(a)** nom **[(b)** *montium* could occur in extreme NE India**]**. ✿ 1400-2800. Forest. ▽ *sit*; *chip*; rattling *chichichichi*.... **R4**

8 Chestnut-bellied Nuthatch *Sitta castanea* (1827-31) 13cm. Dark underparts contrasting with fairly well-defined white cheeks on ♂ distinctive. ♀ from 6 by underpart colour with lower breast not markedly paler than belly but more vinous on upper breast; scalloped undertail-coverts. Races **(a)** *almorae* **(b)** *cinnamoventris* **(c)** nom. ✿ <1830. Usually in open broadleaved forest. ▽ *chit-chit*; high *seet*; *chip*; clear rippling *whee-whee-whee-whee-(whee)-*.... **R2**

9 White-tailed Nuthatch *Sitta himalayensis* (1834-5) 12cm. The diagnostic white patch on the centre of tail can be difficult to see in the field (the white spots on the tips of the outer tail feathers are not diagnostic as this feature is also shown by other species); the white chin and cheeks gradually becoming increasingly cinnamon-buff on the remaining underparts separate this from 8 & 10; underparts are paler (rufous vs chestnut) and the relatively broad black eye-stripe usually flares more markedly behind the ear-coverts than on 6. ✿ S 1500-3400. W >920. Broadleaved (mossy) forest. ▽ ♂*chip*...*(chip)*...; clear whistled *wheet-wit-wit-wit-*....; strong *pee-pee-pee-pee-pee-pee-pee-peeh*. **NA2**

10 White-cheeked Nuthatch *Sitta leucopsis* (1832-3) 13cm. Dark upperparts and black crown contrasting with white face (enclosing eye) and throat (buffier in juv) mark out this nuthatch. ✿ S 2100-treeline. W >1800. Coniferous (and mixed) forest. ▽ Plaintive nasal *quair-(quair)*; *ti-tüü ti-tüü ti-tüü*.... **RA3**

11 Velvet-fronted Nuthatch *Sitta frontalis* (1838) 12cm. Characteristic blue upperparts; red bill; velvety black forecrown. ♀ (not shown) lacks black supercilium. ✿ <1500(2200). Variety of less-dry forested or wooded habitats. ▽ *chit-(chit)-(chit)*... higher-pitched than 8; rattling *sit-sit-sit-sit-*.... **R2**

12 Beautiful Nuthatch *Sitta formosa* (1837) 16cm. Easily distinguished from other nuthatches by large size with brilliant blue and black patterning on upperparts. ✿ S 1400-2100. W 330-2000. Primary broadleaved evergreen forest. ▽ Similar to other nuthatches but deeper. **RA5**

13 Eastern Rock Nuthatch *Sitta tephronota* (1836) 15cm. Note long bill; whitish breast; cinnamon-buff colour restricted to lower flanks, vent and undertail-coverts. ✿ (300)1800-2750. Rock walls, stony valleys, gorges. Often near streams. ▽ *pit-pit-pit*; loud trilling; loud mellow *twoi-twoi-twoi-twoi-(twoi)-(twoi)*. **R2**

14 Wallcreeper *Tichodroma muraria* (1839) 17cm. Unmistakable. ✿ S >3300. W plains-5000(5730). Cliffs, gorges, quarries, stony riverbeds, old buildings etc. Frequently flicks wings open. ▽ Weak *tseeoo*; *toooée*; *chiwytsee*; *zee´zee ´zee´zee ´zwee*. **R●AW3**

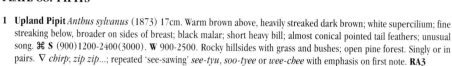

PLATE 88: PIPITS

1 **Upland Pipit** *Anthus sylvanus* (1873) 17cm. Warm brown above, heavily streaked dark brown; white supercilium; fine streaking below, broader on sides of breast; black malar; short heavy bill; almost conical pointed tail feathers; unusual song. ⌘ **S** (900)1200-2400(3000). **W** 900-2500. Rocky hillsides with grass and bushes; open pine forest. Singly or in pairs. ▽ *chirp*; *zip zip...*; repeated 'see-sawing' *see-tyu*, *soo-tyee* or *wee-chee* with emphasis on first note. **RA3**

2 **Blyth's Pipit** *Anthus godlewskii* (1863) 17cm. Hard to separate from 5, 6 & 8. Voice distinctive. From 8 by streaked upperparts; pale lores. Most similar to 6 but on **ad** (or **imm** in part-moult) note squared dark centres to median coverts contrasting with whitish fringes and tips (on 6 pointed centres with less contrasting fringes and tips); smaller; shorter-tailed; slightly shorter, more pointed bill with pinkish base. ⌘ <750 (up to 4250 on passage). Dry fields, grassland, scrub, wasteland. Generally drier areas than 5 & 6. ▽ Explosive *sspzeeu* downwardly inflected at end; also *chup* like 5. **WP3**

3 **Olive-backed Pipit** *Anthus hodgsoni* (1852-3) 15cm. Distinctive small black-and-white patches on rear of ear-coverts. Like 4 but upperparts more greenish-grey, less heavily streaked; supercilium usually white above/behind eye, buff in front, bordered above by thin dark line. Rump unstreaked. Races **(a)** nom **(b)** *yunnanensis*. ⌘ **S** (2450)2700-above treeline. Open grassy areas, clearings, scrub with scattered trees. **W** <2800. Also open forest, forest edge. Commoner in hills than lowlands. When disturbed flies up into tree. ▽ Sibilant *psee(z)* higher than 4; *tsit*; lark-like song. **MAW2**

4 **Tree Pipit** *Anthus trivialis* (1854-5) 15cm. Note buffy-yellowish breast; white on centre of belly; boldly streaked breast; finely streaked flanks; brown upperparts, streaked darker especially on crown; distinct malar stripe; unstreaked rump. Compare 7. ⌘ **S** 2700-3700(4200). Grassy slopes with scattered trees and bushes. **W** <1400. Open habitat with grass, scrub and trees. ▽ *bzee(z)*; *chikchikchik...chia-chia-chia-wich-wich-wich*; *seea-seea-seea...seeeea*. **MPW3**

5 **Paddyfield Pipit** *Anthus rufulus* (1858-60) 15cm. From other pipits (except 2, 6 and imm 8 which see) by band of fine streaks across breast, not on flanks. Smaller than 6 with shorter legs and tail, shorter finer bill; diffuse dark lores; less upright stance; overall paler, more lightly streaked above. ⌘ **S** <1800(3000). **W** Mainly lowlands. Open short grassland, stubble, fallow and wasteland, marshy areas. ▽ High *tseep tseep*; *chip chip*; sharp *twit*; *r-r-ruup*; song perched or in flight with fluttering ascents (*tissip-tissip-tissip*) and parachuting descents (*tit-tit-tit*). **R●2-3**

6 **Richard's Pipit** *Anthus richardi* (1857) 18cm. See 5. ⌘ Moist grassland; cultivation. ▽ Harsh *dschreew* or *psheuw*. **WP4**

7 **Meadow Pipit** *Anthus pratensis* (1856) 15cm. Like 4 but slimmer; weaker-billed; more olive-brown above; streaking bolder on flanks, weaker on breast; head more like 3. ⌘ Grass; fields. ▽ Thin *tseep tseep tseep*. **V**

8 **Tawny Pipit** *Anthus campestris* (1861-2) 16cm. **Ad** Pale sandy, lightly streaked mantle; little or no streaking below; dark lores; broad rufous-buff fringes to tertials. **Imm** More heavily streaked on breast and mantle; from 5's pale race *waitei* by longer tail; slightly paler above; tertial pattern; dark median covert panel; slight buffy tinge to outer tail. ⌘ Mainly plains. Semi-desert, dry fields, open scrub. ▽ Drawn-out *tseep*; *p(i)yoo*; sparrow-like *tch-eulp* or *chir-rup*. **W2**

9 **Red-throated Pipit** *Anthus cervinus* (1864) 15cm. **Ad** reddish throat/breast, duller in winter. **Imm** by bold streaking above, including rump, and below; prominent malar; often pale 'braces' down back; lacks 10's olive secondary fringes. ⌘ Damp grassy/marshy areas, cultivation. ▽ *pseeeu* or *teeez* like 3 & 4 but more drawn-out, plaintive, trailing off. **PW*5**

10 **Rosy Pipit** *Anthus roseatus* (1865) 15cm. **Br** suffused pink on breast/throat. **Nbr** dark above, heavily streaked; from 9 by more olive upperparts; clear rump; olive fringes on secondaries form wing-patch; pale ear-covert spot; very long supercilium. ⌘ **S** >treeline. Alpine meadows, often near snow melt. **W** < foothills. Wet ground. ▽ Thin *tsip* or *tsiep*. **AMW2**

11 **Long-billed Pipit** *Anthus similis* (1866-9) 20cm. Very large, rather uniform pipit; very lightly streaked above; white throat contrasts with rufous-buff underparts; buffy outer tail feathers. Races **(a)** *decaptus* of NW is paler with breast streaking light or absent. **(b)** *travancoriensis* of South India is darker, more richly coloured with heavier breast spotting. When flushed shoots up, then zigzigs away to ground again. ⌘ **S** 600-2900. Grassy and stony hillsides. **W** <2600. Also open scrub, fallow, grazing land; sand dunes. Singly or in pairs. ▽ Subdued *plip...plip*. **RMA2-3**

12 **Nilgiri Pipit** *Anthus nilghiriensis* (1870) 17cm. Note yellowish-buff supercilium and underparts; fine streaking on breast and flanks. Range and habitat indicative. ⌘ (1000)1500-2300+. Open grassy hills with shola pockets. Flies up to top of nearby bush when disturbed. Singly or in pairs. ▽ Soft *sink....sink*; thin *tsip*...(*tsip*)...(*sip*)...(*sip*).... **E3-4**

13 **Buff-bellied Pipit** *Anthus rubescens* (1872) 15cm. Like 14 but darker and less streaked above; pale lores; distinct eye-ring and malar; pale legs. **Br** lacks blue-grey crown/nape of 14; poor supercilium; more boldly streaked breast. **Nbr** flanks, breast more heavily streaked. ⌘ Damp ground, stubble, riverbanks. ▽ High *tsip-it* or *tsiit* like 7. **WP5**

14 **Water Pipit** *Anthus spinoletta* (1871) 15cm. **Br** Grey crown and nape, almost unstreaked pinkish underparts and dark legs. **Nbr** Greyish-brown upperparts; whitish underparts; fairly conspicuous wing-bars; generally dark legs. Less heavily streaked above than other pipits except 8 & 11, which are larger and longer-tailed, and 13, which see. Some show slight streaking on breast and flanks. ⌘ Damp ground, often near water; wet crops. ▽ *tsiip* similar to 10. **WP3**

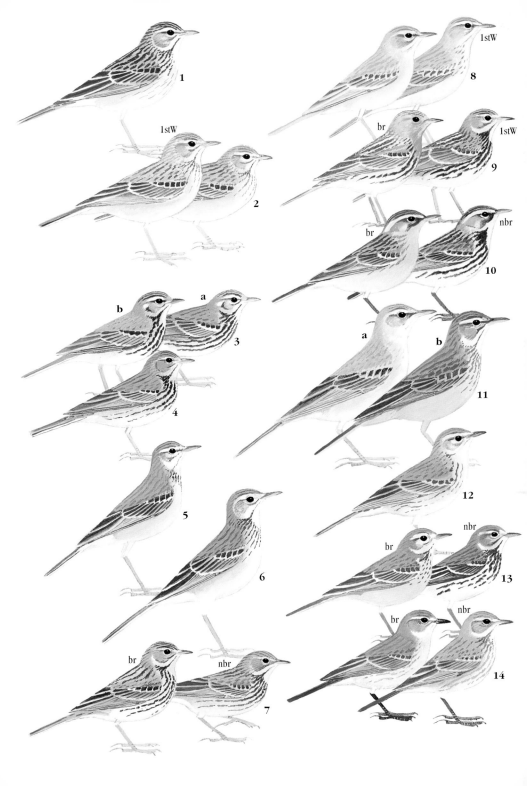

PLATE 88

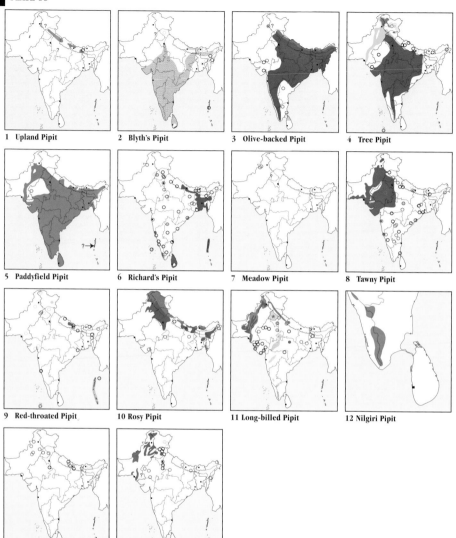

1   Upland Pipit

2   Blyth's Pipit

3   Olive-backed Pipit

4   Tree Pipit

5   Paddyfield Pipit

6   Richard's Pipit

7   Meadow Pipit

8   Tawny Pipit

9   Red-throated Pipit

10 Rosy Pipit

11 Long-billed Pipit

12 Nilgiri Pipit

13 Buff-bellied Pipit

14 Water Pipit

PLATE 89

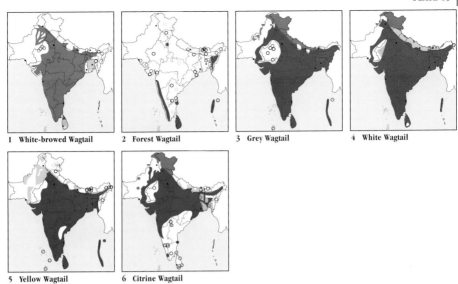

1   White-browed Wagtail

2   Forest Wagtail

3   Grey Wagtail

4   White Wagtail

5   Yellow Wagtail

6   Citrine Wagtail

PLATE 89: WAGTAILS

1 **White-browed Wagtail** *Motacilla maderaspatensis* (1891) 21cm. Pied plumage distinguishes this from all wagtails except black-backed races of 4. From latter by large size, black of crown meeting the bill (i.e. conspicuous white supercilia do not meet) and wing pattern. ⌘ <2200. Usually in pairs near water. ▽ Loud *chiz-zit*; varied jumble of pleasant and squeaky whistling notes, e.g. *peek peek wheechy-whichy-weech...*or *wik wik....ki-ki-ki-tew-tew-teew.* **E2**

2 **Forest Wagtail** *Dendronanthus indicus* (1874) 17cm. The banding on breast and wings give this bird a very distinctive appearance. Has a characteristic habit of swaying its rear end from side to side. ⌘ **S** >1525. **W** Foothills-2200m. Forest, plantations, clearings. ▽ Finch-like *pink-(pink)*; *tsi´fee tsi´fee tsi´fee tsi´fee (tsi´fee).* **WB*3**

3 **Grey Wagtail** *Motacilla cinerea* (1884) 17cm. Distinguished from 1 & 4 by yellow on underparts and from all plumages of 5 by the grey mantle, longer tail, contrastingly yellow rump. ⌘ **S** (1200)1800-3900. Rocky mountain streams. **W** <2000. Near water (mainly streams). ▽ *chi-chip*; *piti, pi-iti, pititi*; *zee-zee-zee-zee-zee.* **AMW2**

4 **White Wagtail** *Motacilla alba* (1885-90) 18cm. The pied plumage separates this from other wagtails with the exception of 1. The black-backed races are distinguished from the latter by their white foreheads, smaller size and different wing pattern. ⌘ Usually in open country. **S** 800-4500. Streams and rivers **W** <1800(5500 on passage). Vicinity of water, damp fields, short grassland. ▽ Sharp *chi-cheep*, harsher than 3, 5 & 6; *chissik*.

Breeding-plumaged males can be identified to subspecies as follows:
Black-backed races:
(a) *alboides*: black ear-coverts. **AM2**
(b) *leucopsis*: white ear-coverts. **W2**
Grey-backed races:
(c) *dukhunensis*: white ear-coverts, black chin and black throat. **W1**
(d) *baicalensis*: white ear-coverts, white chin and black throat. **W4**
(e) *personata*: black ear-coverts. **MW2**
(f) *ocularis*: black eye-stripe. **W4**

5 **Yellow Wagtail** *Motacilla flava* (1875-80) 17cm. Distinguished in all plumages from other wagtails by the greenish- or brownish-toned mantle and back. Shorter-tailed than 3; rump and uppertail-coverts same colour as back (contrastingly yellow in 3). Different authors treat some races as full species. ⌘ **S** 3600-4500. **W** <1500. Damp pastures, marshy areas with short vegetation, margins of rivers, lakes and jheels. ▽ *weesp-(weesp); weechie; wizzie; tsree-ree.*

Breeding-plumaged males can be identified to subspecies as follows:
(a) *beema*: pale bluish-grey head with white supercilium. **BWP1**
(b) *thunbergii*: grey head (darker on lores and below the eye) with very little or no whitish supercilium. **WP2**
(c) *taivana*: head same greenish colour as mantle (darker on lores and ear-coverts) with yellow supercilium. **V**
(d) *plexa* (now usually subsumed in *thunbergii*): dark blue-grey head with short white supercilium, chin usually yellow (sometimes whitish), malar usually yellow (sometimes white). **WP4**
(e) *simillima* (includes *zaissanersis*): slaty-grey or dark blue-grey head, long white supercilium (sometimes tinged yellow), chin usually white (sometimes washed with yellow), malar usually white (sometimes yellow). **WP2**
(f) *melanogrisea* (sometimes subsumed in *feldegg*): dark grey, almost black head (without supercilium). **WP2**
(g) *leucocephala*: white head. **P5**
(h) *lutea*: largely yellow head with pale olive-greenish crown and eye-stripe. **W3**
Birds with blackish head and white supercilium sometimes treated as race *superciliaris* but are probably hybrids between *melanogrisea* and *beema*.

6 **Citrine Wagtail** *Motacilla citreola* (1881-3) 17cm. Breeding-plumaged ♂ easily identified by the entirely yellow head. 5h is similar but has a pale olive-greenish crown and eye-stripe. Br♀ separated from similarly plumaged 3 by yellow supercilium curving round behind the ear-coverts to meet yellow throat, white vent and broad white wing-bars. **1stW** differentiated from 3 by the head pattern (pale surround to ear-coverts), conspicuous white wing-bars and lack of yellow on vent; from similar winter-plumaged 4 by complete absence of black on underparts; from 5 by grey upperparts and head pattern. ⌘ **S** (1500)3000-4600. **W** Mainly lowlands. Marshes, wet margins of lakes and jheels, wet paddies. Generally prefers wetter areas than 5 though often found together. ▽ Calls harsher than 5; *shrreep*; *chiz-zit*.

Breeding-plumaged males can be identified to subspecies as follows:
(a) *calcarata*: black mantle and back. **M2**
(b) nominate: dark/mid-grey mantle and back, broad black hind-collar. **W3**
(c) *werae*: pale grey mantle and back, black hind-collar narrow (sometimes absent). **W2**

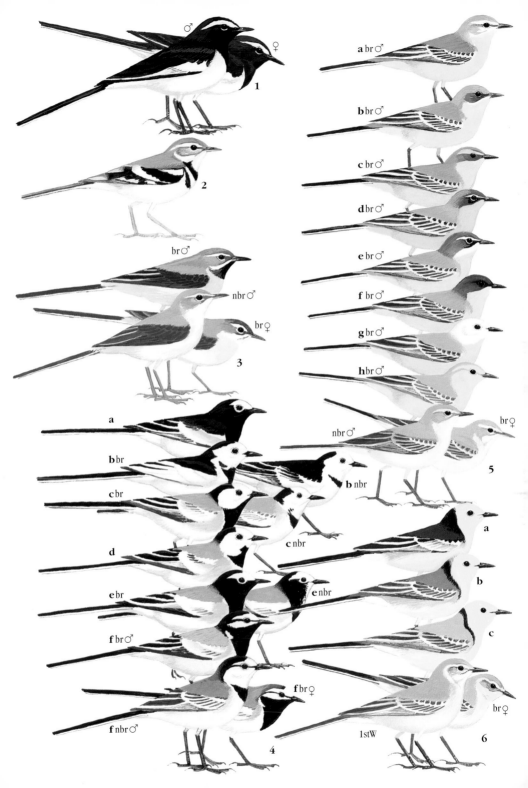

PLATE 90: SPIDERHUNTERS, WHITE-EYES AND SUNBIRDS

1 Streaked Spiderhunter *Arachnothera magna* (1932) 17cm. Very long decurved bill and dark streaking diagnostic. ⌘ S 600-1500(2200). **W** >plains. Dense forest, overgrown clearings, bananas. ▽ *chirrick, chirrick*; *d-d-d.* **RA2**

2 Little Spiderhunter *Arachnothera longirostra* (1931) 14cm. Could be confused with ♀ sunbird but note large size; very long bill (1¹/₂ x head-length); greyish throat and breast merging into yellow belly. ♀7 has white flanks. ⌘ <2100. Moist forest, second growth, bananas. ▽ Harsh *dzit*; *chee-chee-chee-...*; *which-which-which-....* **R3**

3 Oriental White-eye *Zosterops palpebrosus* (1933-6) 10cm. Superficially like ♀ sunbird but short bill, white breast and belly, broad white eye-ring. Similar warblers do not show such a broad eye-ring nor such yellowy-olive upperparts. See also 4. ⌘ <1800(3000). Forested/wooded, mainly hilly, habitats. ▽ Plaintive *cheer*; *prrree-u*; tinkling jingle. **R•1-2**

4 Sri Lanka White-eye *Zosterops ceylonensis* (1937) 11cm. Distinguished from 3 by the slightly larger size, darker olive (less yellow) plumage, slightly larger bill. ⌘ >(450)900. Forest, plantations, gardens. Within its range chiefly at higher altitudes than 3, though ranges overlap. ▽ Similar to 3 but deeper. **E2**

5 Ruby-cheeked Sunbird *Anthreptes singalensis* (1906) 10cm. The brick-red throat is diagnostic along with ♂'s ruby cheeks. ⌘ <700. Moist broadleaved evergreen forest. ▽ Shrill *chirp*; *wee´eest.* **R3**

6 Olive-backed Sunbird *Nectarinia jugularis* (1913-5) 10cm. ♀ from ♀16 (only other sunbird in its range) by bright yellow (vs yellowish-olive) underparts. ⌘ Forest, scrub, gardens, mangroves. ▽ *sweét.* **R2**

7 Purple-rumped Sunbird *Nectarinia zeylonica* (1907-8) 10cm. ♂ purple throat and yellow underparts with white flanks distinctive, but see also 8. ♀ from 2 by shorter bill and white flanks; from ♀ sunbirds by ashy throat, yellow breast and belly with broad white flanks. ⌘ <2100. Open scrub jungle, second growth, gardens, hedges. ▽ *psee-psit psee-psit psee-psit titrou*; *sisiswee, sisiswee,....* **R2**

8 Crimson-backed Sunbird *Nectarinia minima* (1909) 8cm. ♂ is similar to ♂7 but smaller with a broad carmine breast-band, yellow flanks and without the metallic shoulder-patch. ♀ is only ♀ with a crimson rump. ⌘ (300)1200-2100. Moist evergreen habitats. ▽ Metallic *chick*; high *pseeu*; *chweew*; high rapid *see-see-whi-see-see-siwee.* **E3**

9 Purple-throated Sunbird *Nectarinia sperata* (1910) 9cm. ♂ purple throat, dark red breast/upper belly, blackish lower/belly vent. ♀ breast usually tinged reddish, often as streaking; from all ♀ but 10 & 11 by blackish uppertail; smaller than 10 & 11, shorter-billed and usually more olive. ⌘ Moist forest, second growth, gardens. ▽ *chip chip.* **R•5**

10 Loten's Sunbird *Nectarinia lotenia* (1911-2) 12cm. ♂ from br ♂11 by long decurved bill; dark matt-brown (vs glossy purple-black) belly. Bright yellow tufts under wing visible chiefly in display. Imm/eclipse ♂ like eclipse ♂11 but longer bill and uniformly darker above. ♀ bill as ♂, lacks ashy throat of ♀7. Races (a) nom (b) *hindustanica.* ⌘ <1600(2100). Open forest, second growth, gardens. ▽ *chit*; *kecheew...kecheew*; *titti-titu-weechi weechi weechi.* **E3**

11 Purple Sunbird *Nectarinia asiatica* (1916-8) 10cm. Br♂ from most sunbirds by glossy blue-black plumage; from ♂10 by shorter bill and glossy belly. Bright yellow and red pectoral tufts visible in display, preening. Nbr♂ has eclipse plumage with purple-black band from throat to belly. ♀ olive above, blackish tail, variably yellow below. ⌘ <1600(2400). Open broadleaf forest, second growth, gardens. ▽ *chip*; *chweet*; (*chit-chitty*) *cheewit-cheewit-cheewit....***R•AM1**

12 Black-throated Sunbird *Aethopyga saturata* (1925-6) ♂15cm ♀10cm. On ♂ note blackish throat and upper breast, together with red back and sides of neck. ♀ diffuse pale supercilium, yellow rump and greyish-olive underparts. ⌘ (plains) foothills-1800(2000). Dense forest (edge), scrub, second growth, areas of scattered bushes. ▽ *pzit.* **RA3**

13 Green-tailed Sunbird *Aethopyga nipalensis* (1922-4) ♂14cm ♀10cm. ♂ separated from ♂14, 15 & 16 by metallic blue-green head and upper back; from ♂12 also by yellow breast and belly (streaked with scarlet on breast). ♀ very like ♀16 which see; similar to ♀12 & 14 but rump only slightly yellower than upperparts. ⌘ Seasonally 300-2750(3600). Dense forest, scrub, gardens. ▽ Sharp *dzit*; *tchiss...tchiss-iss-iss-iss.* **RA2**

14 Mrs Gould's Sunbird *Aethopyga gouldiae* (1919-21) ♂15cm ♀10cm. ♂ has dark throat with red sides of head; from ♂13 & 15 also by metallic blue tail; from ♂12 & 16 by yellow belly and vent. ♀ grey crown, throat and breast, yellow belly and rump. Races (a) nom (b) *dabryii.* ⌘ Seasonally foothills-3650. Forest, scrub. ▽ *tzit-(tzit).* **RA4**

15 Fire-tailed Sunbird *Aethopyga ignicauda* (1930) ♂16cm ♀11cm. Long red tail of ♂ diagnostic. ♀ olive upperparts without distinct yellow rump-band or white tips to corners of tail; olive underparts; orange-yellow centre of belly. ⌘ S 3000-4000. **W** 1050-2150(2900). Open fir forest, alpine shrubbery. ▽ *dzidzi-dzidzidzi.* **RA3**

16 Crimson Sunbird *Aethopyga siparaja* (1927-9a) ♂15cm ♀10cm. ♂ identified by red chin and throat. ♀ olive upperparts, white tips to outer tail feathers and yellowish-olive underparts; from ♀13 by pale brown (vs dark brown/black) lower mandible. Races (a) *nicobarica* (b) *vigorsii* (c) *seheriae.* ⌘ S <1800. **W** <1400. Forest, scrub, gardens, orchards, groves. ▽ *wehpititi*; *chi-chiwee*; trill. **RA3**

PLATE 90

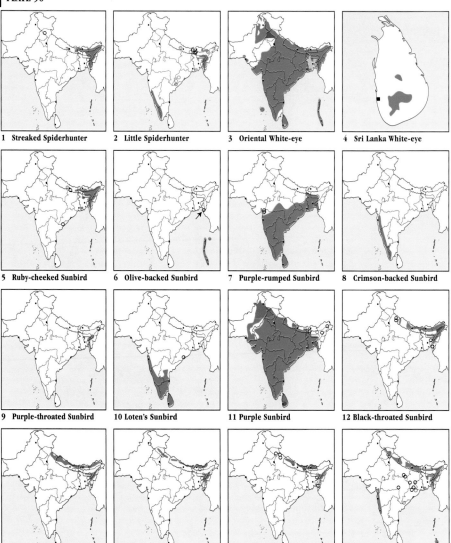

1 Streaked Spiderhunter

2 Little Spiderhunter

3 Oriental White-eye

4 Sri Lanka White-eye

5 Ruby-cheeked Sunbird

6 Olive-backed Sunbird

7 Purple-rumped Sunbird

8 Crimson-backed Sunbird

9 Purple-throated Sunbird

10 Loten's Sunbird

11 Purple Sunbird

12 Black-throated Sunbird

13 Green-tailed Sunbird

14 Mrs Gould's Sunbird

15 Fire-tailed Sunbird

16 Crimson Sunbird

PLATE 91

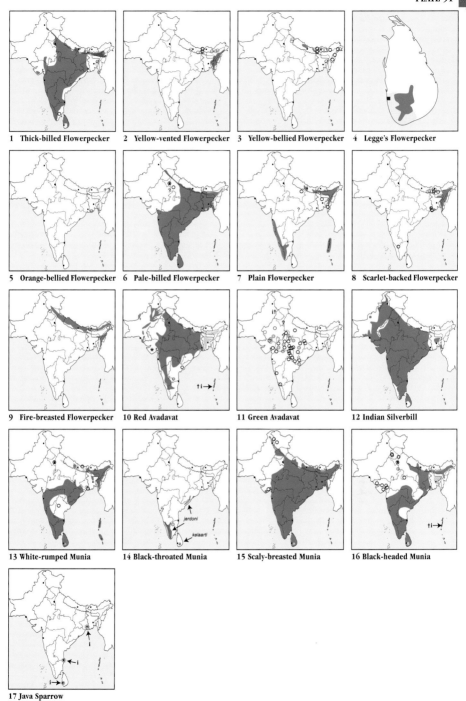

1 Thick-billed Flowerpecker

2 Yellow-vented Flowerpecker

3 Yellow-bellied Flowerpecker

4 Legge's Flowerpecker

5 Orange-bellied Flowerpecker

6 Pale-billed Flowerpecker

7 Plain Flowerpecker

8 Scarlet-backed Flowerpecker

9 Fire-breasted Flowerpecker

10 Red Avadavat

11 Green Avadavat

12 Indian Silverbill

13 White-rumped Munia

14 Black-throated Munia

15 Scaly-breasted Munia

16 Black-headed Munia

17 Java Sparrow

PLATE 91: FLOWERPECKERS, AVADAVATS AND MUNIAS

1 **Thick-billed Flowerpecker** *Dicaeum agile* (1892-4) 9cm. Short thick bill, faint brown streaking on breast and flanks, and orange-red eye distinguish from 6 & 7. ⌘ **S** <2100(3000). **W** <800. Wide range of habitats wherever there are fruiting or flowering trees and shrubs. ∇ *chik*, scratchier than 6; *psit*; *ch-ch-ch-ch-chrr*; *chi-pss*. **RA3**

2 **Yellow-vented Flowerpecker** *Dicaeum chrysorrheum* (1895) 9cm. Only flowerpecker with heavily streaked underparts. ⌘ <2000. Forest edge, orchards, open woodland and gardens. ∇ Short harsh *tzrrp*. **R3**

3 **Yellow-bellied Flowerpecker** *Dicaeum melanoxanthum* (1896) 12cm. Resembles 4 but ranges disjunct. White stripe down centre of throat and breast separates ♀ from similar ♀♀ of 5 and 9. ⌘ **S** 2000-3600. **W** 1400-1800. Tall trees in open forest and forest clearings. ∇ Agitated *zit-zit-zit-zit*. **A3-4**

4 **Legge's Flowerpecker** *Dicaeum vincens* (1897) 9cm. Unmistakable; only other flowerpeckers within its range are 1 and 6. ⌘ <900. Primary forest in Wet Zone and adjoining hills in Sri Lanka. ∇ *tsit*; *tsee-tsit-(tsit)*. **E2**

5 **Orange-bellied Flowerpecker** *Dicaeum trigonostigma* (1898) 9cm. ♂ unique. ♀ grey throat and breast; orangy lower rump. ⌘ Evergreen forest edge and mangroves. ∇ Harsh *dzip*; descending *tsi-si-si-si-sew*. **R*3**

6 **Pale-billed Flowerpecker** *Dicaeum erythrorhynchos* (1899-1900) 8cm. Like 7 but has pale flesh-coloured bill. Race *ceylonense* of Sri Lanka, where 7 is absent, has brown lower mandible. ⌘ <2000, lower in winter. Moist-deciduous forest, second growth, plantations, groves and gardens. ∇ Sharp repeated *chik* often in flight; *pseep*; chittering song. **NA2**

7 **Plain Flowerpecker** *Dicaeum concolor* (1901-3) 8cm. Like 6 but blackish bill. **Juv** has pale bill. ⌘ <1200 (1800). Forests and groves. ∇ *chik* like 6; *tsit tsi-si-si-si-si*; *witwitwitwitwitwit*. **R2**

8 **Scarlet-backed Flowerpecker** *Dicaeum cruentatum* (1904) 7cm. Very distinctive ♂. Red rump of ♀ separates from all other similar species. ⌘ <1400. Open forest, groves, orchards, gardens. ∇ Loud *tchik*. **R2**

9 **Fire-breasted Flowerpecker** *Dicaeum ignipectus* (1905) 7cm. Underparts of ♀ pale buff, more olive on flanks. ⌘ **S** 1400-2700(3000). **W** 600-2500. Forest, second growth, orchards. ∇ *chip*; *trik*; *tsit*; *tseet*; *tsitsit-tsitsit-tsitsit*; rapid *kik-kik-chichi-chee*. **A2**

10 **Red Avadavat** *Amandava amandava* (1964) 10cm. The ♀ and **nbr**♂ have red bill and uppertail-coverts. **Juv** has two buffy wing-bars and pale fringes to tertials. ⌘ <1800. Scrub, reeds, grassy areas, sugarcane fields, overgrown parts of parks and gardens. ∇ Thin *tsee*; chirps. **R3**

11 **Green Avadavat** *Amandava formosa* (1965) 10cm. **Ad** distinctive. **Juv** rump tinged with yellowish-green; pink cutting edges to blackish mandibles. ⌘ <1700. Rare resident of hilly areas in central India where it prefers grass, sugarcane fields and scrub including lantana. ∇ Nasal *swee* or *seee*; nasal *pink* gliding into *sss*; chirps. **E*5**

12 **Indian Silverbill** *Lonchura malabarica* (1966) 10cm. White underparts and rump; black pointed tail. Overall paler and without the dark throat, breast and vent of 13. ⌘ <1200. Prefers drier open scrub, cultivation, grassland and light secondary growth. ∇ Sharp *chip*; *cheep*; *tchwit*; soft *seesip*; trilling *zip-zip*. **R●2**

13 **White-rumped Munia** *Lonchura striata* (1967-70) 10cm. White belly, flanks and rump on otherwise dark brown bird. Races (**a**) nom, southern India; (**b**) *acuticauda*, northern India, Nepal and Bhutan; (**c**) *fumigata*, Andamans. ⌘ <1800. Light scrub, secondary jungle, grassy areas and cultivation. ∇ Plaintive peeping; *tr-tr-tr*; *prrrit*; *brrt*. **RA2**

14 **Black-throated Munia** *Lonchura kelaarti* (1971-3) 10cm. Not unlike 15 but upperparts dark brown; face, throat and upper breast blackish; fulvous uppertail-coverts. Races (**a**) nom of Sri Lanka (**b**) *jerdoni* of Indian mainland may prove to be separate species. ⌘ 200-2100. Uncommon endemic inhabiting similar types of habitat to other munias but also bamboo and forest clearings. Generally found at higher altitudes and in moister areas than 13 and 15. ∇ High-pitched nasal *tay* or *toot*; soft buzzing note; chirps. **EA3**

15 **Scaly-breasted Munia** *Lonchura punctulata* (1974-5) 10cm. Scaly lower breast, belly and flanks; reddish-brown upperparts, head, throat and upper breast. **Juv** similar to juv 16 but bill blackish. In large flocks of juvs there are usually some birds with traces of scaling on the underparts. ⌘ <2400. Open areas with grass and scrub, scrubby hillsides, secondary growth, cultivation and gardens. ∇ *kitty-kitty-kitty*; *kit-eeeeee*; *ki-ki-ki-ki-teeee*; *chup*; *tret-tret*. **R(A)2**

16 **Black-headed Munia** *Lonchura malacca* (1976-8) 10cm. Black head, throat, middle and upper breast. **Juv** very similar to juv 15 but bill bluish. Races (**a**) nom (**b**) *atricapilla*. ⌘ <2100. Long grass, cultivation and marshy areas. ∇ Weak *peekt* or *pee-eet*; *chirp-chirp-chirp*; whistling *veet veet*. **R3**

17 **Java Sparrow** *Lonchura oryzivora* (1978a) 16cm. ⌘ Lowland paddyfields, reedbeds, parks and gardens. ∇ Liquid *tup*; *t-luk* or *ch-luk*; sharp *tack*. **I*5** (Feral populations around Colombo and Calcutta [?], formerly also Madras.)

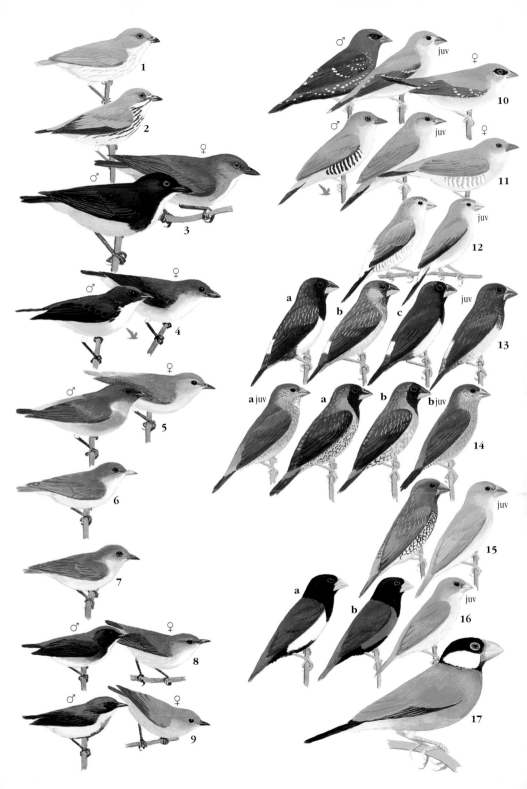

PLATE 92: SPARROWS, PETRONIAS, WEAVERS, CHAFFINCH AND BRAMBLING

1 **House Sparrow** *Passer domesticus* (1938-9a) 15cm. ♂ note grey crown and black of throat extending onto upper breast. ♀ very similar to ♀2 and 4 but has less distinct, pale buffy-brown supercilium behind eye and unstreaked dingy white underparts. ✲ <4000(4500). Common bird in urban areas throughout most of the subcontinent. ▽ Variety of chirps and chirrups; *cheer, cheer, cheer....* **M1**

2 **Spanish Sparrow** *Passer hispaniolensis* (1940) 15.5cm. ♂ from 1 by chestnut crown; flanks and mantle heavily streaked black, duller in non-breeding plumage. ♀ from ♀1 by fine grey streaking on breast and flanks. ✲ Mainly plains cultivation and semi-desert, sometimes in massive flocks. ▽ Similar chirps to 1; *che-uit che-uit che-uit....* **WP3**

3 **Eurasian Tree Sparrow** *Passer montanus* (1941-4) 15cm. Rich brown crown and nape; black patch on white ear-coverts. ✲ **S** 450-2700(3900). **W** Lower. Villages and cultivation. ▽ Like 1 but sharper *chip* or *tet*; metallic *tsooit*; varied *chip chip tsweeet tet....* **RA1**

4 **Sind Sparrow** *Passer pyrrhonotus* (1945) 12cm. Similar to 1 but smaller and slimmer. ♂ has grey crown, hind-nape and sides of neck; smaller, neater black bib; chestnut-brown line around ear-coverts; reddish-brown rump. ♀ has longer, well-defined pale supercilium; greyer crown and ear-coverts; whiter underparts. ✲ Shisham, acacias, scrub and grassland in vicinity of water in Indus floodplains. ▽ *chu-wit chu-wit*; *chup* like 1 but softer. **N*3**

5 **Russet Sparrow** *Passer rutilans* (1946-7) 15cm. Russet crown and upperparts of ♂ distinctive. On ♀ richer brown upperparts, greyish crown, broad creamy-white supercilium and dark eye-line separate from 1, 2 and 4. Races **(a)** *cinnamomeus* **(b)** *intensior*. ✲ **S** 1200-2700(370-4200). **W** 500-1500(150). Light forest and cultivation, often in the vicinity of human settlements in the hills where 1 is absent. ▽ *cheeep* sweeter than 1; *cheep-chirrup-cheweep*. **A3**

6 **Dead Sea Sparrow** *Passer moabiticus* (1947a) 12cm. Distinctive ♂. Pale yellow sides of throat and yellowy-buff supercilium separate ♀ from similar birds. ✲ Tamarisk scrub and bushes, usually near streams. Very localised. ▽ *chelp*; *tchirlp*; rhythmic *chetty-chetty-chetty-chetty-chetty*. **W*2**

7 **Chestnut-shouldered Petronia** *Petronia xanthocollis* (1948-9) 14cm. Combination of white median coverts and chestnut lesser coverts (browner in ♀) is best distinguishing feature; also relatively long fine bill; unstreaked brownish-grey head and upperparts. Yellow on throat often difficult to see; absent on juv. ✲ <1200. Open dry deciduous and thorn forest; trees and hedges near villages and cultivation. ▽ Like 1 but softer and sweeter; *chilp chalp cholp....* **RM2**

8 **Rock Sparrow** *Petronia petronia* (1950) 17cm. Like ♀1 but broad white supercilium; dark stripes on sides of crown, behind and above ear-coverts; breast streaking; yellow throat patch not always obvious (absent in juv). ✲ Locally around 1500. Open stony ground. ▽ Many calls like 1; *chew*; nasal *chwee-ee(it)*; *chwit*; *whewit*; metallic *dliu*; *sup*. **W*4**

9 **[Pale Rock Sparrow** *Petronia brachydactyla*. 14cm. Rather pale sandy-brown featureless bird resembling a lark but with longer wings, sparrow-like pale bill and no streaking. ✲ Rocky hillsides, stony desert. ▽ High nasal *zweeeee*; soft *churr* in flight; *tse-tse-tse-tseeeeeee*. **X** (Not recorded in our region but summer range includes Iranian Baluchistan and it could occur in neighbouring parts of Pakistan.)]

10 **Baya Weaver** *Ploceus philippinus* (1957-9) 15cm. Crown and back of ♀ yellowish-buff streaked brown; breast, supercilium and sides of neck yellowish-buff. Non-breeding ♂ similar but breast and supercilium pale yellow. Not all races shown. Races **(a)** nom **(b)** *burmanicus* from eastern Bihar eastwards: ♂ has variable throat – extreme pale-throated individual shown; white throat in ♀. ✲ <1400. Open country with scattered trees, scrub and cultivation. ▽ Sparrow-like *chit-chit-chit*; *chit chit chit chee-ee-ee*. **R*2**

11 **Finn's Weaver** *Ploceus megarhynchus* (1960-0a) 16cm. Races **(a)** nom **(b)** eastern race *salimalii*. ✲ <300. Very local in terai marshes, tree-dotted grass. ▽ Louder, harsher than 10; *twit-twit-tit-t-t-trrrrr wheeze whee wee we*. **E*5**

12 **Black-breasted Weaver** *Ploceus benghalensis* (1961) 15cm. Blackish-brown band across breast, less marked in ♀. ✲ <300. Reedy marshes and grassland liable to flooding. ▽ Soft *chit-chit*; soft *tsi tsi tsisik tsisik tsik tsik*. **E*3**

13 **Streaked Weaver** *Ploceus manyar* (1962-3) 15cm. Only weaver with heavy streaking on breast. Lightly streaked non-breeding individuals separated from ♂10 by yellow on sides of throat. ✲ <1000. Mainly lowland marshy areas and riverbeds. Prefers reeds and bulrushes. ▽ Loud *chirt chirt chirt...*; repeated *tre tre cherrer cherrer*; *see-see-see-see-see-see o-cheeee*. **R2-3**

14 **Chaffinch** *Fringilla coelebs* (1979) 15cm. Non-breeding birds duller. This and next species are uncommon to rare winter visitors unlikely to be seen in full breeding plumage. Note greenish rump (not visible in illustration). ✲ Woodland, orchards, gardens and cultivation. ▽ *chink*; soft *tchup*; *pweet*. **W5**

15 **Brambling** *Fringilla montifringilla* (1980) 15cm. From 14 by white rump and orange breast. ✲ Woodland, gardens, orchards and neighbouring fields. ▽ nasal *zweeah*; *zwea*; *chup*; *tsit*. **WP2**

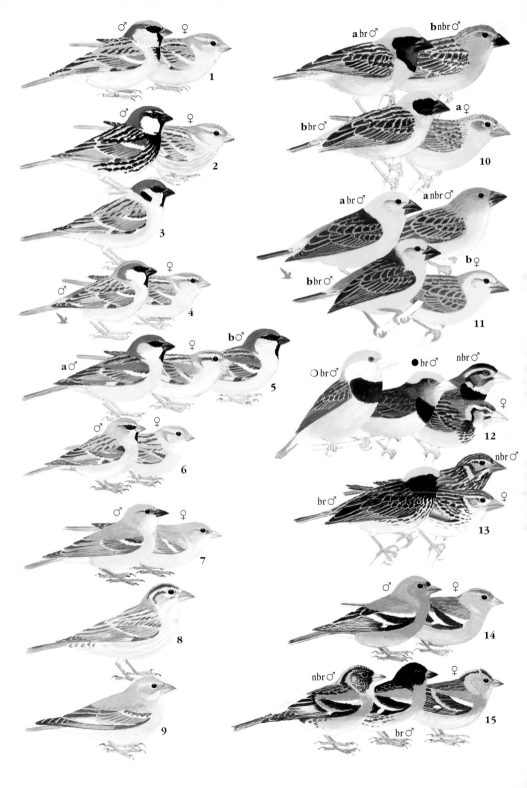

PLATE 92

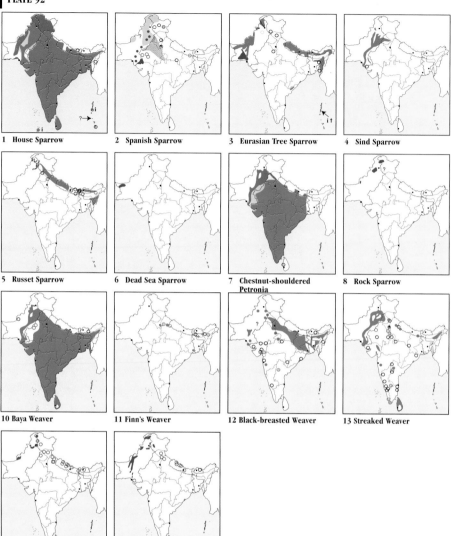

1 House Sparrow

2 Spanish Sparrow

3 Eurasian Tree Sparrow

4 Sind Sparrow

5 Russet Sparrow

6 Dead Sea Sparrow

7 Chestnut-shouldered Petronia

8 Rock Sparrow

10 Baya Weaver

11 Finn's Weaver

12 Black-breasted Weaver

13 Streaked Weaver

14 Chaffinch

15 Brambling

PLATE 93

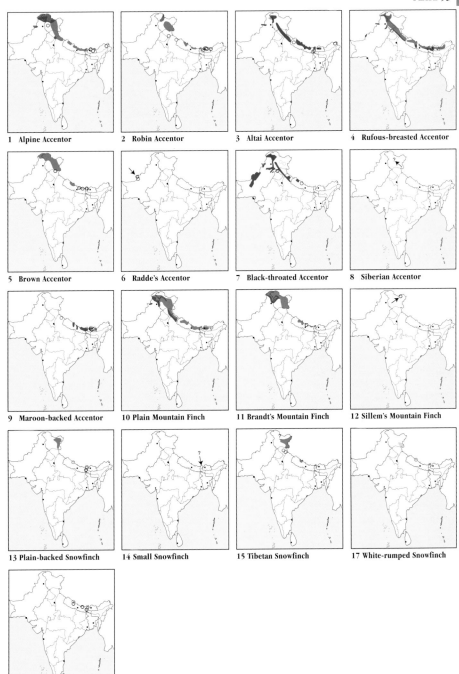

1 Alpine Accentor

2 Robin Accentor

3 Altai Accentor

4 Rufous-breasted Accentor

5 Brown Accentor

6 Radde's Accentor

7 Black-throated Accentor

8 Siberian Accentor

9 Maroon-backed Accentor

10 Plain Mountain Finch

11 Brandt's Mountain Finch

12 Sillem's Mountain Finch

13 Plain-backed Snowfinch

14 Small Snowfinch

15 Tibetan Snowfinch

17 White-rumped Snowfinch

18 Rufous-necked Snowfinch

PLATE 93: ACCENTORS, MOUNTAIN FINCHES AND SNOWFINCHES

1 **Alpine Accentor** *Prunella collaris* (1777-9) 17cm. Grey head and breast; rusty-streaked flanks; barring on throat (only obvious at close range). ⌘ **S** 3600-5500(7900). **W** 1800-4800. Stony meadows, cliffs, moraines, scree slopes; also mountain villages in winter. Not shy. ▽ *chirriririp*; *chit-chittur.* **AM3**

2 **Robin Accentor** *Prunella rubeculoides* (1781) 17cm. Grey head and unstreaked red breast. ⌘ **S** 3000-5300. **W** >2500 (1000). Scrub and bushes in valley bottoms, often preferring wet areas; around upland villages in winter. ▽ Trilling note; *zieh-zieh*; *tililili*; *si-tsi-si-tsi*, *tsütsisi*. **A3**

3 **Altai Accentor** *Prunella himalayana* (1780) 15cm. Breast and flanks streaked with rufous. Supercilium sometimes obscure. ⌘ (1000)2000-4000. Bare rocky ground. ▽ 'Silvery and finch-like'. **W3**

4 **Rufous-breasted Accentor** *Prunella strophiata* (1782-3) 15cm. From 2 by black mask; obvious supercilium; dark streaking on underparts. ⌘ **S** 2700-5000. Dwarf juniper and rhododendron jungle, rocky meadows. **W** (600)1200-3600. Bushes near cultivation, scrub. ▽ *tir-r-r-r-r-t*; *zwitt-twitt*, *twitt*, *twitt*; wren-like song. **RMA2**

5 **Brown Accentor** *Prunella fulvescens* (1784-5) 15cm. Black mask, white supercilium and unstreaked underparts. ⌘ **S** 3300-5100. **W** >1500. *Caragana* scrub; in drier areas than 2. ▽ *ziet*, *ziet*, *ziet*; tinny rattle; short low trilling warble. **A2**

6 **Radde's Accentor** *Prunella ocularis* (1785a) 15cm. Similar to 5 but paler; more heavily streaked mantle; streaking on flanks; slight malar stripe. ⌘ Mountainous, dry rocky areas. ▽ Slurred chatter. **V**

7 **Black-throated Accentor** *Prunella atrogularis* (1786-7) 15cm. Only accentor with black chin and throat. ⌘ <1800(2500). Scrub, orchards, bushes and semi-desert near cultivation; *sarpat* grass. ▽ Soft *trrt*; trilling warble. **W3**

8 [**Siberian Accentor** *Prunella montanella* (1787a) 15cm. Yellowish throat, breast and supercilium. ⌘ Open woodland, forest edge, bushes. ▽ Quiet *tirrl.* **X** (Single dubious record from Ladakh.)]

9 **Maroon-backed Accentor** *Prunella immaculata* (1788) 15cm. ⌘ **S** 2900-4200. **W** (1500)2100-3700. Humid fir and rhododendron forest, second growth, clearings, forest edge near fields. ▽ *zieh-dzit.* **AW3**

10 **Plain Mountain Finch** *Leucosticte nemoricola* (1999-2000) 15cm. Faint supercilium; two thin pale wing-bars. **Juv** from 11 by dark streaking on back. ⌘ **S** (3300)3600-5300 open habitats above treeline. **W** >1500(1000). Villages and open forest. ▽ *chi-chi-chi-chi*; whistling double-note; *rick-pi-vitt*; *diu-dip-dip-dip.* **A2**

11 **Brandt's Mountain Finch** *Leucosticte brandti* (2001-5) 18cm. **Br**♂ distinctive. **Nbr** from 10 by pale pink rump and lesser coverts and scalloping on crown. **Juv** from 10 by paler buff colour; unstreaked upperparts; indistinct wing-bars. Races (a) nom (b) *haematopygia.* See also 12. ⌘ **S** (3900)4200-6000. **W** >3000. Barren, open high-altitude habitats preferring wet areas often near melting snow. ▽ *twitt-twitt-itt*; *twree-eh*; *twee-ti-ti*; *peek-peek*; *churr.* **AW*3**

12 [**Sillem's Mountain Finch** *Leucosticte sillemi* 18cm. Some doubt has been cast regarding the validity of this species; described from two skins collected in 1929 at an altitude of 5125m in the Karakoram Mountains in a disputed border area with Tibet, presently under Chinese administration. Separated from 11 by tawny-cinnamon head; no black on fore crown; unstreaked mantle; paler rump; lack of white fringes on flight feathers, which are drab grey (vs blackish). ⌘ Similar to 11? ▽ Unknown. (May occur in Ladakh.)]

13 **Plain-backed Snowfinch** *Pyrgilauda blanfordi* (1955) 15cm. Distinctive face pattern with 'horns'. ⌘ 4200-5000. Tibetan steppe; enters villages in winter. ▽ Usually silent; rapid twittering. **W*2-3**

14 [**Small Snowfinch** *Pyrgilauda davidiana* (1956) 15cm. Black bib, lores and forecrown. ⌘ Tibetan steppe. ▽ Soft twittering. **X** (Single dubious record from N Sikkim.)]

15 **Tibetan Snowfinch** *Montifringilla adamsi* (1952) 17cm. Black bib; white primary and greater coverts. ⌘ 3600-5200. Open stony ground, scree slopes, fields. ▽ *pink pink*; mewing note; twittering; monotonous single repeated note. **A2**

16 [**White-winged Snowfinch** *Montifringilla nivalis* (1951) 18cm. Black bib and large white wing-patch formed by white coverts and secondaries. ⌘ Barren alpine habitats. ▽ *peeshew*; *tsee*; twittering. **X** (Could occur in Safed Koh of Pakistan.)]

17 **White-rumped Snowfinch** *Pyrgilauda taczanowskii* (1953) 17cm. Grey head with blackish lores and whitish supercilium; only snowfinch with white rump, but see also 12. ⌘ Tibetan steppe. ▽ *duid duid*; *duid ai duid*, *duid*, *duid*, *ai.* **W*4**

18 **Rufous-necked Snowfinch** *Pyrgilauda ruficollis* (1954) 15cm. Similar to 13 but lacks 'horns' and bib; chestnut on nape, sides of neck, ear-coverts and sides of breast; different flight pattern. ⌘ (2200)4200-4800. Barren steppe, grassy plateaux. ▽ soft *duuid*; chattering alarm. **R*W*(B*)5**

PLATE 94: FINCHES

1 **Eurasian Siskin** *Carduelis spinus* 12cm. ♂ black bib and forehead. ♀/juv from ♀/juv 5 by yellow at base of tail. ⌘ Fir, alders, larch, birch and hedges. ▽ *tseelu*; *tsu*; twittering. V

2 **European Goldfinch** *Carduelis carduelis* (1987-9) 14cm. Races **(a)** *caniceps* [**(b)** *subulata* could occur in N Pakistan] **(c)** *major* (vagrant). ⌘ S (1500) 2400-4200. W (75) 1900-2400. Orchards, forest, fields. ▽ *deedelit*; *chirik*; twittering. A2

3 **Yellow-breasted Greenfinch** *Carduelis spinoides* (1990, 1992) 14cm. **Ad** distinctive head pattern. Races **(a)** nom **(b)** *heinrichi*. **Juv** from juv 4 by pale supercilium, yellow on underparts and sides of neck. ⌘ S 1800-4400. W (150) 900-1500(2700). Forest, forest edge, gardens and scrub. Flocks in winter. ▽ *beez*; *weeeeeee-tu*; twittering. A2

4 **Black-headed Greenfinch** *Carduelis ambigua* (1991) 13cm. **Ad** dark hood (less contrasting in ♀). **Juv** Wider yellow base to flight feathers than 3; lacks pale supercilium and yellow at side of neck. ⌘ 2800-3100. Fields, meadows and forest edge near cultivation. ▽ *tit-it-it-it-it*; *tzyeee*. A?5

5 **Tibetan Siskin** *Carduelis thibetana* (1993) 12cm. ♂ from 1, 3 and 4 by lack of black on head; unstreaked appearance. ♀/juv lacks yellow in wing of 1, 3 and 4 and yellow at base of tail of 1. ⌘ 1000-3800. Fir, birch, hemlock, alders. ▽ *tsuu-ee*; twittering *tirrillilit*. A*W3

6 **Eurasian Linnet** *Carduelis cannabina* (1994) 13cm. Pink of winter ♂ more obscure. ♀/ juv from 7 by white rump, streaked chin and throat. ⌘ <2400. Open country and cultivation. ▽ *tsit*; *chi-chi-chi-chi-chit*; *too-tee*; twittering. W*3

7 **Twite** *Carduelis flavirostris* (1995-6) 13cm. ♀ from ♀6 by buff rump streaked with brown; unstreaked chin and throat; in winter by yellow bill. Races **(a)** *rufostrigata* **(b)** *montanella*. ⌘ S (3400) 3600-4500(4800). W Not much lower. Open country with *Caragana*, cultivation and scrub. ▽ *tsweee*; twittering. A3

8 **Fire-fronted Serin** *Serinus pusillus* (1998) 12cm. ⌘ S 2400-4000(4500). W (750) 1500-3300. Hillsides with bushes and stunted trees, screes, dwarf juniper, forest edge, fields. ▽ *tree tree*; *chiririiri*; twittering; *dzhewee*. A3

9 **Red Crossbill** *Loxia curvirostra* (2032) 15cm. Bill shape diagnostic. ⌘ (1500) 2600-4000. Conifers. Erratic in movements. Follows good crops of fir cones on which it feeds. ▽ *kip kip....* A●?3

10 **Scarlet Finch** *Haematospiza sipahi* (2034) 18cm. ♀ olive-green with orange-yellow rump-patch, cf. ♀ 95.14 & 95.21. ⌘ S 1600-3100. W 600-2600. Open pine and oak forests, streamside vegetation. ▽ *too-eee*; *kwee-i-u*. A*4

11 **Brown Bullfinch** *Pyrrhula nipalensis* (2036-7) 17cm. General ashy-brown colour. Scaly forecrown. ⌘ S (1800) 2100-3000(3900). W >1500. Dense fir, oak and rhododendron forest. ▽ *pearl-lee*; *chuwerly*; soft twittering. A4

12 **Grey-headed Bullfinch** *Pyrrhula erythaca* (2038) 17cm. ♀ from 14 by vinaceous (vs orange) underparts, less extensive black on face separated by a white border from grey of head. Ranges do not overlap. ⌘ S 2500-3800. W (1700) 2000-3200. Fir, rhododendron, willow and buckthorn. ▽ Triple *soo-ee*. A*4

13 **Red-headed Bullfinch** *Pyrrhula erythrocephala* (2039) 17cm. ♀ has yellowish-green nape. ⌘ S 2400-4200. W >(1000) 1500. Mainly deciduous forest. ▽ *phew-phew*; *phew-plít*; *cher-peri*. A2

14 **Orange Bullfinch** *Pyrrhula aurantiaca* (2040) 14cm. Juv♂ is like ad♀ but head same pale orange colour as breast. ⌘ S 2700-3300. W >1600. Open fir, birch and mixed forest. ▽ *tew*; *tew tyatlinka-tlinka*. EA3

15 **Gold-naped Finch** *Pyrrhoplectes epauletta* (2035) 15cm. ⌘ S 2800-3900. Rhododendron, ringal bamboo. W 1400-3600. Dense vegetation in forest, forest edge, scrub. ▽ *peeu peeu*; *pi-pi-pi-pi*. A4

16 **Hawfinch** *Coccothraustes coccothraustes* (1981) 18cm. ⌘ Mostly in the foothills. Orchards, groves, gardens, wooded hills. ▽ *tzik*; hard *pwit*; *teee*; *tzeep*. W*3

17 **Black-and-yellow Grosbeak** *Mycerobas icterioides* (1982) 22cm. ♂ similar to 18 but black thighs, little or no orange wash to hind-collar and rump, black of plumage dull, bill a brighter greenish-yellow. ⌘ S 1800-3500. Pine, silver fir and deodar forest. W >(750) 1500. Also oak forest. ▽ *pir-riu pir-riu pir-riu...*; *chuck*; *prr-troweet-a-troweet*. A3

18 **Collared Grosbeak** *Mycerobas affinis* (1983) 22cm. ♂ from 17 by yellow thighs, chestnut-orange wash to hind-collar and rump, black of plumage glossy, bill dull yellowish-green. ⌘ S (2700) 3000-4200. W >(1100) 1800. Oak, rhododendron and mixed forests. ▽ Ringing *ki-ki-ki-kiw*; *pip-pip-pip-pip-pip-pip-ugh*; *kurr*; *hi-diddle-diddle-the-fiddle*. A3

19 **Spot-winged Grosbeak** *Mycerobas melanozanthos* (1986) 22cm. ♂ from 20 by black rump, yellow breast, pale tips (spots) to secondaries. ⌘ S 2400-3600. W >(600) 1200. Mixed forest. ▽ *krrrr*; *typo-tio*. A4

20 **White-winged Grosbeak** *Mycerobas carnipes* (1984-5) 22cm. ♂ from 19 by dull yellow rump and belly, black breast, larger white wing-patch. ⌘ S 3000-4200. W >(1500) 2700. Pine, juniper, fir and rhododendron forests. ▽ nasal *chwenk*; *wet*; *wet-et-et*; *wil-ye-go-ame*. A3

See also Japanese Grosbeak 95.22.

PLATE 94

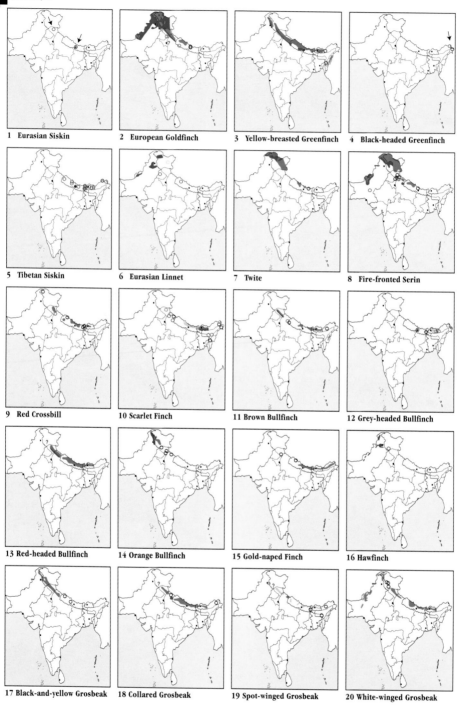

1   Eurasian Siskin   2   European Goldfinch   3   Yellow-breasted Greenfinch   4   Black-headed Greenfinch

5   Tibetan Siskin   6   Eurasian Linnet   7   Twite   8   Fire-fronted Serin

9   Red Crossbill   10 Scarlet Finch   11 Brown Bullfinch   12 Grey-headed Bullfinch

13 Red-headed Bullfinch   14 Orange Bullfinch   15 Gold-naped Finch   16 Hawfinch

17 Black-and-yellow Grosbeak   18 Collared Grosbeak   19 Spot-winged Grosbeak   20 White-winged Grosbeak

PLATE 95

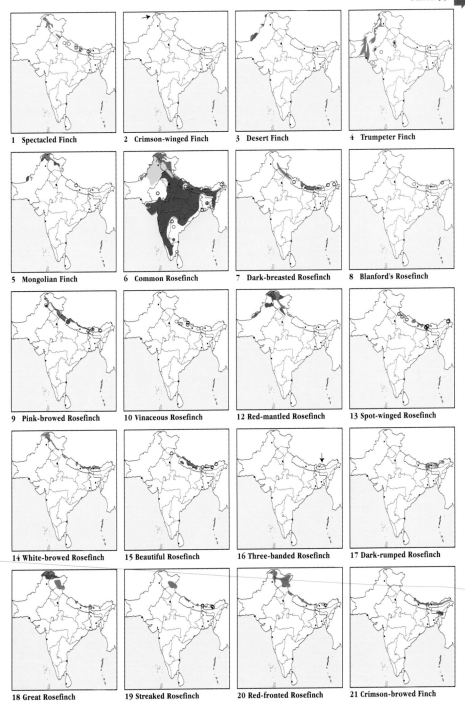

1 Spectacled Finch

2 Crimson-winged Finch

3 Desert Finch

4 Trumpeter Finch

5 Mongolian Finch

6 Common Rosefinch

7 Dark-breasted Rosefinch

8 Blanford's Rosefinch

9 Pink-browed Rosefinch

10 Vinaceous Rosefinch

12 Red-mantled Rosefinch

13 Spot-winged Rosefinch

14 White-browed Rosefinch

15 Beautiful Rosefinch

16 Three-banded Rosefinch

17 Dark-rumped Rosefinch

18 Great Rosefinch

19 Streaked Rosefinch

20 Red-fronted Rosefinch

21 Crimson-browed Finch

303

1 Spectacled Finch *Callacanthis burtoni* (1997) 17cm. Distinctive 'spectacles'. ⌘ **S** (2400)2700-3000(treeline). **W** (800)1800-3000. Open coniferous forest. ▽ Plaintive *pweee*; *ueh-eh*; *twee-yeh*. **EA4**

2 Crimson-winged Finch *Rhodopechys sanguinea* (2009) 18cm. From 3, 4 & 5 by blackish crown, dappled brown back, throat, upper breast and flanks. ⌘ High-altitude semi-desert biotope. ▽ *chu-chily*; *dy-lit-di-lyt*; *chee chee*; *chu-cheech-chu-chwili...chwilichip*. **V**

3 Desert Finch *Rhodospiza obsoleta* (2008) 15cm. **Br**♂ separate from 2, 4 & 5 by buffy-brown rump, black bill and lores. **Juv** like ♀ but dark-tipped yellowish bill; less pink in wings; similar to juv 4 & 5 but more white in wings; blackish primaries; dark-tipped bill. ⌘ <1400. Open country and cultivation with trees and bushes; orchards. ▽ *prruii-prruii*; nasal *shureeah*; *pink pink pink* **B*W*3**

4 Trumpeter Finch *Bucanetes githagineus* (2006) 15cm. **Br**♂ Red bill, red wash to underparts and pale greyish-brown head distinctive but see also 2, 3 & 5. **Nbr**♂ like ♀ but yellow bill; both lack pink and white in wings of 3 & 5. **Juv** has no pink in plumage and is like juv 3 & 5, which see. ⌘ <foothills/3000. Bare hills, semi-desert. ▽ Song and calls have nasal buzzing quality: *che*; *eech*; *chit*; *chääääääää*. **R•2**

5 Mongolian Finch *Bucanetes mongolicus* (2007) 15cm. **Br**♂ is like 4 but with yellowish bill, pinkish supercilium, much white in wings, paler underparts and brownish legs; from 3 by yellowish bill, pinkish supercilium and rump. **Nbr**♂ like ♀ but slightly pinker. **Juv** from juv 3 by all-pale bill and brownish primaries; from juv 4 by slight streaking above and whitish edges to secondaries and tertials. ⌘ **S** 3000-3900. **W** 1500-3000. Steep rocky slopes and ravines, barren plains. ▽ *djou-voud...djoudjou-vou...*; slow *do-mi-sol-mi*. **R•M3-4** (erratic)

6 Common Rosefinch *Carpodacus erythrinus* (2010-3) 15cm. ♂ crimson rump, breast and head, brown upperparts tinged red/pink, white belly and vent, no supercilium, brownish eye-stripe. ♀/*imm* no supercilium, 2 buffy/whitish wing-bars, streaked upperparts and breast, whitish belly and vent. Races **(a)** nom **(b)** *roseatus*. ⌘ **S** 2000-3900(4200). **W** <2400. Bushes, open forest, scrub, cultivation. ▽ *twee-ee*; *tweeti-tweeti-tweeou*. **AM2-3**

7 Dark-breasted Rosefinch *Carpodacus nipalensis* (2014-5) 15cm. ♂ overall very dark with dark red breast-band and long thin bill; this and 17 are only ♂ rosefinches without red/pink rump; from ♂17 by rosy-red forehead, redder supercilium and throat. ♀ unstreaked and darker than other ♀♀. ⌘ **S** 3000-4400. **W** (700)1800-2700. Rhododendron, silver fir, meadows with bushes above treeline, clearings, bushes, cultivation. ▽ Plaintive double whistle; wheezy *chair*; monotonous chipping. **A2**

8 Blanford's Rosefinch *Carpodacus rubescens* (2016) 15cm. ♂ duller, darker red on crown and rump than 6 and without latter's brown eye-stripe; rosy-red below, the wash extending down over greyish belly and flanks (buffy-white in 6). ♀ is paler than 7 with faint (vs obvious) wing-bars and rufescent rump; absence of streaking separates from all other ♀♀. ⌘ **S** 2700-3800. **W** 1300-3050. Conifer and conifer/birch forests. ▽ *sip*; *pitch-ew pitch-it chit-it chit-ew*; persistent clacking. **A4**

9 Pink-browed Rosefinch *Carpodacus rodochrous* (2017) 15cm. ♂ pink supercilium (redder above lores and on forecrown), unstreaked pink underparts and rump, streaked brown back; see also 12, 14 & 15. ♀ like ♂ 10 but has long buffy-white supercilium; throat a little whiter than rest of underparts. ⌘ **S** 2800-4200. **W** (600)1200-2400(3000). Open fir and birch forest, willow, dwarf juniper, oak, scrub, grassy slopes, gardens, villages. ▽ *swee-et*; *per-lee*; *chew-wee*. **A3**

10 Vinaceous Rosefinch *Carpodacus vinaceus* (2017a) 13cm. ♂ fairly uniform, deep wine-red with paler rump and pink supercilium. ♀ streaked, no supercilium or wing-bars, olive-brown above, warm brown below. ⌘ **S** 3050-3200. **W** 1050-3050. Dense bushes and glades in bamboo. ▽ *zieh*; *pwit*; *weeeep*; *tip*; *pink*; *zick*; *pee-dee*, *be do-do*. **A?5**

11 [Pink-rumped Rosefinch *Carpodacus eos* 13cm. Extremely similar to 15 but smaller and inhabits higher altitudes; ♂ is slightly darker, the pink on throat/ear-coverts is a little more extensive and there is a little more red on lores, side of forecrown and sides of chin; ♀ indistinguishable. ⌘ 3950-4900. Bushy dry valleys, cultivation. ▽ *pink*; *tsip*; *piprit*; *tvitt-itt-itt-itt*. **X** (Could stray to Arunachal Pradesh.)]

12 Red-mantled Rosefinch *Carpodacus rhodochlamys* (2018) 18cm. ♂ separated from most rosefinches by distinctly large bill and silvery-white streaks on feathery pink supercilium, ear-coverts and throat; the rather similar but smaller 9 has the supercilium meeting across the forecrown (brown in 12); 14 has different supercilium, much darker line through the eye and distinct wing-bars. ♀ has a fairly distinct supercilium and is heavily streaked throughout including belly; ♀9 is smaller, with a buffier ground-colour, especially below, and much reduced streaking on belly; ♀14 has orangy rump. ⌘ **S** 2700-3800. **W** foothills-2600. Dry alpine shrubs, thorny scrub, gardens, cultivation. ▽ Wheezy *quwee*; sharp *wir*. **A3**

13 Spot-winged Rosefinch *Carpodacus rodopeplus* (2019) 16cm. ♂ identified by deep vinous-brown upperparts, long pale pink supercilium (redder around face), rows of pink spots on wing-bars and tertials, dull pink rump. ♀ is relatively

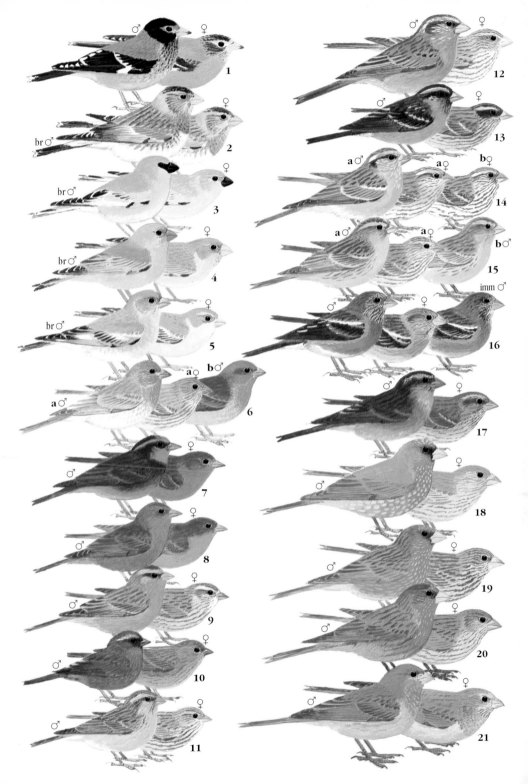

dark, streaked above, with long buffy supercilium, two diffuse pale wing-bars, pale spots on the tertials, buffy streaked with dark brown below; from ♀9 by large size, large bill and darker brown upperparts; from ♀10 by supercilium, large size, heavier streaking; from ♀15 by large size, dark mask through eye, distinct buffy supercilium and warm buffy underparts; from ♀17 by spotted wing-bar, bolder streaking on breast, longer clearer supercilium. ⌘ S 3050-4000. W 2000-3050. Dwarf rhododendron, grassy slopes, dense forest undergrowth, damp ravines. ▽ Canary-like *chirp*; wheezy *schweee*. A3-4

14 White-browed Rosefinch *Carpodacus thura* (2020-2) 17cm. ♂ supercilium pattern is distinctive – silvery-pink with a white spot at the rear. Note also red lores and dark line behind eye. ♀ orange rump streaked with brown distinguishes from other ♀♀ except 21 and 94.10, which see. Races **(a)** nom orange-buff throat and breast of ♀ distinctive. **(b)** *femininus*. ⌘ S 3000-4200. W 1800-3900. Alpine meadows and shrubbery, forest edge, bamboo. ▽ *pupupipipipi*; *pwit pwit...*; buzzy *deep-deep, deep-de-de-de-de*; bleating *veh ve ve ve ve ve ve.* A3

15 Beautiful Rosefinch *Carpodacus pulcherrimus* (2023-4) 14cm. Very like, perhaps even conspecific with, 11 which see. ♂ similar to ♂9 but paler pink below and on supercilium, streaked crown, heavily streaked, greyish-brown (vs warm brown) upperparts, thinly streaked breast and flanks. ♀ from ♀9 by heavier streaking above, whitish underparts, paler crown and ear-coverts. Races **(a)** nom **(b)** *waltoni*. ⌘ S (3600)3800-4200(4500). W 2100-3600. Alpine shrubbery, open scrubby slopes, forest and cultivation edge. ▽ *trip*; *trilp*; *chillip*; *cheet-cheet*; *chaaannn.* A2

16 Three-banded Rosefinch *Carpodacus trifasciatus* (2026) 17cm. Triple wing-bar and head-pattern diagnostic. ⌘ 2000-3000. Light conifer forest. ▽ Usually silent. **V**

17 Dark-rumped Rosefinch *Carpodacus edwardsii* (2025) 17cm. ♂ has very dark plumage with pale pink supercilium and throat; from ♂7 by little or no red on forehead and upperparts, streaked mantle, paler pink supercilium and throat; from ♂13 by brown rump, dark breast-band and no pink spotting on wing-bars. ♀ has fairly dark plumage but easily separated from ♀7 by its streaking; more similar to ♀13 but less heavily streaked below, less distinct supercilium (streaked) and little/no wing-bar scales. ⌘ S 3200-3900. W (1000)2000-3700. Rhododendron; juniper; fir; birch; scrubby hillsides. ▽ Metallic *twink*; rasping *che-wee.* A4

18 Great Rosefinch *Carpodacus rubicilla* (2027) 19cm. Very similar to 19; best distinguished by the paler sandy-brown, almost unstreaked upperparts. At close range note ♂'s rounded white spotting on crown and underparts (vs thin, slightly wedge shaped-streaks on 19). ⌘ S (3300)3900-4800(5350). W (1500)2600-4500. Rocky alpine meadows and scrub. ▽ Slow *weep*; low chuckles; *twink*; *twit*; subdued whistle; brief twitter; *fyu-fyu-fyu-fyu-fyu-fyu.* A3

19 Streaked Rosefinch *Carpodacus rubicilloides* (2028) 19cm. Very like 18, which see; from 20 by upperparts with slight red tinge, red extending to hind-crown (vs forecrown and supercilium only), no dark line through eye, reddish (vs brown) wash on belly. ♀ from ♀20 by paler underparts (whitish belly vs brown) and shorter, deeper bill. ⌘ S 3700-4800. W 2200-4800. Alpine scrub and willow. ▽ *twink*; *sip*; *dooid dooid*; *tsee-tsee-soo-soo-soo.* A2

20 Red-fronted Rosefinch *Carpodacus puniceus* (2029-31) 20cm. Not unlike 19 & 21, which see. ⌘ S (3900)4200-5500. W (1500)2700-4550. Steep rocky slopes. ▽ Wheezy *chirp*; cat-like *m-a-a-a-u*; soft *twiddle-le-de*; *are you quite ready.* A4

21 Crimson-browed Finch *Propyrrhula subhimachalus* (2033) 20cm. ♂ from 20 by unstreaked greyish-brown belly, deep red rump and reddish tinge to relatively unstreaked upperparts. ♀ olive-yellow supercilium and upper breast diagnostic. ⌘ S 3500-4200. W 1800-3600. Scrub near treeline, light forest with dense undergrowth. ▽ *chirp*; *ter-ter-tee*; bright, varied warble. A4

22 [Japanese Grosbeak *Eophona personata* (not illustrated). 21cm. Typical grosbeak build. ♂ black of face, throat and crown extends below/behind eye but not onto ear-coverts; powerful yellow bill; pale grey body washed with brown on upperparts; whitish rump; black wings with white primary patch; black tail. ♀ slightly duller than ♂ with brownish-grey rump. (Beware the similar Chinese Grosbeak *Eophona migratoria* which could also occur as a winter vagrant but ♂ has black-tipped bill; black of head extends over ear-coverts; greyish-brown body; primaries broadly tipped with white; ♀ is similar to ♂ but has grey head with blackish face; primaries narrowly tipped with white.) ⌘ Well-wooded areas; edges of cultivation. ▽ Hard *tak, tak*; 4-5 fluty notes. **X(V?)** (Single record from E Arunachal Pradesh, NE India, as yet insufficiently documented.)] See also grosbeaks on Plate 94.

PLATE 96

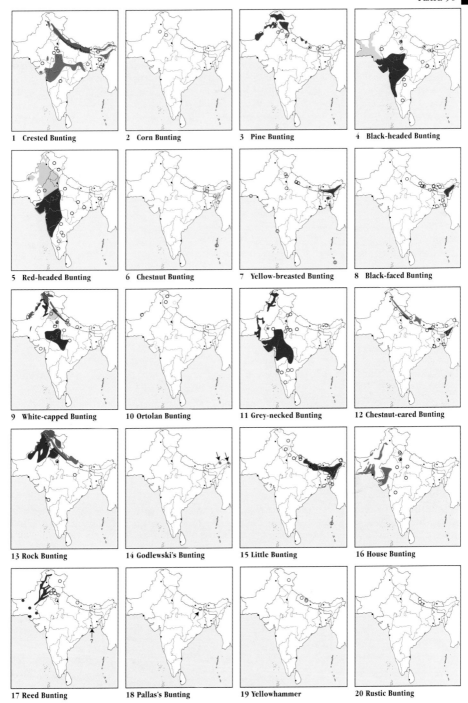

1 Crested Bunting

2 Corn Bunting

3 Pine Bunting

4 Black-headed Bunting

5 Red-headed Bunting

6 Chestnut Bunting

7 Yellow-breasted Bunting

8 Black-faced Bunting

9 White-capped Bunting

10 Ortolan Bunting

11 Grey-necked Bunting

12 Chestnut-eared Bunting

13 Rock Bunting

14 Godlewski's Bunting

15 Little Bunting

16 House Bunting

17 Reed Bunting

18 Pallas's Bunting

19 Yellowhammer

20 Rustic Bunting

PLATE 96: BUNTINGS

1 **Crested Bunting** *Melophus lathami* (2060) 15cm. ♀ crest; from larks by thin pointed bill; rufous wings and tail. ⌘ <2400. Scrubby hillsides, fallow fields. ▽ *tip*; *pink*; *tzit-tzit-titiweechyweeo*; *which...which-whi-whee-which*. **RA3**

2 **Corn Bunting** *Miliaria calandra* (2041) 18cm. From larks, pipits and rosefinches by jizz; from other buntings by bulky build and extensive streaking below. ⌘ Waste ground, cultivation. ▽ *tik*; *tchrrp*; *trree*. **V**

3 **Pine Bunting** *Emberiza leucocephalos* (2042) 17cm. ♀/**imm** like 19 but without any yellowish tones. ⌘ Dry bushy slopes; fallow fields and stubble in hilly country. ▽ *pit*; *trp*; *dzee*. **W3**

4 **Black-headed Bunting** *Emberiza melanocephala* (2043) 18cm. Many ♀♀ are similar to **imm** and cannot safely be distinguished from ♀/imm 5. ⌘ Plains. Grain crops and grasses. ▽ *tweet*; *tzit*; *dzee*; *prriu*; *tizik*. **WP3**

5 **Red-headed Bunting** *Emberiza bruniceps* (2044) 17cm. See 4 & 6. ⌘ **S** 1600-2400. **W** plains(<4600 on passage). Grain crops and grasses. ▽ *chip*; *ziff*; *prrit*; *tleep*; song *zreet zreet zeeti-teezi-churri-churri-trrr*. **B*WP3**

6 **Chestnut Bunting** *Emberiza rutila* (2045) 14cm. ♂ from ♂5 by chestnut upperparts. ♀/**imm** from ♀/imm 7 & 8 by unstreaked rufous rump. ⌘ <4500. Rice stubble, bushes near cultivation, forest edge. ▽ *zick*; *teseep*. **W5**

7 **Yellow-breasted Bunting** *Emberiza aureola* (2046) 15cm. ♂ from ♂4 by white shoulder-patch; chestnut breast-band and nape; in winter no black mask but dark ear-coverts and yellowish supercilium. ♀/**imm** note yellowish crown-stripe; 2 whitish wing-bars; rump with rufous and dark brown streaks. ⌘ <1500. Fields, grassland, bushes. ▽ *tzik*; *trssit*; *tsee*. **W2-3**

8 **Black-faced Bunting** *Emberiza spodocephala* (2047) 15cm. ♂ olive-grey head merging into black face. ♀/**imm** from ♀/imm 3, 6, 17 & 19 by unstreaked olive-brown rump. ⌘ <1000(1300). Long grass, bushes, scrub, bamboo; usually near water. ▽ *tzii*; hard *tzik*. **W4**

9 **White-capped Bunting** *Emberiza stewarti* (2048) 15cm. Greyish-white cap, black mask and throat of ♂ distinctive. ⌘ **S** 1200-3600. **W** <1400(2500). Rocky, grassy slopes, grassy scrub. ▽ *tit*; song *chew*- repeated 10-12 times. **M2-3**

10 **Ortolan Bunting** *Emberiza hortulana* (2049) 15cm. Greenish-grey head (usually) and breast-band; obvious whitish eye-ring; pale yellow throat and submoustachial stripe (but see 11). **Imm** like imm 11 but more boldly streaked, including rump; darker flight feathers. ⌘ Dry open country, sparse scrub. ▽ *siee*; *plit*; *tew*; *twick*; *chip*. **V**

11 **Grey-necked Bunting** *Emberiza buchanani* (2050) 15cm. **Br**♂ is similar to 10 but grey (vs greenish-grey) head; no breast-band; creamy-white (vs pale yellow) throat often mottled with rufous. **Br**♀ like ♂ but streaked on head and breast. **Imm** from imm 10 by finer streaking; brown rump almost unstreaked; upper breast often with rufous mottling. ⌘ Dry scrubby hills. ▽ *click*; *tcheup*; *trip-trip*; song *dzeee-zeee-zeeeo zee-zee-deo*. **W(B*)3**

12 **Chestnut-eared Bunting** *Emberiza fucata* (2055-5a) 15cm. Chestnut cheeks contrast with remaining plumage. Races **(a)** nom **(b)** *arcuata*. ⌘ **S** 1650-2700. Bushy and scrubby hillsides. **W** <1600. Marshy areas, cultivation. ▽ *pzick*; *zii*; *chutt*; song *chick-chick-he'll get used to you-chick*. **AW4**

13 **Rock Bunting** *Emberiza cia* (2051-2) 16cm. From 14 by black (vs chestnut) head markings; from 16 by unstreaked throat and head; black lateral crown-stripes; overall richer colouring; rufous (vs brown) rump; white (vs buff) outer tail feathers. ⌘ **S** 2000-4600. **W** 600-2100(3600). Bushy rocky slopes, juniper, open pine forest, field margins. ▽ *seea*; *tzi*; *tsee*; *swip*; *chelut*; *swee*, *swee*, *trrr*; song *chet-reyt-tsit-trrt-chet-tsit* and variations. **AM2**

14 **Godlewski's Bunting** *Emberiza godlewskii* (2053-4) 17cm. See 13. ⌘ 1500-4200. Similar to 13. ▽ Similar to 13. **A*?4**

15 **Little Bunting** *Emberiza pusilla* (2056) 13cm. Note rusty-chestnut crown-stripe, ear-coverts and fore-supercilium; black lateral crown-stripes; no moustachial stripe; pale eye-ring. **Imm** head pattern less distinct. ⌘ <2000(3050). Scrub, bushes, stubble, grass, cultivation, orchards. ▽ *tik*; *tzit*. **W2**

16 **House Bunting** *Emberiza striolata* (2057) 14cm. Overall paler but could be mistaken for 13 which see. ⌘ Rocky ground with sparse scrub. ▽ Nasal *chwer*; *tzswee*; song *which-which-wheech-whichy-which* **R*3**

17 **Reed Bunting** *Emberiza schoeniclus* (2058-9) 16cm. **Nbr**♂ has head pattern obscured by pale fringes to the black feathers. ♀/**imm** lack chestnut rump of 3, 19 & 20; from 15 by large size; heavier bill; brown (vs chestnut) ear-coverts; black moustachial stripe; no eye-ring. ⌘ Reeds and bushes near water. ▽ *tsiu*; *tseek*; *chink*; *chup*. **W3**

18 **Pallas's Bunting** *Emberiza pallasi* (**not illustrated**) 14cm. Like 17 but br♂ dark mantled (heavily streaked blackish); fairly prominent white wing-bars; grey lesser coverts; in other plumages by grey (vs rufous) lesser coverts. ⌘ Waterside vegetation in winter. ▽ *chleep*. **V** (Recent record from Nepal.)

19 **Yellowhammer** *Emberiza citrinella* 17cm. ♀/**imm** from ♀/imm 3 by yellowish tinge. ⌘ Open habitats with trees and bushes; cultivation. ▽ *tzik*. **V**

20 **Rustic Bunting** *Emberiza rustica* 15cm. Rusty hind-neck, rump and streaking on flanks. ♂ has distinctive head pattern. ⌘ Open woodland, cultivation. ▽ Fine *tzik*; *tsiee*. **V**

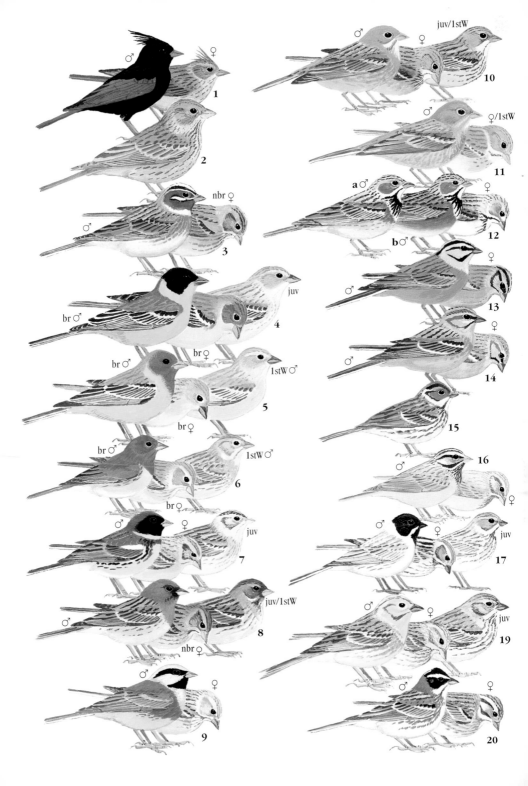

NIGHTJAR WING AND TAIL PATTERNS

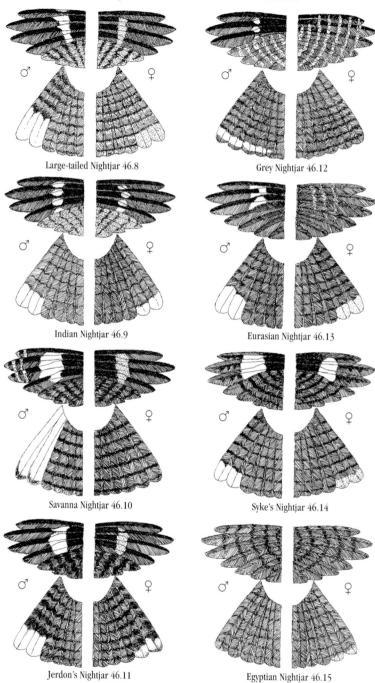

Large-tailed Nightjar 46.8

Grey Nightjar 46.12

Indian Nightjar 46.9

Eurasian Nightjar 46.13

Savanna Nightjar 46.10

Syke's Nightjar 46.14

Jerdon's Nightjar 46.11

Egyptian Nightjar 46.15

TAIL PATTERNS OF WHEATEARS, COMMON AND WHITE-TAILED STONECHATS

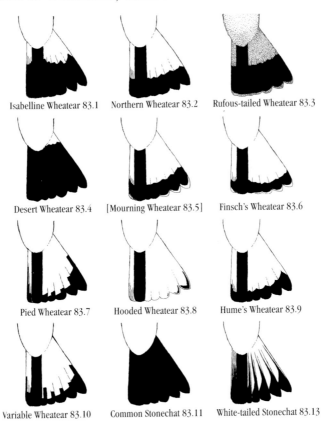

Isabelline Wheatear 83.1   Northern Wheatear 83.2   Rufous-tailed Wheatear 83.3

Desert Wheatear 83.4   [Mourning Wheatear 83.5]   Finsch's Wheatear 83.6

Pied Wheatear 83.7   Hooded Wheatear 83.8   Hume's Wheatear 83.9

Variable Wheatear 83.10   Common Stonechat 83.11   White-tailed Stonechat 83.13

SNIPE TAIL PATTERNS

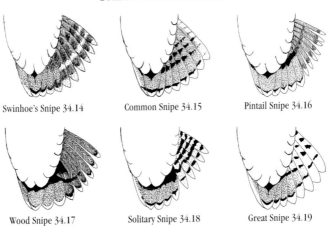

Swinhoe's Snipe 34.14   Common Snipe 34.15   Pintail Snipe 34.16

Wood Snipe 34.17   Solitary Snipe 34.18   Great Snipe 34.19

GLOSSARY

See also page 15 for diagrams of bird topography.

Allopatric Refers to species occurring in geographically separated areas, i.e. ranges not overlapping.

Altitudinal migrant A species found at different altitudes at different times of the year, especially breeding higher in the mountains and wintering lower down.

Aquatic Living or growing on or in water.

Arm The base of the wing from the carpal joint to where it joins the body; often used in describing seabirds and birds of prey.

Arboreal Tree-dwelling (may also frequent bushes).

Avian Pertaining to birds.

Avifauna The community of birds (species) found in a given region.

Axillaries Feathers of the axil ('arm-pit') where the underwing joins the body.

Bamboo Plant family related to the grasses but usually with thick woody stems; important varieties in South Asia include maling, reed and ringal bamboos.

Bare parts Those parts of a bird not covered in feathers, i.e. bill and legs, sometimes also bare skin around the eye, or on the head and neck.

Basal Related to the base, e.g. of the bill or tail.

Biotope Region characterised by certain environmental conditions and inhabited by a particular community of flora and fauna.

Bird wave Mixed flock or mixed hunting party.

Buff(y) A very pale (yellowy-)brownish colour.

Bulrushes Perennial grass-like herbs with thick triangular stems, usually found in marshy areas.

Cap Contrastingly coloured area at the top of the head, usually from the top of the crown down to more-or-less the level of the bill and eye.

Caragana Spiny shrubs of dry Himalayan steppe country, mostly with yellow or orange-yellow flowers.

Cardamom A tropical spice plant of the ginger family.

Carpal Pertaining to the carpal joint (bend of the wing); the joint itself.

Casque An extension on the upper side of the bill, chiefly in hornbills.

Cere Bare fleshy skin at the base of the bill, chiefly in raptors.

Cheek Area on the head below the eye, usually including the ear-coverts.

Collar Distinctly-coloured band around the neck.

Conspecific Belonging to the same species.

Corvid Bird of the crow family.

Coverts Feathers covering the bases of flight and tail feathers.

Covey (Family) group, usually applied to 'game' birds.

Crepuscular Active during the twilight of dawn and dusk.

Decurved Downcurved.

Deodar A species of cedar tree *Cedrus deodara* of the Himalaya.

Dimorphic (dichromatic) Occurring in two distinct plumage types, usually related to gender, e.g. species where males and females appear different are said to be sexually dimorphic (dichromatic if the difference is only one of colour).

Disjunct Completely separated, not overlapping, usually referring to distribution ranges.

Distal The part farther away from the body, e.g. distal half of the bill or tail.

Diurnal Chiefly active during the daytime.

Duar The eastern part of the *terai* from West Bengal eastwards.

Eclipse plumage Post-breeding plumage, especially in ducks, when for a short time males resemble females.

Endemic Restricted to a given country or region.

Epiphyte A plant which grows on another plant.

Facies Subdivision of a region or biotope; general aspect.

Family A group of related genera.

Feral Species which were once domesticated but have escaped and adapted to living in the wild.

First-winter (1stW) plumage The plumage worn by a bird in the winter of its first calendar year.

Flight feathers In this work denotes the primaries and secondaries. Other authors sometimes include the rectrices.

Frugivorous Fruit-eating.

Fulvous Reddish-brown, reddish-yellow or tawny.

Genus (plural genera) A taxonomic grouping of closely related species. Birds of the same genus share the same initial scientific name.

Ghat Slope, as in mountain or steps down to a river, e.g. Western Ghats (mtns parallel to the W coast of peninsular India).

Gonydeal Related to the gonys.

Gonys The angle on the bottom edge of the lower mandible, especially obvious on gulls and terns.

Gorget A band of a distinctive colour across the throat or upper breast.

Granivorous Grain- or seed-eating.

Gregarious Associating in groups or flocks.

Gular On or of the throat.

Gular stripe Dark stripe down the centre of the throat.

Hand The outer part of the wing from the carpal joint to the wing-tip; often used in describing seabirds and birds of prey.

Hawking Catching insects in the air.

Hepatic "Liver-coloured", usually referring to the reddish-brown morph of some female cuckoos.

Immature Not yet adult (may include juvenile).

Invertebrates Animals without backbones, e.g. worms, snails, insects.

Iris Membrane around the dark pupil (centre) of the eye – often brightly coloured and of some diagnostic value in birds.

Jheel Shallow lake, pond or marshy area.

Jizz A bird's overall 'character' produced by a combination of features and habits which can be difficult to define but make it recognisably of a particular species, genus or family.

Juvenile A bird in its first full plumage after fledging.

Lantana Low shrub with small pink, red and white flowers. Introduced from tropical America, it has spread uncontrollably, replacing the native undergrowth throughout large parts of the subcontinent.

Littoral Pertaining to the sea-shore.

Loranthus Epiphyte, such as mistletoe, the fruits of which are much loved by flowerpeckers.

Mandible One of the two sections that form the bill, *viz.* upper mandible or lower mandible.

Melanistic Refers to individual birds which appear unusually dark due to an excess of the pigment melanin in their plumage.

Mesial 'Of the middle', usually referring to the dark stripe down the centre of the throat found on some raptors.

Mirror Subterminal white spot or patch on the outer primaries of a gull.

Montane Of the mountains. In this work usually refers to altitudes above 1500m.

Morph A normal plumage variant of a species unrelated to age, sex or season, occurring alongside other plumage type(s) within a given population.

Nalla(h) or **nullah** A small ravine, stream or ditch, usually without water in the dry season.

Near-endemic A species is considered near-endemic if the majority of its range lies within the subcontinent.

Nocturnal Mainly active at night.

Nomadic Given to erratic or poorly understood (seasonal) movements.

Nominate The subspecies which was named first. The subspecific name is then the same as the specific name, e.g. *Gyps indicus indicus*. See also *trinomial system*.

Non-passerine A bird which is not a passerine (which see).

Nuchal Of or on the nape.

Paddy Rice growing in a field.

Passage migrant A species which occurs on migration between its breeding grounds to the north and its wintering grounds to the south, chiefly in 'spring' and/or 'autumn'.

Passerine Sparrow-like bird. Order of birds which includes most typical small to medium-sized songbirds, such as larks, finches and thrushes, as well as families such as swallows, pittas and babblers.

Patagial In vultures refers to a pale bar visible on the lesser underwing coverts parallel to, and between, the leading edge of the wing and the pale bar along the centre of the underwing coverts.

Pelagic Living chiefly out to sea.

Plumage A bird's feathering.

Polyandrous A female mating with more than one male.

Polygynous A male mating with more than one female.

Primary projection On a folded wing the distance from the tip of the longest tertial to the wing-tip.

Proximal The part nearer (to the body), e.g. of the bill or tail.

Race In this work used to signify subspecies.

Raptor Diurnal bird of prey other than owls, e.g. hawk, eagle or falcon.

Rectrices Tail feathers.

Remiges Flight feathers, i.e. primaries and secondaries.

Rictal Of the gape (usually describing the bristles near the base of the bill, or a spot behind the mouth).

Riverain/riverine Of or along a river.

Rufous Light reddish.

Rufescent A colour somewhat lighter than rufous, a slight reddish tinge.

Scree A steeply sloping mass of loose stones and rocks.

Shaft-streak Thin line of distinct colour along the shaft of a feather.

Sheesham (shisham) *Dalbergia latifolia,* a kind of rosewood tree.

Shola Strictly speaking refers to montane elfin forest in the highlands of southern Indian and Sri Lanka, but loosely applied to any patch of evergreen forest in that region.

Speculum A contrastingly coloured panel (usually iridescent) on the secondaries of ducks.

Storey Forest level, i.e. lower or under-storey = undergrowth and bushes; mid-storey = tops of tall bushes, small trees and lower branches of tall trees; upper storey = tree canopy.

Streamers Greatly elongated projections, usually from the tail feathers.

Subadult An identifiable stage achieved prior to full adult plumage in some species, such as raptors and gulls, which take several years to attain full maturity.

Subspecies A population of a given species which differs to some definable degree from other populations/subspecies of the same species.

Subterminal Just before the end, e.g. of the tail, usually referring to a band of distinct colour.

Supraloral Above the lores.

Sympatric Refers to species occurring together in the same area, i.e. ranges overlap.

Tank Artificial pond, lake or reservoir, often near a town or village and of ancient origin.

Tawny Yellowish-brown.

Taxon Term used for a subdivision in the classification of organisms, e.g. species or race.

Taxonomy The scientific classification of organisms.

Terai Originally a wide belt (25km–45km) of marshy jungle and grasslands that stretched along the Himalaya between its foothills and the plains of northern India and Nepal – now largely drained and cultivated.

Terminal The end; the part furthest away (from the body), e.g. of the tail.

Terrestrial Ground-dwelling.

Tooth-brush Tree *Salvadora persica*.

Trinomial system The scientific system of giving three latinised names to a bird population, e.g. *Gyps indicus tenuirostris*, where the first name is that of the genus, the second that of the species and the third that of the subspecies.

Trousers Loose feathering on the tibia of some birds.

Underparts Under surface of the body including the throat but not the sides of the head.

Upperparts Upper surface of the body.

Vermiculations Fine wavy lines, often not discernible at a distance.

Vinaceous The colour of red wine.

Wattle Bare pendulous skin growing from the head, frequently brightly-coloured as in some lapwings and mynas.

Wing-bar A contrastingly (usually pale) coloured band across the wing. In passerines this is most commonly formed by the tips to the greater and/or median coverts; in shorebirds by pale bases to the flight feathers.

Wing lining Term denoting the underwing-coverts, sometimes including the axillaries.

Zygodactylous Having two toes pointing forward and two back, e.g. as in cuckoos and most woodpeckers, as opposed to most birds which have three forward and one back.

USEFUL ORGANISATIONS

Many organisations are concerned with birds, birdwatching and conservation in the Indian subcontinent, and we can only give a selection of the more important ones here. Foreign-based birders will find membership of the Oriental Bird Club (OBC) of particular value. Locally based birdwatchers are encouraged to join their local club or national organisation as well as the OBC. The publications sent to members are a useful source of information on birds and birding in the region.

INTERNATIONAL

BirdLife International (formerly ICBP) is the world's leading international bird conservation organisation. It supports, organises and co-ordinates bird-related conservation schemes through its network of national partners around the world and monitors the status of all endangered species. Members receive the quarterly magazine *World Birdwatch* and an annual report. Address: Asia Division, Wellbrook Court, Girton Rd, Cambridge, CB3 0NA, UK. Tel 01223-277318; fax 01223-277200.

Oriental Bird Club (OBC) aims to encourage an interest in the birds of the Oriental region (including South Asia) and their conservation; liaise with and promote the work of existing regional societies; collate and publish material on Oriental birds. Members receive two bulletins and a journal *Forktail* annually. Address: c/o The Lodge, Sandy, Bedfordshire, SG19 2DL, UK; Website www.orientalbirdclub.org; Email <mail@orientalbirdclub.org>.

OrientalBirding is an email discussion group for all those with an interest in the birds of the Oriental region. Membership is free. To join send an email to <orientalbirding-subscribe@egroups.com>. The email can be blank or with the subject 'subscribe'.

South Asian Natural History Discussion Group is another useful Internet forum. To join email <Listproc@lists.princeton. edu> leaving the 'subject' heading blank or with the word 'subscribe'. In the body of the message you should write 'subscribe nathistory-india' (without the quotation marks) together with your email address, first name and last name. There is no membership fee.

Wetlands International mission is to sustain and restore wetlands and their biodiversity for future generations. Asia Pacific Regional Office: 3A37, 4th Floor, Block A, Kelana Centre Point, Kelana Jaya, No. 3 Jalan SS7/19, 47300 Petaling Jaya, Selangor, Malaysia. Tel +603 704 6770; fax +603 704 6772; email <wiap@wiap.nasionet.net>; web address http://ngo.asiapac.net/ wetlands.

World Pheasant Association (WPA) is the leading international conservation and research association for all galliforms. It undertakes and supports many projects in the Indian subcontinent, both materially and financially. Members receive *WPA News*. Address: P.O. Box 5, Lower Basildon, Reading, RG8 9PF, UK. Tel 0118-984-5140; fax 0118-984-3369; email <wpa@gn.apc.org>. The South Asia Regional Office address is c/o WWF-India, 172-B Lodi Estate, New Delhi 110 023, India.

World Wide Fund for Nature (WWF) is one of the world's leading conservation organisations and is very active in the Indian subcontinent, being the primary force behind many important wildlife protection projects, as well as doing much work in education and research. Members are sent regular newsletters. See below for the addresses of national head offices.

NATIONAL

Bangladesh

Nature Conservation Movement (NACON) is instrumental in wildlife conservation, education and surveys (including the Asian Waterfowl Census) in Bangladesh. Address: 125-127 (2nd Floor) Mohammedia Super Market, Sobhanbag, Dhaka 1207.

Wildlife Society of Bangladesh carries out wildlife studies, encourages conservation and supports academic zoology. Address: c/o Dept. of Zoology, University of Dhaka, Dhaka.

Bird records for Bangladesh should be submitted to Dr David Johnson, House 52, Road 11, Banai, Dhaka. Tel (res) 884215; email <dave@dhaka.agni.com> or Paul Thompson, ICLARM, House 75, Road 7, Banani, Dhaka. Tel (res) 982535, (off) 873250; fax 880 2 871151; email <iclarm@dhaka.agni.com>.

Bhutan

Royal Society for the Protection of Nature (RSPN) aims to improve public awareness of environmental concerns, as well as monitor and conserve rare and endangered species. Members receive two newsletters *Thrung Thrung* annually and the quarterly magazine *Rangzhin*. Address: P.O. Box 325, Thimphu.

WWF has been engaged in wildlife conservation in Bhutan since 1977. Address: P.O. Box 210, Thimphu.

India

Bombay Natural History Society (BNHS) was founded in 1883 and is still one of the leading organisations of its kind in Asia. It promotes research, conservation and education in all aspects of Indian flora and fauna. Members receive the magazine *Hornbill* and the *Journal of the BNHS* (published three times a year), one of the most important sources of information on the natural history of the subcontinent. Address: Hornbill House, Dr Sálim Ali Chowk, Opp. Lion Gate, Shahid Bhagat Singh Rd, Bombay 400 023. Tel 022-2843869/2843421; fax 022-2837615; email <bnhs@bom4.vsnl.net.in>.

Newsletter for Birdwatchers appears six times a year and carries an interesting selection of bird-related news, surveys etc. Applications for subscriptions should be addressed to: S. Sridhar, Navbharat Enterprises, No. 10 Sirur Park 'B' Street, Seshadripuram, Bangalore 560 020. Tel 080-336 4142/336 4682; fax 080-336 4687.

Salim Ali Centre for Ornithology and Natural History (SACON) is a government agency whose remit is to act as a focus for natural history research and conservation. It publishes research reports and the *SACON Newsletter*. Address: Kalampalayam PO, Coimbatore 641 010, Tamil Nadu. Tel 0422-807973/807983; fax 0422-807952; email <lv@sacon.ernet.in> or <centre@sacon.ernet.in>.

Wildlife Institute of India (WII) is primarily known for its work in providing professional training to India's protected area managers and wildlife biologists. It also pursues wildlife research projects, provides consultancy services and is building a wildlife information database. Address: P.O. Box No.18, Chandrabani, Dehra Dun 248 001, Uttar Pradesh. Tel 0135-620912 to 620915; fax 0135-620217; email <wii@giasdl01.vsnl.net.in>.

Wildlife Protection Society of India (WPSI) has as its primary aim the prevention of poaching and the illegal wildlife trade but it is involved in all major conservation issues in India. Address: Thapar House, 124 Janpath, New Delhi - 110 001. Tel 011-6213864; fax 011-3368729; email <wpsi@vsnl.com>.

WWF-India is the country's largest conservation NGO. Address: 172B - Lodi Estate, New Delhi 110003. Tel 011-4633473/4627586.

Zoological Survey of India (ZSI), as its name suggests, is the government agency responsible for surveying India's faunal wealth. It maintains a number of regional offices and collecting stations throughout the country and publishes many of its results in book form available from Publications Division, ZSI, 2nd MSO Bldg, 13th Floor, 234/4 Acharja J. C. Bose Rd, Calcutta 700 020. The Head Office is at Prani Vigyan Bhawan, M Block, New Alipore, Calcutta 700 053.

Nepal

Bird Conservation Nepal (BCN – formerly the Nepal Birdwatching Club) is the oldest and most important bird study and conservation organisation in Nepal. Members receive the quarterly newsletter *Danphe*. Address: Post Box 12465, Kathmandu.

WWF has been active in Nepal since 1967. Address: P.O. Box 7660, Lal Durbar, Kathmandu.

Pakistan

Ornithological Society of Pakistan (OSP) was created in 1993 to promote wildlife study and conservation throughout the country with a particular focus on birds and their habitats. It publishes the *Pakistan Journal of Ornithology*. Address: Near Chowk Fara, Block 'D', P.O. Box 73, Dera Ghazi Khan 32200.

WWF has been active in Pakistan since the 1960s and is the country's largest conservation NGO. Address: Ferozepur Road, 54600 Lahore; mail: PO Box 5180, 54600 Lahore. Tel + 92-2-86-360/586-429; fax + 92-2-86-358; tlx 082 44866 pkgs pk.

Sri Lanka

Ceylon Bird Club (CBC) is one of the most active and oldest ornithological organisations in South Asia, having been founded in 1943. The CBC Rarities Committee evaluates all Sri Lankan records of new and rare birds. Members receive the monthly newsletter *CBC Notes*. Address: 39 Chatham Street, Colombo 1. Tel ++94-1-328625/328627; email <birdclub@sltnet.lk>.

Field Ornithology Group of Sri Lanka (FOGSL) has as its aims the conservation and study of birds and their habitats. It is closely associated with the University of Colombo and publishes the quarterly *Malkoha*. Address: c/o Department of Zoology, University of Colombo, Colombo 3. Fax ++94-1-337644; email <fogsl@slt.lk>.

REFERENCES AND FURTHER READING

It is neither possible nor appropriate to cite all of the many references used in preparing this guide. The following may be of particular interest to readers:

Field guides

Ali, S. (1996) *The Book of Indian Birds*. 12th revised and enlarged edn. BNHS, Bombay.

Ali, S., Ripley, S. D. & Dick, J. H. (1996) *A Pictorial Guide to the Birds of the Indian Subcontinent*. 2nd edn (reprint with corrections). BNHS/OUP, Bombay.

Fleming Sr., R. L., Fleming Jr., R. L. & Bangdel, L. S. (1979) *Birds of Nepal*. 2nd edn. Avalok, Kathmandu.

Harrison, J. & Worfolk, T. (1999) *Field Guide to the Birds of Sri Lanka*. OUP, Oxford.

Henry, G. M. (1998) *A Guide to the Birds of Sri Lanka*. 3rd revised and enlarged edn. OUP, Delhi.

Ripley, S. D., Rasmussen, P. C. & Anderton, J. C. (in prep.) *Birds of South Asia: A Field Guide*. University of Texas Press.

Sonobe, K. & Usui, S. eds. (1993) *A Field Guide to the Waterbirds of Asia*. Wild Bird Society of Japan, Tokyo.

Woodcock, M. (1980) *Collins Handguide to the Birds of the Indian Sub-Continent*. Collins, London.

Handbooks and reference works

Ali, S. & Ripley, S. D. (1971-1999) *Handbook of the Birds of India and Pakistan*. 10 vols. OUP, Delhi & Oxford.

Ali, S. & Ripley, S. D. (1987) *Compact Handbook of the Birds of India and Pakistan*. 2nd edn. OUP, Bombay.

Baker, E. C. S. (1922-1930) *Fauna of British India: Birds*. 2nd edn. 8 vols. Taylor and Francis, London.

Collar, N. J., Crosby, M. J. & Stattersfield, A. J. (1994) *Birds to Watch 2 - The World List of Threatened Birds*. BirdLife International, Cambridge.

Cramp, S. *et al.* (1977-1994) *Birds of the Western Palearctic*. 9 vols. OUP, Oxford.

Cramp, S. *et al.* (1997) *Birds of the Western Palearctic*. Concise edn. 2 vols. OUP, Oxford.

del Hoyo, J., Elliott, A., & Sargatal, J. eds. (1992-1999) *Handbook of the Birds of the World*. Vols I-V. Lynx Edicions, Barcelona.

Grimmett, R., Inskipp, C. & Inskipp, T. (1998) *Birds of the Indian Subcontinent*. Christopher Helm, London.

Inskipp, C. & Inskipp, T. (1991) *A Guide to the Birds of Nepal*. 2nd edn. Christopher Helm, London.

Inskipp, T., Lindsey, N. & Duckworth, W. (1996) *An Annotated Checklist of the Birds of the Oriental Region*. Oriental Bird Club, Sandy, U.K.

Lamsfuss, G. (1998) *Die Vögel Sri Lankas : ein Vogel und Naturführer*. Heidelberg : Kasparek Verlag.

Martens, J. & Eck, S. (1995) *Towards an Ornithology of the Himalayas: Systematics, Ecology and Vocalizations of Nepal Birds*. Bonner Zoologische Monographien, Nr. 38. Bonn: Zoologisches Forschungsinstitut und Museum Alexander Koenig.

Ripley, S. D. (1982) *A Synopsis of the Birds of India and Pakistan*. 2nd edn. OUP/BNHS, Bombay.

Roberts, T. J. (1991-1992) *The Birds of Pakistan*. 2 vols. OUP, Karachi.

Wijesinghe, D. P. (1994) *Checklist of the Birds of Sri Lanka*. (Revised edn.) Ceylon Bird Club, Colombo.

Photographic guides

Grewal, B. (1995) *Odyssey Nature Guide to Birds of the Indian Subcontinent*. 2nd edn. Guidebook Company Ltd., Hong Kong.

Grewal, B. (1995) *A Photographic Guide to Birds of India and Nepal*. New Holland, London.

Grewal, B. & Pfister, O. (1998) *A Photographic Guide to Birds of the Himalayas*. New Holland, London.

Site guides

de Silva Wijeyeratne, Gehan (in prep.) *Pica Traveller Sri Lanka*. Pica Press, Mountfield, U.K.

Inskipp, C. (1988) *A Birdwatchers' Guide to Nepal*. Prion Ltd, Sandy, U.K.

Kazmierczak, K. & Singh, R. (1998) *A Birdwatchers' Guide to India*. Prion Ltd, Huntingdon, U.K.

Regional works

Ali, S. (1945) *Birds of Kutch*. OUP, Bombay.

Ali, S. (1949) *Indian Hill Birds*. (Reprinted 1979). OUP, Bombay.

Ali, S. (1962) *Birds of Sikkim*. OUP, Bombay.

Ali, S. (1969) *Birds of Kerala*. OUP, Madras.

Ali, S. (1977) *Field Guide to the Birds of the Eastern Himalayas*. OUP, Delhi.

Bates, R. S. P & Lowther, E. H. N. (1952) *Breeding Birds of Kashmir.* (Reprinted 1991). OUP, Delhi.

Ganguli, U. (1975) *A Guide to the Birds of the Delhi Area*. New Delhi.

Harvey, W. G. (1990) *Birds in Bangladesh*. University Press, Dhaka.

Kalpavriksh (1991) *What's that Bird? A Guide to Birdwatching, with Special Reference to Delhi*. Kalpavriksh, New Delhi.

Neelakantan, K. K., Sashikumar, C. & Venugopalan, R. (1993) *A Book of Kerala Birds*. WWF-India, Trivandrum.

Robertson, A. & Jackson, M. C. A. (1992) *The Birds of Periyar: an Aid to Birdwatching in the Periyar Sanctuary*. Tourism and Wildlife Society of India, Jaipur.

Tikader, B. K. (1994) *Birds of Andaman & Nicobar Islands*. Zoological Survey of India, Calcutta.

Field guides to neighbouring regions

King, B., Woodcock, M. & Dickinson, E. C. (1975) *A Field Guide to the Birds of South-East Asia*. Collins, London.

Jonsson, L. (1992) *Birds of Europe with North Africa and the Middle East*. Christopher Helm, London.

Leader, P., Carey, G., Round, P. & Worfolk, T. (in prep.) *A Field Guide to the Birds of China, Tibet and Taiwan*. Pica Press, Mountfield, U.K.

Lekagul, B. & Round, P. D. (1991) *A Guide to the Birds of Thailand*. Saha Barn Bhaet, Bangkok.

Meyer de Schauensee, R. (1984) *The Birds of China*. Smithsonian Institution, Washington DC.

Porter, R. F., Christensen, S. & Schiermacker-Hansen, P. (1996) *Field Guide to the Birds of the Middle East*. Poyser, London.

Robson, C. (2000) *An Identification Guide to the Birds of South-East Asia*. New Holland, London.

Family monographs

Baker, K. (1997) *Warblers of Europe, Asia and North Africa*. Christopher Helm, London.

Byers, C., Olsson, U. & Curson, J. (1995) *Buntings and Sparrows: A Guide to the Buntings and North American Sparrows*. Pica Press, Mountfield, U.K.

Chantler, P. & Driessens, G. (2000) *Swifts: A Guide to the Swifts and Treeswifts of the World*. 2nd edn. Pica Press, Mountfield, U.K.

Cheke, R. A., Mann, C. F. & Allen, R. (in prep.) *Sunbirds: A Guide to the Sunbirds, Flowerpeckers, Spiderhunters and Sugarbirds of the World*. Pica Press, Mountfield, U.K.

Cleere, N. & Nurney, D. (1998) *Nightjars: A Guide to Nightjars and Related Nightbirds*. Pica Press, Mountfield, U.K.

Clement, P., Harris, A. & Davis, J. (1993) *Finches and Sparrows: An Identification Guide*. Christopher Helm, London.

Feare, C. & Craig, A. (1998) *Starlings and Mynas*. Christopher Helm, London.

Fry, C. H., Fry, K. & Harris, A. (1992) *Kingfishers, Bee-eaters & Rollers*. Christopher Helm, London.

Gibbs, D., Barnes, E. & Cox, J. (in prep.) *Pigeons and Doves: A Guide to the Pigeons and Doves of the World*. Pica Press, Mountfield, U.K.

Grant, P. J. (1986) *Gulls: A guide to Identification*. 2nd edn. T. & A. D. Poyser, Calton, U.K.

Hancock, J. & Kushlan, J. (1984) *The Herons Handbook*. Croom Helm, London.

Hancock, J. A., Kushlan, J. A. & Kahl, M. P. (1992) *Storks, Ibises and Spoonbills of the World*. Academic Press, London.

Harrap, S. & Quinn, D. (1996) *Tits, Nuthatches & Treecreepers*. Christopher Helm, London.

Harrison, P. (1985) *Seabirds: an Identification Guide*. Revised edn. Croom Helm, Beckenham, U.K.

Harrison, P. (1987) *Seabirds of the World: A Photographic Guide*. Christopher Helm, London.

Hayman, P., Marchant, J. & Prater, T. (1986) *Shorebirds: an Identification Guide to the Waders of the World*. Croom Helm, Beckenham, U.K.

Johnsgard, P. A. (1983) *Cranes of the World*. University of Indiana Press, Bloomington, USA.

Johnsgard, P. A. (1986) *The Pheasants of the World*. Oxford University Press, Oxford.

Johnsgard, P. A. (1988) *The Quails, Partridges and Francolins of the World*. Oxford University Press, Oxford.

Johnsgard, P. A. (1991) *Bustards, Hemipodes and Sandgrouse, Birds of Dry Places.* Oxford University Press, Oxford.

Johnsgard, P. A. (1993) *Cormorants, Darters and Pelicans of the World.* Smithsonian Institution Press, Washington DC.

Jones, D., Dekker, R. W. R. J., Roselaar, C. S. & van Perlo, B. (1995) *The Megapodes.* OUP, Oxford.

Juniper, T. & Parr, M. (1998) *Parrots: A Guide to the Parrots of the World.* Pica Press, Mountfield, U.K.

Kemp, A. & Woodcock, M. (1995) *The Hornbills.* OUP, Oxford.

König, C., Weick, F. & Becking, J.-H. (1999) *Owls: A Guide to the Owls of the World.* Pica Press, Mountfield, U.K.

Lambert, F. & Woodcock, M. (1996) *Pittas, Broadbills and Asities.* Pica Press, Mountfield, U.K.

Lefranc, N. & Worfolk, T. (1997) *Shrikes: A Guide to the Shrikes of the World.* Pica Press, Mountfield, U.K.

Madge, S. & Burn, H. (1988) *Wildfowl: an Identification Guide to the Ducks, Geese and Swans of the World.* Christopher Helm, Bromley, U.K.

Madge, S. & Burn, H. (1993) *Crows and Jays: A Guide to the Crows, Jays and Magpies of the World.* Helm, Mountfield, U.K.

Olsen, K. M. & Larsson, H. (1997) *Skuas and Jaegers: A Guide to the Skuas and Jaegers of the World.* Pica Press, Mountfield, U.K.

Olsen, K. M. & Larsson, H. (1995) *Terns of Europe and North America.* Christopher Helm, London.

Restall, R. (1996) *Munias and Mannikins.* Pica Press, Mountfield, U.K.

Summers-Smith, J. D. (1988) *The Sparrows.* T. & A. D. Poyser, Calton, U.K.

Taylor, B. & van Perlo, B. (1998) *Rails: A Guide to the Rails, Crakes, Gallinules and Coots of the World.* Pica Press, Mountfield, U.K.

Turner, A. & Rose, C. (1989) *A Handbook to the Swallows and Martins of the World.* Christopher Helm, Bromley, U.K.

Wilds, C., DiCostanzo, J. & Schmidt, C. (in prep.) *Terns and Skimmers: A Guide to the Terns and Skimmers of the World.* Pica Press, Mountfield, U.K.

Winkler, H., Christie, D. A. & Nurney, D. (1995) *Woodpeckers: A Guide to the Woodpeckers, Piculets and Wrynecks of the World.* Pica Press, Mountfield, U.K.

Sound guides

Ranft, R. & Cleere, N. (1998) *A Sound Guide to Nightjars and Related Nightbirds.* CD. Pica Press, Mountfield, U.K.

Connop, S. (1993) *Birdsongs of Nepal.* Cassette. Turaco, New York.

Connop, S. (1995) *Birdsongs of the Himalayas.* Cassette. Turaco, New York.

Cramp, S. *et al.* (eds) (1998) *The Complete Birds of the Western Palearctic on CD-ROM.* 3 CD-ROMs. OUP, Oxford.

Marshall, J. T. (1978) *Systematics of Smaller Asian Night Birds Based on Voice.* Vinyl record and booklet. American Ornithologists' Union, Tampa.

Mild, K. (1990) *Bird Songs of Israel and the Middle East.* 2 cassettes and a booklet. Bioacoustics, Stockholm.

Mild, K. (1987) *Soviet Bird Songs.* 2 cassettes and a booklet. Bioacoustics, Stockholm.

Roché, J. C. (1990) *All the Bird Songs of Europe.* 4 CDs and 4 booklets. Sittelle, Chateaubois.

Scharringa, J. (1999) *Birds of Tropical Asia : Sounds and Sights.* CD-ROM Bird Songs International BV, the Netherlands.

Sivaprasad, P. S. (1994) *An Audio Guide to the Birds of South India.* Cassette. Privately published, London.

Warakagoda, D. (1997-8) *The Bird Sounds of Sri Lanka.* 2 Cassettes. DHW Library of Nature Sounds, Nugegoda, Sri Lanka.

White, T. (1984) *A Field Guide to the Bird Songs of South-East Asia.* 2 Cassettes. British Library, London.

INDEX OF ENGLISH NAMES

The plate number is followed by the number of the species on that plate. Alternative (obsolescent) names are given in parentheses.

INDEX OF SCIENTIFIC NAMES

The plate number is followed by the number of the species on that plate. Obsolescent names are given in parentheses.

QUICK INDEX TO PLATE NUMBERS

KEY TO DISTRIBUTION MAPS

■ **major city**

〜 **international border**

〜 **state boundary**

▮ **resident (including local and altitudinal migrants)**

▮ **former range (no recent records but may still survive)**

▮ **summer visitor (including summer monsoon)**

▮ **winter visitor**

▮ **passage (autumn and/or spring) visitor**

▮ **known to be occasional, scarce or erratic** ⎤

● **small isolated population (actual range smaller)** ⎟ **colour coded for seasonality as above**

○ **isolated record(s) - one or more in the same area** ⎟

★ **isolated record(s) - exact location uncertain** ⎟ **black denotes unspecified season**

? **uncertain record** ⎦

i **locally introduced or feral**

† **formerly present (believed extirpated)**

+ **occasional breeding / has bred**

× **possible breeding**

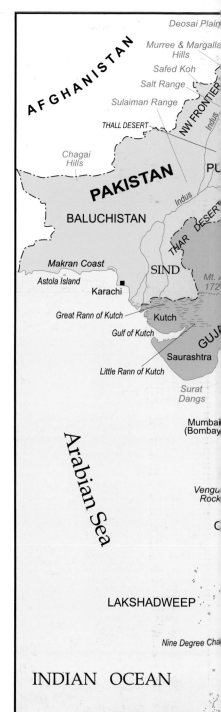